identity, self esteem 274-5

Social Work with Groups

Helen Northen

Social Work with Groups

SECOND EDITION

COLUMBIA UNIVERSITY PRESS
New York 1988

Columbia University Press
New York Guildford, Surrey

Printed in the United States of America

Library of Congress Cataloging-in-Publication Data

Northen, Helen.
Social work with groups.

Bibliography: p.
Includes index.
1. Social group work. I. Title.
HV45.N6 1988 361.4 88-1018
ISBN 0-231-06744-5

Hardback editions of Columbia University Press books are Smyth-sewn and are printed on permanent and durable acid-free paper.

Book design by Jennifer Dossin

Contents

Contents

Preface

The earlier edition of *Social Work with Groups* was the first book to present a group development and social systems perspective on social work services to groups of people. The book continues to be used widely in both generic practice and specialized courses in schools of social work; its theoretical base and applications to practice have stood the test of time. Yet practice with groups has accelerated rapidly over the years as has knowledge about the development, structure, and processes of small groups. These groups help people of diverse ages, socioeconomic strata, and ethnic backgrounds in all fields of practice.

The time has now come to incorporate this additional knowledge and applications to a variety of settings and types of groups, and the second edition of the book is the result.

I have a strong commitment to an integrated method of social work practice that can be applied differentially to varied situations and modalities. A substantial common core of values, purposes, knowledge, and technology defines the profession for its practitioners and for the public. Beyond the generic, however, social workers need to extend and deepen their knowledge and skills in each form of practice. If they are to meet the differential needs of the people they serve, they should be competent in the flexible use of individual, family, and group modalities. Within an integrated view of social work practice this book presents the values, theory, and skills essential to effective practice with growth-oriented or treatment groups.

Comparative analysis of the major writings reveals that many of the values, concepts, skills, and principles are similar and that the differences are more in emphasis than in kind. The trend now is to reaffirm the characteristics common to most social work with groups—what Catherine Papell and Beulah Rothman call a mainstream model. Within the general model there is room for differences in explanatory theories and conceptions of the roles of social workers.

Practice in this book is based on an ecosystems orientation that takes into account the biological, psychological, and social functioning of the members, the social processes and development of groups, and environmental forces. Practice is process oriented and goal directed. The practitioner helps groups to form for particular purposes and facilitates the development of member-to-member relationships and interactions through which the members become able to provide mutual support and aid in working toward their personal and social goals.

This new edition is intended primarily for social work students, faculty, and practitioners who desire to enhance their knowledge and competence in working with groups. Some psychologists, psychiatrists, educators, and even biologists who read the first edition commented on its usefulness to them, suggesting its appeal to a wider readership.

I continue to be indebted to the faculty, deans, students, and alumni of the University of Southern California who have both challenged and supported me in my effort to develop practice theory. I am indebted also to the faculty and students at the University of Alabama, where I spent a year as a visiting professor, and particularly to Ben A. Orcutt who gave generously of her time and talents in our collaborative work in the development of curricula for social work practice. George Getzel and Roselle Kurland provided consultation on the content of the book and generously supplied process records of practice for use in clarifying issues and illustrating concepts and principles. Furthermore, Dr. Kurland read an earlier draft of the manuscript and gave valuable suggestions for additions to the content and clarification of the material; that was a generous and wonderful service. Florence Clemenger, Margaret Hartford, and Mary Louise Somers have offered helpful suggestions concerning the organization and content of the new edition. I am indeed fortunate to have a large social network of former students, colleagues, and friends around the country who are sources of inspiration, stimulation, and support. They all deserve my heartfelt thanks.

Social Work with Groups

1

Groups in Social Work Practice

Enhancement of the psychosocial functioning of people and their environments is the primary concern of social work. The profession of social work has a rich heritage of activities directed toward reforming conditions that degrade the human personality, providing services to meet basic needs, and improving people's capacity for more effective interpersonal relations and role functioning. As people's problems in meeting their basic needs, coping with stressful situations, and developing satisfying social relations have become identified and understood, so, too, has need for knowledge and skill on the part of those persons who are in helping roles.

The profession of social work emerged out of recognition that, if people were to be helped to interact more effectively with each other and within the varied and complex situations of modern life, the nature and quality of efforts to help could not be left to chance. Good intentions must be buttressed with knowledge and competence. As Schwartz has pointed out, "Ends without means must, in fact, have recourse to magic . . . there is a mystical, prayerful quality about exhortations to achieve something important without skill and without method, but merely through the sheer power of intent."[1] A profession requires that complex tasks be performed, not routinely, but through artistic application of principles derived from knowledge. The adaptation of basic principles to particular situations involves judgment and imagination, combined with skill. The knowledge and technical competence of a professional practitioner are used for social ends deemed to be essential to the common good of society. Ends and means are inextricably interwoven: the means used should be consistent with the ends sought. In social work, the ends are rooted in values about the quality of life, knowledge about people and their environments, and competence in the practice of social work.

VALUES

Values are an important determinant of the social worker's selection of knowledge for purposes of assessment, planning, and treatment. They are ideas about what is worthwhile or useless, desirable or undesirable, right or wrong, beautiful or ugly. They include beliefs and ideologies, appreciative or aesthetic preferences, and moral or ethical principles. Translated into ethical principles of conduct, values guide the practice of any profession. They derive from a few fundamental beliefs and attitudes about people and society.

The ultimate value of social work is that human beings should have opportunities to realize their potentials for living in ways that are both personally satisfying and socially desirable. Ashley Montagu has said that "The deepest personal defeat suffered by human beings is constituted by the difference between what one was capable of becoming and what one has in fact become."[2] Most social workers would agree with this statement. Underlying the value of realization of potential are many more specific ones that elaborate its meaning. Implied in the basic value is simultaneous concern for personal and collective welfare for the mutual benefit of all concerned. As Silberman has said, "Successful social work service should benefit the child and the family, the patient and the hospital, the employer and employee, the member and the group; not one at the expense of the other, but for the benefit of both."[3]

A conviction that each person has inherent worth and dignity is a basic tenet of social work. A practitioner who has this conviction holds dear certain specific values. All people should be treated with respect, regardless of their likenesses or differences in relation to others. The principle of individualization is deduced from this value, as are acceptance and self-direction. People should have opportunities to grow toward the fulfillment of their potential, for their own sakes and so that they may contribute to building a society better able to meet human needs. They should have the right to civil liberties and to equal opportunity without discrimination because of race, age, social class, religion, nationality, state of health, sexual orientation, or gender. They should have access to resources essential to the fulfillment of their basic needs.

A conviction that people should have responsibility for each other is another basic value of social work. It is the democratic spirit in action. This value leads to the view that all people should have freedom to express themselves, to maintain their privacy, to participate in decisions that affect them, and to direct their own lives, with an accompanying responsibility to live constructively with other people. People are interdependent for survival and for the fulfillment of their needs. Mutual responsibility, rather than rugged individualism, should prevail. Individuals and groups should assume social responsibility in small and large ways, according to their capacities to do so.

People are interdependent. Konopka eloquently reminds us that "All lives are connected to other lives. . . . It is the vital interrelationship of human beings that is the heart of social group work. The focus is on *freeing* individuals while helping them to support each other."[4]

Interdependence implies mutuality in relationships among persons and among groups and organizations. It acknowledges the diversity of groups and cultures that comprise society. American society, as is also true of many other societies, is made up of a network of ethnosystems, each sharing some common values and characteristics and each having some values unique to members of that group.[5] Each individual, family, and group needs to be particularized, so that there can be opportunities for each social unit to maintain its own culture and to make a contribution to the whole. Interdependence is essential to democracy. A democratic philosophy, according to Pray, rests upon a deep appreciation of the validity and the value to society as a whole of these individual differences in human beings. It conceives of social unity and progress as the outcome of the integration, not the suppression or conquest, of these differences. Accordingly, it tests all social arrangements and institutions by their impact upon human lives, by their capacity to use for the common good the unique potentialities of individual human beings, through relationships that enlist their active and productive participation.[6] Group, as well as individual, differences should be accepted and used for the welfare of all.

The ideology of social work from a broad psychosocial perspective views individuals as whole persons, interacting with others in the systems and the subsystems in which they find themselves. It is humanistic, scientific, and democratic. It is humanistic in its commitment to the welfare and rights of clients and the social systems of which they are a part. It is scientific in that it prefers objectivity and factual evidence over personal biases. It emphasizes that the practitioner's judgments and actions are derived from a reasoning process, based on scientific knowledge to the extent that it is available. It embodies the great idea of democracy, not as a political structure, but as a philosophy governing relationships among people, based on reciprocal rights and obligations, and directed toward the welfare of the individual, family, group, and society.

PURPOSE

The purpose of social work, related directly to its primary values, is improvement in the relationship between people and their environments. A recent definition of social work by the National Association of Social Workers states that

> social work can be defined as the professional activity of helping individuals, groups, or communities improve their social functioning and creating societal conditions favorable to this goal. It can be further described as consisting of the professional application of social work values, principles, and techniques to one or more of the following ends: helping people obtain tangible services;

providing counseling and psychotherapy to individuals, families, and groups; helping communities or groups provide or improve social and health services; and participating in relevant policy-making forums.[7]

Within the general purpose of the profession, social work with small groups may be directed toward helping the members to use the group for coping with and resolving existing problems in psychosocial functioning, toward preventing anticipated problems or maintaining a current level of functioning in situations in which there is danger of deterioration. Further, it may be directed toward developing more effective patterns of group and organizational functioning and removing environmental obstacles. With any group, the specific outcomes sought vary with the desires, needs, capacities, and situations of the members who comprise the group and with the purpose and nature of the group itself. Although there is a considerable body of knowledge and skills applicable both to groups with a general purpose of enhancing the social functioning of the members and those with a major purpose of achieving a collective task, the major focus of this book is on the former.

A THEORETICAL PERSPECTIVE

What a social worker does in practice is for a purpose. It reflects values and is based on knowledge. All social workers need considerable knowledge about the processes of biopsychosocial development and social change. They need to understand the social and psychological components of typical stresses and problems in social living and the available alternative means for coping with stress and resolving problems. They need to understand environments as ecological systems with their cultural, racial, political and economic realities and to understand the structures and processes of social systems from the dyad to larger organizations. Knowledge about social welfare problems, resources, services, and social policies is also relevant for all social workers. Such knowledge is derived from the biological, psychological, and social sciences and selected and adapted for social work purposes in the form of concepts, middle range theories, and principles.

The practice described in this book is within a contemporary intersystem approach that takes into account the multiple and complex transactions that occur among persons within their families, other membership and reference groups, and organizations. An intersystem approach is relevant to social work because social work situations involve people's coping with changing environments or with changes in their own capacities to deal with their surroundings. Maas says that these situations "call for altered patterns of interaction between persons and their social contexts."[8] The changes that can be made depend in part on the options and responsiveness of environments and on people's capacities and developmental potentials.

The intersystem approach is based on an ecological or ecosystem perspective. Ecology is the study of the relationship of plants and animals to one another and to the biological and physical environment. In the words of Cook, "The study of the interrelationship of living things with one another and with the basic natural resources of air, water, and food is called ecology, after the Greek oikos for house."[9] Ecologists use the term ecosystem to refer to a community of associated species of plants and animals together with the physical features of their habitat.[10] The essence of ecology is that no organism can live alone: there is a web of interdependence among all living things and between these organisms and the physical environment in a given habitat. The environment provides the condititons and nutrients essential to survival and growth or it provides obstacles to survival and growth. It has been said by Henry and Rebecca Northen that "The capacity of living things to adapt to new environments and conditions is one of the marvels of nature. The wonder is not only that so many forms of life have evolved but also that the forms are so neatly suited to all the available niches that earth offers."[11] Organisms change, and are changed by, aspects of their physical and social environments. A neat fit between the organism and its environment is essential to survival and satisfactory development. The fundamental principles of ecology concern adaptation, dynamic flow of energy, cycles of materials and nutrients, diversity and stability, succession, cooperation and competition, mutualism or symbiosis, and geometric growth of populations.[12]

Ecology has become popularized by environmentalists, psychologists, sociologists, anthropologists, and social workers who are searching for ways to understand the interrelationships among people and between people and their environments. Each discipline makes its own modifications of the scientific base, selecting some major concepts from the whole.

Knowledge about the interrelationships between people and their environments has been a major theme in group work, as will be seen in the next chapter. Recently, however, Germain, Meyer, and their associates have perhaps given most attention to the use of ecological concepts in social work practice with individuals, as well as groups. Germain states that an ecological perspective is "concerned with the growth, development, and potentialities of human beings and the properties of their environments that support or fail to support the expression of human potential. . . . In an ecological view, practice is directed toward improving the transactions between people and environments for all who function within them."[13] Social workers tend to use ecology as a metaphor or as a perspective rather than as a theory, because the totality of ecological concepts and principles has not been applied directly to the practice. Rather than use the metaphor, it might be more precise to use the term *intersystems network*, as Chin has proposed.[14] This concept makes it possible to understand systems of different levels of complexity from cell to society and the network of systems that comprises the environment or social context of a person, family, small group, or larger organization within a given habitat at a given time.

In the approach to practice described in this book, a group is viewed as a complex, open, goal-directed, and adaptive system. Attention is paid to the individuals who comprise the group, the group's structure and process, and the environments of the members and of the group. Human problems arise from multiple interconnections among biological, economic, environmental, sociocultural, and psychological factors, often referred to as a biopsychosocial framework for understanding people in their social contexts. It is a form of practice oriented to process and interpersonal relationships and in which leadership is primarily facilitative. It differs from models of practice that are based solely on behavioral or cognitive theories, are highly structured, emphasize the achievement of concrete tasks or changes in habits, and in which leadership is largely directive.[15] Both major orientations to practice share the broad purpose of improved social functioning but have some different specific goals and interventions.

Within the intersystem perspective, numerous theories are used to explain the conditions and processes occurring in a group at a given time. Of special importance are concepts from ego psychology that explain the behavior and development of the members who comprise the group and theories about group development, structure, and interaction. Since the group is a powerful environment for its members, its development and operation must not be left to chance.

The group is an environment or context, but it is also a means or instrument for growth and change of its members. Another set of theoretical propositions is, therefore, important: principles about the means by which professional practitioners enable persons to move toward the achievement of their goals and work toward improvement of social institutions and environmental conditions. Of special import for work with groups is knowledge of the process by which practitioners enable groups to form and to develop into viable social systems. Other knowledge is essential as it contributes to the competence of practitioners to render appropriate services to people.

SUPPORTS FOR PRACTICE

Social workers derive sanction to practice from governmental bodies, the profession of social work, the clients themselves, and, except in private practice, a social agency. Governmental bodies sanction practice in a variety of ways. They establish legislation and appropriate funds for specified services, provide a legal base for the operation of voluntary agencies, grant special privileges such as tax exemptions to charitable organizations, and determine whether or not practitioners should be licensed or registered. Through its organizations, the profession of social work sanctions practice by defining standards for and conditions of practice. It has programs that certify competence, accredit professional education, establish codes of ethics, provide channels for complaints against members, and encourage the development of theory and research. Social agencies also authorize particular forms of practice. Kaiser has explained how the nature and quality of practice is "profoundly affected and to some extent determined by the purpose, function, and structure of the institution in which it is carried on."[16]

The social agency's influence on service may enhance greatly the ability of practitioners to meet the needs of their clientele, or it may impede them from giving appropriate and qualitative service. For private practitioners, the specific conditions for the provision of services are set by their perceptions of the needs of certain potential clients and their professional interests and competence, within the standards set by certification and accountability to funding sources. Ultimately, the sanction comes from the people who use the services, for social workers cannot perform their roles unless the participants grant them the necessary status. The knowledge about sanction is generic to social work with individuals, families, groups, and organizations.

COMMON CHARACTERISTICS OF PRACTICE

In the provision of direct services to people, social work practice consists of a constellation of activities performed by a practitioner in a planned and systematic way and designed to lead toward the achievement of the purpose for which service to a particular group is initiated. The common characteristics of the practice of social work are many and interrelated. They have been stated in different forms by different writers, in either a few abstract generalizations or in specific terms. Some of the essential characteristics of social work practice that apply to work with individuals, families, and other small groups are the following.

1. Social work practice is purposeful. The specific purposes toward which the service is directed are determined by the needs of the persons being served within the purpose of the profession. Purposes are defined through a process in which both the worker and the clients participate, and they change as do the needs of the clients.
2. Social workers develop and sustain professional relationships with

individuals, families, and groups. Acceptance, empathy, genuineness, and self-awareness are components of the social work relationship.

3. They engage in the interrelated processes of social assessment, formulation of plans for service, implementation of the plans, and evaluation of outcomes. The interventions are based upon an understanding of individuals and groups in varied social situations.

4. They engage in assessments that take into account interacting biological, intrapersonal, interpersonal, and environmental influences on development and behavior in order to understand the needs and capacities of clients. The assessment is flexible, changing as the needs of the clients become better understood.

5. They, in collaboration with clients and often also with other personnel, develop a plan for service that specifies the needs or problems, the goals to be pursued, the most appropriate modality of practice, the targets of change efforts, and the structure and content of service.

6. They select and make flexible use of a variety of procedures and skills, dependent upon the assessment, the plan for service, and the phase of process.

7. They individualize their clients and groups. Individualization occurs when a person's needs and capacities and the unique qualities of the environment are understood and taken into account by the practitioner.

8. They clarify their roles and seek congruence between the clients' and the workers' perceptions of role expectations.

9. They center their attention simultaneously on relationships and on the verbal and nonverbal content of the interview or group session.

10. They, through the purposeful use of verbal and nonverbal communication, enable their clients to express feelings, attitudes, and opinions and to contribute knowledge that enlightens the content of the transaction.

11. They participate collaboratively with individuals and groups in decision-making processes that empower the clients to use the social environment toward improving their life situations.

12. They facilitate the participation of clients in all aspects of the service. The rights of people to make and implement their own decisions are respected within certain understood limits.

13. They, being aware of the significance of a time sequence in the provision of service, engage in professional activities that are appropriate to the stage of development of the client system at a given time.

14. They make use of agency and community resources, contribute their knowledge toward the development of new or improved services, collaborate with others who are serving their clients, and participate in efforts to influence desirable changes in policies and procedures on behalf of clients.

15. They make flexible use of individual, family, group, and community modalities from whatever the initial point of contact with a client, moving from an individual to a group or wider community or from the community to a small group or individual, on the basis of the needs of clients and the availability of appropriate services.

UNITS OF SERVICE IN SOCIAL WORK PRACTICE

The recipient of a social service may be an individual, a group, a subsystem of a group, or some larger collectivity. The group may be a family or other natural group such as a gang, or it may be a group formed specifically for a social work purpose. It may be an intergroup, composed of representatives of other groups or organizations. The specific constellation of persons who receive the service is a client system.

A person may be viewed as a biopsychosocial system who, from birth, is a member of a family and an extended family and who subsequently becomes a member of friendship, educational, recreational, religious, and cultural groups, and civic associations. The person and the groups to which he belongs both influence and are influenced by the physical, political, and social environment. A client group is a social system that is part of the social agency system, and so on. At whatever level a system is defined, it is viewed as an interdependent part of other systems in continuous interaction with their environments. An ecosystem perspective assures that a practitioner will focus on the system-in-environment gestalt. The concept of ecosystem alerts the worker to the fact that, as Somers emphasizes, the individual, the group, and the environment are "inextricably interrelated and the condition of each is bound to affect the other."[17]

When social workers enter into a relationship with a client system, they have their own status within the system and a distinct role to perform in helping the members to move toward the achievement of their purposes. Regardless of the system that is the unit of service at a given time, the workers use knowledge about people in groups and larger systems. Even in working with persons singly, workers need to understand the transactions of those persons within their families, membership groups, and communities. In this sense, there is nothing unique in the knowledge about human behavior and social systems required for service to individuals as compared with service to groups. The generic concepts and principles of practice are applicable to work with any size of client system. But there are indeed differences in the way practitioners relate to and behave with a group as contrasted with one person, derived from the differences in the structure, function, and development of varied social systems.

A small group is a particular kind of social system produced by persons in interaction with each other and with other social systems. As Eubank has defined it:

> A group is two or more persons in a relationship of psychic interaction, whose relationships with one another may be abstracted and distinguished from their relationships with all others so that they might be thought of as an entity.[18]

A small group, normally consisting of two to twenty people, is usually thought of as one in which members are able to engage in direct personal relations with each other at a given time. The essential emphasis is pithily stated by Homans, "small enough to let us get all the way around it."[19] The idea is for every member to be able to relate face-to-face with every other member. Davidson explains that the group is greater than the sum of its parts because "a system consists of the interdependent parts plus the way the parts relate to each other and the qualities that emerge from these relationships."[20]

SELECTION OF GROUPS AS UNITS OF SERVICE

Within a generic or integrated approach to social work practice, groups may complement or supplement individual, family, or community modalities, and they can be supported by these other modalities. Individual and group formats may be combined or used in sequential order, depending upon the needs of the particular clients at a given time. The dimension of mutual aid operates in groups, which is one primary factor that differentiates group work from other modalities of practice. Mutual aid goes beyond self-help and help from others. It is people helping each other. People grow and change through their relationships and interactions with others. The fact that people need people is the raison d'etre for social work practice with groups. The need is presented dramatically by Schutz in his introduction in *The Interpersonal Underworld.*

> Laurie was about three when one night she requested my aid in getting undressed. I was downstairs and she was upstairs, and . . . well.
>
> "You know how to undress yourself," I reminded.
>
> "Yes," she explained, "but sometimes people need people anyway, even if they do know how to do things by theirselves."
>
> As I slowly lowered the newspaper, a strong feeling came over me, a mixture of delight, embarrassment, and pride; delight in the realization that what I had just heard crystallized many stray thoughts on interpersonal behavior, anger because Laurie stated so effortlessly what I had been struggling with for months; and pride because, after all, she is my daughter.[21]

When the mutual aid process operates, dynamic forces are released that are often referred to as change mechanisms or as curative or therapeutic factors. These forces make the group the preferred modality under certain circumstances. Unlike the one worker to one client system, there are multiple relationships and interactions to be understood and used for particular purposes. To make viable decisions about the appropriate use of groups, the practitioner needs knowledge about the unique processes that operate therein and the goals that can best be reached through a group service.

Contributions to clarifying the dynamic forces in small groups have been made by social psychologists, psychiatrists, and social workers. The first major research was conducted by Corsini and Rosenberg in 1955.[22] These authors analyzed three hundred articles, from which one hundred sixty-six different statements about change mechanisms were identified. They classified these statements into nine categories: ventilation, acceptance, spectator therapy, intellectualization, universalization, reality testing, altruism, transference, and interaction.

In 1970, Yalom reported on what he called the curative factors that operate in long-term psychotherapy groups for adults and tested these factors against the members' views of how they were helped through the group experience.[23] The factors are as follows: instillation of hope, universality, imparting of information, altruism, the corrective recapitulation of the primary family group, development of socializing techniques, imitative behavior including modeling and vicarious learning, cohesiveness, catharsis, and interpersonal learning. Yalom emphasized that interpersonal learning is a particularly important force in groups. It involves "the identification, the elucidation, and the modification of maladaptive interpersonal relationships."[24] In 1975, he added existential factors to the list.[25]

The first major social work contribution was made by Marks, who described the reasons why groups are the preferred means of help for emotionally disturbed boys in residential treatment.[26] Another major report was the result of deliberations at a conference on the use of groups, primarily in adult psychiatric settings.[27] Several similar dynamic forces were identified in these major reports and in subsequent writings.

The dynamic forces that have been most frequently identified as applicable to the practice of social work with groups may be summarized as follows.[28]

1. Mutual support. A climate of peer support, in addition to support from the worker, reduces anxiety and facilitates self-expression and willingness to try out new ideas and behaviors.

2. Cohesiveness. The mutual acceptance of members and commitment to the group make the group attractive to its members. When

members feel they belong to a group that has meaning for them, they are influenced by other members and by the norms of the group. When the members provide mutual support, acceptance, and empathy, the group fulfills the basic human need to belong, sometimes referred to as social hunger.

3. Quality of relationships. When the relationships among the members provide a blend of support and challenge, Goldstein notes that there is the "relative safety of controlled intimacy."[29]

4. Universalization. The realization that similar feelings and difficulties are common among the members lessens the sense of being unique and alone. Self-esteem and mutual esteem are enhanced by the recognition that others have difficulties, too, and yet are likeable and worthy people. Members discover the reassuring fact that they are not the only ones with troublesome emotions and experiences. Such discovery makes such feelings and events less frightening and controlling of behavior.

5. Instillation of hope. By identifying with the group and unconsciously perceiving the group's expectations of positive outcome, members may become influenced by optimistic goals of others and move toward them. They perceive how others have endured similar problems and coped with them successfully.

6. Altruism. Self-esteem and personal identity are enhanced as members learn that they can extend help to others and get something helpful back. People relate better to others who appreciate and use what they can contribute.

7. Acquisition of knowledge and skills. Opportunities afforded for self-expression and for trying out and mastering social skills have a beneficial effect upon the members' self-esteem and enjoyment of being with others. The group is a safe place to acquire needed knowledge; to risk new ideas, efforts, and behaviors; and to learn valued social skills.

8. Catharsis. Expression of feelings and disclosure of ideas and experiences, as these are accepted by others, lessen anxiety and free energies for work toward the achievement of desired goals.

9. Corrective emotional experiences. Groups provide opportunities for members to correct earlier dysfunctional relationships with family members or other persons of significance in the members' lives. Actually, the entire group experience is a corrective emotional experience. As the practitioner treats the members with empathy, acceptance, and genuineness, the members come to emulate these qualities in their interactions with each other. This quality of mutual caring and concern is a rare experience for many members, and they bloom as they experience it. In addition, through identification with the social worker or other members, a person may internalize, often unconsciously, the positive behavior and attitudes of others. By recognizing and working through transference reactions to the worker or other members, persons may come to understand and modify their irrational behavior and thus relate to

others in more realistic ways. Transference is a process whereby people respond irrationally to other persons as if the person with whom they are interacting is a parent, sibling, or significant other person from the past.

10. Reality testing. Groups provide a dynamic context in which multiple perspectives are shared. The other members are used as sounding boards for sharing and comparing feelings, opinions, and facts. The information given by other members often includes unexpected and profoundly insightful perspectives. Responses from peers are often more candid and explicit than are those that come from the worker or persons not in the group. The group becomes a protected reality in which to test different ways of dealing with other people. If a mistake is made, a member can try again, whereas in the outside world, there might well be negative consequences. Members observe others, receive feedback, and engage in reflective thinking about the feedback. As they do so, they come to understand their patterns of feeling, thinking, and behaving and the impact of these patterns on their interpersonal relationships and role performance. Distortions of reality are reduced with reevaluation of self in relation to others. Such reevaluation is a step toward changes in self-defeating attitudes and behaviors.

11. Group control. Through behaving in accordance with the group's expectations, members reduce their resistance to authority, suppress inappropriate behavior, endure frustration, and accept necessary and fair limitations. Temporary group controls serve as a means toward the goal of appropriate self control.

These are the dynamic forces of mutual aid. Findings from research generally support the importance of these forces in positively influencing the members' group experience. Findings also suggest that some factors are more important than others for different types of groups and even for different members of the same group.[30] By which of these means a particular member is helped depends upon his interpersonal needs, environmental resources, and the purposes, structure, and composition of a particular group. Furthermore, these dynamic forces need to be viewed as potential benefits; they are not present automatically in groups but need to be fostered by the practitioner.

CRITERIA FOR SELECTION OF A GROUP MODALITY

Through understanding the dynamic forces that can be mobilized in groups, it is possible to develop criteria for selecting a group experience for a given person or category of people.

An important principle of social work practice is that the means used should be consistent with the ends sought. When the purpose of service is some form of enhancement of social relationships, the group is usually the preferred modality. In a study of definitions of group work from the first one in 1920 up to 1964, Hartford concluded that there was consensus that one important purpose of group work was to help people to resolve problems in social relationships and also to help "normal people to grow socially."[31] Sonia and Paul Abels state this purpose in another way—work with groups "ought to be directed toward the strengthening of mutual and reciprocal relationships";[32] and Goldstein's formulation is that groups often aim to correct maladaptive patterns of relationships.[33]

The particular dynamics of groups, as described previously, make them ideal social contexts for coping with deficits or difficulties in social relationships. A small group in which these forces operate affords an ideal environment in which people can be helped to work on dependence-independence conflicts, sibling rivalries, conflicts with authority, rejection, withdrawal, loneliness, and loss. Even when the major problems are in the functioning of the family system, usually indicating a service to the family unit, a member of the family may benefit from a group experience. Some people may not be able to bear the anxiety of family sessions or may not be able to overcome a fear that other members will retaliate for their disclosure of previously unexpressed feelings and ideas. When the boundary of the family is quite closed to new inputs, multiple family groups may stimulate the members to new ways of expressing feelings, assigning roles, communicating with each other, and making decisions.

A second purpose of social work service that usually calls for the use of a group is the enhancement of social competence, usually a preventive service. For purposes of preventing problems in social functioning, the group is clearly the predominant modality, according to Caple's research.[34] The goals are to help the members to function more adequately in their vital social roles and to cope with changes in role expectations as they move through life transitions.[35] The need for services stems from lack of adequate knowledge, social experiences, and skills for coping with an anticipated event or situation, usually a new phase of psychosocial development or a transition to a new or changed role. Examples are prospective adoptive parents who may not have accurate knowledge about the many considerations that ought to go into making an appropriate decision, or children moving into a new developmental phase or educational level. Other clients may lack skills in applying for jobs, being appropriately assertive, or using available community resources. Many patients and their relatives need to learn new or changed roles that accompany physical disability, or they need to be resocialized into changed role expectations.

On the basis of extensive study of socialization theory, McBroom concluded that a group is the most effective and natural modality for intervention in enhancing social competence because social competence can be developed only through relationships with other people.[36] Similarly, Germain and Gitterman assert that when there is a common set of life tasks, groups provide multiple opportunities for human relatedness, mutual aid, and learning task-related coping skills.[37] And Solomon states that group methods provide rich opportunities for empowering clients who belong to stigmatized minority groups. Competence is power: empowerment is a process whereby people are enabled to enhance their skills in exercising interpersonal influence and performing valued social roles.[38]

A third interrelated purpose of social work for which a group is often the preferred treatment is the development of capacities to cope with devastating events, such as a life-threatening illness, divorce, rape, or physical violence.[39] Support and stimulation from peers aid members to disclose and manage emotions, release tension, enhance damaged self-esteem, and discover new ways of coping with stress and with the reality of the situation. Some research indicates that people who have had traumatic experiences often feel isolated, lonely, and depressed. Such people are more likely to have serious difficulties in coping realistically with the consequences of the event than those with supportive social networks are.[40] Such people are particularly suitable for a carefully planned therapeutic group experience.

Groups are also, of course, the modality of choice for services aimed primarily, not toward helping clients within direct service, but toward staff training, collaboration, planning, and social change. Such task groups are, however, beyond the scope of this book.

The remainder of the book sets forth the knowledge and skills essential for the development of groups in which the dynamic forces operate and in which the members work toward the purposes of enhancing social relationships, developing social competence, or coping with life transitions and role changes. In developing effective groups, practitioners make use of the generic values, knowledge, and skills of social work, adapting them to the needs of particular clients and to varied group situations.

2

The Group as a Unit for Social Work Practice

In social work practice, the small group is both a social context and a means through which its members modify their attitudes, interpersonal relationships, and abilities to cope more effectively with their environments. As Somers has said, the social worker thus recognizes "the potency of social forces that are generated within small groups and seeks to marshall them in the interest of client change."[1] A group can become a powerful growth-promoting environment, with power to support and stimulate its members toward the accomplishment of individual and corporate purposes. Positive results are not, however, assured. Quite the contrary, a group may have very little influence on its members, or it may have a potent influence that is destructive for its members or for society. The development of a group must not, therefore, be left to chance. To make effective use of groups, social workers require a body of knowledge about small groups and ways of influencing them.

The person who hopes to become knowledgeable about small groups finds a fascinating, diverse, and sometimes confusing array of theoretical formulations and research reports for consideration. A review of research by Lakin indicates that the number of books and articles relevant to the study of small groups continues to burgeon.[2] Most of the research has been done on short-term groups that were organized for experimental purposes, necessitating caution in generalizing the findings to other types of groups. Terminology is a problem, too, in that different terms are sometimes used to designate quite similar ideas, and the same terms often denote somewhat different concepts. Nevertheless, a framework of basic concepts occurs frequently and has acquired enough common meaning to be communicable to others.

MAJOR SMALL GROUP THEORIES

The approaches to the study of small groups that are most widely known have developed since 1930. The works of such early sociologists as Cooley, Eubank, and Simmel provided impetus for further refinement of concepts and for empirical research.[3] In a recent review of the literature on small groups, Hare identified three schools of thought that have made major contributions to understanding small groups: (1) group dynamics as it has developed from the pioneering work of Kurt Lewin's field theory; (2) sociometry; and (3) interactional process analysis of groups as social systems.[4] In addition, psychoanalytic theory has been used to some extent in these major theoretical approaches to understanding small groups and has made some contributions of its own as well.

Perhaps the best known theoretical approach to the study of small groups is field theory, associated with the work of Lewin and his associates. Its basic thesis is that an individual's behavior is a function of the life space or field, which consists of the person and his environment viewed as one constellation of interdependent factors operating at a given time. The focus is on the gestalt, the totality of factors as they interrelate in a defined situation. Behavior is a function of the interaction of personality with the environment. The personality includes the psychological and physical systems. The environment includes the immediate social group, the family, work group, and other groups to which the person belongs. It also includes the cultural system made up of the mores and norms of the person's nationality, racial, religious, and other reference groups. Lewin said that "to understand or to predict behavior, the person and his environment have to be considered as one constellation of interdependent factors."[5] Within a group, regarded as a system, there is a continuous process of mutual adaptation of members to each other, labeled as "dynamic interaction." Lewin's conceptualization is, indeed, in harmony with the intersystem, ecological, and biopsychosocial perspectives that are prevalent in today's direct service practice.

Sociometry, a method for depicting and measuring interpersonal attraction in groups, was developed primarily by Moreno and Jennings.[6] It uses field theory, with special emphasis on small groups as networks of affective relations, as these relations are identified by the stated choices of persons for others with whom they would like to associate in defined situations. It deals with the reciprocity of positive choices that bind members of a group together and with individual differences that account for a member's acceptance or rejection by others. Its major thesis is that the full realization of the individual's personality and the effective functioning of social groups depend upon the spontaneity with which given individuals accept others as coparticipants in specified activities.

Group interaction itself is the focus of the research conducted by Bales and his associates, referred to as interaction process analysis.[7] The group is viewed as a system of individuals in interaction for the purpose of solving some problem. The focus is on patterns and sequences of communicative acts of members. To solve problems related to the achievement of the task of the group, members either seek or give information, suggestions, or opinions. Members also deal with the socioemotional problems of managing tension and maintaining an integrated group.

Groups are never in a state of static equilibrium; they swing back and forth between the emotional and task realms. The problem-solving process has certain sequential phases that follow each other in a fairly regular manner, each phase being dependent upon the preceding one and each influencing those that follow.

Within the interactional analysis approach, Homans' work had as its objective the development of a set of concepts drawn from observations of groups.[8] The essence of Homans' theory is that the group is an adaptive social system, surviving and evolving in an environment. The whole is determined, not only by its constituents, but also by the relation of the parts to one another and to the environment. The environment is defined as everything that is outside of the group's boundary. Interdependence characterizes the relations of variables within the group and also the relations of the group to its physical and social environment. Members come together to form a group, motivated by their interpersonal needs and concern for a task. What emerges is a pattern of activity—whatever people do—that satisfies personal needs and gets tasks done. The verbal and nonverbal interaction patterns of activity established among the members move back and forth between socio-emotional and task areas. An internal structure of interpersonal relations develops, interacting with the external system. The structure consists of norms; status and roles; and an affective structure. The group creates its own structure that consists of a set of norms, based on values, that differs in some ways from the culture of the external system influencing the group's norms and goals. A status hierarchy of roles develops through which power and influence are distributed. Sentiments are exhibited in the affective structure of liking and disliking among the members and result in greater or lesser degrees of cohesion.

Many factors influence the group's interactions, including the environment, the size and composition of the group, the structure of interpersonal relations, its capacity for adaptation, and the parallelism between what successful operations on the environment may require and what the group itself created. Homans tried to discover the relationships among the elements of the group. For example, he proposed that the closer a person conforms to the group's norms, the higher will be that member's status in the group; and an increase in the frequency of interaction among the members increases the strength of the favorable sentiments toward one another and the activities carried out together.

Psychoanalytic theory contributed to knowledge about groups in terms of the influence of earlier social experiences on group behavior and the unconscious processes operative in group formation and interaction. Unconscious emotional factors partially explain the nature of the emotional ties of individuals with the leader and among the members and such processes as scapegoating, contagion, conflict, and cohesion. In addition to Freud's own work, some of the principal contributors to the application of this theory to groups are Bion, Durkin, Redl and Wineman, Scheidlinger, Slavson, and Yalom.[9]

Research on small groups continues at an accelerated pace. It continues to deal primarily with controlled experiments in laboratories and with aggregates of people, rather than with groups in natural settings. There has been continued emphasis on group pressures toward conformity, group cohesion, stages of group development, and conceptualizations of groups as social systems. Increased attention is being given to research on encounter and therapy groups, including the therapeutic forces operating therein.[10]

The major orientations to the small group tend to be supplementary to each other, rather than contradictory. Although there is not full agreement on a conceptual framework, a number of concepts are used over and over again by different authors. The selection of concepts for use in practice is related to the underlying theory and to the purpose and type of group to which the theory should apply. For social workers, a framework of concepts about the structure, process, and development of small groups alerts them to what they should take into account in seeking to understand what is occurring in a group and thus enhances their sensitivity to certain important variables that otherwise might be overlooked.

Most social work practice with groups was based on an intersystem perspective, even before contemporary knowledge about complex adaptive systems and human ecology had been conceptualized. In *Social Process in Organized Groups,* published in 1930, Coyle analyzed the literature on all kinds of groups and larger organizations. The first chapter is titled "The Organized Group in its Social Setting." Groups are viewed as forms of reciprocal relations. Internal group influences interact interdependently with influences from other social systems. Characteristics of the community milieu such as ethnic stereotypes, social class differences, dislocations of families, and the pluralistic nature of society affect individuals and the groups to which they belong. A major theme is that a group must be viewed within the multiplicity and complexity of organized life. Coyle wrote:

> the nature and quality of the community life . . . permeate the life of all the associations within it. The reciprocal action of individuals, groups, and the total milieu creates each organization and determines its functions and processes.[11]

In addition, Coyle identified a set of concepts for understanding the interacting processes of groups. Her work clearly set a precedent for social work's contemporary emphasis on ecological or intersystem perspectives on practice.

UNDERSTANDING INDIVIDUALS AS MEMBERS OF GROUPS

The intersystem perspective takes into account both the members and the processes that operate within the group and in the environment. One body of essential knowledge, therefore, explains the behavior of the members who comprise the group. Because social workers aim to enhance the psychosocial functioning of people, the selected knowledge needs to encompass the interrelations among biological, psychological, economic, and sociocultural components of human behavior and development. The members need to be distinguished in terms of their distinct psychosocial development, motivation, and potential for relationships. Falck notes that an individual cannot, in reality, be psychologically apart from a group. This idea is explained in terms of knowledge about the psychosocial development of individuals from initial narcissism to increasingly mature and reciprocal relationships with other members of the family and broader social networks.[12] A given group's functioning, at any point in time, can be influenced primarily by individual, group, or environmental factors or, as happens most frequently, by a mixture of all three. Since modern ego psychology and ecosystems theory are compatible, ego psychology is well suited to enlightening our understanding of the members of groups.[13]

Ego psychology builds on but also diverges from early psychoanalytic theory in important ways. Ego psychologists give central importance to the functions of the ego—a dynamic force for understanding, coping with, adapting to, and shaping external environments. When stress upsets a person's dynamic equilibrium, the ego responds through the use of protective defenses or problem-solving efforts. Significant experiences from the past may influence a person's capacity to cope with stress and to relate effectively to other people. Adaptation occurs through changes in health, in psychological functioning, in interpersonal interactions, or in the environment. Cognition, affect, and behavior are interrelated processes. As Howard Goldstein expressed it:

> Emotions are incomprehensible without some kind of cognitive designation, vague though it may be; cognitions are empty of meaning without reference to their emotional energies, and behavior would appear random if its cognitive motives and emotional forces were absent.[14]

The primary function of the ego in perceiving and adapting to reality encompasses many interrelated clusters of activities: reality testing; judgment; self-regulation and control of drives, affects, and impulses; development of object relationships; problem solving; use of protective defenses; autonomous functioning; competence; and synthetic-integrative functioning.

group provides motivation for the achievement of goals. The social worker needs, therefore, to help the members to identify and clarify the varied goals of the individuals who comprise the group and to find the common ground within these particular goals. If a group sets its own goals, they will tend to be progressive, so that the members move from one to another under their own motivation.

Socioemotional Ties. Fundamentally, the purpose of the group and the compatibility between persons determine what the nature of the group is and often, in fact, whether or not a group will develop. This fact points to the necessity for concern with the affective forces of attraction and repulsion among members of a group that comprise the emotional bond among the members.[26] Acts of communication in a group convey positive and negative expressions of emotion, as well as of opinions and facts. Both in verbal and nonverbal ways, the members communicate their feelings toward each other. Phillips notes that in every human relationship, there are "emotional reactions to one's self, to the other person, and to the specific content of the material expressed."[27] The varied responses of persons toward others are means through which they attempt to satisfy their own needs for relationships with others and to avoid threats to self.

Schutz has postulated three basic interpersonal needs: inclusion, control, and affection.[28] Persons differ in the extent to which they seek out and desire meaningful relations with others as contrasted with their desire for and use of privacy. Each person, to a certain degree, indicates a desire to have others initiate interaction toward him or to leave him alone. A person expresses behavior toward others in terms of inclusion or exclusion as well. People differ, too, in their need to control others and in preferences for being controlled by others. The balance of power may be stable or shift in different situations. Although everybody needs to love and be loved, people vary between preference for intimate, personal relationships or for more impersonal and formal relationships with others. Again, persons behave toward others and prefer that others behave toward them in certain ways with respect to affection. The responses of persons toward others and of others toward them may or may not be reciprocated. Bronfenbrenner has a similar formulation but places greater emphasis on reciprocity. He identifies the basic needs as reciprocity, balance of power, and affective ties.[29]

The way in which persons relate to each other is the heart of the group process. The attitudes that people have toward each other are naturally somewhat ambivalent. Human relationships are characterized by various positive ties—love, affection, empathy, cordiality, and positive identifications. These are associative and tend to unite people. Relationships are also characterized by various negative ties—hatred, hostility, repulsions, fears, prejudice, and indifference. These are dissociative, separating in their effect. When persons come together, they may accept each other, reject each other, or be indifferent to each other. They may seek to establish intimate, personal relationships or behave in an impersonal manner. They may prefer that others respond to them with a particular degree of closeness or distance. A positive orientation to others is often reciprocated by the other, but not necessarily. There may or may not be compatibility between the needs of persons for relative intimacy or distance. The extent to which persons find acceptance in a group depends upon the complex interaction between their own needs and attributes, those of other individuals, and the social climate of the group. Each individual is like all others in many ways; yet he is also a unique human being. Each member of a group has many things in common with other members but also is different in many ways. Similarities and differences in such characteristics as age, gender, religion, race, nationality, education, and economic status are influential in determining the place a person will find in a group. Other important factors are the similarities and differences in the members' goals and aspirations; the nature of their needs and problems; their capacities, achievements, and interests; the opportunities and deprivations of their environments; and the groups to which they belong and those to which they aspire.

The combination of affectionate or hostile feelings between members is very subtle at times. It is difficult to know the reasons for liking or not liking others. Positive or negative feelings may be based on distortions in interpersonal perception. A person may have false perceptions of another owing to ineptness in communicating intent. A child, for example, tries to express friendly interest in another child through a push, but the gesture is misinterpreted as one of hostility. Ignorance of the nuances of language of various subcultural populations often leads to the use of words that hurt, when no hurt is intended. People tend to stereotype others, that is, to perceive them according to preconceived notions about what they will be like or how they will behave, representing failure to individualize them and to recognize them as they really are. There is a tendency to stereotype persons who differ from oneself in such characteristics as race, religion, gender, social class, appearance, or age. Certain distortions in perception of other people are connected with mental illness as part of a constellation of serious problems in the perception of reality.

A person may have a false perception of another based on transference reactions.[30] Many relationships have within them feelings, attitudes, and patterns of response transferred from other, earlier relationships, particularly those with parents. The person misunderstands the present relationship in terms of the past. He tends to relive earlier attitudes with the persons in his present situation and reacts in ways that are not logical or appropriate to the current relationship. A transference reaction may be functional or dysfunctional to a relationship. Emotional attitudes and behavioral patterns evolved in the course of family living and other meaningful earlier groups are subject to transfer in various degrees in subsequent group relationships. In a group, transference reactions may be enacted toward the leader, who may represent a parental or other authority figure to the members. Such reactions may also be directed toward other members of the group who have the emotional significance of siblings to the member who distorts the current relationship. Only by observing both the transference and the reality characteristics of a relationship, and by noting how they contrast, overlap, and interact, is full justice done to the process of assessment.

As members interact with each other and with a professional practitioner, identifications may be formed. Identification is one form of imitation whereby a person feels like another person. It is a process through which a person adopts some real or imagined attitude, pattern of behavior, or value of another person and through which the desired aspect becomes integrated into the ego. It becomes a part of a person's sense of identity. It is largely an unconscious process, for the person is seldom aware that he is modifying some aspect of self to be like another person. Positive identifications are based on admiration of another person, but there can also be negative identifications based on fear. In the latter instance, identification is a defense; Anna Freud demonstrates how anxiety may be warded off through identification with an aggressor.[31] This often happens when a group is influenced by one member who initiates behavior that immediately stimulates the others to participate in similar ways. As a group develops cohesiveness, positive identification takes place also with the group as an entity. The values and norms of the group then become incorporated into the personalities of the participating members.

Groups require that members be able to give to others and to receive from them and that they be interested in and concerned for each other. In many groups, members do not have the ability to perceive other members as distinct personalities and to be concerned about them. Mature object relationships, characterized by love of others, are in contrast to the immature, narcissistic relationships of some group members, whose needs are expressed by the phrase, "I want what I want when I want it." In such narcissistic relationships, the orientation is toward the self rather than toward give and take with others. The behavior toward another person is motivated primarily by the individual's own needs and impulses. Other persons are used primarily for self-gratification. In any group, there will be variations in the members' abilities to relate to others in ways that are fairly realistic, that indicate mutuality of concern for and interaction with each other, and that tend toward identification with the positive values and norms of the group. For a collection of individuals to become a group, or for an existing group to survive, the positive unifying forces must predominate over the negative, divisive ones.

As described earlier, a feeling that one is accepted in a group and that one, in turn, accepts other members is a powerful therapeutic factor. Acceptance denotes the quality of being regarded favorably by the group to the extent that continued interaction with others is possible without undue threat. As a person feels accepted, her self-esteem rises. She becomes more open to new ways of feeling and thinking and feels comfortable enough to reveal some of her feelings, aspirations, and concerns to others. She can dare to look at the unacceptability of some of her behavior, using that knowledge for growth and change. As she feels accepted, a member tends to enhance her identification with the group, which, in turn, enhances the group's impact on her attitudes and behavior.

One major reason that the group can become a potent force for development and change is that group practice builds on the powerful fact of interdependency of people. This is mutual aid. To be sure, it is mutual aid in a group with a professional worker who has a distinctive role in the group. The group provides a give-and-take situation that may reduce feelings of inadequacy or difference and of dependency on the worker. In any healthy relationship, each participant carries a contributing, as well as a taking, role. Overton and Tinker emphasize that "Shrinkage in self-esteem and resentment occur when people are only the recipients of help—they relate better to people who use and appreciate what they can contribute."[32] Altruism is one of the therapeutic forces. This very potential poses problems, however, for many persons who are inadequate in their abilities to enter into the give and take of group participation. The potential value of the group will depend upon whether indeed a member can be helped to find acceptance and to move into interdependence with others. This process results in a feeling of belonging to the group, another of the major dynamic forces in groups.

As people become acquainted with each other and develop positive or negative ties toward each other, a structure of relationships develops. Statuses and roles become differentiated, and transitory or relatively stable subgroups form.

Status and Roles. Status refers to a person's position relative to others in a hierarchy of statuses in a given group.[33] Through a process of evaluation in a group, the members rank each other, with or without awareness of the process. The basis for such rankings depends upon the values and aspirations of the members. A person has a different status in each group to which he belongs or, for that matter, at different times in the same group. He also has generalized status in the community, which may be achieved through such means as education, income, or competence. Or this status may be ascribed to a person on the basis of certain factors other than achievement: color, ethnic origin, money, age, gender, physical condition, ancestry, or style of living. A person brings this status with him into the group. Depending upon the social agency setting, a member may already have a status that labels him as deviant, for example, as an offender, school dropout, foster child, or patient. The bases for members' ratings of each other are thus brought with them into the group from earlier life experiences, their current membership and reference groups, and their cultural values.

Values on which members of a group rate each other may be in agreement or in conflict with those of the group leader and the surrounding society. The rating pattern may be predominantly task centered or may reflect deep emotional needs. A rank is often related to a person's likability, the nature and degree of competence or other resources that she has to offer to the group, and ability to exert power over other members of the group. The ranking process may be unrelated to or even inconsistent with the overt purposes of the members but relevant to their unavowed aims. Also, the ranking process may be relative to the influence of subcultural values, for example, the bases for prestige in adolescent peer society or within a profession.

One's status in a group determines the amount and kind of influence, responsibility, and control that he has relative to other members. A reputation, once acquired, tends to be more stable than the actual behavior of a person. Reputations shape expectations and draw out behavior that accords with such expectations; thus prestige is one determinant of behavior. High status is a source of positive self-image and vice versa. The extent to which this is so relates to the importance of the group to the person and the way in which status in the group is related to status in other groups of significance to the person.

The concept of role is one of those most frequently referred to in the literature on small groups; yet there is no single agreed-upon definition of the term. Many definitions of role are similar to the one proposed by Bronfenbrenner: "A role is a set of activities and relations expected of a person occupying a particular position in society, and of others in relation to that person."[34] As Stein and Cloward point out, whenever the question is asked, "What is the proper way to behave in this situation?" or "What is really expected of me?" there is an implied problem of role definition.[35] People tend to organize their behavior in terms of the structurally defined expectations assigned to each of their multiple social roles. Each position has its organized role relationships that comprise a role set, "that complement of role relationships which persons have by virtue of occupying a particular social status," as defined by Merton.[36] This idea of role set emphasizes the importance of relationships among and between members of a group. Although a role is associated with each of the multiple positions that a person occupies, there may be multiple roles associated with a single status.

When a person enacts or performs a role, she is responding to a set of expectations that others have for her behavior, but she is also acting in accordance with her own expectations and motives. No two persons enact a role identically. When a person meets the expectations, she usually receives positive feedback; when she fails to meet expectations, negative sanctions are likely to be applied. There may or may not be consensus among significant others concerning the expectations for role performance. The expectations for behavior both influence and are influenced by the individual in the role, by the social sytem and its component parts, and by the expectations and demands of the wider social milieu. The roles of a person are not static but undergo constant definition and redefinition as the person acts and as other persons respond to her actions.

Roles become differentiated as definitions develop about what is to be done in what way by whom. When a division of labor becomes stabilized over a period of time, expectations for performance of the responsibilities become institutionalized. Thus the family has conventional roles of husband-wife, wife-mother, son, and daughter. These roles are examples of those that are assigned automatically to a person by society on the basis of age, gender, and marital status. In a peer group, there is the basic role of member, associated with the position of being in a particular kind of group. In the member's role set are his relationships with the social worker, other members of the group, and various people in the external system who have expectations concerning his attributes and behavior. Such diverse expectations need to be articulated sufficiently for effective operation of the status and role structure. Shaw cites evidence from research that role conflicts will ordinarily be resolved in favor of the person or group that is most important to the occupant of the role.[37] The extent to which conflict concerning expectations is reduced determines the effectiveness of the group's role system.

For social work purposes, an influential group is one in which the member's role is defined as a collaborative one in relation both to other members and to the social worker. The person is not only in a help-using or client role but also in a help-giving role to others. There is a mutual aid system to be built on and used. The word *member* implies that one belongs to the group and that he participates in interdependence with others. The members are participants in all aspects of the social work process—the selection of goals, the determination of means, and the processes of assessment and evaluation. To put it another way, the group operates as a democratic system. This emphasis does not deny the special authority of the worker to influence individuals and the group's structure and processes; it does, however, indicate the way his influence is to be used. Nor does emphasis on mutuality deny the development of leadership functions among the members of the group. It means that members are given freedom of choice within the definition of the group's purpose, their abilities, and the rights of others. Members are encourged to do as much for themselves and for each other as they are able. Each is expected to contribute according to his ability and each is assured that his contribution is valued. The roles of both worker and member are clear to all concerned, and so are the expectations for officially differentiated roles as these are developed in the group. This conception of roles implements professional values.

As a group becomes organized, certain members may acquire a position related officially to the purpose and structure of the group, for example, officer, coordinator, or committee member, each with its particular expectations. These positions are acquired as a result of certain choices that the person has made or that the group has made for her, usually a combination of both. Authority to influence others in certain ways is inherent in these institutionalized roles. These roles are part of the formal, organized structure of the group.

In addition to the institutional or task roles, every group develops a set of personal or, more accurately, as Radin and Feld call them, contextual roles.[38] In the small group, these are often illustrated by such labels as the shy one, the scholar, the clown, the scapegoat, and the rival. Individual patterns of behavior become evident, some of which may become differentiated into roles as the group develops particular expectations for a member and the member perceives these behaviors as expected of him. These patterns of behavior may not become roles in the strict sense of the term. Nevertheless, they are influenced by the members' own expectations and those of others in the group or society in which they are participants.

The roles that emerge in a group may be constructive for both the individual in the role and for the group, or they may be mutually destructive. Hartford notes that the establishment of roles leads to stereotypes: "a person may be so typed within the group that he cannot move out of the set of expected behaviors. Thus he may be caught in a type of behavior he cannot change and his participation and contribution may be limited."[39] In order to understand these roles the social worker needs to consider what there is about the person that accounts for his role in the group and what there is about the other members and the group situation that accounts for the fact that the group expects one of its members to behave in this way. A complex combination of individual and group influence is at work.

Subgroups. As members of a group come to discover what they have in common, various subgroups and alliances develop that express common interests, mutuality of feelings of attraction or repulsion, or needs for control or inclusion. These subgroups reflect the personal choices, interest, and interpersonal feelings of the members, not always on a conscious level. Members with reciprocal interpersonal needs tend to find each other. Isolates, pairs, and triads combine to form a pattern, often described as the interpersonal structure of a group.

The smallest subgroup is the pair or dyad, which is the most intimate and personal of all patterns of relationships. Dyadic relationships include mutual pairs in which the give and take between the members is about equal; courtship pairs in which a person is seeking and the other being sought after; dominant-dependent pairs in which one tends to control and the other to defer; sadist-masochist pairs in which one is attacked by the other but seems relieved by it; and complementary pairs in which the qualities and needs of one supplement those of the other.[40] In the pair, harmony brings greater advantages than in any other relationship, and discord brings greater disadvantages.

The triad, or group of three persons, is another subgroup to be understood. It is famous in fiction as the love triangle for the reason that a third person has an effect on the pair; in a group of three, there is almost always the rivalry of two for the affection or attention of one. The triad may consist of a mediator and two others between whom there is conflict. There may be a two-person coalition against one. A third person may increase the solidarity of the pair or may bring discord into the relationship. Often a triad evolves into a pair and an isolate or, through the addition of another person, into a double pair.[41] Larger subgroups comprise various combinations of isolates, dyads, and triads. As the group increases in size, subgroups tend to become more prominent.

Subgroups develop out of the interplay of the members' perceptions of likeness and difference, common attributes, and common interests. For some persons, membership in a subgroup may reflect apprehension about meaningful involvement with the group, so that the subgroup becomes a nucleus of security for fringe members of the group. Especially in large groups, subgroups may enhance the cohesiveness of the group, since they may further enable the group to meet the needs of members for intimacy, control, and affection beyond what is possible in the total group. A subgroup may temporarily cut itself off from participation in the life of the group. Two or more rival subgroups may emerge, each with its own indigenous leader, resulting in a reduction of cohesiveness. Or the conflict between subgroups may provide the means by which issues are recognized and problems are solved. For some isolates in the group, membership in a subgroup may be an indication of progress when such a person is able to relate more frequently in a subgroup that is functioning on a mature level. Members of subgroups may be in almost continuous or sporadic interaction with each other.

In the formation of subgroups, the generalization that "birds of a feather flock together" is contradicted by the equally accepted idea that "opposites attract." There are indications, however, that proximity in school, work, or residence; the presence of similar individual characteristics such as age, gender, race, and ability; common interests and values; and complementarity in patterns of needs influence the differential degree of intimacy among members of a group. The more lasting subgroups often stem from strong identifications or mutuality of symptoms. In evaluating the emergence of subgroups, the basic questions concern the way in which they relate to the group as a whole, whether there is cooperation or conflict among the subsystems, and whether they are functional for the particular tasks of the group at a given time. Subgroups may at times interfere with the group's effectiveness and cohesion, but they may at least as often contribute to individual and group development.

Values and Norms. A distinctive culture, consisting of values expressed through a set of norms, is a property of any stable social system. Once a set of norms is accepted, they influence the goals toward which members strive, the ways members relate to each other and to significant persons in the environment, the nature and operation of the content of the group, and the means for resolving problems.[42]

A norm is a generalization concerning an expected standard of behavior in any matter of consequence to the group. It incorporates a value judgment. It is a standard to which the members of a group expect each other to adhere. It differs from a rule that is externally imposed on the group by the leader, the organization's policies, or law. A rule becomes a norm only when it is accepted by most members, when it encompasses values and behaviors that members expect of themselves and each other. A set of norms defines the ranges of behavior that will be tolerated within the group and introduces a certain amount of regularity and predictability in the group's functioning because members feel some obligation to adhere to the expectations of the group, which they have had a part in developing. A norm implies that certain rewards and sanctions will be invoked for conformity to or deviation from the norms of the group. Since these positive or negative sanctions are often expressed through granting or withholding acceptance and prestige, the nature of the expectations and the manner in which they are enforced play an important part in a group's development. The norms of a group cannot be too far beyond the capacities of the members if they are to be relevant to the functioning of the group. Norms, once developed, tend to become stable. They become susceptible to change, however, when they are deemed inadequate to a particular situation, usually at a time of crisis.

Essentially, the process through which a set of norms is developed is one of identification of the members with what is valued and accepted by the group. Group norms are the product of social interaction based on some consensus about values, yet they are very much the property of individuals, influencing their actions even when they are alone or in other groups. A classic experiment illustrates this point. Sherif demonstrated that an individual's specific judgments about the movement of a light in a dark room tended to converge in a direction consistent with the group's range and norm of responses. A conclusion of the study was that when a person, after the range and norm of responses has been established, faces the same situation alone, he perceives the situation in terms of the range and norms that he brings from the group.[43] Therefore, the norm formed in interaction with others becomes the individual's own norm. A necessary condition for this internalization of social norms is participation in reciprocal interaction with others.

The development of norms is based on the general psychological tendency to experience things in relation to some reference point or standard. Individuals facing an unfamiliar situation tend to form a common basis for reaction to it, rather than develop a unique mode of reaction. Each person brings a set of cultural values and norms into the group. These values confront those of other members, the social worker, the agency or organization, and the surrounding environment. Through communication, these diverse values get translated into a common system of norms that regulates the behavior of all participants in the process. Gradually, those norms are selected that are appropriate to the needs of the group and new ones are developed, as deemed necessary for the pursuit of the group's purposes.

Acceptance of the norms of a group aids in the establishment of procedures and in the coordination and control of the participation of individuals. Control in a social group refers to the social interactional patterns by which the behavior of group members is influenced, restrained, or directed. Norms serve as the principal means of control within a group. They provide pressures toward conformity. As stated by Thibaut and Kelley, "They serve as substitutes for the exercise of personal influence and produce more economically and efficiently certain consequences otherwise dependent upon personal influence processes."[44] Since norms convey expectations and indicate requests that others may not properly make of a person, they protect him from the misuse of power by another. Since norms are usually based on agreement among members, the need for personal power to enforce the norms is reduced and responsibility for enforcement is shared among the members. Norms that are accepted and complied with will become intrinsically rewarding and thus reduce the need for external control. They thus provide a means for regulating behavior without entailing the costs and uncertainties involved in forcing conformity to imposed rules through use of interpersonal power.

The survival of a group is dependent, to some extent, upon the development and acceptance of a set of norms that governs the behavior of its members. Each group applies pressures on its members to conform to group norms, through various subtle and direct means of reward and punishment. Persons conform to these pressures or they resist them, depending upon numerous circumstances. Shaw and Moscovisi both present findings from research to indicate that there are differences in ability to resist pressures from others related to the person's status, sense of identity, need to rebel, or strength of conviction.[45] People try to meet the requirements of groups to which they most want to belong—hence the degree of attractiveness a group has for a particular person is an important factor. They are more apt to conform to the values of others who have high prestige in the group. They tend to conform on important issues and differ on minor points. They are more apt to conform to the group's standard if it is supported by a large majority of the members. Fear of psychological punishment or of being rejected by others force persons to conform to norms that otherwise they would not accept. Finally, the pressures toward conformity vary with a person's perception of the group's attitudes toward nonconformity; that is, if there is a norm that differences are to be recognized and valued, there is a wider range of tolerance for deviance than in groups that do not value differences. It is to be remembered, also, that when persons conform to group standards they do not thereby give up their individuality. In a very important sense, a person's attitudes and behavior are usually within an acceptable range denoted by the norms of the group.

Conflict between the values of a particular group and those of other groups to which a person belongs or to which he aspires is a common phenomenon. In some situations, the norms of different groups may point in quite different, even opposite directions. Balgopal and Vassil emphasize that the environment in which the group exists has great influence on the behavior of the members. Hostility to authority and patterns of fighting may be in harmony with the norms of the community. The security of members may be dependent upon their acting in accordance with community norms such as, for example, respect for the turf of rival gangs.[46] Dysfunction in normative patterns may occur when there is conflict between imposed rules and the accepted norms of the group and when there is conflict between the group's norms and the norms of the members' other groups. Norms may either facilitate or hinder the group's movement toward its objectives. Furthermore, the same set of norms may provide support for one person and may reduce the creativity and motivation of another. Thus, the nature of the norms, the manner in which they are enforced, and their impact on each individual and on the group as a whole are important determinants of the group's development.

In effect, then, norms suggest what a group sees as important and what it dismisses as insignificant, what it likes and dislikes, what it desires, and what it objects to or is indifferent about. The constellation of norms, based on a group's perception of what ought to be, provides weak or strong motivation for its members to use the group for their mutual benefit. One of the most important tasks of the practitioner, therefore, is to facilitate the creation and management of norms.

The social worker helps the group to develop a norm that accepts experimentation and flexibility. For change to occur, an individual needs to perceive that the group provides opportunities for him to experiment with new or modified ways of relating and responding to people and to things. A system bound by traditional and inflexible modes of response is limited in its ability to consider alternatives. An experimental norm permits the introduction of evidence that may suggest alternative responses. It conveys to members the notion that it is safe to disclose feelings and ideas pertaining to experiences of a personal and sensitive nature. It conveys to members that it is desirable to try out new tasks, make mistakes, and ask for and use help from the worker and other members. Such a norm gives permission for a range of idiosyncratic ways of self-expression, so long as these do not impede the achievement of goals and do not hurt others. It invites opportunity to explore, express, and test experiences in a variety of ways of relating to self, others, and materials. Through such experimentation, members learn that others share similar feelings and problems. Such knowledge lessens the sense of being alone with one's problems and enhances ability to face and cope with the reality of various situations. Members learn, too, that differences are acceptable, useful, and valued: what a wonderful experience that can be.

The small group is most effective in bringing about positive growth and change in its members if it combines effective psychological support for efforts to change with adequate stimulation from others to act as a motivation toward change. What is desired is that members learn to interact with each other so that they mutually support each other. The social worker can do things to help the members to accept the norm of mutual aid for efforts toward growth. The group can be developed in such a way that it provides adequate support for members in coping with their anxieties about the group experience and in their problem-solving efforts. Even when a person is motivated toward change, some feelings of loss and failure are involved in the anticipation of changes. While the group does not remove an individual's anxiety, it tends to help him to cope with it and render it more manageable and therapeutically useful. In a group, support comes from persons in a peer relationship on a level of equality, in addition to that offered by the professional helper. Support comes partly from a feeling of commonality, the "we're in the same boat, brother" theme, the dynamic change mechanism of universality. Knowing that others have similar needs, interests, and problems reduces the sense of stigma that often accompanies being a client.

Support alone is not enough. Interpersonal learning requires changes toward different attitudes and behavioral patterns. Olmsted describes a number of studies showing that the effect of a group upon an individual's motivation is often positive in that a person is more stimulated when in the company of others than when alone.[47] This interstimulation facilitates the member's communication with self and others in terms of perceptions of self-image, adequacy, beliefs, and ideas. It lowers resistance to change. There is a direct experiencing of the self in a variety of interactions with others, which may help to combat the self-confusion and self-diffusion so prevalent in our society. Such positive benefits are not likely to occur, however, unless there is a norm that reinforces the members' sharing of varied feelings, opinions, and points of view.

Groups, including families, tend to promote conformity among their members. Insofar as satisfactions derived from group life become essential, Cartwright and Zander say that the individual tends to conform to the norms of the group in order to gain and retain approval of other members.[48] But conformity is not necessarily a negative thing. According to the Hoffmans,

> It is not solely the province of the anxious, the dependent, the maladjusted; unwitting conformity in the face of ambiguity may be so, but conformity to the socially accepted demands of clearly defined situations seems a perfectly healthy response for a child or for an adult for that matter.[49]

In social work practice, the task for the worker is to influence the development of norms that further the purpose of the group. One such crucial norm to which it is hoped members will conform is that of acceptance of differences. If members conform to that norm, then the group becomes a means for helping a person to find his own identity through a combination of support and stimulation toward change.

Tension and Conflict. The sociologist Cooley said "The more one thinks of it, the more he will see that conflict and cooperation are not separable things, but phases of one process which always involves something of both."[50] Tension, or the threat of it, is essential for human development. According to Buckley, "tension is seen as an inherent and essential feature of complex adaptive systems: it provides the go of the system, the force behind the elaboration and maintenance of structure."[51]

The word *conflict* tends to elicit frightened or hostile responses, yet conflict itself is an important ingredient in development and change. It can be destructive in its impact on the self, other members of the group, or society. Yet it can also be a constructive building force in group relations. It is a natural and necessary component of group process, created through the ways people communicate with each other.

Conflict encompasses a wider range of behavior than its usual images of violent struggle and war. Conflict occurs when at least one person feels he is being obstructed or irritated by one or more others. Three basic elements characterize the conflict situation: there are two or more identifiable focal units or parties to the conflict; the parties perceive incompatible differences that create frustration; and there is interaction between the parties around the differences. Conflict is the behavior as contrasted with the emotions, such as fear or hostility, that are often connected with it. At the intrapersonal level, conflict refers to contradictory, incompatible, or antagonistic emotions and impulses within a person. At the group level, conflicts arise out of the intrapersonal conflicts of the members, misinformation about the objective state of affairs, or differences in goals, values, and norms among the members. At times, conflict has its source in the divergence between the values and norms of the group and those of certain segments of the community of which the group is a part. Differences in goals, values, and norms are due to differing life experiences and socioeconomic resources within a given culture and in other cultures.

The view of conflict espoused here is a social psychological one, consistent with an ecological approach to practice. It recognizes the need to understand the persons involved, the nature of the issues, the responses of others to the conflict, the social environment in which the conflict occurs, and the consequences of the conflict for all who are affected by it. Numerous social scientists agree that conflict is inevitable and has potentially functional and constructive uses, as well as dysfunctional and destructive ones.[52]

The person who has learned to manage her internal conflicts may well be what Sanford has called a more fully developed person than one who has never dealt with serious intrapersonal conflicts.[53] Such a person's range of coping mechanisms and adaptive behavior may be broader and more flexible, and her capacity for empathy may be greatly increased. Conflict prevents stagnation, stimulates interest and curiosity, and makes possible the recognition of problems and the consequent rethinking and assessment of self. Conversely, however, intrapersonal conflicts that are too long lasting, too severe, or too basic to the personality structure may lead to severe intrapsychic disintegration and breakdown in functioning.

At the group level, conflict may lead to enhanced understanding and consequent strengthening of relationships among members because differences are aired and not allowed to remain irritatingly below the surface. Conflict provides stimulation and a basis for interaction. Only through the expression of differences is it possible for a group to delineate its common values and interests. As areas of disagreement are explored, the areas of agreement become clarified. This clarity, in turn, contributes directly to the cohesiveness of the group. Social conflict may have consequences that increase rather than decrease the group's ability to engage in successful problem-solving activities. To focus on the useful aspects of conflict is not to deny that much conflict is destructive and may lead to the disintegration of the group. Thus, the way in which members of groups recognize, resolve, and manage conflict is crucial to the very survival of the group.

Conflict may be realistic or unrealistic. Realistic conflict concerns the means of achieving a rational goal. In unrealistic conflict, the conflict becomes the end in itself, stemming from the irrational, emotional, and competitive processes of the parties involved. Frequently, the parties to the conflict are unaware of the emotional processes that motivate them to enter into the struggle. Most conflicts, occurring as they do within the complex of a human situation, have both rational and irrational elements. Furthermore, they may be both functional and dysfunctional at the same time.

Efforts to resolve conflict occur throughout the life of any group, but there are differences in the nature and intensity of the conflict at various stages of the group's development. The earliest conflicts are around the issues of inclusion and power; later ones are around intimacy, interdependence, and separation. The resolution of major conflicts cannot occur until a group has developed to the point at which the basic consensus within the group is solidly built. An episode of conflict can end in several ways: the group abandons the issue through a shift of topic or activity; the group agrees that resolution is not attainable or undesirable; or the conflict is resolved. Research by Baxter indicates that avoidance of conflict is the prevalent means of coping with it.[54] The result is often an accumulation of unresolved issues. Although avoidance of conflict may relieve tension in the short run, the long-term consequence is dysfunctional.

It is through methods of decision-making that conflict is controlled or resolved. Groups often control conflict through a process of elimination, that is, forcing the withdrawal of the opposing individual or subgroup, often in subtle ways. In subjugation or domination, the strongest members force others to accept their points of view. In spite of its use as a democratic procedure, majority rule is an example of subjugation because it does not result in agreement or mutual satisfaction. Through the means of compromise, the relatively equal strength of opposing forces leads each of the factions to give up something in order to safeguard the common area of interest or the continuation of the group itself. Each side loses something in order to meet a common need. An individual or a subgroup may form an alliance with other factions; thus each side maintains its independence but combines to achieve a common goal. Finally, through integration, a group may arrive at a solution that is new and different from any of the contending alternatives, so no one loses and no one wins. The new solution is both satisfying to each member and more productive and creative than any contending suggestion. It is the latter process that, according to Wilson and Ryland, "represents the height of achievement in group life. It has the potentiality of being personally satisfying and socially useful: such action is the basis of democratic government."[55]

In which of these ways a particular group will attempt to resolve a conflict will depend upon a number of interrelated individual and group characteristics. Among these are the nature of the conflict; such attributes of the members as emotional maturity, values, knowledge of the subject matter, and skills in interpersonal relations; the group's prior experience in working with conflict; and the norms that have developed about the way in which differences are dealt with and problem solved.

Deutsch says that the less intense the conflict, the easier it is to resolve through cooperative means. When conflict is instigated by fears or unconscious processes, when it threatens self-esteem, or when it concerns major issues of principle, it will be more difficult to resolve than when the opposite is true. As conflict accelerates, the degree of commitment to it increases, as does holding on to one's position. Pathogenic processes inherent in competitive conflict such as distortions in perception and self-deception tend to magnify and perpetuate conflict. According to Deutsch,

> The tendency to escalate conflict results from the conjunction of three interrelated processes: (1) competitive processes involved in the attempt to win the conflict; (2) processes of misperception and biased perception; and (3) processes of commitment arising out of pressures for cognitive and social consistency. These processes give rise to a mutually reinforcing cycle of relations that generate actions and reactions that intensify conflict.[56]

The concept of conflict is associated with a number of other concepts: uncertainty, crisis, change, and dynamic equilibrium in a cyclical process. Herrick suggests a model for viewing conflict, with special reference to group situations (figure 2.1).[57] Some uncertainty exists whenever people come together. There is, for example, uncertainty about goals and means toward their achievement, status, adequacy of resources, roles, and norms. Such uncertainty leads quite naturally to conflict. The system is under stress. Its members are involved in attempting to resolve the conflict through the group's usual means. Apprehension increases if

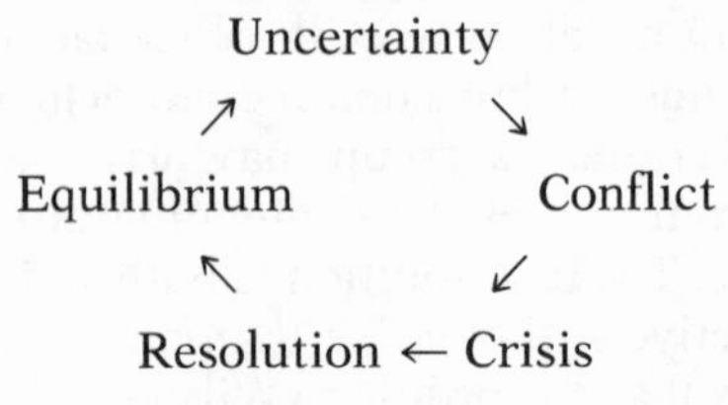

FIGURE 2.1

the conflict becomes intensified and if efforts to control it and to resolve it fail. The conflict may accelerate. A crisis may occur when the conflict reaches its apex, at which time members become aware that they are incapable of resolving the problems basic to the conflict through their customary problem-solving devices. Emotions reach a peak and the group becomes disorganized. A point of maximum disruption and considerable disorganization, accompanied by unusual susceptibility to influence, exists. The group's resources are mobilized for the necessary change, since there is awareness that some change must occur if the group is to continue. The crisis is resolved through more effective means of problem-solving.

Most groups need a period, following the resolution of a conflict with its accompanying changes in the group, to consolidate the changes. The newly achieved consensus reestablishes a steady state. During this period, the members are incorporating these changes into themselves and into the group system in such a way that a certain unity and accommodation exist within the parts. A certain unity must develop out of diversity both within the individuals and in the group, if positive growth and change are to result. Within the group unity, there are seeds for further conflict: the existing stability is usually only a temporary balancing of conflicting forces as changes are being worked through.

In day-to-day practice, a crisis need not occur before appropriate changes are made. Most conflicts can be faced and resolved before they reach a point of crisis. A group in a constant state of crisis usually disintegrates: entropy takes over. The successful resolution of conflicts strengthens the consensus within the group and enables the members to move toward the accomplishment of their goals. As Follett said, "We can often measure our progress by watching the nature of our conflicts . . . not how many conflicts you have, for conflict is the essence of life, but what are your conflicts and how do you deal with them."[58] Efforts to deny differences and to suppress conflicts are unsuccessful over the long run. Such devices lead to stagnation, dysfunction, poor morale, or disintegration of the system. Unity in diversity is a value that recognizes differences, uses them to strengthen the group, and makes it possible for conflicts to be resolved through cooperative processes.

The social worker's concern goes beyond the resolution of single conflict situations to an ability to manage conflict. Since conflict is an inevitable and continuing process in human relationships, one of the worker's tasks is to help members to develop more effective means for dealing with the process of conflict as it occurs again and again within the group. The elements that are crucial to integration as a form of conflict resolution are also the factors that contribute to the effective management of conflict. Mutual acceptance, open communication, and respect for differences make it possible for members to become competent to deal with the conflicts so characteristic of the human condition.

Group Cohesion. Concern with the cohesion of a group is based on the results of studies that indicate that cohesion has an important influence on the group. Cohesion is a group property with individual manifestations of feelings of belongingness and attraction to the group. The concept refers to the attraction that members have for each other and for the group as an entity.[59]

Research indicates that the more cohesive the group, the greater its influence on the members. To the extent that a group is highly attractive to its members, it has the ability to produce changes in attitudes, opinions, and behavior. There tend to be greater satisfaction with the group, higher morale, less internal friction, and greater capacity to survive the loss of some of its members. In groups of high cohesion, the members may disagree with each other, but they also tend to find solutions to problems and conflicts more quickly. In general, groups with high degrees of cohesion are more effective than those with low cohesion are in achieving their respective goals. The outcome for the members is better.[60]

The attractiveness of a group to its members depends basically upon the extent to which it serves the needs of its members. It will become less attractive to a person if it becomes less suitable as a means of satisfying existing needs, or if it acquires distasteful or unpleasant properties. A person usually leaves a group voluntarily only when the forces driving him away from the group are greater than the sum of the forces attracting him to the group, plus the restraining forces against leaving. Many groups survive only because the members have no strong motivation to leave. Such groups are not cohesive and exert little influence on the lives of their members.

When a group becomes a cohesive one, according to research by Levy, the following indications will usually be evident. (1) Regularity of attendance and punctuality predominate, especially in groups in which membership is voluntary. (2) Members feel that they belong, as evidenced by knowing who are members and differentiating themselves from nonmembers. (3) Members increase their expressions of "we" feelings, symbolizing identification of members with each other and with the group entity. (4) Relationships among members become accepting, interdependent, and intimate. (5) Members become highly invested in their participation in the content of the group experience. (6) Members express verbally their satisfaction with being a member of the group and with the way it operates. (7) The social climate is characterized by spontaneity, informality, and appropriate self-disclosure. (8) The group's norms provide pressures toward uniformity. (9) A system of ritual has developed that distinguishes the group from other groups and social networks.[61]

Cohesiveness can, in a sense, be perceived as the result of the interacting processes within the group. Cohesion results from the "scope and intensity of the involvement of members in the group," according to Merton.[62] The attractiveness of a group to its members is proportional to the motivations of the individuals, their attraction to each other, and the ability of the group to meet their needs. Cohesion develops as members come to know each other and as they strive toward the advancement of their shared purposes. Attraction to the group's purpose and participation in activities devoted to the pursuit of that purpose are essential conditions for the development of a cohesive group. A consensus about the common interests of the members develops. In addition to the interest in the purpose of the group, interpersonal attraction is a crucial factor in the development of cohesion. As members explore and test the meaning of the group to them and work through the conflicts over inclusion and power, the group becomes more attractive to them. Mutuality of acceptance among members develops out of shared experiences. It must be remembered, however, that in any group there are gradations and continuous shifts, both in the movement toward the achievement of goals and in the process of acceptance and rejection. Gradually, there is an increase in the extent to which members truly involve themselves in the group. Shared values and norms tend to accelerate the forces of attraction to the group. A basic consensus is established whereby the members perceive events, people, and objects from similar, but not identical, perspectives. Recognition of the differences among them creates conflict, whose resolution provides stimulation toward new and modified common perceptions. The basic process through which cohesion develops in a group is effective communication, which frees members to express themselves, encourages comparisons of likeness and difference, and modifies the attitudes of members toward each other and toward the group.

Strong cohesion may have negative, as well as positive, consequences for the members of a group. Members who are highly attracted to a group may have difficulties in recognizing the negative aspects that should be changed, or they may be unduly influenced by the other members. Overdependency on the group for basic satisfactions may limit the members' involvement in groups in the community. Strong identification with the group, an aspect of cohesion, simultaneously carries the potential for loss of individuation and personal identity. A cohesive group may protect itself against new inputs of information from the external environment; the boundary becomes relatively closed to new ways of thinking, feeling, and behaving. New ideas may threaten the existing satisfaction with the group. In such instances, Evans and Servis note that cohesion becomes the ends, not the means, toward achieving other goals.[63]

A cohesive group does not just develop. A group's cohesiveness is enhanced if the leader's participation contributes to the group's maintenance and further development. The degree of cohesion is demonstrably influenced by its leadership. The social worker, as the technical leader of the group, influences cohesion through the way he uses his professional knowledge and skills in his work with individuals and the group system.

The influence of the degree of cohesion on the individual's and group's progress varies with the purpose of the group and its content. To the extent that the group is viewed as the agent of change, as contrasted with changes being brought about by the worker or activity, strong cohesion during the core stages of development is a major therapeutic or dynamic force for change. Thus, in some forms of behavior modification or didactic educational groups, the state of cohesion may be less important than in therapy, support, or psychoeducational groups in which member-to-member influence is fostered. Cohesion may develop much more rapidly in some groups than in others: a strong sense of commonality among the members and strong felt needs tend to hasten the process. Groups with stable membership tend to become more cohesive than those open groups with frequent shifts in membership and irregular attendance do.

A cohesive group tends to become a reference group for its members. A reference group is an actual group or a category of people to which a person aspires to relate himself psychologically. It serves as a point of comparison against which a person can evaluate himself and others. A person identifies with a reference group and internalizes its values and norms of behavior so that he comes to perceive the group's values as his own. A membership group is not necessarily a reference group, but when a group in which a person is a participant is also a group with which he identifies, then his membership group is also a reference group. As Merton has said,

> Any of the groups of which one is a member . . . as well as groups of which he is not a member . . . can become points of reference for shaping one's attitudes, evaluations, and behavior.[64]

The need, then, is to develop a reference group through which all members can benefit and then help them to find their own identity so that they can function effectively when the group is discontinued. The type of group that is developed cannot be left to chance. It should become one in which the relationships and norms are those that promote growth toward more effective psychosocial functioning.

CONCLUSION

A social worker, then, has a model of a type of group in mind toward which he or she makes efforts to direct attention. Briefly, it is a group in which: (1) there is a shared purpose; (2) the role of member is defined as a collaborative one; (3) relationships are characterized by a preponderance of positive ties and interdependence among the members; (4) communication is characterized by freedom of expression and openness; (5) subgroups are flexible and functional to the group's development; (6) the values and norms of the group support healthy growth toward adaptive behavior; and (7) conflict is acknowledged and coped with through appropriate decision-making processes. Such a group will be a cohesive one in which the dynamic change forces are apt to operate, resulting in positive results for the members.

In one sense, as Homans wrote, "There is still only one sufficient reason for studying the group: the sheer beauty of the subject and the delight in bringing out the formal relationships that lie within the apparent confusion of everyday behavior."[65] But, for a professional practitioner, the shift out of confusion to understanding is translated into an accurate assessment of the group for use in helping that group to achieve its goals.

3

Social Work Intervention in Groups

The role of the social worker in reciprocal interaction with the members of a group consists of a sequence of patterns of behavior and attributes expected of the practitioner by the profession of social work, employers, licensing organizations, and the persons who are served. The social worker's is an achieved role, earned through education and experience. Within the group, his actual behaviors are influenced by the group's purpose, content, and structure and the members' needs and expectations. One of the advantages of the use of groups in social work is that stimulation toward improvement arises from a network of interpersonal influence in which all members participate. Thus, the practitioner is one important influence, but so also is each member of the group. The agent of change is the group.

Through mutual aid, the dynamic forces emerge and facilitate the positive use of the group by its members. These factors, presented in the first chapter, are what make the group the modality of choice in many situations in which people have need for help in improving their interpersonal relationships, combating low self-esteem, coping with life transitions and traumatic events, and developing skills essential for satisfactory role performance. These forces do not operate automatically; far from it, the worker's major task is to facilitate their development and use in relation to the group's goals. Social workers influence the quality of group interaction. They cannot not influence the group's patterns of communications, norms, roles, subgroups, and problem-solving processes. The focus on individual needs of members is important also but cannot in reality be separated from what is going on in the group as a system. What goes on in the group is dependent upon interactions among the members and the impact of environmental forces on individuals and the group. In providing service to a group, social workers do not limit their focus to the internal workings of the group. They often engage in conferences with members or their families, briefly or as part of a treatment plan. They are engaged continuously with the organization that sponsors the group and with numerous systems in the community. Thus, they have a constellation of subroles to fulfill: counselor or therapist, resource provider, educator, liaison or broker, collaborator, and consultant.

The primary task of the social worker is to facilitate the group process, so that the group truly becomes the prime influence on the behavior of its members. A committee of psychiatrists wrote:

> The key question, we believe, is whether we therapists can become completely aware of the ever changing and flowing reality of this process, and then conceptualize from our awareness. . . . Process may be viewed as the dynamic interaction of all the phenomenological aspects of the therapy, encompassing all overt as well as covert interactional expressions of feelings, thoughts, and actions occurring over time. . . . We need to appreciate what went before, what is happening now, and dimly what is portended in the future.[1]

Facilitating the process of the group toward goal achievement involves motivating and assisting members to participate actively and collaboratively in the process. The worker is concerned with participation in the process because the primary means of help when using a group are the support and challenge that members give each other, supplemented by the worker's direct contributions to the work of the members. Changes in attitudes and behavior occur when members are actively involved in the group—when they are able both to give and to take from others. They benefit from perceiving both their likenesses to and differences from others. Thus, the focus is on the development of meaningful group interaction without losing concern for individuals. Sharing of feelings, thoughts, and experiences is necessary so that each member can become aware of what others are feeling and thinking and use this knowledge for appraisal of his own feelings, thoughts, and actions. The satisfaction of each member is essential to the development of cohesive groups that influence their members positively. The worker needs, therefore, to make sure that the group becomes a mutual aid and mutual need-meeting system. He attempts to maximize the dynamic forces so that the group becomes the primary instrument of help. Focus on the group does not negate the importance of the individual. When the focus is on interpersonal interaction, neither the individual nor the group is submerged: both are viewed as equally important. Neither can be fully understood without the other.

PROBLEM SOLVING

The essential process used is one of problem solving, which, according to a review by Somers, has been incorporated widely into theories of social work with groups.[2] Problem solving emphasizes a process of reflective thinking used for coping with questions and difficulties. It integrates feelings with rational thought processes and takes into account both conscious and unconscious elements. Emotions influence cognitive processes. Perlman has pointed out that "in actuality, too, problem solving in social work probably proceeds, not linearly, but by a kind of spiral process in which action does not always wait upon the completion of assessment and assessment often begins before data collection is complete."[3]

Dewey's steps provide the model for reaching some decision and action.[4] The steps in the process are as follows.

1. Recognize the difficulty. Some state of doubt, hesitation, perplexity, or difficulty is recognized by one or more persons. The leader often observes patterns of behavior, conflicting messages on the part of members, silence in response to questions, or comments that indicate some doubt or concern that was not recognized by the group.

2. Define, specify, and then explore fully the problem and the goals. The process involves formulating specific questions or aspects of the problem and its component parts. The difficulty, as initially presented, may not be the problem selected for focus. In exploring the ramifications of the situation, it may become evident that there is a core difficulty underlying the stated one. Either the core problem or some facet of it may be selected for work. The process involves analysis of the problem to clarify who is concerned about the difficulty and what it means to those concerned about it. In this step, there is ventilation and exploration of feelings about the problem. If the problem is a complex one, a particular aspect might be chosen as the immediate focus of worker-group interaction. A series of decisions is made in defining and selecting a problem.

Each member of the group may have different feelings in kind and intensity about the nature of the difficulty and the hoped-for outcomes. There may be different perceptions about the nature of the problem, stemming from differences in life experiences, personal and cultural values, and norms. It is not unusual for members to be caught up in a vicious cycle of arguing and disagreeing, accusing and defending, without awareness of the issues that led to the dysfunctional behavior. Unless the sources of conflict can be defined and some goals for change identified, there cannot be opportunity for change. Before a problem can be solved, the participants in the process must arrive at a common understanding of the issue.

3. Consider alternative proposals for solution. Proposals for solutions are elicited from the members or may be offered by the leader. Facts need to be obtained in order to assess the suitability of each proposal to the achievement of the goal. The choices to be made need to be based on realistic available alternatives. The only alternatives available are those that are within a cognitive field of experience related to past personal experiences, social and cultural characteristics, and the social and physical environment of the participants. The potential consequences of the alternatives need to be considered, even though there might be unanticipated consequences of the choices made.

Considerable reflective thinking on the meaning of the possible solution to the members and significant others is essential in considering alternatives for action. Alternatives are based on different constellations of values, norms, resources, and role sets. Thus, some understanding of self and situation is required for analysis of alternative choices: one's attitudes, emotions, values, and norms of behavior influence decisions about which alternatives are acceptable and which are not. The possible choices are influenced by the availability of support systems in the family and community. Many blocks to problem-solving are imposed by society. There may be a lack of appropriate resources or rigid policies that deter any viable choices. Certain stigmatized groups are objects of discrimination and thereby lack power to achieve their goals. As alternatives are considered, some will be recognized quickly as either not feasible or not worth further consideration; one or more will be seen to have the potential for sound decision.

4. Decide which alternative to accept, necessitating the exclusion of other proposals, and evaluate the probable consequences of the decision. As in all steps of the process, the result is not based only on rational thinking; unconscious factors, values, experiences, and external factors are powerful forces in choosing. Often, there is a spontaneous recognition that a particular decision seems right. Sometimes the choice is arrived at through a cognitive process of summarizing the problem and goals, the advantages and disadvantages of each alternative, and the reasons for the particular choice. Depending upon the way the group has learned to recognize and manage conflict in the past, a solution that is reasonably acceptable to all will develop or the conflict will be solved by means of elimination of dissenting members, subjugation of some to the power of others, compromise, or majority rule. Members often need help with rethinking the proposed choice in light of their goals, the resources available, the strength of motivation to implement the decision, and the consequences of the anticipated decision.

5. Plan a course of action for putting the decision into operation and clarify the roles of worker and members in implementing the decision. The plan involves clarifying the actual steps to be taken and the persons to be involved in the process.

6. Implement the decision and evaluate the results. When an individual or group acts on a decision, another series of subproblems need to be faced. There may be a need to find an alternative way to enact the decision. Obstacles may be encountered in the abilities of the individual or group or in the environment. Once an effort to act on the decision has been made, the results need to be evaluated. There may be a sense of great success, or the results may not bear much resemblance to what was intended. The effectiveness of problem-solving depends largely on the relationship of members with the worker and with each other.

USE OF RELATIONSHIP

The nature and quality of the social worker's relationship with individuals, subgroups, and the group as a whole has an important effect on the development of the group. The use of relationship is of primary importance in motivating members to discover and develop their capacities, to feel self-esteem, and to accept and use the contributions of the worker. Perlman has described relationship as "a human being's feeling or sense of emotional bonding with another."[5]

The social worker develops a unique relationship with each member of the group. Of equal importance is the ability to facilitate relationships among members. As stated by Phillips,

> the worker's relation to each member is important, but if he is to accelerate the group relations and help members to use them, he will need to modify the many diverse, individual strands of his relationship with the members so that they will be in process with each other and so that he will have a connection with the group as a whole.[6]

In one sense, then, the social worker's focus is on the group.

Within the group, whatever the worker does that is directed toward a particular member influences the group as a whole. Coyle said it this way:

> It seems to me that the primary skill is the ability to establish a relationship with a group as a group. This involves the capacity to feel at ease, in fact, to enjoy the social interplay among members and to be able to perceive both individual behavior and its collective manifestations . . . as well as to become a part of the relationships and to affect them.[7]

If the social worker has a connection with the group as a whole, the worker also simultaneously views the individuals, the network of relationships, the group, and the environment. This complexity makes special demands on the worker. The worker seeks to develop and maintain a relationship that is sensitive to the feelings of members toward her and toward each other as these influence the climate of the group. Within these expectations, there is ample room to respond appropriately to different members in different ways at different times.

Numerous theorists have demonstrated that the three primary ingredients of the worker's relationship with the members are acceptance or nonpossessive warmth, empathy, and genuineness.[8] Levine describes the practitioner's role as a nurturer of these qualities in the initial phase, gradually moving to the facilitation of these qualities among the members as the group develops.[9]

Feeling accepted by another human being tends to make a person feel that he is of some worth to another and that he is understood by the other. Evidences of an attitude of acceptance are showing genuine interest in a person, giving him recognition, listening sensitively to what he says, paying attention to what he does, conveying a desire to be helpful, and really caring about the person. In an atmosphere in which a person feels he is of basic worth, he is free to explore his interests and capacities, discover his own identity, and set forth realistic aspirations for himself. Acceptance does not require the approval of behavior; it does, however, convey the hope that the person will be able to move away from self-defeating behavior toward the realization of his potentialities.

The value on which the concept of acceptance is based is the innate dignity and worth of people. As representatives of a profession and of society, social workers are the bearers of values, but feeling accepted makes it possible for the members to feel secure and worthy of respect and consideration, even when the workers cannot approve of their behavior. Thus, acceptance does not mean that the workers do not make judgments about the members of the group but rather that, although they evaluate, they do not condemn. The workers' evaluations of members and the group are made against the norms thought to be conducive to human welfare. This evaluation is based also upon an understanding of the person, the group, and the environment.

Empathy is closely related to acceptance but involves specifically the capacity to feel with another person.[10] It is the ability to project oneself into the feeling and thinking of another person in order to understand what he experiences. A person's intimate feelings and concerns can be discovered and evaluated only if the social worker and the members are involved in the same situation. When the worker can feel with the member, then the member tends to feel free to communicate his feelings and concerns. When persons sense that the responses to their messages are attempts to understand, rather than to judge, it is not necessary for them to cling to defensive distortions of communication. The capacity for empathy demands that a person have warmth of feeling that comes through in communication with others.

Empathy requires the presence of several sets of behavior: (1) imaginative consideration of the other person in his situation or, as Konopka says, feeling what it would be like to "walk in his shoes;" (2) a process of sensitive anticipation of the feelings and concerns that members may bring to a given session; (3) accurate perception of the members in their situations; (4) facilitation of members' expression of both their positive and negative feelings; and (5) separation of one's own feelings from those shared with members. Accurate reception of messages from the members is complemented by accurate feedback to them. Empathy is a process. Being closely linked to intuition, it is not primarily intellectual. The most distinguishing feature of empathy, compared with other kinds of fellow feelings toward others, lies in the fact that the person's ego boundaries and coherence of self are maintained. The practitioner not only identifies with the member insofar as he experiences what the member feels but also perceives and shares in the member's feelings as though they were his own. A professional detachment follows that makes possible an objective analysis of what the worker has perceived. Empathic communication is facilitated when there is identification on the basis of a common purpose or quality sufficient to give the group at least a fair degree of cohesion. An anonymous English writer is credited with the statement that empathy means "to see with the eyes of another, to hear with the ears of another, and to feel with the heart of another."[11] Empathy is not to be confused with sympathy. In sympathy, attention is on the assumed parallel between one's own feelings and situation and the feelings and situation of another.

Several degrees of empathy have been defined operationally, ranging from unawareness of the feelings of a person to a level at which "the message 'I am with you' is unmistakably clear."[12] Accurate empathy requires the verbal facility to communicate one's understanding in language that is clearly understood by the other person. The worker communicates feelings of empathy through the consistency of his verbal and nonverbal acts, which convey an honest desire to understand, avoiding such statements as "I know" or "I understand" when indeed he does not and cannot. How much more useful to say, "No, I really don't but I want to be able to." It is possible to enhance ability to empathize with others through imaginative consideration of other persons in their situations and through awareness of one's feelings toward other people and situations.

Objectivity, essential to empathy, is the capacity to see things and people as they are, without bias or prejudice. The worker's focus is on the needs of the members. Being aware of her own values and feelings, she is able to refrain from imposing them on others. She is able to evaluate realistically the feelings expressed toward her. In perceiving other persons, there is a tendency toward a halo effect, that is, to see only positive qualities in persons who are liked and only negative qualities in persons who are disliked. Self-awareness lessens the likelihood of making faulty judgments about others.

Objectivity involves understanding the motives of members in their reactions toward the worker, so that the worker is realistic in evaluating the feelings and behavior expressed toward him. It involves as well understanding one's own reactions to the covert or overt feelings expressed by members. Self-awareness is pursued, not for the satisfaction it brings the worker in his introspective activities, but for use in practice wherein some of his own feelings and reactions may hamper his ability to understand others or to use himself appropriately as he interacts with individuals, the group, and systems in the social environment. The worker needs sufficient self-acceptance and security to permit disengagement from his own feelings in order to be able to focus on the feelings of others. Dealing with such feelings necessitates some emotional maturity. Self-centeredness is incompatible with group leadership. Indeed, if the worker is preoccupied with his own feelings and reactions during a group session, rather than focused on the feelings and reactions of the members, he may not be able to empathize with the member or act appropriately in response to the interaction.

Genuineness or authenticity is the third ingredient of a helping relationship. An effective practitioner does not present a facade. To be genuine does not mean that the worker discloses her own feelings, problems, and experiences to the members, except for a carefully thought through purpose. It does mean that the worker does not deceive the member about self or situations. Genuineness requires considerable self-awareness so that he worker's verbal messages become consonant with her feelings and she is able to control her negative or defensive responses in order that they will not be harmful to others. What is effective is the absence of phoniness and defensiveness. Honesty and freedom from defensiveness provide a model for the member to emulate.

Members of groups usually develop realistic views about and appreciation of the worker and of each other. Some members may, however, perceive the social worker unrealistically, owing to erroneous expectations of his role in the group. Or they may transfer reactions from earlier relationships onto the worker and thus distort their perceptions of him. Transference is the attribution of feelings and desires from earlier relationships onto the worker or other members. These reactions derive from early childhood experiences not only with parents and parent surrogates but also with such authority figures as teachers, physicians, and employers. They also derive from and are further developed in relationships with siblings and peers. They may be exhibited through either positive feelings and reactions that facilitate the development of harmonious relationships or negative ones that inhibit them. Relationships in the group are particularly complex because of multiple transference reactions. The worker can be perceived in different ways by different members, who often symbolically find siblings or parents in the group. The reactions are largely unconscious, manifested in the present through such behavior as excessive seeking of approval, attempting to please by excessive compliance or ingratiation, asking personal questions, offering favors or gifts, clinging to the worker or another member; or through projection of hostility, provocative behavior, destructiveness, tardiness, testing the worker's interest in them, or unrealistic complaining.[13]

Some social workers find it difficult to initiate and sustain effective relationships in groups because they become overwhelmed by the intensity and multiplicity of feelings and problems expressed. The intricacies of the relationships create challenges for the worker. To be able to accept, empathize with, and communicate authenticity is not easy;

the need for these qualities may strain the capacities of the worker. Awareness of one's own responses is essential in order to avoid distortions of perceptions to the extent that this is possible. When it is the worker who transfers feelings and reactions from earlier relationships onto one or more members, the term *countertransference* is used. Countertransference components of the relationship need to be recognized, and if they are inimical to the progress of an individual or the development of a group, they need to be understood and controlled.

Awareness of one's own values is crucial to understanding and helping others, for people's values determine many of their choices and actions. In writing on psychotherapy, Buehler has said:

> One cannot live without encountering the problem of values. . . . Nor can one be a therapist without bringing certain convictions about values into one's work. These convictions may or may not be specifically communicated to the patient, but they help determine the goal he sets for himself and his patient; and they are consciously or unconsciously reflected in his questions, statements, or other reactions.[14]

Herein lies the need for self-awareness so that social workers can honestly and openly recognize their own values, distinguish them from those of the members, and act on the basis of knowledge about the distance between their values and those of the members, rather than deny that values do enter into practice.

Knowledge about the range of values held by persons within our American culture and its many subcultures may help the social worker to separate his values from those of others. Understanding and coming to terms with the values of his own important reference groups is necessary for anyone who hopes to understand the values of other people. Konopka points out that the worker needs "to realize that he sees others through the screen of his own personality and his own life experiences. . . . This is why a social worker must develop enough awareness of at least the make-up of his own particular screen."[15] Fortunately, the worker may correct this screen through careful analysis of his own behavior in relation to others and through the use of supervision or consultation. Such efforts help him to take into account his own bias, even though he cannot completely eliminate it and thus make it possible to understand better the persons with whom he works.

If a social worker can come to accept, empathize with, and be genuine with the persons with whom she works, she will not need to worry about using the professional relationship for purposes inimical to the well-being of the members. To relate to others with these qualities it not dependent upon long duration of the relationship. The worker's attributes can be conveyed in short-term, as well as long-term, involvement. The worker can communicate these intentions to the members of the group only if she truly possesses the qualities.

There is considerable research to support the view that the quality of the relationship is a necessary condition for successful outcome. Numerous studies of both worker-individual and worker-group relationships confirm "the potency of relationship in bringing about positive outcomes."[16] There is also evidence that, in spite of their importance in determining outcomes, many practitioners do not have high levels of warmth, empathy, and genuineness; but there is also evidence that these interpersonal skills are not innate and that they can be learned.[17]

A professional relationship conveys acceptance, empathy, and genuineness. It also carries authority in that the social worker assumes some degree of leadership in influencing the initiation and development of the group. Pigors explains that this authority is vastly different from the exercise of authoritarian power over others for personal gratification or for the achievement of one's own ends.[18] The authority is derived from knowledge, professional skill, and power invested in the worker by the agency or other institution. It is also derived from the power the members give the leader to influence them. The nature and degree of the worker's influence on individuals and the group process vary with the capacities of the members to cope with the demands of group life, to participate in the group, and to make their own decisions. When members are unable to cope with a situation, the worker actively uses his authority. On the other hand, when the members are able to participate responsibly, the worker supports the group's autonomy. When, on rare occasions, the worker must use coercive authority because members are hurting each other, destroying property, or engaging in such behavior as child abuse which must by law by reported, the coercive authority is vested in the professional role and in its legal sanctions.

The social worker does not first form a relationship and then get to work. The relationship develops as the worker helps the members to work on the socioemotional and problem-solving tasks of each stage of group development.

PROCEDURES AND SKILLS

Relationship is a crucial element of practice with groups, but effective problem-solving requires that the social worker make other contributions to developing and intervening in the group interaction. While the caring relationship develops, practitioners make differential use of verbal and nonverbal acts that help members to achieve goals related to the enhancement of their functioning. How to describe the complex constellation of means by which workers use their personality, knowledge, and professional skills to help a group is a thorny problem. Writers use different terms to describe the sets of interventions from which practitioners select a particular one, according to their cumulative understanding of the person-group-environment situation at a given time. These clusters of interventions are often referred to as procedures, techniques, or skills. The word *procedure* refers to a particular course of action or manner of intervening in some process. A technique is a set of specific interrelated actions that carries out the intent of a procedure. Skill denotes proficiency or expertness in the use of procedures. In spite of different preferences for terms, there is considerable agreement about types of interventions used to achieve particular goals.

The major procedures or clusters of technique are support, structuring, exploration, education-advice, confrontation, and clarification. This typology of procedures is based on Fatout's content analysis of major books on social work practice and on the research of several other social workers.[19] Other writers have developed inventories of techniques or skills that can be incorporated into the categories used here.[20] These procedures are used in work with varied types of groups, although the frequency of their use may vary and some may be emphasized more than others. In a comparative study of socialization and treatment groups, Horowitz found that the same skills are used with both types of groups: they are generic.[21]

Support. If the social worker is to contribute to the members' achievement of their goals, she needs to give them sufficient support so that in time their major support will come from the group itself. While the group is still forming, and at times during its later stages of development, the social worker supports a member, a subgroup, or the group as a whole. Support means to sustain or keep steady, to offer hope, to express faith and confidence, or to give approval to someone. The intent is to enhance a sense of self-esteem and security. What is supported are the strengths and constructive defenses of a person, in order that he may maintain a level of functioning or attain a better one. The aim is to support the ego in its efforts to cope with new or difficult situations.[22] In systems terms, the steady state needs to be maintained in reasonable balance so that stress is not beyond the members' coping capacities.

The relationship between the social worker and the group is itself a means through which the members are supported in their efforts to use the group for their mutual benefit. The worker sets the tone for mutual support through expressing his own caring and the expectation that members will become able to do this, too. To a large extent, the members support each other as they become aware of their common purposes, aspirations, interests, and needs and as they work out their positive and negative feelings toward each other. They become supportive of each other as they feel security and trust in the worker, as they come to identify with him, and later integrate some of his patterns of supportive behavior into their own personalities. In addition to relationship, the primary skills involved in support are the appropriate use of attending, realistic reassurance and encouragement, setting realistic expectations, and use of environmental resources.

Attending is essential in supporting one member, a subgroup, or the group as a whole. It is the ability to pay undivided attention to what is being said or done. Its purpose is to convey a message of respect and a feeling that what is being said or done is important. While essentially silent, the worker is actively observing, listening sensitively, and following the flow of verbal and nonverbal communication. He notes not only the manifest content but also the feelings behind it. He sends back cues that he is interested in and understands the information through such nonverbal means as head nods, leaning toward the speaker, murmurs, and occasional paraphrasing or requests for elaboration. He involves the group in whatever is going on, even while paying attention to one member, through scanning the responses of all to the comments of one member.[23]

Encouragement is another powerful means of support. Many members need considerable encouragement to participate actively in the group. The worker encourages members to do so through such means as inviting participation or recognizing a particular contribution made by one member to another member or to the group as a whole. She expresses confidence that improvement in some area of concern to a member is possible and that she can be counted on to do her part to bring it about. She shares her belief that participation in the group will be beneficial. Some realistic hope is necessary to develop and sustain motivation to enter into a group, remain in it, and make optimal use of the opportunities it provides. Hope is one of the dynamic forces that facilitate positive changes in individuals and the group's development. Members develop positive motivation when they are encouraged to remain in the group and to participate in varied discussions and social experiences in which they can feel success.

Members belong to many groups and social networks in their communities. Their relatives and other significant persons may or may not support the person's membership in the group. These people need to be encouraged to give active support to the member or, at least, to not sabotage the group experience. These persons may, in turn, need support from the worker in facilitating the member's use of the group.

Provision of realistic reassurance is an important skill in the use of support. Reassurance tends to reduce feelings of insecurity and anxiety. Persons often come into a new group, especially if they have been referred to it for help with a problem perceived by a relative or person in a position of authority, with feelings of stigma, abnormality, or guilt. A moderate level of stress may motivate a person to attain a goal, but when it is extreme, it is disruptive and incapacitating. The worker provides reassurance through encouraging disclosure of feelings, accepting the feelings, and noting the universality of them when this is so. He encourages or limits the extent of the expression of feelings so that those expressed can be coped with at a given time, and thus he reassures members that the group is a safe environment. When realistic reassurance cannot be given, it is often helpful to acknowledge the difficulty and to suggest that ways can be found to improve the situation. False reassurance is not helpful; it usually stems from the worker's need to make things better or to deny the reality of the problematic situation. Along with encouragement, realistic reassurance instills hope that things can be better and thereby enhances motivation for trying to change oneself or one's situation.

Defining realistic expectations provides support to members. When they are clear about what is expected, the energies of members can become mobilized around the accomplishment of goals, rather than be tied up with anxiety and uncertainty about their own capacities, rights, and responsibilities in the situation. One realistic expectation is that members will become able to support each other, building upon the basic need of people to give to, as well as to take from, others. The question is how to set realistic expectations without arousing the members' fears that they will disappoint the worker or fail in the tasks. The worker needs to demonstrate that he will continue to accept the members, regardless of their performance.

Support from the social worker and other group members needs to be augmented by support from parents or other relatives and from other social systems that directly influence the members and their use of the group. Since a group is a social system that should be viewed as connecting with other social systems, it is influenced by and, in turn, influences these other systems. Interviews with family members and other significant persons in the member's social orbit may result in encouragement for the member to remain in the group and in the provision of whatever resources are necessary for that to happen. When a child is the group member, the minimal involvement of the parents is that of granting permission for the child to be served for a particular purpose. Relatives may be helped to consider how they can alter some of their behavior toward the child. Marital partners may support or sabotage the group treatment of their partners. Joint or family interviews may often result in an increase of supportive behavior. The focus should be on strengthening the relationship of the member to the family and of the family to other social institutions. In residential settings, the attitudes of other social workers and members of other professions likewise may or may not provide support for the clients' use of a group service.

To serve groups effectively, the worker needs to work collaboratively with other social workers and with members of other professions such as education, law, psychiatry, medicine, and theology. Conferences with other personnel, such as teachers or nurses, are usually focused on members who are having difficulty. The content may be an exchange of information, joint planning for integrated service to the person, attempts to modify the behavior of others toward the member, or reports on the member's progress with the hope that this will start a chain reaction in the member's favor.

Use of Structure. People are influenced to move toward the achievement of their goals through participation in a group whose structure meets their needs and provides direction for their interactions. The objective of structuring is to create an optimal milieu for work. Structuring includes techniques to assure the flexible use of policies and administrative procedures, preparation for sessions, the use of space and time, the definition of limits, and the focusing of discussion and activity.

The policies and ways of work of an agency provide a framework within which the worker and the members operate. To work together effectively, the worker and members need to be clear about the policies and procedures concerning purposes of service, use of time, duration and frequency of sessions, fees, principles of confidentiality, and the major focus and content of the group. Such agreements provide a boundary within which the worker and members are free to operate. These policies and procedures should be used flexibly and changed in accordance with the needs and capacities of the members. Achieving clarity about the structure of the service reduces ambiguity and confusion and thereby provides support so that energies can be released for working toward the agreed-upon goals. Within the requirements, the plan for a particular group provides the framework for the group's operations.

Before each group meeting, the worker prepares for it in order to enhance its value for the members. She reviews pertinent records or other data to clarify the direction of her efforts. She follows up on members who might have been absent the time before; she makes decisions about whether new members should be admitted or visitors allowed to attend. She secures the necessary equipment and supplies to be used by the group and sets the stage by arranging the physical environment, because space carries psychological meaning for those who use it. It provides a boundary and anchor for a given set of actions.[24]

Nationality and other subcultural differences, as well as personality factors, account for the fact that people prefer greater or lesser distance from others, and the worker needs to be sensitive to these differences. People who desire closeness with particular others usually choose locations close to them, while those who prefer distance tend to sit farthest from others. Those who intend to participate less actively will probably seat themselves farthest from the central action. Some flexibility in the arrangement of physical facilities allows some choice for the members.

Limits, restrictions on behavior, are important forms of structuring. They define the boundaries of acceptable behavior. In defining limits, the worker intends to help a member of the group as a whole to adapt to the realistic demands of the situation. A person needs to learn to meet these demands and to be protected from the destructive tendencies of self and other. Limits provide a sense of safety, diminishing fears of going too far and losing control of oneself. Initial rules are replaced by the group's own norms as sources of limits. Such limits are more acceptable than the use of power by the leader in the form of punishment or negative criticisms. Some people need to learn to overcome too rigid conformity to policies and rules in order to develop spontaneity in relationships and to use their capacities in more creatively adaptive ways. They need permission to try out different modes of behavior. The social worker needs to balance the use of permissiveness and limits based on differential assessment of the individuals and the group as a whole. Structural controls are not an end in themselves but serve as a means to the goal of self-control and self-direction.

One important technique of structuring is focusing, that is, guiding the flow of verbal communication or the sequence of an activity toward content that is relevant to the group's purpose at a given time. The intent is to maintain the focus of attention, bring it back to a previous situation, or move to a new issue. The worker monitors the pace of the group so that the members do not become confused or lose interest. He tries to ensure, for example, that each member has an opportunity to participate so that the domination by one member or a subgroup does not persist, that agreed-upon norms are not violated, and that situations detrimental to one or more members are recognized and dealt with. Members do expect practitioners to provide guidance so that the most productive use is made of the time available. When members do not do so, the worker comments or asks questions that focus the members' attention on an issue of importance to their use of the group. The worker may reinforce the importance of continuing further what is going on, call attention to the observation that one member's contribution has not been picked up on, comment that the group seems to have shifted its attention, or request that the group stay with the discussion longer. Whatever the comment or question, he seeks responses from members to it and may need to elaborate on the reason for his concern.

As members communicate with each other, the remarks of one often set off free associations with other related topics, resulting in scattered discussion and loss of attention to the matter at hand. They may change the subject or engage in chit-chat or prolonged joking or avoid sensitive areas, or they may permit one or a few members to ramble on and monopolize the time. Messages from the worker that hold to a flexible focus convey the expectation that members can deal with issues in greater depth rather than skirt around them. The skill is not simply in holding members to a focus but in using judgment about when and how to do it. All groups need to have some light moments for friendly exchanges or respite from a too-demanding discussion or social experience. Even when a focused intervention is clearly indicated, the comments or questions can be taken as punishment unless they are accompanied with acceptance and empathy and made in nonthreatening, supportive ways.

Exploration. Exploration is one of the dominant sets of techniques used in social work practice with groups. It is a means for examining a situation by bringing facts, opinions, and feelings into the open so that sufficient understanding of the person-group-situation configuration is obtained to work toward goal achievement. It is used to elicit necessary information, to bring out details about relationships and experiences as the members perceive them, to examine the feelings connected to the relationships and experiences, and to search for alternative explanations and solutions. Along with support and structuring, it lays the groundwork for techniques more directly intended to influence the psychosocial functioning of each member and the functioning of the group as a unit.

Exploratory techniques are used (1) to elicit information, feelings, and thoughts about the external circumstances relevant to each member and to the group, the members' understanding of the group's purpose, goals, and ways of work and (2) to ascertain the feelings and patterns of behavior of individuals and the relationships among the members of the group. In most exploratory work, there is almost simultaneous effort to obtain information to increase the worker's understanding of the members in their environments and to direct discussion or activity into productive channels for understanding self, other people, and situations. It is assumed that, as people disclose more about themselves and their situations to others, they reveal themselves not only to others but also to themselves, which sets in motion a process of clarification. Through exploration, the worker helps the members to recognize and identify the various aspects of a particular situation.

Exploration of feelings has been given much attention in practice theory. Support is an essential condition for the expression of genuine feelings and concerns. When they feel supported, members find courage to express feelings and thoughts that would be suppressed in usual situations, to expose some of their vulnerabilities, and to dare to risk trying new things. As feelings of love, satisfaction, and happiness are expressed, these feelings are reinforced if the responses to them are supportive. Feelings of anger, sadness, hopelessness, hostility, and fear are also often expressed, usually leading to a reduction in anxiety. If a person can recognize the universality of his feelings, as well as their unique meaning to him, his anxiety tends to lessen. Some anxiety is, however, helpful and used for productive work in problem-solving. Feelings often lose some of their intensity and hold on a person once they are expressed to and accepted by others. But more important, once expressed, feelings are open to examination and clarification. Clarity about feelings can lead to changes in behavior. By being able to identify and describe a feeling, for example, a child may learn to substitute verbal symbols for harmful action. Ability to associate emotions with words supports the ego's capacity to cope with them.

Exploration includes, but goes beyond, ventilation. Yalom, in writing about therapeutic factors in groups, has said: "the open expression of affect is without question vital to the group therapeutic process; in its absence a group would degenerate into a sterile academic exercise. Yet it is only a part process and must be complemented by other factors." He suggests that it is the "affective sharing of one's inner world and then the acceptance by others" that seems of paramount importance.[25] Not merely releasing the feelings but also exploring them with the other members are what is important. Facilitating the group process involves bringing out similarities and differences among the members. Through exploratory questions or comments, the worker elicits the members' common and diverse attitudes, feelings, and ideas. He avoids engaging one person in a dialogue for an extended period of time, with others acting as an audience. When that happens, other members tend to become passive or bored, and the group becomes an ineffective means of help.

Although disclosure of facts about oneself and one's situation and the feelings about these facts is of value, expression may often need to be contained. A member may get gratification from talking about himself without being able to make progress toward any change. He may get caught up in his own sense of hopelessness or helplessness in a repetitive recital of content. Furthermore, other members may react negatively to the monopolization of time by one. Their responses to the nature and amount of self-disclosure by one member need to be assessed. The worker may need to stop the outpouring of feelings to seek elaboration of the material or its meaning to the other members.

The social worker uses many different specific techniques within the category of exploration. One major set of techniques is purposeful inquiry, through which the worker gives direction to the members' efforts to ascertain, expand, and clarify information. She asks questions and makes comments to guide the members in providing essential information, referred to as the skill of probing. She may ask direct questions to secure specific information about a member's characteristics, experiences, situations, or the meaning of these to him. She may ask more general leading questions that request elaboration of a question or comment. She may, for example, request that a member explain what happened, what the trouble seems to be, or what might be done about it. Such probing for information may be necessary to encourage the flow of verbal communication, to amplify details, to clarify ambiguities, and to test out the perception that members have of their problems or the processes of treatment. In a group of young children in a hospital, for example, the worker asked a five-year-old boy why he had an IV on his arm. He said it was to keep him puffed up so he'd look normal—without it, he'd go down like a balloon. Another boy said he was in the hospital because his mother had just come home with a new baby that she liked better, so she traded him in. Another said that it was because "I peed too much." The perceptions may be accurate or distorted, a necessary piece of information for the worker.[26] The challenge for the worker is to explore in ways that do not feel like cross-examination, as often happens when one question after another is asked. Questions should be used sparingly and in forms that do not elicit yes or no answers but that invite elaboration of a subject.

Usually comments are more effective than questions in encouraging members to reflect on pertinent matters. The techniques used are summarizing, reflecting, suggesting elaboration of ideas, sharing observations, restating ideas, and stimulating communication among members. A brief summary of what has been said before, a reflecting back to an individual or the group of a feeling or opinion, or a suggestion about what it might be helpful to talk about next are comments that aid the members toward fuller exploration. In some comments, the worker shares an observation with the group. The reactions to the observation then provide additional information. The request from the worker may be that members share with each other their reactions to what they have observed about a member, each other, or the process among them. The worker may restate an idea to verify his or the group's understanding, which tends to make it the possession of the group, as well as makes its meaning clear. Whenever this happens, the core of common experiences of the group is broadened, and this, in turn, facilitates communication among the members.

Purposeful silence and sensitive listening are powerful aids to self-revelation and examination of self and situation. Purposeful silence often indicates that a worker is listening and following what is being said. Such a stance tends to induce the talker to continue in the same vein. In other instances, purposeful silence indicates that a client is expected to mobilize his thoughts and then express them. A worker's personal need to fill in a short period of silence with words often interferes with members' efforts to get ready to share pertinent information.

Exploration is one of the most frequently used clusters of techniques in work with groups and is an essential part of problem-solving. When the practitioner gives inadequate attention to exploration of the nature and meaning of problems and alternative solutions, the results are often less than those desired. Inadequate consideration of alternative explanations and solutions leads to faulty assessment by the worker and the members and, therefore, to poor solutions or decisions. Solomon has shown how lack of attention to alternatives impedes the empowerment of oppressed populations, but her warning is applicable to work with any group.[27] Some practitioners tend to shortcut exploration out of a desire to reach a resolution to a problem quickly. They accept a member's or the group's first proposal: the focus is on action—"what are you or we going to do?", rather than on the means to achieve the best possible action—"how can we make a good decision?" "what is really going on here?" "what seems to be contributing to the difficulty?" as perceived by all of the members. Some practitioners may also be uncomfortable with the ambivalence, differences, and uncertainties that exploration often accelerates. So, in a rush to bring certainty to an issue or get busy with a task, workers may avoid or shortcut exploration. The process of exploration furnishes a necessary foundation for moving beyond eliciting and elaborating information to using the information for other helpful purposes.

Education and Advice. People often change if they know what is desirable and effective with respect to rational self-interests. Lack of knowledge contributes to ineffective functioning. Assimilation of information from the social environment is central to the process of problem solving in a group. Positive change may be influenced by an educational process that offers tools and resources useful to the members. One of the major tasks of the social worker, according to Schwartz, is to contribute data—ideas, facts, and value concepts—that are not available to the members and that may prove useful to them in attempting to cope with the part of the social reality involved in the problems with which they are working.[28]

Knowledge is one road to ego mastery; it is a source of power.[29] Sharing information, rather than withholding it, provides the best safeguard against dependency upon the worker. Knowledge is provided or new skills taught when the material is clearly relevant to the members' situations and when they do not have ready access to the information. The information that is shared needs to be accurate: the worker needs to know the facts and how they relate specifically to a particular member's or the group's needs.

People often need new information or reinforcement of knowledge in order to make sound decisions about themselves and other persons who are significant to them. They often need specific details about community resources and their use. They often need to understand general principles of human growth and development or the implications of an illness or physical handicap for themselves or their families. They may need to learn some basic skills that can help them to enter into new relationships more effectively, as for example, appropriate approaches to a teacher, stepparent, or prospective employer. They need information about laws that affect them concerning such events as abortion, marriage, adoption, divorce, discrimination in housing or jobs, and consumer protection.

The purpose of education is to provide new knowledge and skills required for coping with a particular situation. McBroom notes, for example, that parents often need specific help in understanding their children.[30] Messages regarding parenthood are often confusing and lead to insecurity. Results of parent education, she points out, have been disappointing in that minimal changes in behavior result from formal classes and informational brochures. But social work groups are often effective when education is an important part of help. A group experience makes available peer support to increase confidence and competence in helping the child to master developmental tasks. Likewise, learning of new roles, for example, as parents or as patients who need to adjust to major physical impairments, can help individuals to find appropriate modes of expression and action.

Ability to communicate with other people is basic to effective psychosocial functioning. Unless a person understands the intent of messages sent to him, he cannot respond in ways that meet the expectations of the sender of the message. Likewise, unless a person can convey his intents to others in such a way that they can be perceived with accuracy, he cannot make his desires known. When a person cannot understand others, he tends to become anxious. Many difficulties in interpersonal relations and role performance derive from inability to make clear one's desires, feelings, and ideas. If members do not participate actively in the communicative network within a group, they miss an opportunity to give to others and to receive validation of their feelings and thoughts from others.

There is a close interrelationship between facility in verbalization and exposure to and use of experiences in the physical and social environment. Stimulation from dealing with a variety of nonhuman objects, within supportive social relationships, seems essential to the development of adequate verbal skills. The basic speech skills are acquired during the preschool years. The progression is from experiencing many objects to learning the verbal symbols for things, people, and experiences. Dearth of language skills may often be reflected in poor performance at school or work. In working with members of groups who have suffered early deprivation in this respect, development of skills in verbal communication may be dependent upon the provision of experiences with objects and people to make up for these lacks.

With small children, the worker may teach them the elements of verbal communication: how to label the sights, sounds, colors, and things they encounter. She may teach them how to ask questions or make a request of an adult or another child. Often children need to talk about those things with which they have direct experience in the group, so that social experiences and conversations go hand in hand. With older children and adults who have difficulty in the use of verbal communication, the worker may need to provide indirect modes for practicing communication through such experiences as role playing, sociodrama, use of microphones, word games, or charades. She moves them, however, into direct verbalization as soon as they are ready to benefit from it.

Decision making is a way of actively using information. Effective decisions are dependent on adequate knowledge about the nature of the issue, the conditions in which it is imbedded, the people affected by it, and what can be done about it. In addition to resolving a particular problem, social workers often help the members to learn a process useful for coping with other problems: how problem-solving skills can be applied to other situations.

Decision making is an integral part of the problem-solving process. As Max Siporin has said,

> Making sound decisions and implementing them are fundamental aspects of all adaptive thinking and action. They are fundamental to problem-solving, and are involved in the task of assessment, planning, intervention, and corrective action in normal life and in the helping processes. We make both routine and non-routine, fateful decisions all of our lives, in secure situations or uncertain ones. . . . Choices are best made when people are informed and can actively and willingly participate in their making.[31]

Through questions, comments, and active teaching, the social worker contributes to the client's understanding of how to cope with problems. He often needs to teach the steps to be taken and provide information concerning alternative solutions and the consequences of choice. He may teach, through demonstration, ways of doing things that implement decisions. For example, a decision to budget income may need to be followed by learning about and practicing budgeting. A decision to have a conference with a school principal may need to be rehearsed before the actual experience.

The appropriate use of education, including suggestion and advice, is a crucial skill. It is based on exploration, involving searching for information, exploring alternative solutions to problems, and encouraging members to share their knowledge and skills with each other. The worker may provide relevant data, teach the steps in the problem-solving process, seek responses to the information given, and ask members to apply the information or skills to their own situations. The teaching methods may include verbal presentations of information or the use of such media as audiovisual aids, role playing, and demonstration. They also involve the selection and use of persons not in the group to provide information or teach relevant skills.

Information is given in ways that relate clearly to the purpose of the group and the goals of the members. The worker does not rigidly follow a fixed agenda or outline. She pays attention to the psychosocial and cognitive needs of the members at a given time. She offers the information briefly in language that can be understood by the members, and in a tentative manner, making clear that it is open to examination by members who may question and refute it. The worker clarifies to what extent the information given is based on facts or opinions. When the worker observes nonverbal cues that indicate doubt or skepticism or disagreement with the information, she encourages expression of feelings and alternative ideas. "You look puzzled; you may not agree with that; that seems to upset you; or how do you see it?" are comments and questions that stimulate the members to come to grips with the issue being addressed. There may be a need to go beyond imparting information to assisting members to recognize and cope with their emotional reactions to the information through the use of exploration and clarification. Kane has reminded us that education and therapy are closely akin.[32] Emotions and relationships can obscure educational messages, and members need help to bridge the cognitive and affective aspects of learning.

Giving suggestions and advice is a special form of education. Reid and Epstein emphasize that the worker offers suggestions to serve two functions: to give specific recommendations that, if carried out, may further the attainment of the members' goals and to provide an important source of emotional and cognitive stimulation.[33] He shares his opinions, based on knowledge, and explains the reason for the recommendation, a form of information giving. He offers advice cautiously, so as not to hamper the members' efforts to arrive at their own decisions. He offers such advice as tentative ideas for consideration by the members, rather than as commands. Although workers are often hesitant to give advice for fear of encouraging dependency, they probably do so more often than they acknowledge. Members resent advice at times and do not use it, but this is most often true when advice was not sought or when it was inappropriate to their needs.

Members often want and need suggestions and advice from workers. They may perceive lack of advice as lack of interest in helping them. In a study of groups by Lieberman, Yalom, and Miles it was found that the members valued direct advice or suggestions given by the practitioner or other members of the group about how to deal with some life problem or important relationship. Those who made large gains in treatment marked this item as important significantly more often than those who made few gains did.[34] In another study, by Sainsbury, it was indicated that clients tended to reject advice when it was perceived as an order to do something, but it was accepted when perceived as a suggestion for their consideration.[35] This finding suggests that it is the way advice is given that makes a difference in its usefulness. In still another study, on the use of advice by eight social workers in a parent-counseling program, Davis concluded that working class parents received more advice than those of middle class status did; all of the social workers gave some advice; and parents' reactions to advice tended to be more negative than positive. Parents also said, however, that they liked the workers to give advice and none wanted less advice than they received. This paradox may be resolved, according to Davis, by realizing that advice may serve an important therapeutic function other than guiding actions. It may stimulate a person to think of alternative ways for dealing with problems.[36]

Advice is generally accepted by, and useful to, a person if it is what he really needs, if it is presented in a way that connects it to the current life situation, if it is ego-syntonic, if it is presented in a manner that conveys genuine interest in the person's welfare, and if the person's own decision-making processes are engaged in responding to the advice.

Education is used not only with members but also with significant people in their behalf. A worker may, for example, give information to a teacher about a child's family situation or to a prospective employer about the kind of jobs that can be performed by a client with a particular handicap. He may give advice in the form of a recommendation, for example, that a child in residential treatment be moved to a cottage more appropriate to his current needs. It is to be remembered that it is ethical to intervene with others about members only if it is done with their informed consent, except under the most unusual circumstances.

Confrontation. Confrontation is a form of statement that faces a person or a group with the reality of a feeling, behavior, or situation. Its dictionary meaning is to face boldly, to bring a person face to face with something. Its purpose is to interrupt or reverse a course of action. It is a form of limiting behavior that faces a person with the fact that there is some inconsistency between his own behaviors or between his own statements and those of other sources, that his behavior is irrational, or that it is destructive to self or others. It is concerned, not with the meaning of the behavior, but with stopping it and redirecting the course of the discussion or activity. Although usually viewed as dealing with negative behavior, it may be in the form of challenging positive attitudes or performance as well.

Confrontations usually challenge a client's defenses, such as denial, rationalization, projection, or displacement, or they challenge unacceptable behavior. They upset the person's emotional balance, creating temporary discomfort or anxiety, and thus unfreeze the system and make possible a readiness to change in order to reduce the discomfort. A confrontation disconfirms the acceptability of what is happening. It provides information that contradicts distortions or blindness to facts, directly and openly. It provides a force that challenges obstacles to the achievement of goals. Overton and Tinker say that confrontations are direct statements, but they need not be harsh: the firm challenge should be "with an arm around the shoulder."[37] There is a vast difference between confrontation that is accusatory, such as, "Stop lying to me" and one that deals with denial by such a statement as "I know it's hard for you to tell me, but I already know that you are in serious trouble with the police," accompanied by a gentle tone of voice.

Hallowitz and associates report that there is some empirical evidence for the view that, when it is accompanied by a high degree of empathy, confrontation is an effective therapeutic technique; when employed by practitioners with little empathy, it is not.[38] Citing various studies, Nadel concluded that a challenging comment by a worker may be effective with certain clients who need more than a reduction of restraints to express their unconscious negativism.[39] A challenge is a form of confrontation: it calls into question and takes exception to what is being said or done. Confrontation may be of a person's verbal or nonverbal behavior or of the interactional patterns among members of groups.

Confrontation needs to be based on sound assessment of both individuals and the group. It is not the worker alone who uses confrontation. The members confront each other, often quite bluntly, requiring that the worker evaluate the impact of such statements on particular individuals and on the group, following up in whatever way seems necessary. The worker may ask the group itself to evaluate the consequences of such confrontations on the progress of individuals and the movement of the group. In order to find patterns of behavior, the worker may comment on omissions and contradictions in the descriptions of the members. A comment that seeks to understand what happened tends to be more effective than questioning why it happened. It tends to focus on the chain of events, and this makes clear the nature of the behavioral pattern to the members.

Clarification. Techniques of clarification are widely used in practice with groups. The term encompasses a variety of techniques intended to promote the members' understanding of themselves in relation to significant other persons in their lives and in relation to their roles in varied situations. Yalom refers to the process of clarification in groups as interpersonal learning.[40]

A major theoretical assumption that underlies clarifying techniques is that feeling about and perceiving oneself differently and feeling about and perceiving others differently can do much to alter behavior, attitudes, and relationships. It is assumed that a person may be able to alter his behavior or undertake new activities if he has a clear idea about what he wants to do. Current experience can be used as a corrective in modifying attitudes and behavior if the members are helped to examine and reevaluate the nature of significant experiences, situations, and people, and the consequences of their ways of functioning. Techniques for enhancing awareness often help members to work through obstacles to solving a problem or achieving a task. If members understand the nature and perhaps also the origin of these obstacles, they are often able to overcome them.

Social workers often want to help the members of a group to recognize and identify the various aspects of a social situation, then extend or elaborate on that understanding, and move ahead to clarify the problems and the situations. Three major aspects need clarification by the members of a group: the social situation, which includes the outer environment, the agency, and the group; the patterns and content of communication; and the attitudes and behavior of the members in various social situations.

Members of groups often do not have adequate understanding of situations in the community that influence their attitudes and behavior. A lack of resources, presence of a gang culture, racist or sexist attitudes, substandard housing, and lack of public transportation are examples of community conditions that negatively influence their daily lives. Some members may have distorted or one-sided views of varied institutions and groups in the community or of the legal requirements for certain privileges, such as driving a car, remaining on probation or parole, using public buildings, or providing day care for children. When they can distinguish between problems within themselves and those occasioned by conditions over which they have little control, they can focus their energies on coping with these matters. When such distortions are corrected, the members can then move to learning how to use the available resources to meet their needs. In some groups, they can learn how to become active in working toward social change.

Members often need help to correct their misunderstandings of the agency as it influences the service given, or they may need help to clarify their perceptions of the group itself. The members may simply need information about these matters or may have misperceptions about some aspect of the agency or the group that requires clarification as a prelude to correction. Attitudes and responses to the social worker may be brought into the group's discussion as may attitudes and responses to each other. Clarification of such matters tends to remove obstacles to a sound relationship between the worker and the group and among the members. It makes it possible for members to turn their attention to working on other problems of concern to them. Clarification of the nature of the group and agency is predominant during the early stage of the group's development, as will be seen in a later chapter.

Clarification of distortions in communication is often essential. In a group, the network of communication is more complex than in a one-to-one relationship. Each member's messages need to be understood by all and to be responded to in appropriate ways. Within the interacting processes of the group, corrections of distortions of the intent and content of communication may be delayed. Some messages may get lost in the welter of competing messages so that responses are missing. Lack of a core of common experiences may make communication difficult, requiring considerable clarification of the intent and meaning of any message.

There is often a need to help persons to check out the intent of a message with the message as perceived by others, through such means as questioning others about what they understand and requesting restatement of the message sent. When a person has expressed an emotion or an idea, a reaction is expected that contributes to the extension, clarification, or alteration of the original message. When a person is aware of the results produced by his own actions, his subsequent actions are influenced by this knowledge. Some members of groups need to be asked to listen to others, to indicate when a message is not clear, and to offer correction of messages, when requested. There may be double-bind messages, those in which the latent message contradicts the manifest or cognitive message or in which one set of words contradicts another. Words may convey one attitude or request, and tone of voice a different one. In double binds, there is often no right response, so that the person is caught in a dilemma and may become anxious, inactive, or withdrawn.

Flexibility in adapting to the needs and interests of others in pursuit of one's own realistic goals requires the ability to perceive the relevant factors in a social situation realistically and to act in accordance with this understanding. Improvement in functioning is enhanced when realities are faced and appropriate coping methods are developed. Almost every person has some difficulty in perceiving himself accurately in relation to other people and to the environment. Distortion may stem from bias, isolation, lack of knowledge or experience, a frame of reference not shared by others, strong emotion, or unconscious transference reactions.

In a sense, a small group is a microcosm of society, providing for its members an opportunity for reality testing, that is, for testing their perceptions against those of the worker and their peers. The group situation may be likened to a wall of mirrors through which are reflected various views of different aspects of each member. The members come to see themselves in and through the group, gradually discovering their own identity. Positive evaluation from one's peers is a source of reassurance and satisfaction; negative evaluation is painful but often a valid source of learning about oneself. When perceptions of reality are affirmed or challenged by peers, the impact may be more powerful than when this is done only by a professional helper.

People have a tremendous store of images that are residuals of experiences with which they were associated earlier. Negative symbols associated with earlier life experiences of a hurtful nature tend to remain. Hobbs explains how these residuals need to be divested of their anxiety-producing potential.[41] In Heine's study of client reports on their experiences with therapists of different theoretical orientations, there was considerable consensus that the most helpful procedure, in addition to the relationship, was the recognition and clarification of feelings that clients had been approaching hesitantly.[42] Another study, by Lieberman, Yalom, and Miles, found that the qualities or relationship were necessary ingredients in successful outcome but only when combined with work toward improved cognitive understanding.[43]

Behavior, attitudes, and values are organized and supported by self-image. A person's self-image may be different from the ways others see her; her definition of the situation may be different from that of others; or her image of others may be out of line with their own perceptions of themselves and of each other. One or all of these may be present. In order to change, a person needs to disconfirm some assumptions she has made about herself in relation to others or to situations. Bennis explains that when information does not support these ideas, there may be readiness for change. If a system is stable, the steady state may be disrupted through lack of confirmation or through disconfirmation of that idea about self or others; through induction of guilt or anxiety; or through the removal of barriers by creating a milieu of psychological safety.[44] Some upset in the system motivates a person to change, but too much stress may lead to disintegration.

Perceptions of self in relation to others may be changed through bringing to consciousness and then understanding the previously suppressed material. Through finding the connection between past experiences and current responses, a person may come to recognize that the present is not the past but that some past experiences are disturbing the present. A person may modify his defenses when he sees their irrationality or harmfulness; he becomes more clear about them and their effect on his functioning. Many maladaptive patterns of behavior can be modified with little or no clarification of the relation of past to present, but some destructive patterns may be modified only if a person examines and reevaluates significant past experiences and their consequences for current functioning and future living. Growth in ego capacity is encouraged by facing and coping with the reality of one's feelings, thoughts, and behavior. In working toward adaptive change, some understanding of one's behavior is often an essential prerequisite to change in that behavior.

Insight is a surprise response that occurs when a person is prepared to recognize the truth of an observation. It involves a new perception of the relationships among knowledge, emotion, and experience. Blum has described it as "Ah-ha" learning that occurs when a person integrates an idea that has relevance to his past or present feeling or behavior.[45] It may occur with a sense of great suddenness. It involves connections between affective and cognitive aspects of perception and behavior or connections between past and present.

One major set of techniques is used to clarify the person-situation configuration. These techniques are often referred to as forms of feedback, as suggested by Brown.[46] They include the skills of reflecting back, paraphrasing, suggesting connections between events or behavior, commenting on patterns of behavior, naming and describing emotions, and exercising cautious self-disclosure.

Reflecting or paraphrasing is a way of mirroring behavior as it is observed by another. The worker or another member may rephrase a person's statement so that he can see his problem and situation more clearly or in a new way. Sometimes a person is not sure what he has said, because there were so many confused thoughts and feelings connected with the words. When the worker or a member of the group can express what he heard, the sender of the message can decide whether this is what he really said or meant to say. Members who did not clearly hear another person may respond with a request for clarification. It may then be possible for members to pursue the subject in more depth. Such an act may also enlist the participation of other members, since the worker's reflection of client activity is like an invitation to react further to what is being said.

Another technique is to make a statement connecting two events that are obscure to one or more members so as to help them understand logical connections between aspects of their own behavior or emotions or between their behavior and that of others. The worker may offer a comment that identifies the common ground between people. Such statements may call attention to the common needs, problems, or interests of two parties who may be in conflict. They may call attention to common feelings that underlie apparent differences. Still another technique is to identify patterns of behavior. Discussion directed toward understanding the feelings and behavior of members toward one another is one form of clarification which Yalom calls process illumination. A worker may share her observations of repetitious forms of behavior in order to enhance the members' understanding of patterned responses or episodes of behavior. She may identify emotions by naming them and describing them, which helps the members to conceptualize what they are experiencing. The worker may identify some of her own emotions by naming and describing them when she thinks that such sharing will contribute something important to the group.

In the process of clarification, group leaders need to remember that such defenses as denial, displacement, or projection are self-protective devices that need to be respected and often supported. In some instances, they may be opened up to examination gently, in nonthreatening ways. The members of the group are often most effective in recognizing defenses in each other, as they reflect on each other's behavior. Comments by the worker such as "I wonder what is happening now" or "Have you ever noticed that . . . ?" can open up group discussion that leads to recognition of defenses in ways the members can deal with successfully. Sometimes, members can use simple explanations by the worker of the way a defense works or, for example, of how the conscience can be too harsh in its demands. Such contributions help the members to objectify and understand the meaning of bits of behavior, emotion, and experience. Putting connections into words helps toward their integration into the personality.

A major form of feedback consists of interpretations about the meaning of behavior. An interpretation is a statement that explains the possible meaning of an experience or an underlying motivation for behavior, or it is a seeking out of reasons for a particular difficulty in psychosocial functioning. The purpose of interpretations is to bring into conscious awareness such feelings and experiences as are not readily acknowledged or verbalized and to aid the members to integrate these new understandings. Interpretative statements are generally not offered until other forms of clarification have been used. They are directed toward the conscious or preconscious level of the personality. They are not offered by the worker until the members have tried to find their own meanings. When the worker adds his contribution to the group's own efforts, he participates according to his judgment that the group is ready for this, that the members are almost ready to acknowledge the meanings themselves, and that there is a strong worker-group relationship to support and sustain the members in their work.

Interpretative statements are usually made in tentative forms of suggesting that something may account for something else, commenting that there are explanations for an event and requesting that the members think of alternative ones, or putting an explanation in the form of a question that asks for consideration of its applicability to the particular situation. In a sense, any interpretation is a tentative hypothesis or a hypothetical question based on the worker's knowledge of people in their environments.

Interpretations are used selectively to enable members to tie some aspects of their past experiences to the present situation. Reviewing past situations is a tool for helping people to learn from experience. Reviewing patterns of experience and behavior may make it possible for a member to take a different turn, based on evaluation, toward more effective functioning. Hutten has said that "allowing clients to talk with feeling about past traumas when they are reevoked by present experiences is one of the opportunities we do have to intervene 'preventively' in relation to the future."[47] She notes that the discovery of continuities of experience can reopen a person's potential for further development. Coping capacities can be released when past experiences can be integrated into the personality "instead of having to be cut off or kept at bay by heavy psychic expenditure."[48]

SKILLS IN GROUP INTERACTION

The mutual aid process is at its apex in groups in which the members accept a working agreement; develop accepting and caring relationships; share feelings, knowledge, ideas, and experiences; develop patterns of communication, norms, and roles appropriate to the purpose of the groups and the needs of the members; recognize and resolve conflict; and become attracted to the group. These characteristics of groups were described in the preceding chapters. The social worker makes use of all of the preceding skills as he assesses and influences group properties and processes.

Relationships. The social worker develops and sustains relationships. He conveys and models acceptance, empathy, and genuineness; separates his own feelings, values, and concerns from those of others; accepts the expression of feelings and reactions of members toward worker and other members; and makes flexible and sparse use of professional authority. He introduces topics and activities that help members to get acquainted, provides opportunities for participation in activities that promote sharing and cooperation, suggests ways of doing things together that will bring satisfaction to the members, encourages appropriate self-disclosures, accepts what is disclosed, seeks responses of the members to the disclosures, and asks members to make emotional connections to the feelings of others.

Support. The social worker supports the members. She attends to individuals and the transactions among them and instills hope. She provides realistic encouragement and reassurance to reduce fears and uncertainties; articulates the feelings, concerns, and ideas that are common among the members; and accredits the members' efforts to share. She recognizes and accredits contributions made by particular members to other members or the group. She sets realistic expectations and uses environmental supports.

Structure. The social worker structures an optimal milieu for work. A major responsibility is to influence the creation and maintenance of a physical and social environment that supports the members in maximizing the use of the group for meeting their mutual needs and achieving agreed-upon goals. He designs and arranges rooms that are conducive to ease of communication among the members and to effective participation in discussion and/or activity-oriented experiences related to the purpose of the group. The worker uses policies and procedures flexibly, prepares for sessions, defines limits, optimizes use of space and time, adheres to a flexible focus, and clarifies the working agreement.

Exploration. The social worker, within the general purpose of the group, explores the common needs, interests, and hoped-for outcomes that provide a focus for the work at a given time. She engages the members in adequate exploration of facts, feelings, ideas, and alternatives. She makes comments or asks questions to elicit information, directed to the group or one of its subsystems; reflects what has been said; suggests elaboration of feelings and ideas; restates them; and summarizes content. She recognizes and accepts similar and different messages, encourages ventilation of feelings and responses, listens sensitively, and uses silence purposefully. She requests that the members engage in purposeful inquiry in their search for alternative decisions and explanations.

Education and Advice. The social worker provides the group with the information needed to acquire social skills or solve problems. He teaches communication and problem-solving skills, gives suggestions and direct advice sparingly when based on assessment, provides information to persons in the environment on behalf of members, and provides social experiences to test the application of knowledge and skills. He uses activities, demonstrations, and audiovisual aids as tools in teaching.

Confrontation. Sometimes it is necessary for the social worker to challenge dysfunctional attitudes, behaviors, and group processes when these create obstacles to progress and to accompany the challenges with support and empathy. He evaluates the impact of confrontational statements on particular members and on the group and either supports or challenges them.

Clarification. The social worker influences the development of a system of communication that is group centered as contrasted with a leader-centered pattern, one in which there is a reciprocal interplay among the members and one in which differences are to be recognized and valued and in which members feel safe to express themselves. Such a system depends on clarity of communication among the members. To establish such a system, the worker models sending messages that are clear and congruent, listens sensitively to the members, and checks out understanding of messages sent. She invites participation through giving active encouragement, attending, scanning the group, and making nonverbal gestures of support. Through comments and questions, she requests sharing and seeks responses from other members to the questions or comments of one. She encourages self-disclosure appropriate to the mood and content of the group at a given time and checks out its meaning.

She asks members to redirect messages from the worker to persons in the group or the group as a whole. She remains purposefully silent at times to stimulate members to contribute to the process and asks members to check out the intent of their messages against the perceptions of others. She restates major ideas to verify their meaning to individuals and the group and encourages the flow of verbal communication, requests amplification of details and ambiguities, and tests for common and diverse perceptions of issues. She uses language and examples that identify members with the group, emphasizing the "we" and "our" as symbols of belonging.

The social worker helps the group members to find realistic explanations for their behavior and the impact of prior experiences on them and for the behavior of other people and environmental conditions. He assures the group that it is safe to open up for discussion subjects that were previously taboo. He asks the members to suggest connections between diverse experiences and to evaluate the consequences of interpretations for those to whom they are directed and for the group. He supplements what members are able to do with each other by contributing information, clarifications, and alternative interpretations essential to the group's deliberations. He offers interpretations in tentative form and requests feedback from the members about the meaning his message had for them. He engages the group in considering how what they have learned can be used in other relationships and situations in the environment.

All of these skills involve give and take among the members with the worker in providing mutual support and mutual help for the benefit of all. The selection of skills is always specific to a situation. No one skill results in positive changes; rather a constellation of skills is used to meet the particular needs of members of particular groups. There are clear indications from the study by Lieberman, Yalom, and Miles that practitioners who convey acceptance, empathy, and genuineness; provide support for the members' efforts; use a cognitive framework that enables members to understand themselves, other people, and their situations; and facilitate the group processes so as to ensure the working of positive forces generally have the best results.[49] In the use of any of the skills, the mutual aid potential of the group is furthered when the object of the worker's intervention is the group as a whole or the interrelations among the parts, as contrasted with work with one member at a time.

The social worker uses these sets of skills regardless of whether the level of communication is primarily verbal or primarily activity oriented or a combination of both. To make effective use of activity-oriented experiences, a perspective on their use is essential to effective practice, the subject of the next chapter.

4
Use of Activity-Oriented Experiences

Activity-oriented experience is a phrase that describes the content of groups when members engage in patterns of action that go beyond talking. Verbal communication is related to the social experience in which the members are participating. Program is a word that is frequently used to designate patterns of activities; yet it is a confusing word because it also is defined as a list of the events to take place in meetings or as everything that enters into the group experience. In addition to talk and nonverbal symbols, shared social experiences occur in groups. Talking and doing are integral components of most social experiences and can be purposefully used to achieve differential goals. Almost all social experiences require some verbalization. Informal conversations occur in the midst of activities. Group discussion is used to make decisions about activities, to plan for them, or to talk over problems encountered in performing them. The use of activities is based on knowledge that improvement in social functioning comes from mastering experiences, usually combined with cognitive understanding of the experience.

VALUES OF ACTIVITY-ORIENTED EXPERIENCES

The use of activities supplements or complements verbal exchange. The guiding principle is that activity-oriented experiences can make purposeful contributions to the achievement of the goals of particular members and of the group as a whole when they are based on the needs of members. In effective practice, activities are used to serve the purposes of a particular group. They make a variety of contributions to the members and to the group's development.

Activity-oriented experiences may be used to: (1) enrich the social worker's assessment of particular members' needs and group interaction through direct observation of the behavior of members as they interact around some activity; (2) reduce stress and satisfy needs for pleasure and creativity, which are essential to mental health; (3) facilitate verbal communication of feelings, ideas, and experiences; (4) stimulate reflective and problem-solving discussions, leading to understanding of selves, others, and situations; (5) enhance the development of relationships among the members and the cohesiveness of the group; (6) provide opportunities for giving to other members or persons in the environment; (7) develop competence in basic skills appropriate to phase of psychosocial development and that enhance self-esteem; (8) enhance competence in making and implementing decisions; and (9) make better use of or change some aspect of the environment.[1]

The value of certain activity-oriented content for purposes of assessment has long been recognized. When members are engaged in working alone or together on some task, the social worker can observe directly the capacities and problems of the members. He can observe their behavior as they interact with others in varied situations. Perceiving their performance in varied situations helps both the members and the worker to recognize the members' responses to situations, the things that give satisfaction as contrasted with those that frustrate, the conditions under which individuals approach new relationships and materials and those in which they avoid them, the situations in which they are able to engage in cooperative activity and those in which they cannot share, and the tendencies toward hostile aggression or withdrawal from people or activities. An example is of a cooking group for single men at a senior center.

> All of the members were relatively isolated: they had few or no friends. Some were recent widowers who had little contact with members of their families, and all were living on low, fixed incomes. Because they did not know how to cook or manage in the kitchen, they were eating most of their meals in neighborhood restaurants, using a large proportion of their limited incomes toward this expense, with the result that most of the men were having only one meal a day. Therefore, a cooking group was formed. The members planned a menu, shopped for the food, cooked it, and then ate together. In the course of each of these activities, the difficulties they had in relating socially to others were reflected. The behavior of each man that contributed to his social isolation became apparent and could be assessed and then addressed in and through the group. The activity of cooking could not be separated from experience in planning and interpersonal learning.

Since many activities free people to express and thereby reveal their attitudes, feelings, and desires more fully than they are able to do in words, the social worker has a rich source of information for use in understanding the members. Activities may be used to assess the members in the group and group structure and processes. Some groups have been formed for the specific purpose of assessing the motivation, capacity, and readiness of prospective adoptive applicants and assessing children's capacity to use psychotherapy.[2]

The promise of pleasure inherent in many activity-oriented experiences should not be underestimated as a therapeutic force in the life of individuals and the group. Play and laughter are indispensable tools for maintaining good health and a sense of well-being. Pleasurable activities reduce stress and enable people to gain new perspectives on themselves and their situations, and creativity may bring deep satisfaction. Social workers perhaps give more attention to the expression of negative emotions of anger, hate, and sadness than to the positive ones of love, affection, and joy, which are also important for effective social functioning. Many children have not learned how to have fun with others, and many adults find it difficult to engage in pleasurable activities. The work ethic and emphasis on success in work or education may lead to guilty feelings for enjoying oneself. At times of crisis and stress, it is difficult to be playful. Inability to pursue pleasurable activities is characteristic of mentally ill people; ability to play and have fun is essential to sound mental health.[3] Group discussions that primarily focus on problems or serious decisions and interactions among members are often laden with conflict. Activities can provide gratifications that reduce stress and sustain members as they encounter the more painful features of the group experience. They can tap in on people's strengths and past successful and pleasurable experiences. For example, a singing group was formed in an inpatient psychiatric hospital. This was one of the few groups for which the members did not have to be reminded to come because the members truly enjoyed singing together. The worker soon discovered that every single group member had had a successful and positive experience in a school chorus or glee club, this in a group whose members had great difficulty in functioning successfully and whose members had been hospitalized many times.

Action is a crucial means through which people communicate with each other. Activity-oriented content is useful to facilitate verbal communication with clients of all ages, and verbal communication facilitates the nonverbal expression of feelings and behavior. Activity-oriented experiences are essential for young children and people, whatever their age, who have low tolerance for communicating or lack of ability to communicate verbally in effective ways. Some activities tend to lower defensive barriers to verbalization, and so they are often used to facilitate discussion. Engaging in some activity permits a person to enter into conversation as he is ready to do so, without the sense of pressure that is often present when discussion is the only activity. This is not meant to imply that some anxiety, discomfort, or pressures toward verbal participation are not useful motivations. Rather, it is meant to emphasize the value of aiding discussion under circumstances in which the members could not participate otherwise or in which the quality and content of communication are enhanced through such devices.

Frequently, the discussion stimulated by an experience is of as much value as the activity itself is.

> Members of a group of sixth graders had difficulty expressing their thoughts and feelings verbally. The group was divided into two subgroups, and each was asked to do a collage, using pictures from magazines. In its collage, one group was asked to address, "what's good about being your age and in the sixth grade?" The other was asked to address what's "bad" about it. When the collages were completed, each group was asked to explain to the other why it selected its particular pictures. The members had no difficulty explaining their choices. Some very similar pictures were included in both the "good" and "bad" collages, which helped the members to acknowledge and discuss some of their ambivalent feelings, especially around increasing independence from their families.

Speech is but one means of communication, but it is a basic tool for all human beings. Nonverbal communication must usually be understood in verbal terms before it can be integrated and used by a person. Verbal skills are essential to success in education and to the successful fulfillment of almost any social role. Numerous simple devices may be used with a group to open up or extend verbalization. The display of a thing that is a symbol of an unexpressed interest or concern may open up discussion. Examples are books or magazine articles on the discipline of children for use in a parent education group or on boy-girl relationships, sex, or drugs for use with adolescents. A family of dolls or a doll house is often used with young children; a movie, a painting, or a drawing that portrays people in situations somewhat similar to those of the members is useful with clients of all ages. Some persons find it much easier to talk into microphones, toy telephones, or through puppets and games than directly to the worker and other members of the group. The "I'm only pretending" quality to such devices makes them useful when members are not yet ready to face their feelings, thoughts, and situations directly. Such experimentation with props often leads to direct verbal expression.

> In one group of economically disadvantaged black children in the second grade, the girls often pretended to be what they feared—lightning, thunder, abandonment, and death. They played house, exposing their feelings about being punished, not loved, and discriminated against by their parents. They played school, exposing their feelings of failure and being disliked by teachers and other pupils. They played games in which white children always won out over black children. In a more directive type of play, the leader set up situations with which

the members needed help. The play period was followed by a short period of group conversation in which the children reviewed their play, and the leader gave information or clarified misperceptions that the children seemed to have. Through such means, the children engaged in problem-solving processes.

The quality of pretending is also present in role playing, an activity in which a group observes some of its members enacting roles in a skit for the purposes of analyzing some real-life situation in which a group is interested. The spontaneity in role playing makes it possible for members to more freely communicate their feelings and thoughts to others. The taking of roles often reveals underlying ambivalence and resistance that a person feels but has not been able to express verbally. The activity reveals to the participants and other members the feelings that need to be dealt with in order for goals to be achieved. It makes it possible for participants to recreate the experience of a personal situation and then be directed toward understanding of it.[4]

In groups of children, play tends to predominate. In play, for example, the child expresses feelings and ideas about the world he cannot verbalize. As he relives experiences in play, he expresses anger, hate, love, joy, and other emotions. Not only does the unpleasant character of the experience not prevent the child from using it as a game, but also he often chooses to play out the unpleasant experience. In work with young children, play materials should be simple: dolls and toys that do not break easily, materials that have high projective values such as finger paints, crayons, puppets, darts, toy telephones, and tape recorders. In hospitals, for example, dolls and medical or nursing kits enable youngsters to experience their feelings and then correct their misperceptions about diagnosis and treatment.[5] In one military setting, coloring books that depicted the deployment of the father were used with children. These pictures encouraged the expression of a range of ambivalent feelings about the absence of the father from the home.[6] In another instance, young children who had been sexually abused learned to express their feelings through puppets who told the long-held secrets. The puppets provided just enough distance—a safety factor. Children who have been molested have often been warned to keep it a secret or face dire consequences. One child, talking through a puppet, poured out details of his abuse. Suddenly, he tossed the puppet out of his hand. The worker asked, "what happened to pac-man?" The child replied, "He is dead. He got killed because he told the secret."[7] It is important for children to express their secrets so they can release anxiety and begin to deal with the traumatic events.

Activities, combined with discussion, seem to be best suited to the needs of adolescents. The underlying reason is that activities are consonant with the action-prone temperament, giving teenagers an opportunity to become comfortable with the leader and each other, and thus enable them to talk about feelings and problems. Adults, too, benefit from using activity-oriented experiences as a stimulant to discussion of problems. One example is Mazza and Price's report of the use of poetry and music in a group of college students who were depressed. Poems and songs were presented that accurately caught the moods of the members and to which the members were encouraged to react. These experiences provided a nonthreatening vehicle for the expression of feelings and helped the members to become engaged in treatment. Feelings and reactions were brought to the surface, where they could be dealt with.[8] In another example, some members of a group in a rehabilitation center were playing a song on a recorder called "Don't Fence Me In." The recording continued until all members of the group were present and had listened to it. A discussion about the selection of that particular song led to greater self-disclosure than ever before about how fenced in all of the members felt by the hospital's restrictions and then later by the restrictions imposed by their physical conditions.

Self-disclosure is essential before feelings and experiences can be understood and their negative impact on the quality of daily living mitigated. Reflective and problem-solving activities and discussion may lead to understanding of self, other people, and traumatic experiences. That this is possible even with children is indicated in the record of a group composed of severely neglected and abused eight- to ten-year-old children.[9] These children had been released for adoption but had serious developmental lags in their ability to form and sustain relationships, characterized by distrust of adults, inability to have fun and relate to other children, and deep feelings of rejection and insecurity. Telling a story about the birth of a child and the development and experiences of the child and family, combined with the use of pictures of people cut from magazines, were the major activities in the early meetings.

> In one session, after a story was told by the worker, the members of the group were asked to tell about the new baby in the family. Jennifer looked at a picture of a baby and said, "This baby's got a black eye." (There was no sign of a black eye in the picture.) When the worker asked how the black eye could have occurred, Thomas said, "someone punched her." The members became agitated and could not continue the discussion. A little later, however, Beverly talked about her broken bones and trips to the hospital. Thomas talked about being scared he would be beaten. Others started to talk, too. Often, only partial ideas were offered, but agitation and frustration were expressed through body movements and fights among the members. As the members came to recognize they all shared having been abused in the past, they began to be more able to relate to each other.
>
> Later, after having developed some trust in the worker, the children

involved themselves further in story telling. They wove the story together with some of their life experiences. They came to distinguish their birth mothers and rejecting foster mothers from their present accepting foster parents by calling them "old mommas" and "new mommas." Ben told the members that they needed to pray for "old mommas" and "old poppas, too." The children began to express the idea that the "old" parents could no longer hurt them and that not all parents abused their children. They moved to talking about their current "good" homes and what their proposed adoptive homes would be like. Although these talks were often disconnected and intertwined with other activities, these children were capable of some understanding of their feelings and past events and separating that out from the current reality, preparing them for being able to belong in an adoptive family.

Creative writing is another form of activity that has been used with adolescents and adults to achieve particular benefits for the members. In one example by Lauer and Goldfield, patients in a mental health setting wrote about subjects of their own choosing, read their productions aloud, and then participated in group discussion through which their feelings, thoughts, and experiences were expressed and then clarified.[10]

Properly selected experiences facilitate the development of relatedness and serve as an aid in sustaining and deepening relationships. Heap notes that group membership, by definition, "provides a context for meeting others and thereby breaks into the spiral of isolation, rejection, and social failure."[11] Activities may stimulate the members' interest in and involvement with each other and the opportunity to develop satisfying relationships and to repair dysfunctional ones. Having something to do, even such a simple thing as doodling, sharing a cup of tea, or playing a name game, reduces anxiety about one's acceptance by others and encourages interaction with others. As people interact together, they become aware of their feelings toward each other—their shared interests, ways of expressing selves, difficulties, and capacities. Shared experiences provide an opportunity for the members to cooperate or to compete: the group becomes a testing ground for assessing themselves and learning to handle cooperation and competition. Since a major therapeutic force is interpersonal learning, every possible medium should be used to help members to learn from each other.

Activities are often used to enhance the relationship among the members and thereby also the cohesion of the group. Members develop meaningful relationships with each other through shared experiences. Each experience provides a somewhat different kind of opportunity and challenge in relating to other members of the group. By providing fresh experiences common to the members that differentiate this group from other groups, identification with the group is enhanced. Some people share more fully of themselves when they engage in activity that is more varied than "just talk"; hence their identification with each other is apt to be enhanced. Experiences in which each member participates enhance mutual understanding and tend to equalize status. They make for group-centeredness by stimulating interaction around a current shared experience.

Activities allow the members of a group to give to others. Children may express their positive feelings toward each other through exchanging valentines, making gifts, and sharing their talents by teaching each other how to do something in which they excel. Even young children derive therapeutic benefits from altruism when what is given springs from their own desire rather than from their feeling that it is expected.

Psychosocial functioning is enhanced as people learn to communicate effectively and have reasonably accurate perceptions of self, other persons, and situations. Clarification of attitudes and behavior in relation to varied social situations may, however, be beneficial only if it helps a person to master problematic situations. Apparent changes in feeling and thinking need to be tested in the crucible of experience. It is especially important to have opportunities to master tasks in areas in which members of the group have previously found themselves lacking. Thus, experiences in doing need to complement experiences in talking. According to Rae-Grant, Gladwin, and Bower, social competence—the ability of people to interact effectively with their environments—"leads to increased ego strength and this stronger ego is in turn inherently better able to cope with conflict and anxiety."[12] This may, in turn, lead to increased group competence: a spiral of success is set in motion.

Psychosocial functioning is strengthened also as people acquire confidence in their abilities to perform roles in ways that are personally satisfying and that meet reasonable expectations of others. Mastery of tasks enhances self-esteem. Especially relevant to issues of self-esteen are groups that engage in the completion of a project.

> One example is of a group of thirteen- to fifteen-year-olds who made a videotape about their neighborhood. To do this, the members interviewed elderly persons who had lived there for years about changes and conditions. They had to learn to operate video equipment, interview people, take pictures, and put all of the material together. They had to learn to relate to elderly residents, who often perceived teenagers as negative and troublesome. Thus, many new learnings contributed to enhanced self-esteem. And the product—the completed videotape—was something of which the group members were very proud.

When groups engage in planning and completing a project, both process and product need to be considered simultaneously by the worker. The process of participation is important but so, too, is the end result.

When the worker demands that the members do the best they can, self-esteem is enhanced. When the members recognize that the efforts of all of them are needed to accomplish the task, they develop a sense of empowerment through group effort and participation.

Self-esteem is a necessary ingredient of social competence. Many members of groups are burdened by a sense of low self-esteem. Often, they have been the victims of the negative valuations of others; have been discriminated against because of their race, sexual preference, or gender; or have been labeled as deviant. They have had innumerable experiences with failure in family, educational, work, or friendship roles. Heap writes that: "Such low self esteem is self-nourishing, since it conditions the expectations and behavior with which new situations are met and thereby maintains the likelihood of new failure. It also frequently inhibits clients from risking new encounters at all and causes their withdrawal into a stultifying but protective passivity."[13] In working toward the aim of self-esteem, it is particularly important that the members achieve a sense of success in whatever they are doing, through group support and mutual achievement. The shift from an attitude of "I can't" to "I'll try" to "I can" is a powerful motivator for success in social functioning.

Varied experiences contribute to strengthening the ego's capacity to cope with the give and take of social relationships and expectations for performance. As Maier says, the group can be used as an "arena for trying out and living out new experiences."[14] Through selected experiences, members come to discover the consequences of their behavior and the means for coping more effectively with difficult tasks. They may demonstrate to each other their actual competence and be faced with questions about success and failure. The culture of the group is crucial in the appropriate selection and use of experiences. There needs to be a norm that accredits trying and learning and one that helps members to face a realistic appraisal of their efforts, without blame or negative criticism for failures. The group becomes a safe place to risk new ways of practicing what members find hard to do.

In using activity-oriented experiences to enhance social competence, the worker needs to assess the extent to which persons have mastered the tasks associated with each phase of human development relative to their age, gender, ethnicity, health, and environment. In helping clients to achieve competence in the performance of particular tasks or roles, the worker primarily uses an educational process. Goldstein differentiates the educational role of the social worker from that of the school teacher. In social work, "the learning process is primarily directed toward the acquisition of knowledge that will aid in the completion of certain tasks or in the resolution of problems related to social living."[15] In order to adapt more effectively, people need the necessary knowledge and skills.

Some groups are composed of members who have encountered serious obstacles to their development. In such instances, the group can provide new and better opportunities and a supportive environment for learning. One recent example, from Wayne and Feinstein, illustrates the use of activities in groups for parents of children who had identified problems in school. Two types of groups were organized—activity and discussion.[16] For some parents, activity groups were judged to be most suitable. These tended to be persons who were more cautious about verbalizing feelings, or foreign-born parents who were still struggling to learn English. Many mothers who joined the activity groups were suffering from feelings of apathy and isolation. In a safe and supportive environment, communication flowed between verbal and nonverbal modes of expression and moved from superficial to meaningful levels. Erikson's concept of mastery as the key task in the latency stage of development was found to be just as relevant for adults who had been underachievers and who were suffering from low self-esteem. In addition to activities, common concerns about parenting and school were discussed, decisions were made, and solutions to mutual problems were sought. The activities served several purposes: enhancement of relationships, opening up discussion, and mastery of tasks.

Another project was a family life education camp, established for the treatment of child abuse. The program had as its goal to teach parents new and constructive parenting skills and to eliminate child abuse. The emphasis was on four major concepts: self-esteem, gratification of needs, mutual sharing, and empowerment. Through the development of skills, self-esteem was enhanced and parents learned ways to gratify themselves without becoming emotionally dependent on their children for satisfying their psychosocial needs. Through mutual sharing, parents could apply these skills to finding and using friendly support systems in the community. By learning to take responsibility for their parts in the abusive events and in the group activities and discussions, they developed power to control their own lives. The use of didactic and experiential techniques accompanied the use of verbal discussion. Oppenheimer concluded that most effective in the "treatment of an abusive parent was a massive dose of hope, self esteem, and education."[17]

In child welfare, there is professional concern about fostering the strengths of natural parents in order that children may be maintained in their own homes. Working with parents to make this possible requires both development of their skills and knowledge. Talking it out in treatment is frequently secondary to activities engaged in with parents—teaching them household management and role-playing ways of understanding children's needs. Whittaker asserts the need to aid natural and foster parents to develop better child-rearing practices and to aid the children to develop essential skills for living. When a child is first placed in a residential facility, he states that "the basic purpose of child helping should be to teach skills for living."[18] Competence needs to be developed in basic social skills such as how to make a friend, how to let someone know you like him, how to join a game, how to defend onself with peers without resorting to fighting, or how to negotiate with an adult. Mastery of these skills enhances self-image and increases the likelihood that more and more difficult challenges will be attempted. These skills can be carried over from the group to daily living in the community.

Demonstration, role-playing, and rehearsal are common tools used to prepare clients for dealing with a demanding or threatening anticipated event. Planning with the members to try something out, then reporting back, evaluating the effort, and planning next steps help to build confidence to try new ways of dealing with stressful situations. Participating actively and responsibly in the effort to change one's behavior is a step in building competence and confidence. The worker maintains a relationship, encourages the members to try out new patterns of behavior, and offers support for experimentation with new behavior that may prove rewarding. Mutual support from each other is an important motivating force.

Members of groups often need to enhance their competence to make and implement decisions, the outcome of problem-solving. In one sense, all purposeful discussion within the group aims at some decision or choice. The decision may be effected within the personality of a member as it influences his feelings or behavior. It may affect the group itself through the form of corporate agreement or action. The decision may be a very minor one or one of major concern either to the individuals concerned or to the life of the group. All the steps in the problem-solving process come into play: identifying and exploring the problem, securing proposals for solution, analyzing the proposals, and making a decision. Based on clarification of the problem and the situation, a choice is made, and if put into practice successfully, the executive function of the ego is strengthened.

Once a decision has been made, it needs to be implemented. Activity-oriented activities are often used to prepare the members for making appropriate decisions and for carrying them out. The worker may use types of activities that focus on discovering alternative solutions to problems and making choices from among them. For example, a group of mothers role played two different approaches to requesting that the school principal provide privacy for their children in taking showers in the gym, leading to consensus about what to do and how to do it. The worker may teach or demonstrate ways of doing things that implement decisions. An example is of a group of twelve-year-old boys who decided to invite a girls' group to share an event with them. The boys were reluctant to extend the invitation and tell the girls what they would be doing together. The worker needed to clarify with them the content of the meeting and then engage them in a rehearsal of how they would invite the girls.

Groups may be directed toward constructive attempts to make better use of or to change some aspect of the environment that affects the group itself or the well-being of some of the members. Activity-oriented experiences in the group should be related to the lives of the members in their families and communities. When people are unable to influence the forces that affect their lives, they develop a sense of powerlessness.[19] Social work help should not only focus on strengthening the ego's coping capacities and the functioning of groups but also reduce obstacles in the environment when that is possible of achievement by the members of the group. Effective social action promotes both social growth and improvement of environments.

Lubell provides an example of patients' successful efforts to improve their hospital ward.[20] A group of patients treated by peritoneal dialysis completed an eight-session group whose focus was on the impact of medical, family, and social factors on their lives. At the end of that group, they requested and secured an extension of time to focus on problems in the ward. To combat boredom, the younger patients organized a film program, improved the television rental service, and conferred with the dietitian on menu changes. The older patients spearheaded a move to become more involved in planning and taking responsibility for their own treatment. They complained about negative experiences with a new dialysis machine and the nurses' refusal to disconnect it when the pain became unbearable. The record reads:

> I suggested that the patients invite the head nurse and physician to a meeting so that they could discuss the issues directly with them. With hesitation, group members supported this idea and asked me to extend the invitation to the staff. I then described this invitation to the doctor and nurse as an opportunity both to enlist the patients' support for the planned changes and to encourage them to move toward responsible self-care. I also warned staff that they should expect some anger and demands and discussed briefly with them ways of handling the situation. The staff seemed pleased with the opportunity to present some of their thinking to the patients, and the meeting went well. Together, staff and patients decided that as soon as the patients complained of pain, the nurse would disconnect them from their machines without waiting for the physician's permission. In turn, the patients agreed to tolerate the discomfort as long as possible while the staff made various technical adjustments.

In a group of residents in a long-term care facility, Berman-Rossi reports that one common theme, as is true in many institutions was dissatisfaction with the food.[21] With the social worker as mediator, the group met with staff from the dietary department several times, resulting in better understanding between patients and staff and some important changes in the menus. As they achieved some success, they felt more in control of their lives: they felt empowered. Similar benefits are reported by Lipton and Malter in their work with a group of patients with spinal cord injuries who were dissatisfied with nursing routines and inadequate sharing of information by physicians.[22] Still another example is that of Lee's work with homeless women in a shelter that combined work toward preparing the members for successful living outside the shelter with efforts to make the shelter more responsive to the needs of the residents.[23]

Examples of social action activities demonstrate also their use in community settings. A threat was made to close a clinic for disabled children. The parents' groups were eager to do what they could to prevent closure. They mobilized a mail and telephone campaign and interested a local radio station and newspaper in the cause. The staff developed viable proposals for funding. As a result of these efforts, the administrator agreed to withdraw the plan to close the clinic. Germain and Gitterman report that:

> Services to this needy group of children and their parents were safeguarded. In addition, the parents' self esteem, competence, and sense of identity and autonomy were enhanced by their having taken action on their own behalf in a matter of deep concern to them.[24]

A typical theme in groups of adolescents is conflict with parents concerning rules, discipline, and privileges. In one group, following an outpouring of complaints, the worker asked the members what could be done about it. The first responses were that nothing could be done; then there was a shift to asking the workers to talk to their parents; and then a decision was made to plan for and follow through on a joint meeting with parents.[25] In another example, when a group of adults who were enrolled in a job-training program learned that legislation was proposed that would reduce funds for the program, the members decided to contact and work with the local Welfare Rights Organization to defeat the legislation.[26]

Decisions to take action in relation to some obstacle in the environment are made through the use of a group problem-solving process and the carrying out of activities necessary to implement the decision. Voluntary participation in social action is growth producing for the members when action is taken with, not for the members. Empowerment, as both Pernell and Solomon demonstrate, is both a process and a goal.[27] As people learn how to solve problems, they gain some power over their lives, enhance their self-esteem, and reduce feelings of hopelessness and helplessness. In small or large ways, they also make environments more responsive to the needs of people beyond the group.

Not all of the members' needs can be met in the group itself: often resources outside the group can be used so that the members may become more effective in their roles in the outside environment.

INDIVIDUAL AND GROUP ASSESSMENT

The use of activity-oriented experiences as a full-fledged medium for growth and change necessitates their appropriateness to a given situation, based on individual and group assessment. Members respond in different ways to the same activity. Members who are very shy and fearful, for example, should not be pushed to try things that create anxiety beyond their capacity to cope with it. They need help to move from parallel participation to group interaction. Members who are very rivalrous can work on this problem through engaging in such activities as role-playing and, when ready, competitive games; they will need help to learn to handle wins and losses. Where self-esteem is low, the activity needs to be one in which successful completion is assured. Members of any age who have had few satisfying social experiences will need a great deal of support from the worker in daring to try new experiences, whereas those who have had numerous satisfactory social experiences are more able to translate the skills learned elsewhere into the group.

Creative use of activities designed to contribute to the resolution of particular members' problems in relationships is illustrated in an article by Bittner on work with a group for mothers and their young children whose purpose was to alleviate dysfunctional mother-child relationships.[28]

> The S family was referred to a child development center by its pediatrician who was concerned about Lisa, age two and a half. She was extremely shy and unable to relate to people; the relationship between mother and child was pathological. Mrs. S was unable to give up extensive early symbiosis with Lisa. Treatment of the marital couple had resulted in some progress, but the relationship between mother and child remained unchanged. So Mrs. S and Lisa were referred to a group composed of four mother-child pairs. The goal was to help Mrs. S and Lisa to differentiate from each other.
>
> The content of the group was designed to further its purpose. Coffee was available for adults and fruit juice for children; name tags were different colors for mothers and children to differentiate mother from child and one person from another. The meetings began with a song which addressed everyone by name and encouraged eye contact and there was a similar closing song. These rituals were used to ease the transition in and out of the group and to enable mothers to connect with each other. Toys for children were selected for the specific

> purpose of helping them to move away from and back toward their mothers.
>
> In the early meetings, Mrs. S would clutch Lisa tightly in her lap and insist that Lisa was too frightened to move off. A wooden rocking boat served as a vehicle for moving Lisa away from and back toward her mother. The boat was placed close to the mother's chair so that mother and child faced one another. The mother sat the child in the boat and rocked it while the worker pointed out how the child was moving away from and then coming back toward the mother, providing a safe way for trying out separating from each other. Other play materials included a slide and a barn and small animals with which Lisa gradually became able to play. Mrs. S, who was extremely shy in relating to other members of the group, gradually became able to participate in discussions about her relationship with Lisa and how to help Lisa to progress in her social development.

Such examples demonstrate the in-depth knowledge of human development and psychosocial assessment that underlies the therapeutic use of activity-oriented experiences, and they also demonstrate creativity and flexibility in the use of materials and equipment.

The content of a group experience needs to be sensitive to the values and norms of the culture of the members. Delgado, for example, points out that activity-oriented approaches are especially beneficial to members of Hispanic backgrounds.[29] The activities used need to be related to the interpersonal and environmental issues with which the members are currently dealing. They need to be supportive, stress cooperation rather than competition, and be consistent with a typical present-time orientation. He cautions that the emphasis on action means, not that the members do not benefit from discussions pertaining to psychosocial difficulties, but that it is the interweaving of doing and talking that is important.

Edwards and associates make similar points concerning successful work with American Indians.[30] They used an activity-discussion group for enhancing the self-concept and identification with being Indian of girls, aged seven to eleven. The content consisted of a variety of activities typical of the Indian culture. Talking supplemented doing. For example, when there was conflict in playing games, the game was terminated, and the members were asked to talk about how they were feeling, how important it is to listen to others and speak for oneself, and how conflicts are resolved. They discussed ways of handling negative remarks about American Indians. They were encouraged to share what they learned in the group at home. In the final meeting, which took place in the home of the leader and was attended by the members' families, the girls reviewed and demonstrated what they had learned in the group. A research evaluation showed positive changes in self-concept and a high correlation between the positive responses of the girls to an activity and the emphasis placed on that activity in the group. The authors caution that activities need to be used differentially with the four hundred eighty-one separate and distinct tribal groups.

In addition to understanding the personal strengths and problems of the members and their cultural identifications, it is equally important that the worker assess the group in its stage of development at a given time.[31] Suitable activities in the first stage are usually those that help members to become acquainted, release tension, and provide for a sense of quick accomplishment. They should not require intimacy and closeness or stimulate aggressive behavior. They should have some clear structure but also allow for some flexibility in order to provide a safe environment for interaction among the members. With some groups, the provision of simple refreshments fosters comfort in interacting with others. When the group moves into the stage of dissatisfaction, activity-oriented activities should provide opportunities for the members to work through conflicts, help them learn to share and handle competition, and require them to make decisions. As members move into the mutuality-work stage, activities may require a higher level of interaction among the members, more self-disclosure, greater individuation, higher demands for competence and facing failure, and opportunities for generalization to the world outside the group. In the termination stage, the content often repeats earlier experiences so that members become aware of their progress, becomes more oriented to the situations of individuals, and emphasizes movement away from the group toward the community. Some groups will use rituals or goodby parties as one means of handling powerful feelings of loss that are expressed symbolically through food, picture taking, and gift giving.

SELECTION OF ACTIVITY-ORIENTED EXPERIENCES

Some social workers avoid the use of activities because of the faulty notion that their use requires that they have special skills in a host of cultural, recreational, and social activities. More important are knowledge of person-environment interactions and skills in assessment. Essential to the use of any form of content is an assessment of each member's needs and problems, capacities, and interests; of the tasks that are typical of each phase of psychosocial development; of the stage of group development; and of the particular issues being dealt with in the group at a given time. It can be assumed that any social worker has had varied experiences in group living and in social and cultural activities. It is out of these life experiences, with special efforts to recall the many things one has done in the past, that ideas for activities come. The worker can capitalize on his own interests and skills, provided that their use will meet the needs of the group. In some groups, outside resources can be used. The most simple everyday tasks, too, may be the most valuable for the group, and these are readily learned by workers. Furthermore, there are excellent resources available in the form of books on games, crafts, simulations, role playing, dramatics, dance, arts, and experiential exercises that might be used by social workers.[32]

A simple activity may be used to accomplish more than one purpose if it is adapted to the changing needs and capacities of the members. An illustration is of a group of adult mental patients in a day treatment center.

> The goals of the group are to assist these regressed patients to learn to relate to each other, to express their feelings and thoughts appropriately, and to develop the social skills necessary for living in the community, with the hoped-for result of lessened social isolation. In the first meetings, the group played very simple name games in order to become acquainted and feel comfortable with each other. The game was played with tennis balls, an acceptable adult form, each with a member's name written on it. The activity has been modified, almost on a weekly basis. One week the members tossed the balls around and had to name the member they were throwing to. Another time, they shot baskets in teams, with more agile members demonstrating the activity to others. At a more recent meeting, the members wrote down some of their favorite things on the balls, mixed them up, and then tried to identify whose favorite thing was on the ball they picked. The leader made adaptations of the activity to move the group toward more complex interaction and verbal communication as part of the activity. Almost nonverbal and afraid to risk trying in the first meeting, members now choose and talk about what they dislike as well as what they like, they address each other directly, and express pleasure in helping each other. When problems in relationships have occurred within the activity, the members have become able to participate in simple discussions that recognize the difficulty, express negative as well as positive feelings, work out the difficulty within the group discussion period, and then see how successful the solution is the next time. Thus, the activities have been a means for reducing social isolation.

In this group, playing with tennis balls took on great symbolic significance, creating a bond among the members. The deliberate progression made it possible for the members to identify how their self-esteem and ability to relate to others had changed over time as they tried adaptations of the familiar and as they discussed the meaning of the activity to them and the difficulties and pleasures they encountered in engaging in progressively more complex demands for doing and talking.

In activity groups, it is easy for inexperienced social workers to overemphasize the activity and give inadequate attention to the members' feelings, interpersonal relationships, and group development. The result may be resistance to the activity of the group, lack of commitment to the project, and the deterioration of the group. The label of activity group means that the focus is on, not the activity itself, but on ways to use the activity, along with verbal content, to achieve particular goals in the realm of psychosocial functioning.

Social workers need to learn to understand the meaning of play, gestures, and other actions just as they need to understand the verbal language of the persons they serve. Words and actions are seldom separable. Many activities make use of words but within a framework of playing, rehearsing, or learning something new, one step removed from the demands and consequences of performance in the world outside the group. The development of facility with language remains an important aspect of ego adequacy. It is easy for a social worker and a group to come to rely on activities as a means of avoiding verbal sharing of feelings, problems, and plans, in which cases activities serve as a defense against interpersonal learning and intimate relationships. Understanding is equally important, whether the medium of communication is verbal, nonverbal, or a combination of both. The two tools of conversing and doing are closely interrelated. The essential question for the worker is when and under what conditions can reflective discussion, decision-making, or an action experience contribute to the achievement of the goals of the individuals who compose the group or to the development of the group as a system.

In using an activity-oriented experience, social workers assess the usefulness of a particular activity in furthering the group's purpose. It is essential that the following questions be considered:

1. *Purpose.* What purposes can be achieved through the use of a particular activity-oriented experience?
2. *Relationship demands.* Can the activity be done alone, in subgroups, by the entire group? What intensity of relationship is required? How much closeness and intimacy are required? Does the activity foster withdrawal from relationships or movement toward others at an appropriate pace? Does the activity suggest cooperation, competition, sharing, blocking, demanding, or attacking behaviors? Is the activity individual or group oriented?
3. *Required skills.* What does the experience require in terms of physical movement, coordination, cognitive ability, language skills, and obedience to rules?
4. *Impact on behavioral expression.* Does the nature of the activity it-

self tend to free, inhibit, or control impulses? What are the extent and forms of control by the worker and by participants—those that are personalized as contrasted with those that are depersonalized in that they come from rules or the nature of the material being worked with? What are the freedoms and limits imposed by the activity? What are the implicit and explicit rewards for participating successfully in the activity and how abundant or scarce are they? How are they distributed?

5. *Decision making.* Who makes the choices and how widespread are opportunities for individual choice and group decision making?

6. *Appropriateness to life situations.* How suitable is the form of content to the life situation of members? What opportunity is there for carryover to situations outside the group?

7. *Cultural sensitivity.* What cultural attitudes and values are perceived as being connected to the activity? What are the anticipated attitudes related to cultural backgrounds toward participation in a given activity? How can the activity be adapted to the ethnic, racial, or social class backgrounds of members and the surrounding culture?

8. *Timing.* How ready are the members to make positive use of an activity at a given time, both within a session and at different times in the group's development? Is the time it takes to do it appropriate to the members' interests and attention spans?

9. *Availability of resources.* What supplies, equipment, space, or knowledgeable persons are essential to the use of the activity?

The social worker takes responsibility for helping the group to select and use experiences. His contribution may be one of introducing, supporting, modifying, or enriching the experience that a group is engaged in at a given time.

Activity-oriented experiences are purposeful. They are means by which the group moves toward the achievement of its specific goals for individuals and the group as a unit within the context of the agency and the wider sociocultural milieu. Thus, clarity of goals for the use of a particular experience is essential. The worker needs to clarify the nature of the hoped-for outcome and what from this experience might be carried over to other experiences both within and outside the group. Almost any form of activity may be modified so that it can be used in relation to the needs and capacities of the members and the readiness of the group at a given time. Many different experiences may be used to achieve the same objective. Among the appropriate ones, members' interests, the worker's preference and competence, and the availability of materials and facilities may guide the selection and particular use of an experience.

Competence can be achieved by people only to the extent that there are opportunities available to develop it. Many opportunities can be provided within the group, but a given group cannot do it all. The social worker, therefore, refers members to other resources in the community. When desirable opportunities are not available, the worker has a responsibility to use appropriate channels to report the lacks to responsible organizations in the community and to cooperate with others on projects aimed to secure more adequate services.

5

Planning: Purposes of Groups in Social Context

Many complex forces determine the meaning and value a group will have for its members. In order that people be served effectively, sound preparation for the initiation and subsequent development of a group is essential.

Before the formation of any group, a complicated set of circumstances determines whether or not a group will be developed and served by a social worker. According to Siporin, planning is "a deliberate rational process that involves the choice of actions that are calculated to achieve specific objectives at some future time."[1] It is a decision-making process through which is determined the means for achieving objectives. The social worker, often in collaboration with others, makes certain choices concerning the nature of the services and resources to be made available to particular clients. Although planning, like assessment, is an ongoing process, certain decisions need to be made before the first group meeting. The plan is based on knowledge of social contexts, types of groups, agency policies and procedures, and assessment of clients in their networks of interacting social systems.

Planning is necessary because social workers seek to provide individualized services to meet human needs. Meyer has suggested that the primary focus of social work is individualizing, which is a process of differentiating particular people from the mass.[2] It involves paying attention to both the uniqueness of individuals and families and the characteristics they share. Within common human needs and situations, particularized needs are to be taken into account. Thus, assessment and planning are interrelated processes.

Kurland has noted that planning has been a neglected process in social work with groups and that "the price for lack of thoughtful and thorough planning is high."[3] Frequently, the price is paid in excessive dropouts, sporadic and irregular attendance, low cohesiveness, inadequate sanction for the practice, and lack of successful outcomes. It is paid also in workers' lack of confidence in their competence to take on new types of clients and new responsibilities. On the other hand, the price of thorough planning is high in aiding workers to use themselves effectively. Evidence is provided by Main's research in which she concluded that the degree of development of individual assessments, treatment goals, and plans for each member was positively associated with the degree of the appropriateness of the worker's use of self with individuals and with the group.[4]

Within the social context of service, preliminary planning includes decisions concerning (1) the needs and problems of the prospective group members, (2) the purpose of the group related to the goals of the members, (3) the composition of the group including its membership and the number and type of personnel, (4) the structure of service, (5) the content of the group, (6) pregroup contacts with prospective members, and (7) collaboration within the agency and with resources in the community. The needs of the members guide decisions concerning the purpose, composition, structure, and content of the group and the ways in which members will be selected and prepared for entry into the group. Influential people within the social context provide the sanction and support for the services offered and rendered. Figure 5.1 depicts the essential components of the planning process as presented by Kurland, with slight modification.[5] All parts of the planning process are interrelated, and decisions are based on assessment of people in their situations and on the organization's purpose, function, and policies. In relation to each of the components of planning, there are alternatives to be chosen based on the professional judgment of the practitioner; the potential members' preferences and capacities; the organization's policies, procedures, and resources; and the external constraints and supports.

THE SOCIAL CONTEXT

The social context, as it affects the planning process, includes the agency or institution in which practice takes place, the community in which the agency exists and the communities served by the agency, the organization of the profession into fields of practice, and the types of groups used in social work practice.

The immediate social context for service is usually a social agency or a multidisciplinary organization in which social work is one component as in schools, hospitals, clinics, prisons, residential institutions, business, or industry within a given community. The organization is a complex network of people in interlocking social systems, such as boards of directors, advisory committees, administrators, clerical and paraprofessional personnel, and practitioners from one or more professions. Within the organization, certain people have the authority to define the parameters of services to be given and the conditions under which they are given. Except in private practice, a social agency or other organization sanctions certain practices and forbids others. It has policies concerning preventive, developmental, or rehabilitative functions; eligibility re-

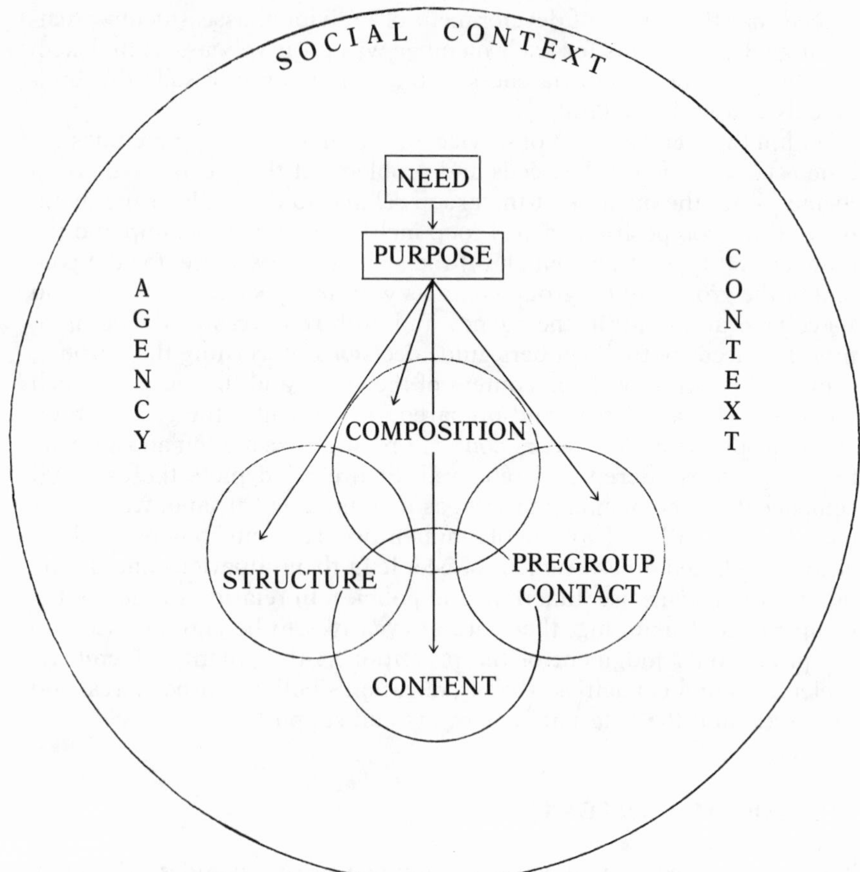

FIGURE 5.1. Pregroup Planning Model.

quirements, including fees for services; the types of clients to whom service will be offered; the resources available to client and practitioner; and even the theoretical base to be used by practitioners. Its structure, policies, and procedures influence matters of access, continuity, equity, and quality of services.

The agency's functions and policies are, in turn, defined partially by numerous laws, governmental regulations, or external financial arrangements. Confidentiality, for example, is compromised by legal requirements to report incidents of behavior such as child abuse. Statutes and court decisions govern commitment of patients to mental hospitals and patient rights. Many agencies are required to use the Diagnostic and Statistical Manual (DSM III-R) of the American Psychiatric Association in order to secure reimbursement of funds for services to clients. Too often, Yalom said, "The powerful invisible presence is the third-party payer—the financial denizen who has a shocking degree of influence over admission and discharge decisions" and about every aspect of a plan for service.[6]

Since social workers serve directly the changing needs of clients, channels need to be provided through which they can participate in review and modification of policies that influence the kind and quality of services provided. Systems of reporting need to reflect accurately the kind, as well as the quantity, of services given to particular people with what kinds of needs and characteristics. Procedures of accountability and evaluation of outcome need to be in harmony with the goals of practice. Social workers need to use their influence to work toward clear policies that safeguard the clients' rights to privacy and informed consent and yet are flexible in such matters as intake, eligibility, fees, forms of service, assignment of workers, and workloads. Their commitment is to make it as easy as possible for prospective clients to have access to and continuity of services to meet needs and for practitioners to have access to needed resources.

Unless group services are a well-established program in an organization, their presence tends to disrupt organizational arrangements, for they require a new stance toward clients and a shift from the familiar and comfortable one-to-one style of work. The use of groups may create a subtle redistribution of power and control between staff and clients. To be effective, groups must be sanctioned and supported by all parts of the organization.[7]

Two myths about groups tend to persist among practitioners in some agencies. One is that groups are second-choice modalities of help, with individual treatment viewed as preferable for almost all clients. In spite of clear evidence to refute this stereotype, it persists. The second myth is that groups are the most economical means of serving people and are primarily used, therefore, to save money. Certainly it is economical to use a group to impart information or teach knowledge and skills: there is usually little benefit from teaching one individual at a time. Some socialization groups are designed for enhancing the social skills of their members and may not require highly individualized planning, treatment, and leadership by professional social workers. Other socialization groups, composed of members who have missed out on opportunities for mastering the skills appropriate to developmental stages, require the most careful planning and competent professional leadership. This is true also of groups used for purposes of preventing or treating problems in social-psychological functioning, as in counseling and therapy. Such groups are seldom timesaving. It takes time to plan well, interview each prospective member before the first meeting, and have occasional interviews with members to supplement the group experience. Group meetings are usually longer than individual interviews are, and the record-keeping process is more complicated, as is the process of evaluation. The point is that a group should be used when it is the modality of choice in a given situation—not as a cheap and second-class type of service. It should be used when people need other people to achieve something of importance for all of them.

If administrators or other personnel who are expected to refer clients have misconceptions about the use of groups to further the agency's purpose, the result will probably be lack of adequate sanction for groups and lack of referrals to appropriate groups. To overcome such resistance, there needs to be recognition of the fears and fantasies that people may have about groups and there needs to be education about the goals of groups, the dynamic forces operating therein, and the ways in which the various forms of help work. Administrators and practitioners need to understand what is being offered, for whom it is indicated, what brings about change, and how outcomes are to be assessed.[8] In planning a new group, the social worker needs to remember that the group is always part of the larger system in which it is imbedded. Its success depends upon cooperation from key staff members. Analysis of the system is essential for answering the following questions: which professionals and other personnel have the authority to determine that a new group should be organized or an applicant may join a group; which staff members are competent to work with a particular kind of group; what are the attitudes of administrators and key staff members toward the group; what population groups are served by the agency and which should be served; what is the relation of the agency to the community; and what is the nature of interagency cooperation in the community?

The sanctioning of a service depends upon understanding the goals of the service, the means used to achieve the goals, and the ways in which the program contributes to the basic purposes of the organization. Administrators and line personnel cannot support a service unless the social workers are clear about the contribution that particular groups will make to the well-being of clients and to the mission of the organization. Unless a tentative plan is carefully made and changes in it are then negotiated with all parties who will be affected by the service, there is little chance of success. In order to have a group, there must be plans for selecting and involving members, appropriate rooms for meetings and other facilities, a suitable schedule that members can meet, and a plan for coordinating the group experience with other components of the members' treatment and other aspects of their lives. If plans are not made in the best interests of all concerned, the organization does not receive the full benefit of social work expertise.

The nature and effectiveness of team practice vary greatly within organizations. Particularly in mental hospitals and residential treatment centers, various forms of counseling and therapy may overlap. Even though there are seldom, if ever, enough appropriate services to meet the needs of clients, there may be competition for serving "the best patients" or for securing the best rooms, time, and scarce resources. In some organizations, interdisciplinary teams exist in which social workers have clearly defined and respected roles and a recognized body of knowledge to share with colleagues. In other settings, teams may be dominated by physicians, nurses, psychiatrists, recreation workers, school principals, or attorneys. In the latter instances, the social worker's professional autonomy is endangered. The authority to make decisions resides in a hierarchy of power, as contrasted with colleagial relationships among staff.[9] If social workers are to be able to engage in autonomous practice, they must be clear about their professional identity, the purposes of the profession, and what knowledge and skills they have to offer to clients and to those with whom they work. They must, of course, demonstrate professional competence.

When a team of personnel is responsible for a given client, early planning about the division of responsibility among the persons involved can assure good service. It can also alleviate later misunderstanding. Agreement also needs to be reached concerning what information will be shared and what is confidential between each practitioner and the member. Each participant needs to understand the goals and values of each of the other persons who has some part in the constellation of services being provided to the client. Each needs to respect the specific contributions of the others, as well as be willing to share some tasks with others. In any teamwork, there needs to be a mutuality rooted in respect for the different contributions of each member to the team. This, as Coyle has said, "is the crux of the relationship. No mechanical division of function can provide the basis for it. True mutuality is a matter of attitude, not layout."[10] It is a matter of each party's being deeply concerned about tendering the best possible network of services to those who need them most.

The physical environment of the sponsoring organization may or may not facilitate the effective use of groups. The physical appearance of the agency gives messages concerning the extent to which people are welcomed and respected. One major question for workers is whether the physical space can be arranged so that it facilitates effective communication among the members of groups. It is important that spatial arrangements provide for adequate privacy for the group and, at the same time, for desired social interaction. Physical settings influence behavior. Proshansky, Ittelson, and Rivlin demonstrate that:

> Physical settings—simple or complex—evoke complex human responses in the form of feelings, attitudes, values, expectancies, and desires, and it is in this sense as well as in their known physical properties that their relationships to human experience and behavior must be understood.[11]

Settings are characterized by continuous changes amidst regularity and stability. They include other people and their behavior, as well as walls, corridors, doors, arrangement of furniture, light, and decorations. The behavior of people and the physical characteristics ae interdependent. A change in any component of the setting affects other components and thereby alters the characteristic behavior patterns of the people in that setting.

Communities in which agencies are located vary greatly in their physical features, the uses of land, and the characteristics of their populations by socioeconomic status, age, race, nationality, and religion. They have a complex pattern of formal and informal social structures and networks that influence the quality of daily life. Many specialized public and voluntary organizations serve every community, often working at cross-purposes and without knowledge of each other's activities. Some communities have many more accessible resources for health, education, and welfare than others do, and usually, the poorer the people, the fewer the resources. In order to be effective, social workers need depth of understanding of the community—its institutions, deficits, resources, and networks of relationships. Planning for groups should take into account the needs of the varied segments of the population, the resources that might be used as part of or in addition to the group experience, and the influence of neighborhood conditions on the behavior of the prospective members. The plan for service needs to include the work that will be done with significant other persons in the environment.

Conditions existing within the sponsoring organization and the environment influence the decisions and actions of the social worker. Indeed, they determine to what extent a particular practitioner has the autonomy to make important decisions in collaboration with colleagues and prospective clients. Within certain restraints, the practitioner makes an organizational analysis, based on answers to the following questions.

1. How will the purpose of the projected group further or change the agency's goals? How can the relation between the group's and the agency's goals be made explicit?
2. Does the agency's philosophy, attitudes toward group services, and its history of experiences in work with groups tend to present obstacles or supports for the success of the group? If they exist, how can negative attitudes be overcome?
3. What resources in terms of staff time, funds, space, and materials will the agency commit to the group?
4. In what ways does the nature of the agency's place and reputation in the community influence the population's use of groups and the availability of resources for the group?
5. What agency policies and legislative requirements will have a di-

rect impact on plans for the conduct of the group? If these are not conducive to the welfare of the members, can exceptions be made?

6. What are the arrangements for collaborative work with social workers and interdisciplinary staff?

7. What arrangements for interagency coordination and collaboration need to be made? What will be the worker's contributions to such joint efforts?

Such an analysis is essential to determining the feasibility of developing a group or program of groups at a particular time. Seldom do social workers have the authority to develop new groups on their own. They need to have the sanction and support of all people who will influence the development and course of the group and who will be influenced by the group. Even in private practice, they often work with other practitioners and depend upon organizations for referrals.

On the basis of the organizational analysis, Gitterman describes the problems and means for getting sanctions for a new group.[12] In some instances, groups are well established in the organization, and the development and conduct of groups is a regular part of job descriptions. Organizational sanction and support are assured, except when changes are to be made in the nature of groups or additional types of groups are to be added to the organization's program.

Decisions need to be made about what particular persons or task groups to approach first. One influence in making such a decision has to do with the position of the practitioner who initiates the group—an honest self-appraisal of how he is viewed by others in terms of visible competence, the persons and task groups with whom he has the closest contacts, and the quality of his interpersonal relationships with particular people. The task may be as simple as presenting a prospectus to a supervisor or administrator and securing that person's approval. Often, there is need to confer with other staff members whose work will be affected by the group such as physicians, nurses, and technicians in hospitals; houseparents in children's institutions; or other social workers in community agencies who might make referrals or to whom some members might need to be referred. Here the major strategy used is collaboration. There is open discussion of the problems that can be dealt with through a group modality. A group problem solving process is used to explore client needs, identify organizational problems that might interfere with the success of the group, propose and evaluate alternatives, and develop a plan for the group. The result is a prospectus to be used in describing the group to clients and personnel.

Persuasion is another strategy to be used under certain conditions, primarily when there is doubt about or resistance to the proposal. Resistance may occur when the idea of a group service threatens the self-interest of persons who will be affected in some way by the group. Some staff members might see the presence of a group as "taking my clients away from me" or "they'll criticize and complain about me in the group." They may regard the group as an additional burden if they are expected to participate in any way, such as making referrals, reminding members of the time of meetings, or making a room available for the group's use. The need is to convince them that a group can benefit both the participants and the organization. To make a strong case for a group, the worker needs to be clear about the unmet need for which the group might be the modality of choice and must have thought through a tentative plan for the group, allowing for changes proposed by others. Persuasion is a rational process, but emotional processes cannot be ignored.

Demonstration of the use of a group for a particular purpose is the third major strategy, the others being collaboration and persuasion. Other staff members may have very little knowledge about the values of groups, the purposes for which they are used, and the ways in which they are started and operate. It is usually not difficult to get permission to try out a group based on a sound prospectus, for demonstration does not imply long-term commitment to the service. But when the service is successful, the doubters may well be convinced. Demonstration itself is not enough, however: other people must be kept informed of how the group is meeting particular needs of the members and contributing to the organization.

The interactional skills described in chapter 3 are just as applicable to working with an informal aggregate of staff or a task group as to working directly with growth-oriented groups. The task group may be an ad hoc or established committee, a short-term task force, or a social work or interdisciplinary team. Skills in interpersonal relationships, support, adequate exploration of the situation, provision of essential information, and clarification of aspects of the plan for the group and its potentially positive contributions to the organization are as crucial in working with colleagues, members of other professions, and administrators as they are in working with clients.

A major job for the social worker is to prepare a clear, concise, and cost-effective plan for administrators and colleagues in order to get sanction for the program of groups or for a particular group.[13] In this sense, the worker needs to develop an organizational contract that supports the plan for a particular group or a program of groups.

FIELDS OF PRACTICE

Planning for groups is influenced by the fields of practice in which social workers are employed. Increasingly, groups are being used in all fields:

family and child welfare, education, mental health, health, neighborhood services, law and justice, and occupational or industrial social work. Generally, each major type of group can be used in all of the fields but with some of the same and some different purposes, structures, and types of clientele.

Family and Child Welfare. Groups are organized in public and private agencies that provide services aimed at the enhancement of the social functioning of the family and the welfare of children.[14] In work with public assistance clients, groups may be organized to orient applicants to their rights and responsibilities as clients and to prepare them to use resources that can contribute to more adequate family life. For groups of unwed mothers, the purpose may be to help them to use community resources, prevent unwanted pregnancies, achieve better understanding of their situations, and make realistic plans for themselves and their children. Groups of parents may be designed for the purpose of improving their family relationships and coping more effectively with the problems of their children. Groups of couples may focus on working through conflicts in marital or parent-child relationships. The family itself may be the unit of service for the achievement of such goals as improved communication among members, decision making around issues and problems that affect the family as a whole, or the resolution of interpersonal conflicts within the family group.

In child welfare services—really a part of services to families—groups are used for many purposes. Parents of children who have been placed in foster homes may use groups to enhance their role functioning within the family and the community and make changes related to the need for placement of their children. Foster parents, as well as houseparents in children's institutions, often need help in understanding the needs and behavior of the children in their care and learning effective means of performing their particular roles. Parents in protective service programs use groups to help them to confront the complaints that they neglect or abuse their children and to understand and solve the problems that contribute to the violence. Many children in foster care require special help with their self-esteem and relationships with foster parents and other adults in positions of authority. Children who have been adopted may make productive use of groups to better understand and accept their adoptive status, and parents of adopted children likewise often need help to cope with the special aspects of adoptive parenthood. Likewise, both children of divorce and their parents use groups to ease the trauma of family breakup. In children's institutions and group homes, the living group itself may be served in order to help the residents with the interpersonal conflicts that are inevitably a part of group life.

Neighborhood Services. A polyglot constellation of neighborhood-based agencies provide services for people of all ages who reside in a given community.[15] Settlements and community centers provide a variety of socialization, treatment, and task groups. As in the past, groups are organized to help refugees and new immigrants to adapt to life in a new country and make appropriate use of available resources in the community. Socialization groups for children and adolescents aim to help them to develop social relationships with peers and acquire the social skills essential for satisfactory passage through a developmental stage. Jewish community centers may serve groups of children and young adults to enhance their sense of Jewish identity and reduce tensions between their identification with Jewish cultures and other significant reference groups. Other religious and ethnic organizations may provide groups for similar purposes. Senior centers provide groups for older adults to help them to adapt effectively to changing roles, retirement, and loss of spouses and close friends and to develop new relationships and use appropriate resources in the agency or community. Such groups combat increasing isolation and provide some intellectual and social stimulation essential to satisfying living.

These various growth-oriented groups may engage in social action projects to influence the environmental conditions that have a direct impact on their own and their families' lives. Some of these activity-oriented experiences were described in the preceding chapter. Examples are projects to improve the physical environment, policies, and programs of the center itself; effect changes in the local schools' schedules and resources; develop support networks; prepare members for active participation in community organizations and voter registration campaigns; lobby for changes in housing or the enforcement of public health measures; or overcome obstacles to the use of community resources. These agencies also develop task groups whose purposes are to study, plan for, and implement improvements in environmental conditions inimical to healthy individual and family functioning.

School Social Work. Social work in schools, ranging from early childhood development programs through services to university students, makes use of groups as a primary modality of practice. Pupils bring family and neighborhood problems into the school, often creating so much stress that the educational process is impeded. Groups are provided to help children and adolescents who are having academic and social difficulties to improve the performance of their roles as students and peers and make better use of educational opportunities. When large numbers of pupils have a common family problem that interferes with their use of education, the school may provide the necessary psychosocial help.

For example, groups of children whose parents are being divorced are being formed to help the children express their feelings, understand their responses to the event, and dispel common misconceptions about their responsibility for the breakup of the marriage. Groups that address sexuality and pregnancy are increasingly being used. Groups are used for preventive purposes to help new pupils make the transition from one school to another or from one level of education to the next. Winters and Easton point out that in school social work the small group is the most effective modality for achieving personal growth in making life transitions and improving interpersonal relations.[16] Group services are compatible with the culture of the school, where groups are viewed as the natural unit of service.

Mental Health. The group modality may be a treatment of choice in many cases of mental illness.[17] The symptoms may vary, but a considerable portion of hospitalized patients have decompensated as a result of interpersonal stress. A large majority of patients have chronic interpersonal problems, such as isolation and loneliness, poor social skills, sexual concerns, conflicts around authority, and difficulties in dealing with anger, intimacy, and dependency. Groups address these concerns directly because, as Yalom writes, "the group is the therapeutic arena *par excellence* in which patients learn to explore and to correct maladaptive interpersonal patterns."[18]

Mounting evidence indicates that group therapy is the preferred modality in mental hospitals. In one major research project, for example, patients who had relatively short-term group therapy showed significantly greater improvement in social competence and in affective and cognitive functioning than those did who were not in group therapy, even when the latter were hospitalized for twice as long. The patients who had group therapy were also more likely to obtain group experiences in the community after hospitalization, and there is substantial evidence that groups are particularly effective modalities for aftercare treatment.[19]

Inpatient groups are formed to meet the needs of patients who remain in the hospital for shorter or longer stays and who have more less severe symptoms. For example, patients hospitalized for only a few days and too sick to participate in groups that require verbal facility need to be placed in groups that provide for highly supportive, pleasant, and successful experiences in working on social relationships through the use of simple games and exercises. Other short-term groups are designed for patients able to verbalize specific goals and work toward their achievement. Still other groups are designed for patients hospitalized for longer periods of time who can benefit from the therapeutic use of verbal group interaction.[20]

The discharged mental patient has needs similar to those of inpatients. He is often "clinically improved but socially diabled."[21] The purpose of groups for such persons may be to help them to maintain and enhance their social relationships and to become more socially able. Mental patients, as they are discharged from a hospital, often face many fears and realistic problems in finding a place to live, reestablishing themselves with relatives, and returning to or securing employment or financial aid. They are fearful about their abilities to stand the test of living in the community. In addition, they carry a new burden, for they have been branded with a stigma of mental illness. They need, therefore, a group in which they can find acceptance and support as they learn to cope with their problems.

Health. Medical hospitals and clinics and voluntary health organizations exist to promote health and to prevent and treat illness. Within these general purposes many patients or their relatives need help with the psychosocial problems that impede the patient's recovery.[22] The rationale for providing group services in health settings is derived from the nature of the difficulties faced by patients and their families, combined with the fact that the dynamics that operate in groups are exceptionally well suited to meeting the needs of people whose normal interpersonal relationships have been disrupted by illness or disability or whose premorbid problems in relationships have aggravated the illness or handicap. These people often suffer from a sense of loss, depression, anxiety, hopelessness, helplessness, low self-esteem, negative self-image, discrimination, and superstitious fears.

The particular reactions vary, of course, with the individual. Illness is not just a private matter but also a social one. The patient is affected by the medical event as are members of his social network; they, in turn, influence the nature and course of the illness. In the words of Falck: "The situation is social, the event is social, and the intervention is social."[23] The illness or handicap of one member of a social network upsets the steady state and requires shifts in the role expectations and role behavior of all concerned. A serious illness or handicap in a person requires complementary adaptations by other family members, friends, and colleagues. Each person influences and is influenced by all other persons in the system. Other people may support or fail to encourage realistic adaptation; they may sabotage efforts to cope. The stress created by the illness is aggravated when other problems exist in the family or at work or school. Groups have special value in helping patients and their families cope with the emotional distress and changes in social living occasioned by the illness or disability.

The purpose of a particular group may be to help parents of hospitalized children to understand how some of their behavior has a negative influence on the child's recovery and to become more cooperative in their relationships with hospital personnel. Or groups may be used to help children cope with the anxieties connected with the diagnosis of their illness or with treatment procedures. They may be focused on helping long-term patients learn to live with the handicap or to make decisions about their futures when they return to the community. The goals of other therapeutic groups may be to relieve social isolation and alienation; enhance capacity to understand and cope with the emotional reaction to the illness, handicap, or threat of death; find effective ways of coping with the stresses and strains related to changes in roles and living situations; or learn to communicate with others about the situation in more appropriate ways.

Formal and informal educational groups may be organized to impart knowledge and develop competence in areas of common interest to their members. They are frequently used to prepare patients for hospitalization, surgery, or other types of treatment and to provide accurate knowledge about or cognitive understanding of the illness, its treatment, and the demands it commonly makes on patients and relatives. They are used in community settings to promote health and provide information about patients' illnesses and the need for early diagnosis and treatment.

Self-help and support groups are offered by voluntary health organizations to provide support and mutual aid for patients in coping with stress or to enhance the self-esteem of persons who feel stigmatized owing to other people's ignorance about their illness or handicap. Such groups are composed of the patients suffering from a particular chronic or life-threatening illness, such as AIDS, cancer, muscular dystrophy, or Alzheimer's disease, or of persons who abuse drugs and alcohol. Groups are also held for the relatives of patients, for patients and relatives together, or for caregivers. With such groups the social worker, rather than be the leader of the group, may refer clients, organize new groups when a need for such is indicated, consult with indigenous leaders or members at their request, and develop indigenous social networks.

Law and Justice. Organizations in the field of law and justice view their purpose as one of helping clients learn new attitudes and patterns of behavior in harmony with society's norms of law-abiding behavior. Groups are used primarily for resocialization to correct inadequate earlier socialization so that the offender can learn to function as an acceptable member of a community.[24] Groups may focus on the initial adaptation of new residents to a correctional institution, the modification of unacceptable behavior, or the preparation for return to community living. In work with gangs in the community, the purpose is usually to effect more satisfying and socially acceptable behavior.[25] Specific goals for work with a gang may be on several levels: to decrease group disturbance, violence, and delinquency; to provide some satisfactions and new relationships with the community and some new perceptions of the world and the person's roles in it; and to help members with particular problems in relation to school, employment, health, or legal situations. There is, therefore, a combination of concerns for the group and the member, for community protection, and for group assistance and guidance. One or more of these purposes is usually cited for the use of groups with adolescents or adults on probation or parole.

Occupational Social Work. Occupational social work, also called industrial social work, is the least well developed but the most rapidly expanding field of practice in social work. This field makes use of groups for purposes of education, support, and therapy.[26] Groups for potentially employable adults may focus on the enhancement of motivation, realistic assessment of the feasibility of particular types of employment, and preparation for job applications and interviews. Groups are used to orient new employees to the workplace—its facilities, culture, policies, and expectations.

The problems that workers have in their families and communities have an impact on their job satisfaction and productivity. When employees become new parents, for example, they benefit from membership in groups that can help them to carry a new role without endangering their roles as employees. Drug abuse and alcoholism, for example, are problems that are often dealt with in groups in industrial settings because, in addition to their impact on employees and their families, they often have a negative impact on the work itself, through errors in judgment and excessive absenteeism or tardiness. Many employees need ongoing support groups when they work in dangerous situations or those that are otherwise exceedingly stressful, for example, nurses and other personnel who serve patients with fatal illnesses or staffs of universities who have frequent and often stressful direct contact with students. They need stimulation and support from their colleagues in understanding their situations and coping with the pressures on them that contribute to burnout. Preretirement planning groups are formed to aid retirees to understand their benefits and make satisfactory transitions to new or changed roles.

The work situation itself creates stress for many employees who feel threatened by the demands for new skills or increased performance, have inadequate facilities and equipment, or have problems in relationships with their supervisors or others in positions of authority. Some have work schedules that disrupt usual patterns of time and relationships, as in irregular hours or "graveyard" shifts. Threats of temporary layoffs or permanent reductions in the work force create stress for all employees affected by them.

The preceding descriptions of purpose in varied organizations are meant, not to be exhaustive, but rather to serve as illustrations of the similarities and differences in purposes for groups that are used in social work. Note that, although organizational auspice is an important determinant of the focus of the service, there is a considerable amount of overlapping. Organizations that on the surface seem quite different may offer services with very similar goals and to persons with similar needs. Many of the policies and procedures that govern the specific way a service is given vary, however. Note also that it is difficult to describe purpose without also describing the clientele for whom the service is intended.

DETERMINATION OF NEEDS FOR GROUP SERVICES

Knowledge of the community, agency, and professional contexts is essential in order to identify the needs and problems of people who may be helped through group experiences. So, too, is knowledge of human development from a broad psychosocial perspective, of the personal and environmental obstacles that prevent optimal development, and of the supports that maximize it. People have needs to master the basic tasks of each developmental stage, to cope effectively with the transitions and crises they face in the process of living, and to have opportunities for meeting their basic needs for health, education, financial security, recreation, and social relationships.

The needs of people are identified through various means. When people apply for a service, they perceive that one or more of their needs are not being met adequately. Many people have, however, needs of which they may or may not be aware, or they do not know what services can best meet their needs. Some people's needs for group experiences are identified by agency personnel in the process of assessment, when they recognize that a group may be the most appropriate form of help or may supplement or complement other services. Some people's needs are met through reaching-out services in the community. Knowledge about the characteristics of a community's population and its resources contributes to the identification of such needs. Different persons may perceive needs similarly or differently. The social worker's and agency's perception of needs may or may not be in harmony with the needs as perceived by prospective clientele. An essential task for the worker in the planning process is to clarify needs and reconcile different perceptions of needs that have priority at a given time.

The group process is a powerful force in assisting people to meet their needs in the realms of social relationships and role functioning. Several types of problems appear to be most amenable to the use of groups.[27]

1. *Lack of knowledge, skills, and experience.* Lack of opportunities to secure information, develop social skills, and try out new experiences are hazards to effective functioning. In many instances, socialization has

been neglected or inadequate in one or more important areas of social living. Adequate performance of vital roles is dependent upon such resources. Skills are not limited to specific behaviors, but more importantly, the need is to master an array of communication, relationship, and problem-solving skills. As persons take on new roles, they are expected to master the attitudes and skills essential for successful performance, and they may be ill prepared for that task.

2. *Coping with life transitions.* Transitions are defined as periods of "moving from one state of certainty to another, with an interval of uncertainty and change in between."[28] They include the passage from one chronological stage in the life cycle to another. They include shifts in roles or significant life events, such as giving up a vital role through retirement, unemployment, divorce, widowhood, or physical and psychological changes. Whether the event is sudden or gradual, some degree of stress accompanies the transition. In addition to the need for knowledge, skills, and material resources, people need to cope with the threats to their past security and competence through understanding their emotional reactions to the transition and using a problem-solving process to make decisions about the future. People with these needs are not emotionally sick; their difficulties are normal problems in social living. For example, as young children enter school, they require separation from family or other primary caretakers for increasing periods of time and must learn to relate to teachers and other pupils and to meet new social and academic expectations. The new demands that face the children create stress for their parents as well. At another stage in the life cycle, elderly people become anxious or face changes or losses in their vital social roles, social relationships, and economic resources. A person passing through a transition may or may not be in a state of crisis. The crisis occurs if the stress becomes acute, disrupting the steady state to such an extent that usual problem-solving methods fail.

3. *Unresolved crises.* Groups are often used to alleviate a crisis in the lives of individuals or families. A person is in a state of crisis when

> an emotionally hazardous situation, so interpreted by the person(s) involved, creates stress which becomes unbearable at the point when some precipitating event places demands on the person(s) for coping resources not readily available. A severe anxiety state sets in, and is not easily dispelled because of lack of effective problem-solving means . . . habitual coping means do not suffice.[29]

Events that often precipitate a crisis are medical diagnoses or accidents, natural disasters such as fires and earthquakes, unemployment, rape, or other physical and psychological violence. Such situations are especially stressful when they coincide with maturation to a new developmental stage.

4. *Loss of relationships.* Separation from some significant person or group is a source of difficulty for many people. Separation of children from parents due to death, divorce, incarceration, or foster home placement is a major problem for both children and parents. Loss of meaningful relationships with relatives and friends usually accompanies placement of elderly persons in retirement or rest homes, particularly when relocation is not voluntary. Loneliness, a sense of loss, and grief accompany separation from others. Death of a loved one is, of course, the most devastating form of separation, at whatever phase in the life cycle it occurs. The survivors must cope with intense feelings of loneliness, isolation, guilt, grief, and depression. They must cope with changes in status and roles and economic and social circumstances. In addition to the emotional reactions to the loss of the deceased person, the survivors experience strains in relationships with other people and difficulties in developing new relationships or deepening existing ones.

5. *Interpersonal and group conflict.* Conflict in central life relationships is frequent, predominantly between marital partners, partners living together outside marriage, parents and one or more siblings, or other relatives. There may be conflict in other relationships also, such as those between close friends, pupil and teacher, worker and supervisor, or colleagues. Conflict may be overt, as evidenced in uncontrolled arguments or physical violence or in spouse and child abuse, which have become major problems for social work intervention. Conflict may be covert and expressed through such means as withdrawal from open communication or displacement of hostility onto other people, as when one member of a group becomes a scapegoat or rejected isolate. Conflicts may stem from lack of complementarity in basic needs, such as degree of intimacy or distance, love and affection, dependency-independency, and authority and control. They often have their source in conscious or unconscious differences in values, goals, expectations, traditions, and customs.

Cultural conflicts are prevalent in many societies. There may be conflict among persons and between groups, based on cultural differences, prejudice, and discrimination. Interpersonal dissatisfactions and conflicts are often based, at least in part, on differences in values, norms, and traditions. Ethnic groups have values that may not be understood by others, creating problems for their members in making choices and adapting effectively to their environments. Adaptation to situations is complicated for persons who have been socialized into one culture whose value system conflicts with the value system of one or more other cultures to which the person is expected to adapt. Many people must learn to integrate some aspects of two or more cultures, often made the more difficult because their own culture is devalued by the dominant society.[30]

Members of one culture may become hostile toward the dominant culture when they know that their rights are violated through legal and social inequities and discrimination in housing, employment, education, and health care. Feelings of distrust, suspicion, resentment, and hostility may characterize relationships between members of groups who differ in regard to race, ethnicity, or religion. The result may be negative stereotyping, interpersonal and intergroup tensions, even violence. A person may hold attitudes that restrict his own choices or may be the victim of the attitudes of others toward him. He may be torn by internal conflict, stemming from differences in the values and norms of his various reference groups. Variations among cultures, then, can result in a variety of intrapersonal, interpersonal, and group conflicts.

6. *Dissatisfactions in social relationships.* People often feel severe dissatisfaction with their relationships. Loneliness is a pervasive social problem: it is among the leading causes of suicide and contributes to physical illnesses and other psychosocial problems. Surveys show that one fourth of the population of the United States suffer from chronic loneliness.[31] Such persons lack affectional support systems. People often perceive deficiencies or excesses in their relationship with others. They may fear entering into intimate relationships or be unable to become intimate when such a relationship is desired. They may feel concern about the adequacy of their sexual adjustment; suffer from extreme shyness or timidity; or feel that they are unable to be assertive in appropriate ways, that they are too abrasive or overly aggressive, or that they are excessively vulnerable to the criticisms of others. Low self-esteem or a distorted sense of identity may prevent them from entering into and maintaining relationships with desired others. A positive and realistic sense of esteem and identity depends, to a considerable extent, upon the quality of relationships within a person's family and within his network of relationships in the community.

7. *Illness.* Members of groups may have problems that have been diagnosed as a medical or psychiatric illness or disability, of which social workers need to be aware. Workers need to understand the problems in psychosocial functioning associated with a particular client's condition. Physical, social, and psychological well-being are intimately interrelated: when a medical problem is suspected, it is necessary to rule out the presence of organic conditions through referral to, or consultation with, physicians. When working in health settings, social workers need considerable knowledge about physical and mental conditions in order to clarify the psychosocial problems with which social work intervention can be effective. Regardless of their views about attaching diagnostic labels to clients, workers are often required by insurance companies or other funding agencies to classify their clients' difficulties according to the categories in DSM III-R.[32] Most social workers agree that, if diagnoses of mental disorders are used, there must also be a psychosocial assessment. The important point is that various social, emotional,

environmental, and economic stresses accompany mental and physical illness and handicaps, which, in turn, often threaten interpersonal relationships and role performance. Whittaker, for example, found that the most severe disturbance in autistic children is the failure to develop satisfactory relationships.[33] This fact means that such children need social work help, since it is in the area of relationships that we can be most helpful.

8. *Lack of resources.* Lack of economic and social resources is the most serious problem facing many clients of health and social agencies. Many people face a frustrating array of social problems occasioned by the lack of adequate income, housing, employment, day care facilities, legal aid, and medical resources. Many neighborhoods lack adequate health, educational, and recreational opportunities, esthetic qualities, and public transportation. In many such situations, the problem is created primarily by external factors to which the client is responding appropriately. Orcutt has pointed out that "all poor people do not have social, psychological, or relationship problems, but being poor greatly increases one's vulnerability."[34]

DETERMINING PURPOSES OF GROUPS

Belonging to and participating in a small group is a basic constructive experience in life for all people. In addition to membership in a family, society provides varied opportunities for people to have such experiences. But the need for social work is evident when there is lack of suitable resources or when persons need professional help in order to maintain a current level of psychosocial functioning or to move toward more effective functioning. Thus, groups have specific purposes that relate to the purpose of social work and that meet specific needs that are in harmony with the functions of the sponsoring organization.

The initial purpose for a group stems from the recognition of certain recurrent needs of people who are within the jurisdiction of an agency —needs that can be met through participation in a group experience. When common needs of applicants or clients are identified and used as a basis for the organization of a group, it is likely that the goals of each member will be related to the general purpose of the group. The initial statement of the group's purpose should be sufficiently broad to encompass several ends, yet specific enough to define the expected outcome. Prospective members need to know what the group is for and of what benefit it will be to them.

Before first contacting prospective members, a worker formulates a tentative purpose for the group that can be shared with, responded to, and modified in communication with the members of the group. The statement of purpose derives from a number of sources—the social worker's purpose of enhancing the social functioning of people; the agency's particular function and purposes; the assessment of needs, problems, and environmental circumstances; the prospective members' perceptions of what they want to have happen as a result of membership in the group; and the group's decision-making processes.[35] Within the general purpose, more specific goals common to the members and specific for individuals are formulated in interviews with members and in the first session of the group.

The purpose is the ultimate aim or end in view. Although a goal is also an aim, the term is used here to indicate more specific aims instrumental to the purpose. A group is, for example, organized to help sixth-grade pupils make a satisfactory adjustment to junior high school. The goals would be related clearly to the needs of particular members of the group. They might include such aims as gaining understanding of the norms of behavior of the new school as these differ from those of the elementary school, developing satisfactory relationships with multiple teachers as contrasted with one classroom teacher, coping with feelings of loneliness due to separation from old friends, reaching out to others and making new friends, and learning about and selecting appropriate extracurricular activities. The achievement of one or more of these goals would contribute to the general purpose of a satisfactory adjustment to the new educational system.

The task for the practitioner is to work with all parties to the agreement so that individual and group goals can be achieved simultaneously. Goals will change as the members interact in the group. During the planning process, however, the task is to formulate the general purpose of the group and explore the prospective members' reaction to it and their preliminary thinking about their own goals as they fit with or conflict with the general purpose.

The worker's preliminary planning is based on understanding the potentials for service to a wide variety of clients with a view toward flexible and imaginative use of agency purposes and policies or to securing an exception to them. If an agency has a variety of alternatives, it is more likely that services will be given that are appropriate to the needs of people. Within a general policy about purpose and services of the organization, the goals agreed upon between worker and clients direct the activities of both the worker and clients. Being able to find some thread of connection between a client's own goals and agency purpose is a crucial problem-solving skill of the social worker.

Some social workers assert that goals must be limited to what clients initially say they want to achieve. Others assert that the social worker uses knowledge about the client-situation configuration to participate actively with the client in a shared goal-setting process. The latter is the perspective taken here: goals emerge from the process of assessment, in which the members participate. The choice of the goal is influenced not only by what the client says he wants but also by what the worker thinks is appropriate and possible. Through sharing their views, the worker and client come to some consensus about the desired outcome.

Clarity of purpose is essential: it provides the basic guide for both the worker and the members of the group. It provides a framework for the social worker's analytic and treatment activities and becomes a primary determinant of the group's motivation and focus. Wide agreement exists that clear goals are important. Siporin summarizes the reason for clarity of purpose:

> Objectives that are clear and explicit evoke investment and commitment. When accepted by the individual, there is also an acceptance of responsibility for action to implement them. They give to the individual a conscious sense of purpose and hope. They stimulate awareness of the interrelationships between purpose, choice, and activity and provide a standard against which to judge performance and progress. When shared with others, objectives provide means for communication, identification, and relationship with others, and when goals become consensual and mutual, they become a basis for joint effort, provide a common frame of reference, and enable communion and community.[36]

Several studies have been made on the use of purpose in social work practice. Failure to clarify goals is a source of problems in ongoing treatment. On the basis of a study in six family service agencies, Schmidt found that when workers made a purposeful effort to formulate objectives and communicated these to clients, a high proportion of clients accurately perceived and agreed with the objectives. When workers did not specify objectives, a majority of the clients did not understand how the service was to benefit them, and a lack of congruence occurred between the goals of the worker and clients. The fact that workers share their views supports, rather than inhibits, the members in clarifying their own goals.[37] Other studies support these statements. Raschella found that clients served in outpatient mental health centers were less likely to drop out prematurely when a high degree of congruence existed between worker and client in the specification of the goals for service.[38] In still another study, Garvin found that early knowledge of the goals and expectations of members helps the worker understand group interaction and predict the degree of investment that members will have in the group. He concluded that clarity of purpose contributes to goal achievement.[39]

The agreed-upon goals are most effective if they relate to the results desired by the client that are directly related to his needs and problems. They are most effective also if they are realistic in terms of the client's capacity, motivation, and resources; are expressed in sufficiently explicit terms to be used as a basis for determining the results of the group experience; and are expressed in terms of positive changes in attitudes, relationships, and behavior. They should refer to an area of improved psychosocial functioning in real-life situations outside the group. The means for evaluation of the group's progress and outcome related to individual goals need to be built into the plan.

TYPES OF GROUPS BY PURPOSE

Several types of groups predominate in social work, each with its own set of major purposes and interrelated goals.

Socialization Groups. Numerous groups are organized to develop members' competence in areas of common need. They may also be referred to as psychosocial educational groups to distinguish them from formal education and from groups that deal only with cognitive aspects of learning. They go beyond imparting information or teaching specific skills to using the group process to help members better understand and cope with the emotional reactions to the information and apply the learning to their life situations, including taking action to change environmental conditions that hinder their growth. Kane has noted that education and therapy are closely akin and that social workers realize that emotions and relationships can obscure educational messages; the need is to bridge transitions between cognitive and affective aspects of learning.[40]

Therapy and Counseling Groups. By far the most prevalent in practice are groups that have a therapeutic purpose. The general purpose of such groups is to help people change or improve in some aspects of their psychosocial functioning that interfere with their ability to develop and maintain satisfying social relationships, resolve interpersonal and group conflicts, and meet their own and others' expectations for the performance of vital social roles. They are used to help members cope with and solve problems and issues that threaten self-esteem and identity, including the resolution of crises and successful adaptation to life transitions.

Support and Self-help Groups. Support and self-help groups have been proliferating at a rapid rate, particularly in the fields of health and family services. The primary purposes of these groups are to control what is perceived to be undesirable behavior such as smoking, eating disorders, and abuse of drugs; to provide peer support and mutual aid in relieving the stress related to difficult life situations such as separation or a serious illness; or to combat discrimination and enhance self-esteem when persons are stigmatized owing to other persons' lack of understanding or prejudice concerning their behavior, illness, or situation. Many support groups require the services of social workers to help the members move beyond only supporting each other to providing aid in coping effectively with the environmental impediments to effective relationships and role functioning. In some self-help groups, the professional worker, rather than be the leader, is likely to refer clients, organize new groups when a need for such is indicated, consult with indigenous leaders or members at their request, and develop indigenous social networks.

Task Groups. Task-oriented groups, organized for the major purpose of accomplishing a particular task, are of many kinds: boards of directors, committees, teams, delegate councils, staffs, and social action groups. Their major purpose may be social planning, coordination of services, policy making, collective problem solving, or social action. They differ from growth-oriented or what Toseland and Rivas call treatment groups whose major purpose is the personal growth of the members.[41] The distinction is not an absolute one. Growth-oreinted groups may often, as indicated earlier, accomplish many tasks, including activities directed to changing some aspect of the environment that is an impediment to their psychosocial functioning. A growth-oriented group may change its purpose to become a task-centered one, as when a group of adult patients suffering from AIDS developed a new agreement to work toward the improvement of the quality of health care for all patients with the disease. The members of task-oriented groups often develop meaningful relationships with each other, share enjoyable activities, and certainly gain in self-esteem and social competence from successful completion of the task. Some task-oriented groups, once the major purpose is accomplished, decide to become a social group or a support group.

The task for the social worker in the planning process is to determine the type of group through which the members' needs can be met and goals can be most readily achieved. Once this has been done, the next decisions concern the composition, structure, and content of the group and the ways to contact prospective members and prepare them for the group experience.

6

Planning: Composition, Structure, Content

The particular constellation of persons who interact with each other is an important determinant of whether or not the participants will be satisfied with the experience and the hoped-for outcomes will be achieved. Regardless of the type of group, a social worker alone or as a part of a team exerts some control over the membership of the group. The degree of control is usually minimal in natural groups and educational groups. It is greatest in formed groups and others in which membership is prescribed or compulsory.

GROUP COMPOSITION

Several ways of determining who the members of a group will be can be delineated. Some groups are characterized by selective intake and placement according to specific criteria that seem relevant to the purpose of the group, for example, therapy and counseling groups. Other groups observe a self-selection process in that the groups are open to anyone who chooses to come. The members are attracted to such a group by its purpose or task; they perceive that the group will meet a personal need. Examples would be some parent education or support groups. In such instances, the worker still has a responsibility to help the members consider whether or not they will benefit from participation and screen out persons who might be harmed by the experience. Still other groups obtain their membership by inclusion of all persons who share a particular status or experience. Examples are living groups in institutions, patients facing discharge from mental hospitals, or ambulatory patients on a pediatrics ward. Persons may or may not have a choice about whether or not they become members of such groups.

Formed groups for which the social worker makes the decision about whether or not to recommend membership to a person occasion the most concern about group composition. "The very fact of group mixture in itself," according to Redl, "may sometimes play a great part in what happens in a group, even when the best conditions and the most skillful professional leadership are taken for granted."[1] If persons are placed in unsuitable groups, they may become a serious disturbance to the group, be harmed by the experience, or drop out of the group. If the composition of a group is faulty, it is less likely to become a viable and cohesive social system. Different results flow from different combinations of people. It is really inappropriate to refer to groups as either homogeneous or heterogeneous; rather, certain common characteristics make for a sense of commonality and certain differences make for challenges toward change. The important point is that there be a good fit between any one person and the other members.

Poor fit is illustrated by a group of patients who had cystic fibrosis. All patients in the medical center were seen as needing a support group and were invited by their physicians to attend the group. The age range was from twelve to twenty-nine. There was a clash of interest between the eight members who were in junior or senior high school and the adults. The younger members needed help with their feelings about the diagnosis, the effects of the illness on their peer relationships, and responses to the knowledge that most patients die at an early age. The adults were concerned with broader issues, such as discrimination in employment, education of the public about the illness, and lack of community resources for patients. Different needs led to conflict, resolved by the young people's dropping out of the group. When a social worker consulted with the leader in charge of the group, the decision was made to divide the members into two groups, based primarily on age. The young people returned, and each group then pursued its particular goals.

The most important consideration in group composition is the purpose of the group. The specific goals and needs of prospective members should be those that can be met through the group's purpose. Whatever the purpose, some common need or problematic situation is essential for providing some focus for the content of group life. Goals of individuals need to be complementary and in harmony with the general purpose of the group.

Criteria for Membership Selection. Knowledge of the factors that influence the participation of people is used by the worker to determine which ones seem most crucial to the purpose and the anticipated focus of the group. There is no such thing as a perfectly composed group, but it is important that the worker know with what he is dealing in this respect. Two basic questions to be raised are: Will a person benefit from the group? Will he be able to participate in such a way that his presence will not interfere seriously with the realization of the purpose of the group for others?

Although there are many opinions about group composition, there has been little systematic study of who fits together in groups. Perhaps the most generally accepted principle is what Redl calls "the law of optimum distance." Groups should be homogeneous in enough ways to ensure their stability and heterogeneous in enough ways to ensure their vitality.[2] This principle is based on the premise that the major dynamics in a group are mutual support and mutual aid among members.

Both the descriptive characteristics of people and their behavioral attributes need to be considered in planning for the group's composition. Considerable agreement exists that homogeneity of goals and some descriptive characteristics provide for feelings of compatibility and interpersonal attraction, leading to mutual acceptance and support and that heterogeneity of behavioral attributes, such as patterns of coping and social skills, provides for the stimulation that ensures the group's vitality. Differences make people aware of options, choices, and alternatives. Levine reports the evidence from research to support this position.[3]

Similarity in descriptive characteristics can enhance the functioning of a group. People hesitate to join groups in which they feel very different from the other members. Members of groups who share the experience of being in a similar stage of psychosocial development tend to face common life tasks to be mastered and certain common interests to be pursued. Levine, in a study of twenty-four outpatient therapy groups of adults, found that similarity of age was the one factor significantly related to interpersonal attraction and freedom of expression.[4] Unless there is some strong sense of common fate that can overcome age differences, groups are most productive when members' ages are fairly similar. Age is a more important factor in relatively short-term groups than in long-term ones. It is also more important in childhood than in adulthood.

Sex-linked values and norms of behavior are important to the development of identity and successful role performance, even though these are changing rapidly. Owing to the fact that gender identity, the subjective sense of being male or female, becomes a major component of personality, expectations and role sets become an integral part of gender identity. In spite of changes, women and men in groups are apt to use power and handle opportunities for intimacy differently. A study of mixed groups by Garvin and Reed suggests that such groups have different effects on men and women and that some of these effects tend to restrict women's options and relegate them to less powerful positions within the group.[5] Daley and Koppenaal studied transition groups for women related to role changes and their effect on age-specific tasks. They found that, compared with co-gender groups, the women's groups facilitated more self-disclosure of feelings and relationships, decreased the likelihood of acceptance of stereotyped roles, and provided greater opportunity for empathy and role modeling for sex-specific conflicts.[6] Mixed groups may be preferred for certain other purposes, as in groups whose members need help to understand and improve heterosexual relations.

A tendency exists for small groups in our society to be based on similarity in cultural values and practices associated with social class, race, religion, and nationality. Differences in such characteristics tend to separate people from one another in work, play, education, place of residence, and life style. These factors may be relevant to the purpose of the group; for example, homogeneity concerning race and ethnicity is appropriate when groups are formed to help members of a minority group accept their own cultural backgrounds as a basis for integrating this facet into their basic sense of identity. Cultural factors may not seem relevant to the purpose of the group, but since cultural differences influence attitudes, patterns of behavior, and interests, they cannot be ignored. They must be recognized. One principle is to avoid having only one person with an important difference in a group, based on knowledge that being the only person with a given characteristic or being a "token" representative of a group is a very difficult situation for most people.

Plans must be made for using differences as positive dynamics toward growth and change rather than as impediments to such movement. In some instances, when there are language differences, bilingual and bicultural workers may be needed. In taking into account cultural values, it is essential that decisions not be made on stereotypes of groups. Solomon asserts that workers need to avoid the fallacy that occurs when inferences are made about the behavior and attitudes of particular persons by endowing them with typical group characteristics.[7]

People with similar medical diagnoses are often placed in the same group. A common diagnosis tends toward the development of empathy among the members and protection from social ostracism. But in relation to certain group purposes, this may be a questionable practice. Handicapped people should have a chance to interact with other people. In one major program described by Kolodny, physically handicapped children and normal children were purposely placed in the same group.[8] Delinquent youngsters have also participated in groups with normal ones. In one research project, Feldman and his associates concluded that children labeled as delinquents could interact with a normal population with at least minimal success and minimal adverse effects on the normal members.[9] In two other projects, it was found that educable mentally retarded clients could be placed successfully in groups with those of average intelligence.[10]

The social worker is concerned not only with the capacities and problems of people but also with modes of coping with the problems. How individuals express themselves, deal with stress and conflict, and defend themselves from threat and hurt influence the nature and content of group interaction. Diversity of ways of coping with problems facilitates the exchange of feelings and ideas among members, provided there is a potential for a strong bond in relation to the purpose and focus of the group. An individual's tendency to withdraw from relationships or to reach out aggressively to other people is especially important. Usually, extremely shy persons are not placed with extremely aggressive ones, because of what is referred to as shock effect on the shy one. Members who are too far from the behavioral level of others in the group may find themselves in intolerable inner conflict, stirred up by the faulty placement. Yalom reports that findings from studies indicate that a person perceived by self and others as deviant derives little satisfaction from membership, is less valued by the group, is more likely to be harmed by the experience, and tends to drop out of the group.[11]

A person's ability to communicate through the use of verbal symbols is another important criterion of group composition. If a group is to make primary use of verbal means of communication, the ability to express oneself clearly is essential. Persons with limited verbal skills often find their problems intensified in groups of active, talkative members. In groups of relatively nonverbal members, however, there is a need for some members to be able to engage in conversation at a level others can come to achieve.

When members live together and their problems are those of communication, relationships, and cooperative living, it is usually desirable to work with the unit as a whole. Examples would be a cottage group in a residential treatment center, a small group foster home, or a family. It is necessary to add the caution that sometimes people need to get away from their families or living groups in order to look at them more objectively and to consider and practice new patterns of behavior that later can be tested out in the living group itself. For this reason, married couples often meet together in groups in which the participation of other couples provides for new inputs into the marital system and opportunities to test out new behaviors. The fact that each couple is a subgroup of a larger group has an impact on the treatment process. The stages in the life cycle of the different marriages and the family and interfamily systems of which the marital pairs are components represent one important criterion for composition. These factors also need to be taken into account in multiple family groups in order to provide sufficient support for all members of the family.

The purpose of the group, combined with a strong common condition, may override other criteria for composition. This situation is most evident when the shared condition isolates persons from others or tends to stigmatize them. One example is of a group for couples in which the husband had epilepsy that could not be controlled through the use of medication. There were five couples in that group. The ages ranged from twenty-four to sixty-nine; the members were from different social classes; all were "Anglo" except for one Puerto Rican couple. But the commonality of having epilepsy was so important that the group became very cohesive. In another group of parents of deaf children in a school, the members varied on descriptive characteristics, but the commonality of having a deaf child made the differences that existed less important than they might be in a different group in which such a crucial commonality did not exist.

Several social workers, as well as psychiatrists, have suggested that persons with certain problems be excluded from groups. Some would exclude persons who are grossly ineffective in communication skills, who lack the capacity to understand their own behavior, or who have weak motivation. They would exclude persons with certain forms of emotional difficulties, for example, narcissistic, suicidal, and psychotic patients, or those who have severe problems with intimacy or self-disclosure. It is true that some persons with such problems may not be suitable for particular groups, but numerous examples of the successful use of groups with these very same populations can be found. Persons with such problems in relationships and role performance are the very ones who most need the mutual aid and support to be derived from membership in an appropriate group. The question is not whether persons with such problems can be helped; rather, it is whether or not there is a good fit between the person and other members of the group, together with a practitioner who has the necessary knowledge and skills to use a group for the members' benefit.

In certain instances, it may be necessary to delay entry into a group until a member's basic needs for survival, from both a physical and social stance, are met. Some persons referred to groups come with great uncertainty about whether or not it will be possible for them to eat, be sheltered, clothed, nurtured, or employed with any continuity and dependability. Some clients may be so overcome with grief or anxiety that they cannot be expected to participate in a group until they have been given immediate help with their particular critical needs on a one-to-one basis. Or some such persons may benefit from concurrent individual and group service. In many instances, such concerns may well be brought into the group experience where the commonality of problems may suggest means of alleviating them, or such concerns may be dealt with through the use of resources beyond the group. The worker may need to work directly with other agencies in the community to secure the necessary resources for one or more of the members.

Selection of Workers. The characteristics of the social worker, as a member of the group with a special professional role, are an important facet of group composition. The issues are primarily concerned with ethnicity, race, social class, gender, and age. Differences in ethnicity between the social worker and members of the group are usually accompanied by differences in socioeconomic status as well. When an ethnic group is also of a minority race, color differences have a great influence on interpersonal relationships. Members from minority ethnic groups have ample reasons to distrust "Anglo" social workers because of the negative valuations that have been attributed to them in most of our society's institutions, which are controlled by the white majority. Members from the majority group may carry over these negative attitudes toward workers who belong to minority groups. Likewise, there are differences among ethnic groups in religious preferences with the accompanying values and attitudes toward such issues as birth control, homosexuality, behavioral expectations, and preferences in food, manners, holidays, and traditions.

The variables of gender and age interact with other factors of difference between the social worker and members of the group. Kadushin reports research findings indicating that clients tend to prefer male interviewers to female ones and older practitioners to younger ones.[12] These preferences may be changing, however, with the rise of women's movements and changing attitudes toward well-qualified younger professional persons.

In considering the desirability of matching workers and members according to factors of difference, Kadushin concludes that with too great a similarity between the worker and clients, there is the risk of overidentification and lack of objectivity; with too great a difference, there is a risk of difficulty in achieving understanding and empathy. Similarities tend to promote an early sense of trust and comfort while differences provide for stimulation toward changed ways of thinking and behavior. The weight of the evidence from research is that competence is a more important consideration than the descriptive characteristics of the worker are as these match or differ from those of the members.

That differences can be overcome by competence is affirmed by Solomon, who sets forth the skills and the underlying knowledge required for the nonracist practitioner.[13] The nonracist practitioner is able to (1) perceive alternative explanations for behavior; (2) collect those verbal and nonverbal cues that are helpful to choose the most probable alternative in a given situation; (3) feel warmth, genuine concern, and empathy for people regardless of their race, color, or ethnic background; and (4) confront clients when they distort or misinterpret true feelings of warmth, concern, and empathy that have been expressed. The same characteristics would be true also of practitioners working with clients who differ from them in other important ways.

Agency Policies. Closely related to purpose of groups and characteristics of people are the agency policies and conditions that influence the particular persons to be included in a group. Administrative considerations play an important part in determining who the practitioner will be and who can become a member. Policies determine such important matters as fees for service, the physical facilities available, the schedule of hours that an agency is open, the geographical areas from which clients come, and the money available for expenses connected with using a service. Size of agency is itself an influence on the number of criteria that can be taken into account in forming new groups. Such practical considerations often make possible the use of only a limited number of other criteria in determining the composition of a group. If various factors are considered in planning for a new group, however, even if they cannot be fully implemented, the practitioner begins his work with knowledge of the influence of composition on the development of the group. Since it is impossible to have a sufficiently large pool of potential members from which to draw, each worker needs to answer these questions: How far from the ideal can be accepted? What are the consequences for persons to be refused entry into a group when they have needs and goals that are appropriate to the group's purpose?

The importance of group composition as a crucial element in planning for social work with groups is underscored by a study by Boer and Lantz. In comparing a group in which composition was planned with another group in which it was not planned, the authors concluded: "The groundwork of membership selection that occurs before the group begins has as much importance in determining member commitment, attendance, and therapeutic results as does the ongoing group process."[14] The results of an appropriate group composition that is in harmony with the purpose of the service, according to Levine, are (1) easier and quicker identification of the members with each other, (2) less difficulty in communication and disclosure of feelings and concerns, (3) harnessing of the power of the group for simultaneous help to each member, and (4) faster, more identifiable problem solving.[15]

Size of Group. In planning a new group, the optimum size should be in relation to the nature of the interaction desired. Hartford reviewed the social science literature on the size of groups and concluded that

> if individual participation, satisfaction, and engagement of the group members in a process that will bring about changes in themselves is the aim of the group, obviously it must be small enough for each person to be heard and to contribute, and also to feel the impact of the group upon his beliefs and behaviors. However, groups should not be so small as to over-expose members or to provide too little stimulation.[16]

That finding still leaves room for the judgment of the worker in determining exactly what size a group should be. Yalom concludes that there seems to be a preference for groups of seven or eight members, with an acceptable range of five to ten.[17] He is, however, referring to semiclosed adult therapy groups; other groups, such as groups of families, need to be larger.

The smaller the group, the more the demand that each member become fully involved in it, and the greater the potential and demand for intimacy of relationships. The less anonymous the actions, feelings, and histories of the participants, the higher the rates of participation and the greater the influence of the group on each member. More time is available for each person to test out his attitudes and ideas with others. The smaller the group, the stronger the group pressures on each individual. The smaller the group, the easier the access of a member to the worker and of the worker to each member. The smaller the group, the greater its flexibility in modifying goals to meet the changing needs of its members. However, too small a group may disintegrate with absences or as some members terminate before the group does. There is, moreover, a lack of adequate stimulation so that some of the dynamic forces that promote positive changes in people are compromised.

As the size of the group increases, each member has a larger number of relationships to maintain. Each member not only has more other members to interact with but also responds to the dyadic and triadic relationships that have developed. There is less pressure to speak or perform and more opportunity to withdraw occasionally from active participation for silent reflection. Beyond the number of approximately eight to ten, formality in leadership emerges and so do subgroups within the larger group. As groups increase in size, more communication tends to be directed toward the worker rather than toward other members and to the group rather than to specific members. The larger the group, the greater the anonymity of the members and the greater the difficulty in achieving true consensus in decision making. A larger group tends to have greater tolerance for domination by a leader, and the more active members tend to dominate the discussion.

Persons differ in regard to the range of relationships they can encompass, on the basis of prior experiences and factors of personality. According to Bales and his associates, "increasing maturity of the personality associated with age permits effective participation in larger groups."[18] But people may be retarded or advanced in their social development. Age does influence size, to some extent. Young children become overstimulated and confused in a group that seems large; they need to work out their problems in relationships with a few as they move toward efforts in cooperation. Latency age children usually need small groups to provide security as they work toward mastery of situations, but there are some cultural differences in this respect. Children from large, economically deprived families are often not ready for the intimacy of a small group. Whereas small groups of six to ten members are usually suitable for counseling and therapy, there are exceptions. The demand for intimacy and active participation may be very difficult for some prospective members, and the greater anonymity permitted in larger groups may be exactly what some persons need at a given time. There is no substitute for sound judgment and careful planning.

Number of Practitioners. An important issue in planning is the decision to have one practitioner or to have co-workers with shared responsibility for giving service to the group. Traditionally, the usual pattern has been one practitioner, regardless of the size of the client system, but some workers espouse the use of more than one worker.[19]

One rationale for the use of co-workers is that this procedure improves the accuracy of assessment and the objectivity of workers. One practitioner may observe something that another misses. Workers' perceptions of the group may become more realistic when they are tested against those of a colleague. The worker who is less active at a given time can note reactions of less verbal participants, as well as of those engaged in the immediate give and take. Middleman raises questions, however, about whether these objectives can be achieved in other ways.[20]

A second major rationale is that co-workers enrich treatment. A division of labor between workers makes it possible for one to focus on major themes of a group nature while the other responds more frequently to individual concerns. Co-leadership makes it possible for one worker to make demands for work while the other one provides necessary support, or one may reinforce the support given by the other. It provides more opportunities for learning new ways of communication and problem solving, since the members can perceive how the workers communicate with each other and handle their differences. Workers thereby serve as models for members. If the co-workers are of different genders, they can model gender roles for members and serve as objects of identification for members of the same gender. They can also model appropriate heterosexual relations. Reed says that these ideas are, however, contradicted by evidence that male-female co-leadership situations may perpetuate gender-stereotyped behaviors in groups, even when both leaders are behaving in nonstereotyped ways for their gender.[21] In a world in which the roles of males and females are changing rapidly, the workers' own views of appropriate roles may be in conflict with those of one or more members or with the members' reference groups. Different perceptions exist concerning definitions of appropriate sex roles. The co-worker relationship when composed of male and female workers is thought to symbolize the two-parent family, making it more likely that the group will provide a corrective emotional experience in which members work through their relationships with parents through transference reactions to workers.

The most frequent use of more than one practitioner is as a vehicle for training practitioners, as distinguished from providing particular benefits to clients. One idea is that workers need the security and support from a colleague in order to reduce their anxiety about leading the group. A less able and less experienced worker can learn from observing another worker and from the feedback he receives from his colleague. Yet, that method of training presents many obstacles for the trainee. Kolodny says that it is an extension of the old apprenticeship model of learning skills.[22] Furthermore, the primary concern should be with what is best for the members of the group. Other means, such as supervision and consultation, can be used to relieve the anxiety of workers and to enhance their skills in assessment and treatment. There are differences of opinion about the impact of observers on a group. If nothing else, they are distracting. If and when they are used, the members need to give their informed consent; time must be given to decision making about the matter. Issues concern the qualifications and motivation of the observers, the nature of contacts between observer and members, and privacy and confidentiality. These, according to Archer, are ethical issues.[23]

In many co-worker relationships, role definitions are not clear. It has been pointed out that George Orwell's observation in *Animal Farm* that "all the animals are equal but some are more equal than others" is true in co-leadership.[24] Waldman, a trainee, noted that "in the group I co-lead, for example, it is always my co-leader who signifies the end of the meeting, and who decides on the time and place of the group meetings. It is also implicit that I will seek out and use feedback from my co-leader about my performance, but that the reversal of this is neither requested nor expected."[25] Being a trainee is often a one-down position fraught with feelings of anxiety and inadequacy when the trainee is given the label of co-leader. If such a pattern of leadership is used, it is necessary to acknowledge the differences between the two workers to each other and to the members.

Other writers also take the position that such forms of co-leadership are not advisable. Pairing a trainee with an experienced leader may create, rather than alleviate anxiety. Mac Lennan describes the problem in this way; "It is, however, a paradox that, while the use of co-therapists may potentially provide a sheltered environment in which to learn, very frequently, because of the complicated relationship between the therapists, the group is harder to lead."[26] The co-leadership relationship is confounded further when the senior leader contributes to the evaluation of the trainee's performance, either formally or informally.

The rationale for the use of only one practitioner with a group concerns the influence of additional workers on the group process. With the addition of a second worker, there is much greater complexity of relationships and communication with which each participant must cope. There are a subgroup of workers and another one of members. Each member must relate to the practitioner subsystem, as well as to each of the workers in it. With two or more workers participating, opportunities for members to participate are lessened. Each member of the group must develop and cope with a relationship with at least two professionals, which dilutes the intensity of the worker-individual relationship and the worker-group relationship. Each member must fathom the differences in expectations that each worker has for her and for the group. Members quickly come to realize that the two practitioners are not truly equal in status, skill, and experience. They usually identify one of them as the primary leader and the other as an assistant. Being an assistant is not the same as fully sharing the authority and responsibility that are implied in the co-leader concept. Ethically, the members have a right to know what to expect of each practitioner and why each one is in the group.

Difficulties that co-practitioners have in working together are likely to be detrimental to the progress of the group. Frequent difficulties are those of rivalry for the love and attention of the members, struggles for power to influence particular members or the group's structure and content, pressures on each worker to prove his ability and to do at least his fair share of the work, and a tendency to divert primary attention from the group to the relationship between colleagues. Too often, also, the workers do not share the same theoretical perspectives on practice, which creates confusion on the members' part in understanding the means being used to help them, unless these differences are discussed adequately in the group. The members may resist the co-leader situation by making unfavorable comparisons, taking sides, making one a scapegoat, pitting one against the other, giving or withholding affection from one, or projecting their feelings about the leaders onto each other.

The practical matter of cost in time and money is a factor to be considered in making decisions concerning the number of workers assigned to a group. The use of two workers is more than twice as expensive as that of only one worker is. Time is spent not only in individual and group sessions. If co-leadership efforts are to be successful, the practitioners need to review together each session, work through their difficulties in roles and relationships, and engage in ongoing planning together.

In one study of fifty therapists in conjoint family therapy, Rice, Fey, and Kepecs found that experienced therapists gradually reached a point of diminishing returns in satisfaction with co-therapy. They came to prefer to work as the sole therapist because they considered this to be a more effective way to serve clients.[27] In a survey of twenty-five faculty members who teach courses on practice with groups, Rothman found that 73 percent favored solo leadership for the education of students, but half of them might use co-leadership in practice under some circumstances.[28] In another survey of psychologists, social workers, and psychiatrists, it was also found that the more experienced practitioners no longer preferred the co-worker role.[29] A review of literature on research on marital therapy by Gurman indicated that no support was found for the view that therapy by co-workers is more effective than treatment by a sole practitioner.[30] Dies summarized five studies on co-leadership in therapy groups and concluded that "Overall, the findings from these five studies suggest that the co-leadership model may complicate the group therapeutic process and actually precipitate problems that are not evident in groups with only one leader."[31] In a survey of residents in psychiatry, Friedman found that the quality of prior co-therapy experience seemed to be directly related to choosing one's own partner and that equal status seemed to be a more important determinant than such other factors as the gender of the co-leader.[32]

Gitterman's opinion is that "the usual and most effective model for the staffing of groups is one worker who possesses substantive knowledge and practice skills."[33] The rationale for solo leadership is that it provides opportunities for more potentially intimate relationships and identifications with the worker and other members. The role of the worker in relation to members is clear to all, uncomplicated by differences in workers' perceptions of that role. Because only one person is in a formal power position in the group, the predominant power is with the members. Less time is taken in worker-to-worker communications, permitting more time for participation by members. The focus of the group is maintained on the members' own concerns and on the group process, rather than diluted by attention to the interactions between the co-leaders. Practically, solo leadership is less than half as expensive of time and money than co-leadership is. What little research evidence there is seems to favor solo leadership in most situations.

More than one worker is, however, essential in some circumstances. There is often a realistic need for more than one practitioner, depending upon the size of the group, the nature of the content, and the needs and problems of the members. Often when members of other professions are involved in the client's treatment, it is desirable that representatives of these professions participate in the group, at least some of the time. Such a plan makes it possible to integrate the contributions of both professions. For example, a nurse or physician may focus on the physical needs of the patients in the group and be responsible for the treatment of the illness, while the social worker is the expert on the psychological and social antecedents and consequences of the illness for both the patient and her family. Another example of the need for more than one practitioner would be an activity group composed of children who are deficient in the ability to verbalize feelings and ideas and who require a great amount of attention within the group. Another would be a large multiple-family group, composed of several families who are also engaged in family therapy. By participating in the multiple-family group, the practitioners are able to further the plan for integrating two forms of help.[34]

The use of more than one worker, when the differences in roles are clearly defined, has potential values. One example, described by Marshall, is the use of aides to assist the social worker in activity groups of emotionally disturbed children and adolescents.[35] The functions of the aides were in the realm of child care activities with six- to eight-year-old children: helping the members of the group on trips by driving the car while the professional worker's focus was on interacting with the members; maintaining safety; assisting with the content of the group by preparing materials, helping to select activities, arranging the room, and teaching or leading a particular activity; and conducting life space interviews with particular members when their maladaptive behavior or troublesome events made this necessary. The effective use of aides requires careful selection and orientation, opportunities for observation, and participation in planning and in postsession evaluation conferences. It seems most appropriate to use more than one worker with large groups as in multiple-family therapy, with activity groups of disturbed children, and with some groups of married couples.

Making Decisions on Composition. In order to influence the formation of a group whose composition will further the achievement of goals, the worker seeks answers to the following questions.

1. Given the needs of the members and the purpose of the group being planned, what persons could benefit most from the projected group and, at the same time, not damage the group experience for others?
2. What are the important descriptive characteristics of the prospective members? What will be the degree of homogeneity or heterogeneity in regard to such factors as age, grade in school or occupation, gender, race, ethnicity, religion, socioeconomic status, intellectual ability, health, and previous group experiences?
3. What are the important behavioral attributes of prospective members? What will be the degree of homogeneity or heterogeneity in regard to such matters as interactional style, patterns of relationships and communication, motivation, and level of psychosocial functioning?
4. What are the important commonalities and differences among the members in regard to their descriptive and behavioral characteristics?
5. What should the optimal size of the group be? If new members are to be added later, what will be the process of their selection?
6. How many practitioners will work with the group? What characteristics and special competencies are important for the workers who will give service to the group? If there is more than one worker, how will the roles and responsibilities of each be defined?

INITIAL ORGANIZATIONAL STRUCTURE

Structure has an impact on the quality of group life. It consists of the relatively stable instruments that determine the distribution of authority and responsibility, the governing procedures, and the manner in which coordination or activity is effected. It gives order and direction to group life. Structure may be formal and official, or it may be informal and unofficial. Where there is a formal structure, there is also an informal one within it that may have as much influence on the members as the formal structure does. The organizational structure ought to facilitate the achievements of the group's purpose.

Types of Structure. Social work groups are organized with two basic types of structure, although there are variations within these types. In one type, often designated as an informal group, the only official roles are those of member and worker. Other informal membership roles emerge out of the interaction within the group itself, as each member comes to influence others and as others respond to this informal influence. Such groups provide a maximum of group-centered communication and spontaneity of individual participation. They favor reflective discussion, informal decision-making processes, and the possibility that each member will have equal access to the worker and to every other member.

In the second major type of structure, relations are organized into well-defined positions. Members acquire roles through being elected, volunteering to do particular tasks, or being appointed by the leader or another member in a position of authority. This form of structure requires that members engage in making corporate decisions and working out conflicts in values and norms as they do so. It provides opportunities to learn to carry responsible roles, use officials appropriately, and experiment with parliamentary procedures. In such groups, the network of communication tends to be formalized, with the expectation that members use official channels for speaking and that they obey rules pertaining to the conduct of the group's business. Such procedures tend to limit the spontaneity and spread of participation among members and dilute the relationships between the worker and each member of the group. In general, when a group has a very formal structure and clearly differentiated official roles for its members, each person's needs and attitudes will be less apparent than in more informal groups: they are masked by the formal procedures. Types of groups with formal structures include interdisciplinary teams, boards of directors, self-government ward groups in hospitals, and some social clubs.

Some groups have had a life span of their own before contact with a social agency, as differentiated from groups organized for social work purposes. For lack of more precise terminology the first are referred to as natural groups and the latter as formed groups. The natural group may be a family, group home, neighborhood organization, work group, discussion group, or some combination of these.

Another differentiation is whether the group members live in an institution or the open community. In institutional settings—such as hospitals, group homes, residential treatment centers, prisons, or homes for dependent children or aged persons—the members of the social work group usually have multiple relationships with each other. In some community-based agencies—such as settlements, schools, senior centers—members of social work groups may also see each other in multiple roles. In other community settings, members of groups see each other only in the group. This is most true in clinics, family service associations, community mental health centers, and such child welfare agencies as those dealing with adoptions, foster care, and protective services.

The initial structure is usually set when the organization of a new group is being considered. But the worker may not have much choice in the determination of the structure, since a natural group already has a system of structural arrangements that the worker needs to understand and respect. Later, whatever the initial structure, it will be changed as the worker and members interact in the course of the group's life.

Open and Closed Groups. In making plans for a group service, a decision needs to be made about whether or not to permit additional members to join after the group has started, that is, to have an open group or to close it to new members after an initial period of time. Actually, there is no clear dichotomy between open and closed groups but rather degrees to which a group is open or closed to new members. The plan for a given group needs to be made with recognition that each new person who comes into a group changes it, alters the interpersonal relations in which the original members are involved, and provides new ideas and ways of behaving to which the members need to adapt. The loss of a member from a group likewise requires an alteration in the network of relationships and communication. In order to make a viable decision concerning stable or changing membership, consideration is given to the characteristics of predominantly closed and predominantly open groups.[36]

Closed groups have many characteristics that make them appropriate for numerous purposes. The dominant purposes of closed or semiclosed groups are related to therapy, socialization, and psychosocial education. In order to achieve their purposes, the members of therapy and socialization groups need an opportunity to develop trust, a sense of belonging, and intimacy with others. Some educational groups are appropriately open to all who wish to come when they are designed to provide specific information and discussion on a particular subject at each session. Psychosocial education requires, however, continuity of work and progression in integrating the information with emotions and applying it to specific situations.

In closed groups, there is an expectation that attendance will be regular, which tends to enhance commitment to the group. The amount, intensity, and degree of commitment are greater when the same others are present in each session. Henry has said it this way:

> when the member can count on the presence, week after week, of the same familiar and trusted others as being those through whom, from whom, and with whom, her or his growth and change and help will occur, the commitment to the experience and investment in it must surely be greater than when the cast of characters changes from time to time.[37]

When the same persons are present, the members perceive their relationships with each other as important and as continuing until the group ends. The members proceed through stages of group development in a fairly orderly way. The primary agent of change is apt to be the group as members learn to give and take, engaging in a mutual aid process. The worker's role becomes increasingly facilitative and less central as shared leadership develops among the members. Continuity of focus on major issues and concerns becomes possible. If a group continues over a long period of time without the entry of new members, however, it can become so stable that there is a dearth of new ideas and ways of behaving that provide the necessary stimulation to move toward desired changes.

In open groups, the dominant purpose is more effective coping with transitions and crises, according to Schopler and Galinsky.[38] Members of these groups usually suffer from stresses in their life situations, resulting from changes in status or physical condition, from separation loss, or a traumatic event. In open groups, the composition shifts from meeting to meeting. Members perceive their relationships with each other as transitory. Mutuality is based more on awareness of a common condition or situation than on interpersonal relationships. Shifting membership upsets the group's steady state as new members enter the groups and others terminate from the group. If such groups are to meet the needs of their participants, it is necessary to develop mechanisms for dealing with problems of entry and exit. There is obviously less continuity in the focus or content, with the need for frequent repetition of purposes, ways of work, and focus of a session. Group development processes are modified. Some groups never move beyond the initial state. In some carefully planned ones, however, Hill and Gruner state that there is evidence that groups develop if a nucleus of members attends regularly.[39] A major advantage of open groups is that they are readily available: people do not have to wait for a new group to begin. When clients suffer from acute distress, they require immediate attention.

The role of the worker is a central one in open groups, because members of groups with irregular attendance are seldom able to share the leadership roles adequately; the members require direction from the social worker. In a large majority of open groups, there is more than one assigned worker. There may also be rotation of workers so that neither membership nor leadership remains stable. It seems obvious that in such groups, each session must be regarded as a group experience in itself.

Several quite different types of groups are lumped together under the term *open group.* The range is from drop-in groups to those that have a regular membership and consistent leadership and admit new members only occasionally.

In drop-in groups, members are self-selected and are attracted to the stated purpose or content of the group. They may come or not as they choose. The size of the group varies from session to session. The only orientation of new members is at the beginning of a meeting, and there is no pattern for planned termination. Nevertheless, some of these groups do develop a core of regular members who transmit the purpose and norms of the group to newcomers; a culture exists in spite of changing membership. These groups have the utmost flexibility and are the most accessible to people who feel a need for what they perceive the group has to offer. If people who try out the group find it is suitable to their needs, they often come regularly for at least several sessions. Examples are groups for adolescents in crisis, suicide prevention groups, and waiting room groups in hospitals. In such groups, the worker cannot assume that any one issue can be worked through in a later meeting. Each session is best viewed as the only one. Members who return will be able to work on a new issue each time.

A variation of the open group is one in which there is a core of members who attend regularly and a number of fringe members whose attendance is sporadic and thereby reflects lack of commitment to the group. Still another form of open group are those with regular membership in which new members are added on a planned basis, often when other members have successfully terminated. The exit and entry of members are planned to take place when the group's development will not be hindered to any extent and when the group is able to integrate new members. Depending upon the frequency of turnover of membership, such groups may resemble closed groups more than other kinds of open groups. In such groups, changes in membership can be used to enhance the members' capacities for accepting new people and separating from others. Many long-term therapy and counseling groups are of this type.

In all kinds of open groups, entry and exit are common themes, contributing some disruption of group relationships among members and the slow development of the group into an effective instrument for change. These groups can be useful for meeting certain needs of people, provided they have a clear sense of purpose, norms appropriate to the form of group, mechanisms for responding to changes in membership, and a plan that motivates a core of members to attend regularly for a period of time.[40]

Duration. Some anticipation of the duration of the group is a part of planning. It is intended that some groups will continue for several months or more and some for as brief a time as a single session. Others range in duration between these extremes. The duration of the service should, of course, be related to the purpose of the group and the particular needs and capacities of the members. Hartford notes that there is an important distinction between the actual and the expected duration of a group.[41] Even though a limit on the duration of a group is set at the very beginning, the members may expect the group to continue indefinitely. On the other hand, although some groups have no clearly designated terminal date, the members may perceive the group as time limited. If a group is viewed as temporary, the members may move in rapidly and focus on the problem or activity but not invest much in interpersonal relationships. They do not engage fully in a mutual aid process. Members of groups who expect to be together longer tend to invest more in their relationships with the worker and each other and in the group's traditions and norms.

Groups of relatively long duration, several months or more, have predominated in social work practice until recently. Such groups have been directed toward the improvement of a constellation of identified problems in the psychosocial functioning of the members or toward the optimal development of members' potentials for effective functioning. If a major purpose is to develop maximum or restore effective functioning in social relationships and social competence, when there are serious obstacles to the achievement of these goals, then short-term treatment is usually inadequate. It takes time for many people to develop meaningful relationships with a social worker and with each other and to use such relationships for their own and others' benefit, to work through the problems, and to stabilize positive gains before the group terminates. Examples of the need for prolonged service are parents with multiple problems that have been present for a long time, seriously disturbed mental patients, and delinquent adolescents.

Short-term groups are of many kinds and meet numerous needs. In some instances, social workers need to extend and adapt their definitions of groups to optimize their use in some settings, for example, medical and mental hospitals. They can adapt their knowledge and skills to work with an aggregate of people who come together for even a brief period of time. Flexible adaptation makes possible brief sessions on hospital wards or waiting rooms where the social worker connects the needs of one patient to the needs of other patients or their relatives. Adaptation makes possible the inclusion of single-session groups in which ongoing relationships cannot develop and in which the focus is on using the interaction among members to meet the immediate psychosocial needs of a collectivity.

In short-term groups, all the phases of development are condensed. The degree of cohesion that develops is dependent upon the attraction of members to the stated purpose of the group, clearly focused content, and relatively strong motivation to belong to the group. Short-term groups seem to be appropriate for several important purposes. Task-centered practice is one form of brief, goal-oriented, and structured treatment used for helping people with a specific problem that can be resolved through the clients' implementation of specific tasks.[42]

Other short-term groups have been used to prepare the participant for a new role, such as becoming a foster or adoptive parent, a recipient of public assistance, a resident of an institution, or a foster child. They have been used for family life education when the focus is to present a limited amount of content, within an atmosphere that makes possible some expression of feelings and ideas and some modification of attitudes and behavior. They have been used to help people to cope with personal or family crises, as when a child is suspended from school or runs away, when a member of a family is arrested, or when there is a new conflict in family relationships or in the family's relationships with significant reference groups. They have been used for teaching parents of child patients to deal with separation from the children, to realize what it means to the child, and to relieve stress and anxiety. With children served by child development centers, diagnostic group sessions may be used to clarify the specific manner in which problems of children are manifested in social situations. Often, a by-product is helping a child accept other treatment. As more use is made of short-term services to groups, both the benefits and limitations need to be studied; more experience and research is necessary to evaluate this trend in practice.

Another trend in practice is toward the use of one-session groups. Such groups are used to provide information, reduce anxiety, and lessen a sense of isolation through interacting with other people who share a similar stressful situation. They have been used with patients and their relatives in waiting rooms in hospitals; with children of military families in which parents are being deployed—a stressful situation for many families; and for patients who are in mental hospitals for only a few days.[43] Such groups are highly structured, with a leader who has a central role in fostering group process and who takes a fairly directive stance. Structure provides support. Yet the worker must, at the same time, remain sensitive to and respond flexibly to individual needs. The worker sets forth clear and limited goals and expectations for the meeting, maintains focus, and moves the group through a stage of orientation; a work stage in which information is provided and reacted to by the members, a specific task is achieved, or a solution to a problem is sought;

and an ending period in which what has been achieved is summarized. Within the structure, there is opportunity to involve the participants in a process of sharing and helping each other.

Several studies have found that, for certain goals, short-term treatment in social work is at least as effective as continued service is. Only the one by Epstein, however, refers specifically to groups.[44] The advantages of short-term treatment are numerous. There are fewer unplanned terminations. A time limit discourages the often potentially destructive development of undue dependency on the worker or the group, enhances a sense of hopefulness that positive changes will occur, and encourages some people to participate when they would be unwilling to undertake long-term treatment. A demand for a high degree of structure and time limits may, however, run counter to the perspectives on time held by different ethnic groups. Cultural variations occur in preferred orientations to past, present, and future time frames. Devore and Schlesinger give the example of American Indians who need to be protected from early intimate disclosure.[45] Some people need considerable time before they are willing to share intimate thoughts and experiences and to enter into open communication with strangers.

Some people need continued service beyond the one to twelve sessions usually considered maximum for short-term service. The issue is not whether brief or longer service can be effective but rather under what circumstances each type is preferable. Numerous demonstration projects of longer term services have led to successful outcomes. These projects have included work with very troubled and disadvantaged young children, disturbed acting-out adolescents, regressed schizophrenic patients, and families with multiple problems.[46] Certainly some people can benefit optimally from brief service; others need a longer period of time. The important point is that, because there is evidence of the effectiveness of short-term treatment for some clients, there should be compelling reasons for deciding on long-term help.

Temporal Factors. Frequency, length, and time of meetings are factors to be considered in planning for a new group. Frequency of meetings has been studied in terms of its effect on participants and on the interaction in the group.[47] As the amount of time spent together increases, the amount of information available, consensus of opinion, and feelings of liking for each other also tend to increase. In open-ended groups that have a rapid turnover of members, frequent meetings may become a means of retaining some continuity of participation. Groups in hospitals, especially on children's wards, may meet every day. Separation from their families and friends, anxiety about medical care, and adaptation to a patient role point to the intensity of the children's needs, requiring frequent meetings. Yalom has made a similar case for frequent meetings with patients in mental hospitals, where the average stay is only one to two weeks and where there is continuous turnover of patients.[48] The only answer to the brief time available and the rapid turnover of members is to hold meetings as frequently as possible.

Crisis intervention groups also tend to meet more often than once a week, owing to the need for quick attention to the upset in the steady state and the attention that must be given to each member's own critical situation. The urgency and the nature of the problem, the members' concerns about it, and the degree to which the group is open-ended are important considerations.

The length of sessions is largely a matter of group purpose and capacities of members for sustained interactions. The most frequent length of group sessions tends to be an hour and a half, which provides time for an opening, and a work segment in which each member may participate actively, and an ending period. Shorter sessions, sometimes only a half hour long, may be as much as young children or seriously disturbed adults can tolerate. As their ability to tolerate longer periods increases, so, too, should the length of the meetings. Environmental factors also often influence the length of sessions as in groups that meet in school during one of the school's regular time periods or when a group must be fitted into a schedule of activities in a mental hospital or day treatment center.

The time of day and the day of the week that a group meets influence its composition and attendance. Some people can arrange to be absent from work or school; absences often add, however, to the stress they already feel. The gains of group participation will have to be perceived as being much greater than the losses in terms of time and money. Some people also react against evening meetings away from home and family, or they fear going out at night, particularly if their homes or the meeting place is located in a high crime area. It may take considerable exploration with prospective members to arrive at a time convenient for them. There is increasing recognition that time of meeting and, therefore, working hours of social workers need to be adapted to the members' situations if services are to meet clients' needs effectively. Accessibility of service should be a primary principle of practice.

Space. The success of a group is influenced by the physical and social environment in which it meets.[49] The adequacy and atmosphere of the room in which the group meets has an important impact on the development of relationships and group cohesion. Some arrangements of space tend to keep people apart, such as chairs in rows or along walls. Chairs arranged so people face each other tend to draw people together. In a room in one agency in which groups of adults meet, the room is bright and light, chairs are informally arranged around a table, and an urn of coffee is provided from which members may help themselves. A contrast is a room with a long board-type table, stiff chairs, and one in which no refreshments are permitted. Another contrast is a room that is dirty, that is full of supplies and equipment not to be used by the group, or that contains broken-down furniture. Such rooms, too often prevalent, do not send messages of welcome and of respect for the group members.

To foster participation in discussion and intimate relationships, the ideal is a room that is quiet and large enough only for the necessary activities and for an informal circle of chairs within such distance that each member can readily be seen and heard by others. The circle is a symbol of closeness. The space in the center provides some distance, and the spaces between the chairs indicate varied degrees of closeness and remoteness. In an open circle, however, no hiding is possible. A table tends to support members and often reduces self-consciousness and allows for a place to put possessions or doodle to reduce tension. When groups meet in schools, churches, playground buildings, or other host facilities, there are always rules and regulations to which all people must conform. A constant location is desirable to reinforce the members' identification with the group and provide a sense of continuity.

Basically, social workers need to think through the impact of the physical setting on the members, do what they can to plan for an adequate setting, and then make the best use of what is available. Within even poor physical facilities, it is possible for workers to create and maintain a physical atmosphere that is consistent, supportive, and trustworthy.

Rules. Rules or procedures that will govern the members' participation in the group need to be clarified. Often, they are in the nature of agency policies and procedures concerning payment of fees, confidentiality, attendance, recording of sessions, informed consent, and bringing observers or visitors to the group. There may also be rules about behavior, such as smoking, drinking, leaving the room, using supplies, or making sexual contacts among members. Members should, of course, have been informed about these policies or rules at the time of entry into the group, should understand the reasons for them, and should have a right to object to them; they become a part of the contract between the worker and the members. In planning for a group, workers need to be clear about what rules are imposed by agency policies over which they have no control but which they need to define for the members. They need to consider whether other rules about the behavior of the members are necessary. Rules should be established only when they are clearly essential to the safety of people or property. Such rules should be firmly related to the situation, rather than based on the arbitrary use of authority.

Decision Making. In planning a group, the practitioner makes decisions about the organizational structure of the group based on consideration of the following questions:

1. What type of group should this one be, related to its primary purpose, degree of open-endedness, and duration?
2. What are the temporal arrangements for the group and the rationale for them?
3. What are the physical arrangements for the group and the rationale for them?
4. What policies and guidelines will govern the conduct of the group and the behavior of its members?

CONTENT

Groups do things. The members talk about certain matters; they convey messages through nonverbal behaviors; and they engage in activity-oriented experiences. Groups vary in the extent to which the content is preplanned, develops spontaneously out of the interaction among the members, or is decided upon by the members through a decision-making process. The nature of the content stems from the purpose of the group, the more specific goals of the members, the members' interests, and the stage of group development.

Development of Content. Occasionally, agency purpose and policies may strongly influence, if not dictate, some of the content to be included in the group experience. For example, agencies serving a particular ethnic or religious population may emphasize the inclusion of certain cultural traditions and activities in its groups; and settlements, Ys, and youth organizations may expect their groups to participate in certain agency-wide activities such as holiday celebrations, sports events, or money-making activities. Such content is more apt to occur in socialization and education groups than in counseling and therapy groups. They might or might not serve the purposes of a given group and might or might not be beneficial to the members of a particular group at a particular time. When groups are expected to participate in such activities, they become a part of the workers' preplanning and orientation of members.

Although the content will, in most instances, be developed by the members themselves with the help of the worker, the practitioner needs to have some tentative plan for proposing what the members will do together. Planning for the first meeting of a new group is particularly important. Research by Henry found that the emotional tone of a meeting and the positive or negative quality of the interactions among the members are altered by the use of certain activities.[50] Since the emotional tone and quality of relationships tend to determine whether or not members will return after the first session, careful attention needs to be given to the nature and sequence of the content.

Decision Making. The questions to be answered concerning content include the following.

1. What will be the general nature of the content of group sessions, that is, exploration of problems, reflective discussion, decision making, educational material, activity-oriented experiences? What is the rationale for these types of content?
2. How and by whom will what content be planned? What agency policies and interests determine the content? How can these be changed or adapted to meet the needs of the group?
3. What will be the nature and sequence of the content for the first meeting of the group? What part will the members have in the process?
4. What space, time, supplies, and equipment will be needed?

ILLUSTRATIONS OF PLANS

The planning process is one of assessing the needs of a defined population and making decisions about the kind of group to be developed to meet those needs. These two sets of skills—assessment and decision making—depend upon knowledge concerning human beings in interaction with their environments, small groups as units of social work service, and the myriad of factors that determine how groups form and develop. Required also are professional judgment, flexibility, and creativity. Although the plans for two or more groups will probably never be the same, illustrations of the process and content of planning may be useful to clarify the framework that has been presented.

A Group in a Mental Hospital

Social Context. Within a large mental hospital, a social work intern was assigned to a ward of regressed and withdrawn schizophrenic patients. Most patients in the hospital are there for very short stays, according to policies that prohibit compulsory hospitalization for more than a few days without a court order. There are, however, several wards for longer term and severely dysfunctional patients who are there voluntarily or have been committed. The hospital has an unusually good treatment program for these patients. It has a policy of encouraging social workers to work with groups of patients, as well as of giving them help individually. The ward has a well-functioning team consisting of psychiatrist, nurses, technicians, and social workers. The social work intern participates in team meetings at which the progress of each patient is discussed and decisions are made concerning any changes in treatment, and he has access to other staff as deemed advisable. Ongoing collaboration with other professional staff on the ward is necessary to ensure that all staff members will support the patients' attendance and help patients to apply learnings from the group to their daily living.

Determination of Need. At a meeting of the ward team, the nurse identified several patients not in groups who needed help in relating more realistically to staff and to one another. The patients' behavior was characterized by apathy, lack of interest in ward and wider hospital activities, and much restless behavior. They sat on benches in a corridor with very little interaction among them. They seldom responded to efforts to engage them in conversation. They were among the newest patients on the ward and had not responded well in therapeutic interviews. They seemed unable to seek and use relationships with other patients: some were even unaware of the presence of other people and unable to respond to comments and questions made by staff in ways that they could be understood. Other members of the team agreed with the nurse's assessment and recommendation that a new group be started for them.

Purpose. The purpose of the group was defined as helping the patients to become aware of and develop supportive relationships with others, at each one's level of capacity to do so and to begin to develop some sense of self-esteem and competence. Within this purpose, specific goals varied with each patient but were most often to help patients feel comfortable in being with others and learn that it helps to listen and be listened to, to help patients identify problems in getting along on the ward and try to lessen those problems, to help patients learn that they are acceptable to others, and to enhance participation in appropriate aspects of the hospital's program. All these goals are directly related to the use of the group for the enhancement of social relationships and role competence.

Group Composition. The decision was made to begin the group with seven patients, small enough for the members to be able to interact with each other and large enough for them not be too frightened by the intensity of too-close relationships. Based on an assessment of the psychosocial functioning of each of the new patients on the ward, the decision was made to include the seven men who seemed most unable to participate in ward activities. Among these seven, however, there were two who were more advanced than the others in their ability to talk and respond to other people. The age range was from twenty-eight to forty. Three black and five white men were included. The social worker was a white male. The common needs of the patients were the primary consideration, but there was no one who might feel too different from the others and there seemed to be sufficient heterogeneity to provide as much stimulation as these men could tolerate.

Structure. It was decided that this would be a closed group, with new members added only in the event of a vacancy, making it possible for the members to develop trust and support from each other over a period of time. It was to be an informal, process-oriented discussion-activity group. Patients who have extreme difficulties in social relationships and low self-esteem need a considerable amount of structure and continuity of experience. They also tend to have, like young children, short attention spans. For these reasons, the group was set up to meet three times a week in order to provide continuity of experience, with meetings lasting only one-half hour until members indicated they could tolerate longer meetings. The duration of the group was tentatively scheduled for three months, by which time it was expected the members would be ready for more advanced forms of treatment. The group was to meet before lunch when the meeting would not interfere with other ward activities and schedules. The meetings were to be held in a pleasant small recreation room, and arrangements were made for the group to have exclusive use of the room, with no interruptions during the scheduled time. Later, patients would be taken out of the ward to test their ability to use more freedom and try out new experiences. When this happens, a case aide will be available to assist the worker in helping the members to use the new experiences.

Content. Because these patients are unable to engage in any focused discussion, and requests to talk are very threatening to them, it was planned that the content of the group would consist of simple, nonthreatening activities and brief discussion periods. Coffee and tea would be offered to reduce anxiety, give the men something to do with their hands, and enhance motivation to come to the group. Beginning meetings would be structured sufficiently for patients to come to know what to expect and develop some sense of security and support. The worker decided to begin the first meeting with a reminder of the purpose of the group and its expectations, emphasizing that the members will benefit from coming. Then there would be a short period of doing something that makes few demands in relating to others and in verbalizing—stretching, a name game, follow the leader, tossing balloons, whatever seems appropriate. Then it would be time to talk in a structured way, often taking turns in saying one thing they felt about coming to the group or one thing they would like to try to do in the group sometime or what their favorite foods are—the possibilities are endless, but they should make a minimum of demands on the patients. In a brief closing, the meeting would be summarized very briefly and a reminder given about the next meeting.

A Group in an Elementary School

Social Context. The group was formed in an elementary school in an inner city neighborhood with a rapidly changing population, which is now about one-third Hispanic. With the influx of new families, the schools are overcrowded and classes are too large. Many of the children are bussed out of the neighborhood to less crowded schools, often going to different schools and having different schedules from their siblings. There are many single-parent families. In other families both parents work, usually at jobs with relatively low wages. There is very poor attendance at parent-teacher meetings and at other school events. The school had a record of high rates of children failing in the second and third grades, and the principal wanted to change these rates. He was able to obtain some additional teacher aides and two additional social workers for the new academic year. In addition to social workers, the school has a half-time nurse, a half-time psychologist, and access to special resources of the school system, such as a school guidance clinic, a tutoring program, a nutrition program, and special classes for mentally retarded, gifted, and physically handicapped children.

Need. One of the new social workers met with the school principal, nurse, psychologist, and second- and third-grade teachers to explore the ways she could be most useful to the school. She had been assigned to the first three grades. One priority identified was to serve a number of third-grade boys who, although of average intelligence or above, were failing in their academic subjects, disrupting the classroom, fighting with other children, and being absent and tardy too often. Efforts by another social worker the year before to work with the boys' families had not been successful. The principal said that one nearby school had organized groups for its troubled children last year and reported greater success with them than with other efforts to help the children individually or in their families. He said he would like to try that here. Discussion of this idea resulted in the decision to begin the program with two small groups—one for boys and one for girls. The division by gender was primarily based on the fact that the girls would not be able to benefit from the much more aggressive behavior of the boys, and some different activities would be needed for boys and girls. In spite of prior lack of cooperation from parents, all the parents signed forms giving their children permission to participate in the groups. An agreement was reached with the principal and teachers that the group workers would not share the childrens' discussion of the families or the school with them unless there was a clear need to do so, in which case they would tell the members that information was being shared. There would be a meeting at the end of each semester, however, to share information about the positive and negative changes in the childrens' behavior and attitudes. The members would be informed about these meetings. The teachers would remind the children of the group meetings, and the workers agreed to be responsible for ending the meetings on time.

Purpose. The purposes of the boys' group were to improve the members' adjustment to school and to help them relate better to peers and teachers, develop more satisfactory classroom behavior, and become motivated to learn. In talks with each boy, the principal and social worker told him he was to be given a chance to be in a club where the members could do things together and talk about things that were hard for them so they could do better in school. They knew the boy could do better; he was not dumb, and the club could help him do better. All agreed to attend the group.

Composition. The decision was made to invite eight boys to join the group, small enough for individualization of needs and large enough to use a variety of activity-oriented experiences, as well as discussion. The major criterion was the severity of the problems in academic and psychosocial functioning: the school wanted to help those who were in most trouble. Those selected shared the problems of having little support at home, limited financial resources, academic failure, unacceptable classroom behavior, and problems in relationships with peers and adults in positions of authority. The age range of the chosen members was eight to nine, their IQs were 95 to 120, five were Anglo, and three were of Mexican descent. All could speak English. The boys used a wide range of means for coping with the demands made on them by the school and the frustrations in their environments. There seemed to be an adequate balance of factors making for homogeneity and those making for heterogeneity to expect the group composition to be satisfactory.

Structure. The group, although called a club, was to have an informal structure of worker and member roles without officers of any kind. The term *club* was used to differentiate it from a class and other types of school activities. The group was to meet twice a week for forty-five minutes to conform to regular periods within the school day, during a period reserved for special activities or study. In this instance, school regulations controlled the length, frequency, and time of meeting. The worker had, however, the major responsibility for suggesting the group meet for the entire academic year because of the range and severity of the boys' problems and their nonsupportive family environments. The only available room was a small, unattractive one adjoining the nurse's office. The worker received permission, however, from the nurse to hang bright and interesting posters on the wall and to bring in a small cabinet for storing such supplies as crayons, paper, finger paints, puppets, and a dart game. The room contained a round table, a dozen chairs, and a set of shelves.

Content. The club was to be an activity-discussion group, with both talking and doing geared directly to the problematic situations of the boys. The plan for the first meeting was to review the purpose of the group with the boys and try to elicit what that meant to each of them, to set a few ground rules for the group and explain how the club would operate and how it would be different from a class or a sports group, to play a get acquainted game in which boys from one classroom would learn something about boys from the other classroom, and to try to interest the boys in drawing pictures showing what they liked or disliked most about school. The content of later meetings might include using puppets and role playing to facilitate the expression of feelings and difficulties, reading out loud simple books on subjects of special interest to the members, directly discussing difficulties and alternative ways of coping with them, and trying out different ways of behaving. The plan would be to move from essentially parallel activities to activities and discussion that require more interaction and cooperation.

Discussion. These two social workers were able to use Kurland's model to plan groups in very different types of organizations and with different client populations. They were fortunate to be in organizations whose administrators and professional personnel supported the use of groups and knew how to, and were motivated to, engage in collaborative teamwork. Without such support, the workers would have had to spend a great deal more time in the preliminary activities of educating other staff members about the roles of social workers, about the ways in which their services can further the mission of the organization, and, within that, about the special values that groups have under certain circumstances. The decisions made in each step of the planning process need to be interrelated, with each decision consistent with and contributing to the overall plan.

7

Selection and Preparation of Members

In planning for formed groups, the prospective member's decision to elect group service or the worker's decision to recommend it is related to the many factors of need, purpose, composition, and structure and to the constellation of services provided by the sponsoring organization. Many different procedures are used by organizations to reach people who need a service, to accept requests for service, and to admit persons into particular groups. But the basic purposes are similar: to help people begin to know about the availability and nature of the service, determine their eligibility for service, ascertain if their goals are sufficiently similar to those of others to be met through a group, and prepare them for entry into a particular group.

APPLICATION AND RECRUITMENT

Recruitment of prospective members occurs in such diverse settings as medical centers, settlements, schools, youth-serving agencies, family service associations, and community mental health clinics to publicize the fact that groups are organized for a given purpose. These groups are usually those provided for psychosocial education or socialization. They are designed for people who are presumed to function within a normal range of expectations: they meet a common human need for help in some aspect of social living. A hospital, for example, publicizes the fact that it has a new wellness program, consisting of six group sessions, that will help participants to maintain and enhance their health. A community center makes known the fact that it is starting a group for parents of preschool children focused on improved understanding of child development and preparation for school entry. A university announces the availability of a group for faculty to help them to overcome writer's block. A child guidance center, in cooperation with schools, announces that groups are available to junior high school students and their parents for help with their reactions to a severe earthquake. A family service association announces that it is starting groups for stepparent families to help the members to understand the special features of such families and to develop appropriate roles in the reconstituted family.

When persons respond to the invitation, there is usually a screening or registration process before the first session of the group. A short interview, before attendance in the group, takes place to provide information about the group, to screen out those applicants who seem not suitable for the service, and to explore how the help being sought matches that being offered. Even though the initial interview is brief and informal, the interviewer is sensitive to the applicant's mixed feelings of positive motivation and apprehension and clarifies his questions. Essentially, the process is largely one of self-selection of clientele who meet the objective criteria established by the organization for group composition, eligibility requirements, and, for children, parental permission for participation in the group. There is the greatest amount of informality in the procedures used in these instances, in order to maximize the accessibility of these services to people with felt needs.

These relatively informal and brief application and registration procedures tend to reduce social distance between staff and clientele. It has been proposed by Cloward that in neighborhood centers located in low-income areas, "where social distance is great, there is little likelihood that efforts to influence members will be effective; where social distance is minimal, the possibilities for influencing members in constructive directions are maximized."[1] Thus, informal entry procedures facilitate the acceptance of social work services by low-income persons. It is suggested that the more formalized the organization, the more likely it will selectively attract persons who have middle-class orientations. Gouldner found a tendency for lower-class clientele to perceive bureaucratic procedures as red tape.[2] The disadvantages of informal approaches are that the practitioner begins her work with a minimal amount of prior knowledge about the prospective members and the members may not have sufficient opportunity to learn whether or not the group is right for them.

For counseling and therapy groups, application and intake procedures tend to be formal, with assignment to a group based on a process of exploration and assessment followed by preparation for entry into the group. Sometimes a short group experience, particularly for young children, may be a part of the preliminary process, used for assessment and treatment planning. Or a conference with an entire family, often in its home, is a part of the process when faulty functioning of the family as a unit is thought to be central to the problem of one or more of its members. In some mental health settings, the period of study and assessment is prolonged: a social worker is assigned responsibility for interviewing applicants to determine their eligibility and to make a psychosocial study of the applicants' problems, capacities, and situation. Applicants may also be seen by other members of the team, such as psychologists, nurses, or psychiatrists. In a meeting of the interdisciplinary team, then, a decision is made about whether or not a case will be accepted and, if so, the type of treatment to be offered. The needs of applicants are assessed in relation to the constellation of individual, family, and group services that comprise the agency's program. People should be assigned to a service immediately whenever possible, rather than placed on a waiting list for service at some future time.

The social worker's relationship with a prospective group member may or may not begin at the point of the person's application for service. It more often begins once the decision has been made that a particular group service is appropriate. Whatever was learned about the person in the application or registration process needs to be conveyed to the worker who will serve as the leader of the group. This worker should then have one or more interviews with the prospective member to initiate a relationship, explore the person's concerns about membership, and prepare him for the meetings.

Reaching-Out Approaches. There has been increasing interest over the years in reaching out to prospective clients who do not seek service. In these instances, there is no typical application process by the recipients of service but rather a seeking out of persons thought to be in need and an active offering of service to them. Outreach services are desirable because many potential clients do not know about services or are resistant to them. Outreach has been defined by Toseland as "a social work practice method that attempts to identify clients who are in need of services, alert these clients to service provisions and benefits, and help them use services that are available."[3] It is one way of promoting access to services. Such procedures are used in schools where the initial concerns are usually expressed by a teacher or administrator who then refers the child for individual or group service. The child or his parents may or may not respond positively, but an agent of the community has decided that help is necessary. This is typical also in the prescription of group services for patients in hospitals. Cases in probation, work with delinquent gangs, and protective services in child welfare are other examples of the approach.

In reaching out to persons who do not seek service, the specific procedures will vary with the organization's function and geographic jurisdiction, the tentative purpose of the group, the potential sources of referral, and the reputation of the organization with those thought to need its help. Public school personnel, probation officers, physicians, police, and courts often refer people to social agencies. Once an agency has established a reputation for being helpful to previously hard-to-reach clients, the volume of referrals tends to increase and the problem then becomes one of limiting intake.

Many children or adolescents are too suspicious of adults or too nonverbal to participate in formal interviews before the beginning of group experience. Information from referral sources helps the staff to assess the need for service and the suitability of a service for the referred persons. Not all persons who are referred are served. Too often, there is inadequate explanation of the purpose and nature of the service and the reasons for making the referral. Too often, also, the persons most in need of service are not the ones referred. Referral agents may have misconceptions about group work, similar to those of prospective members. They may not give the referred person sufficient information to use in making a good decision or following through on the recommendation. The burden is on the group's practitioner to confer with referral agents to ensure that they have the necessary information and positive attitudes about groups to pass on to clients.

A successful outreach program reported by Kilburn took place in a Mental Health Association that organized a program of groups for school-age parents who comprised a population at risk for a variety of physical, social, educational, cultural, and economic reasons.[4] The primary goals of the groups were to increase members' knowledge and use of existing resources, increase the number and type of socially supportive contacts, improve parenting skills, and build a more positive parental identity. An outreach approach was necessary because the agency knew that these young people were not likely to seek services, owing to lack of knowledge about or negative attitudes toward them; fears of retribution or punishment by their own parents, school personnel, and others; and fear of being labeled as a bad parent and having children taken away.

The outreach approach was multifaceted. It included education for staff in organizations who come into contact with adolescents so they would be able to describe the group service adequately. Preliminary interviews with the prospective members were held in their homes—it seemed less threatening to them to begin on their own turf and contributed considerably to the workers' understanding of the young parents and their situations. Transportation to the meeting place was provided, usually in a community facility such as a YWCA. Baby sitters were provided, as was coffee and tea. In addition to social workers, special outreach workers kept in touch with the members and made referrals. Efforts were made to build a social network through which members could call each other, as well as staff, in times of crisis. A formal evaluation of twenty-seven groups that had met twice weekly for twelve weeks confirmed the success of the program. The responses of the former members, on preinterview and postinterview schedules, indicated a very statistically significant improvement in knowledge and use of resources, number and type of socially supportive contacts, and feelings of competence in caring for children.

Agencies have used these and other approaches to facilitate acceptance of needed services. Written invitations to come to a meeting may be effective. So, too, may be introductions of the worker to the person or group by the person making the referral. Street corner visits and telephone calls have been used also by some workers. The particular procedures to be used in reaching members is a matter of professional judgment based on knowledge of the particular people and their situations. Sometimes, when a person or group is wary of the service, the offer of help must be made over and over again. An honest presentation of the service to be offered and the conditions under which it will be given seems to be effective in motivating the prospective members toward a decision to at least try out the group.

In a reaching-out approach, the organization must be very clear about the reasons for choosing to serve one group rather than another, based on needs of people in its catchment area and knowledge of the community. An example is that of a small network of girls, referred by a policeman. It was a subsystem of a larger group that split as a result of a conflict around a boys' gang. In investigating the situation, the social worker learned that the most delinquent subgroup called itself the Spiders, whose members aligned themselves with the Scorpions, a boys' gang. The pattern of delinquent behavior included fighting, truancy, and robbery. The girls were ages fifteen to seventeen in grades nine to eleven in two different schools. Most of the girls were in a special school for students with serious problems in social adjustment. They were of Mexican-American backgrounds. Since the Spiders seemed to be the subgroup with the most serious problems, it was selected for service. The worker secured the girls' names and addresses from various sources, met with them in pairs or triads, and later as a group. Within three weeks, most of the girls said they'd be willing "to try a sponsor."

Services to Existing Groups. Social agencies may offer service to existing groups, or a group may apply for service. In such instances, one major task that faces the social worker is to determine why affiliation with an agency is sought and whether the group's purpose can be achieved within the agency's function. Another task is to determine the membership of the group and its membership policies as these exist. Then it is necessary to secure enough information about each member to make a tentative judgment about the workability of the present composition and size of the group for a social work purpose. If not suitable, are there ways the membership can be redefined for this purpose? Some of the decisions about membership may occur quite naturally as the reason a group is seeking affiliation with the organization is explored. This exploration may be with the group as a whole or with persons who represent the group.

The process of determining the suitability of a group for service may be clarified through an example. A minister telephoned a supervisor in a community center to say that there was a group of troublesome eleven-year-old boys who needed someone to help them. The supervisor went to the church to confer with the minister and later with the boys. The boys wanted a football coach. The supervisor talked with them about this request, explaining that the center did not provide this service, but there was a playground just two blocks away, and he would be glad to see if the boys could have a coach there. The boys said they did not want to go there. Finally, one confessed that they were not welcome there—they had been thrown out. They told tales about the unfairness of the recreation staff about this, but it also became clear that these boys could not participate in organized sports without starting fights and disorganizing the activity. The supervisor said that he understood that it was not easy for the minister, either, to have them here where they were having some of the same troubles they had had at the playground. At first there were denials, but then one boy said that "well, we'll be good if we can have a coach." The supervisor said he could not give them one: what he could do would be to work with the playground director and the boys to reopen the question of their use of the playground, or he could send a social worker to meet with them as a group to help them get along better with each other and the church. They could do things together—even play with a football—and then talk about how the activity went, what they could do to make it better next time, and what troubles they have in getting along with others. Then, when the boys could get along all right and play well together, the social worker would help them find a way to become a team. It took two more conferences before the boys accepted this notion of service. This example illustrates the need for clarity of purpose, based on skill in looking beyond a verbalized request to the underlying need. It illustrates also how a social worker does not meet an unsuitable request for service but offers a suitable alternative.

ASSESSMENT

From the earliest publications on group work to the present, some form of diagnosis or assessment has been described as essential to sound social work practice.[5] Because diagnosis is often associated with illness, assessment has become the preferred term. Many social workers continue, however, to refer to diagnosis, often using that word interchangeably with assessment or using diagnosis when there is an identified mental or physical ailment and assessment for the broader biopsychosocial process. Unlike a medical diagnosis, assessment goes beyond the identification of a problem or illness to an appraisal of the interrelation among biological, psychological, sociocultural, and environmental factors and to positive motivations and capacities. To achieve an accurate appraisal or the meaning of the facts that have been secured, the worker makes appropriate use of typologies of needs and problems, sources of information, and criteria for judging the adequacy of the functioning of individuals or groups and their environments.

According to Siporin, assessment is "a differential, individualized, and accurate identification and evaluation of problems, people, and situations and of their interrelations, to serve as a sound basis for differential helping intervention."[6] It is an ongoing process, not just a first step in practice. From appropriate fact finding about the members and the group system, the practitioner formulates opinions about the nature of the members' characteristics, problems, and potentials. This leads quite naturally and logically to planning for what should be done to enable the members to improve their functioning or to influence changes in the wider social system. The worker later evaluates the impact of the intervention on the members and the group process, which itself involves further fact finding and opinion forming, and so the cycle of understand, plan, intervene, and evaluate goes on in a dynamic way.

It is neither necessary nor possible to have all the facts about persons to make a preliminary judgment about their suitability for a particular group. The worker begins with what facts are relevant to the decision to accept a person for placement in a particular group. He then continues to add to his storehouse of knowledge as he judges what additional information will be helpful in serving individuals and the group as a whole.

In the process of assessment, the goals of the prospective members should be paramount. A person's positive motivations in seeking help or his aspirations are at least as important as his problems are, or, in the words of Mary Richmond, "our examinations of the yesterdays and the todays should be with special reference to the client's tomorrows."[7] If the worker starts with the person's interest in having something be better about self or situation, her subsequent acts are apt to be goal directed. Prospective members may be clear about what they hope for or have only vague feelings of discontent with the current situation. They may be articulate or need much help in expressing themselves. Accompanying the positive motivations toward the opportunity available, resistance to change may be evident. Fear of the unknown and of their own capacities to meet expectations may interfere with their ability to identify some goals related to the group's proposed purpose.

To observe and test for capacities, positive attitudes, areas of successful accomplishment, and supports in the environment are equally as important as knowledge about problems and deficits is. For it is such strengths that can be used and built on in the group. Knowledge of normal growth, development, and behavior relevant to particular subcultures and situations, as well as deviations from norms, is used by practitioners to make possible a valid social assessment of the members and their social situations.

Identifying a type of problem is one important part of understanding it. The severity of the problem needs to be ascertained. Some problems may be as minimal as the need for help in anticipating the demands of a particular stage in the life cycle to prevent a problem from developing. Usually transitional or socioeducational groups are the most appropriate forms of help. Most cases that come to the attention of social workers involve life transitions, changes in roles, and relationships.[8] On the other hand, many problems are severe ones that create tremendous stress for the clients and also often have negative effects on those with whom they interact. Some problems are diagnosed as physical illness or mental disorders. Practitioners need to remember that social work treatment is not directed toward a disorder: it must be tailored to the person-situation gestalt, the network of multiple interacting factors that influence how the person reacts to stressors and pathologic processes.[9] They need to differentiate instances when problems are extensive, pervasive, and catastrophic from instances when change is less problematic. The severity and chronicity of the difficulties have an impact on the kind of service to be provided and the kind of group in which it will be provided.

Guidelines for the Content of Assessment. Crucial for success in helping members use group life toward the achievement of individual and group purposes is the worker's acumen in assessment. The tasks of fact finding and evaluation are somewhat different for each group, depending upon its particular purposes, composition, and structure. Nevertheless, certain guidelines provide workers with a frame of reference for viewing each member in relation to the group and to the external situation. A basic assumption underlying the framework for assessment is that human behavior is the product of the interaction between persons and their environments. Every human being has an interdependent relationship with others and is a component of a number of interlocking social systems. Certain dimensions of behavior can be understood only in terms of the structure and function of these networks of interaction and the member's status and role in them. The practitioner's assessment relates, therefore, both to individuals and the persons to whom they are connected and the significant social systems of which they are a part. At both individual and group levels, the worker is concerned with the nature of stresses from internal and external forces and with the capacity and motivation of the system to withstand stress, cope with change, and find new or modified ways of functioning.

Any group experience occurs in association with continued life experiences at home and in the community. The social worker's relationships, no matter how close, are tangential to those experienced by the members in everyday life. It is these relationships that need to be changed, supported, or strengthened.[10] Within a developmental perspective, the assessment takes into account the interrelatedness of affect, cognition, values, and behavioral patterns. It seeks to ascertain the capacities and limitations of members in each major area of ego functioning, with special reference to self-esteem, identity, judgment, perceptions of reality, adequacy of communication, balance between freedom of expression and rigid control, the appropriateness of defenses and coping patterns, and above all, the range and quality of social relationships.

People need support systems. According to Caplan, "kinship and friendship are the most important types of primary social relationships which can be used as support systems."[11] A support system is one in which significant others help a person to mobilize personal resources, provide the material means and skills essential to meeting a need, and give emotional support to cope with the problems. Networks are composed of relationships among people and are systems of mutual aid. A social work group is a temporary support system. It makes an exceptionally important contribution in helping people develop successful peer relationships, whose importance to the quality of life cannot be denied. Peer relationships "have been shown to be the single most important prognostic factor in the long-term outcome of children and adolescents with emotional disorders and in the prognosis of schizophrenics," according to Grunebaum and Solomon.[12] Most members have both abilities and difficulties in relationships when they enter a group, and the group serves as an arena for working on and improving peer relationships.

External circumstances combine with intrapersonal and interpersonal processes in affecting the adequacy of a person's functioning in a given role at a given time. The major social systems in the community provide resources and opportunities or, too often, barriers to the fulfillment of needs. An adequate assessment takes into account the impact of these systems on individuals, families of members, and the group. A question is the extent to which these systems provide nondiscriminatory access to services for all people and to what extent they create stress and serve as obstacles to effective functioning.

Of great importance in our multiethnic communities is assessment of the impact of ethnicity and race on a person's functioning and the psychological meaning they have for him. Effectiveness of functioning needs to be evaluated within the context of the culture from which people come and the culture with which they identify. In a review of the literature, Jenkins identified the following five major areas of concern about culture that interfere with the provision of appropriate services: (1) lack of recognition of the diversity of ethnic patterns and cultures of client populations; (2) lack of appreciation of language differences and of the importance of bilingualism as a necessary component in work with non-English-speaking clients; (3) the persistence of stereotypes that hamper understanding of ethnic communities, their problems, and their special needs; (4) threats to the survival of an ethnic group as a cultural entity; and (5) lack of recognition of the interrelationship among many factors in understanding how ethnicity influences any person, family, or group–

factors such as differences in age, educational level, and socioeconomic status; recency of migration or immigration; extent of acculturation; and the particular community of residence.[13] The values and traditions of a culture influence a person's or family's opportunities for effective social living. Therefore, according to Lum, it is essential to determine whether cultural factors are useful forces or barriers to the achievement of goals.[14]

Social workers have a special responsibility to assure that their services are appropriate ones. Cooper and Cento give an example of sensitivity to cultural facets of life experiences in a small group developed in a medical center.[15] The group was designed to meet the educational and emotional needs of pregnant Hispanic women. They had been characterized by hospital staff as hysterical and difficult to manage. Group sessions revealed that the patients behaved like that because they had not been prepared for the experience and lacked emotional support. Many were recent immigrants, socially and emotionally isolated, and reacting to foreign customs. They faced cultural and language barriers so that they tended to withdraw when confronted by medical authority and to ignore or misinterpret pertinent information. As the group leader facilitated continuity of care for patients and communication about them among members of the interdisciplinary team, the team members became more sensitive to patients' needs, and communication between patients and staff improved.

Several writers have offered detailed outlines of the content deemed to be essential for making sound assessments.[16] Wilson and Ryland and Toseland and Rivas have given much attention to the interrelationships among the assessment of individuals, the group as a whole, and the group's environment.[17] Practitioners can become overwhelmed by the vast amount of data it is possible to secure unless they have clear guidelines to assist them in exploring for pertinent information and selecting appropriate means for obtaining the desired information. The following questions provide guidelines for assessment.

1. Who is the client in terms of demographic characteristics, stage of development in the life cycle, ethnic background and identity, social class, and family structure?
2. What problem or problems are of concern to the client, the worker, and significant persons in the client's social network? Are the problems suitable for treatment in a group? To what extent are the problems related to changes in roles, developmental tasks, or crises as contrasted with impairments in ego capacities or developmental arrests? To what extent is the problem due to lack of environmental resources or social supports or to lack of fit between the person and subsystems of the environment?
3. How, when, and to whom did the need or problem become evident and what were the precipitating factors?

4. What are the client's attitudes toward self, peers, family members, and persons in positions of authority?
5. What are the range and quality of the person's relationships within the family, with peers, and in the group?
6. What are the capacities and resources within the client and in the network of social systems that can be supported and developed further in behalf of the client?
7. To what extent is the client motivated to become a member of the group? What indicators are there of positive motivation and what are the nature of apparent resistances?
8. What feasible goals, acknowledged by the client, are congruent with the group purpose?
9. Are the agreed-upon goals appropriate to the characteristics of the client and the social situation?
10. What types of intervention are apt to best meet the needs of the particular client?

The amount and nature of the information sought vary with the many facets of the service, particularly its purpose and structure and the practitioner's theoretical orientation. The preliminary assessment cannot encompass all aspects of the person's or group's functioning. In accord with the value of the right to privacy, the information sought should be limited to what is essential for achieving agreed-upon goals. If a service is one of primary prevention or enhancement of normal development, the data obtained are often limited initially to the descriptive characteristics of the clients, phase of development, common experience or status, and certain potential risks to healthy development. Later, during the process of service, the worker elicits additional information as it seems particularly relevant. If the service is a therapeutic or rehabilitative one, helpful treatment cannot be given unless the worker understands the nature, causative factors, and course of the problematic situation and the adequacy of the client's current functioning in particular situations.

Analysis of the Information. To arrive at accurate assessments of the problems and the person-situation configuration, measuring instruments are increasingly being used to obtain and analyze relevant data.[18] Many social workers have tended to make little use of formal instruments, preferring to use the unobtrusive methods in which observation and data collection are part of an ongoing process of interaction between a worker and a group. There has been distrust of devices that might intrude on the developing professional relationship and the exploratory discussion between the worker and members. Some practitioners have learned, however, that selective use of such tools can improve assessment, further the process, and document the outcomes of the helping endeavor. In their book on group work practice, Toseland and Rivas describe self-rating inventories, questionnaires, formal scales, frequency distributions, sociograms, role playing, and forms of simulation that measure certain aspects of social functioning. Numerous instruments have been developed for measuring psychological or social problems of individuals and social interaction, relationships, and cohesiveness. Some of the instruments can be found in Hudson, Levitt and Reid; and Toseland and Rivas.[19] The tools used need to be clearly related to the goals of service and the particular needs of the individual, family, or group being assessed.

When pertinent information has been obtained, the actual assessment consists of the analysis of the person-group-environment configuration. The purposes are to identify the most critical factors operating and to define their interrelationships. The assessment is the practitioner's professional opinion about the facts and their meaning. Somers and Perlman have both referred to this process as one of problem solving by the worker, done through a process of reflective thinking.[20] Lewis states that it is a logical process that also incorporates intuitive insights.[21] Realistic appraisal provides the basis for action that should be guided by facts. What is to be understood are the nature of the need or trouble, the factors that contribute to it, the participants' motivations and capacities, and a judgment about what can be changed, supported, or strengthened in the person-group-situation configuration. Assessment is not completed when a problem or condition has been identified and pertinent data have been obtained from appropriate sources. There remains the need to explain how it has come to be the way it is. The practitioner draws inferences from the data and relates these judgments to the service that must be given. The behavioral science theory used largely determines the inferences made.

Knowledge of the psychosocial development of people throughout the life cycle alerts the worker to what should be observed and checked out if he would serve the members well. Each phase of development incorporates psychosocial tasks to be mastered if the person is to make a successful transition to the next stage. Every culture has norms or expectations used to judge the extent to which a person or a group is functioning adequately. Appraisal of a person's position on a continuum, ranging from very effective to very ineffective functioning, clues the worker in to both capacities and problems. The assessment is made against standards for physical, cognitive, emotional, and social functioning deemed to be within a range of normality for persons within a given stage of the life cycle and within a given culture. These norms need to be differentiated according to such important influences on psychosocial functioning as age, gender, urban, or rural community, school grade or occupation, race, nationality, religion, and economic status.

Although norms are necessary, rapid changes in the conditions of life and in life styles pose problems for both practitioners and members in assessing the adequacy of functioning. So does the fact that clients come from varied cultural backgrounds. One task for the worker is to ascertain the influence of socioeconomic status, race, and ethnicity on psychosocial functioning. Although certain characteristics differentiate one group from another, efforts to define them may lead to negative stereotyping. Persons in positions of power, including social workers, may come to expect stereotyped behavior and plan and act accordingly. Awareness of one's own norms and culture is essential to prevent stereotyping, as is accurate knowledge about other cultures and life styles.

Determining the adequacy of behavior needs to take into account such judgments as whether the behavior is appropriate to the client's stage of development; how long it has persisted; whether it is a reaction to change in circumstances or a devastating crisis; whether it is socially acceptable behavior in the member's culture; whether the behavior interferes with only one or several roles; what the type, severity, and frequency of symptoms are; and whether there are changes in behavior of a kind not expected in terms of normal maturation and development.

The social worker takes into account the facts that all phases of human development overlap, that each person has his own rate of maturation and development within what are average expectations, and that there are many variations within a normal pattern of functioning. A person's feelings about his assigned roles, the way he interprets them, and his responses to the expectations of others give clues to the fit between persons and their environments. A person may adapt well in one situation and poorly in another. The worker is, therefore, concerned with variations in effectiveness of role functioning in different social systems—whether ineffective functioning in one system is affecting ability to adapt elsewhere and whether successful functioning in one system can be used as a bridge to more effective functioning in other systems.

Accurate assessment requires the ability to consider alternative explanations of difficulties. When a causative statement is proposed, the worker has made a choice from among available alternatives: accuracy requires that the selection of alternatives be a conscious one. Solomon gives the example of a girl assessed as being discriminated against in school or, alternatively, as a child having difficulty adapting to a new school in which she feels isolated and lonely.[23] The need is to determine which alternative is more probable through careful exploration of one's own preferences and of the members' situation, including group factors. Explanations are applicable only to a particular case. Lewis points out, for example, that not everyone subjected to social injustice has develoed the same responses; the assessment explains how a particular individual or family was victimized and what the persons' responses were to the event.[24] Strengths, as well as difficulties, are located. Such an approach deemphasizes stereotyping, through establishing the unique, as well as the common, responses to factors that contribute to a particular condition.

The practitioner's decision-making ability is somewhat limited by the need for rapid intervention in many urgent situations. Ultimately, however, skill in rapid assessment is achieved through extensive and thorough knowledge of human behavior. Knowing when and how to alter initial assumptions is also essential to the exercise of professional judgment. The product of an analysis is, according to Siporin, a formulation that integrates the data and draws conclusions about the interrelated factors that contribute to the problematic situation, leading to decisions about interventions to be implemented.[25]

INTERVIEWS WITH MEMBERS

The most frequent source of information for use in assessment is the personal interview in which facts about prospective clients and their situations are elicited. Through direct observation of the nonverbal as well as verbal, behavior, the practitioner derives clues about patterns of relationships and perceptions of self in relation to others. Individual interviews are thought to be especially useful in understanding and clarifying the particular goals that clients hope to achieve and their reactions to the available services and the conditions under which help is given. They offer an opportunity to explore feelings and to secure information pertinent to the selection of interventive actions.

In many instances, interviews with other staff members, relatives of the client, or persons in the person's social network contribute to an understanding of the person's needs, particularly in work with children and in interdisciplinary settings, such as schools and hospitals. In addition, the information gained therefrom may be used in team planning to meet the needs of members and their relatives.

The social worker uses all of her interviewing skills in initial conferences with prospective members. She sets a climate conducive to the task; makes the applicant as comfortable as possible; shares her view of the purpose and nature of the service; assures the person of her and the organization's desire to be helpful; explores with the person how she views the identifying problems that might be suitable for a group form of help and how she feels about groups as the medium of treatment; engages the prospective member's participation in making a decision about using one or more available services; observes and accepts the prospective member's feelings; initiates and develops a time-limited working relationship; secures enough information about the person or group to decide tentatively whether or not the request falls within the organization's purposes and whether the person is suitable for a particular group; and orients the person to next steps and clarifies how he will be introduced to the group, if that is suitable.

There are many reasons for the use of pregroup interviews. When prospective members are prepared through such interviews, they enter the group with a feeling of acceptance by the worker and are at least somewhat ready to engage in relationships with others. The leader can then focus not only on relating to each member but also on promoting communication among the members.

In pregroup interviews, a worker-member relationship is initiated that, it is hoped, is accepting, empathic, and supportive. This kind of relationship enhances motivation to participate, eases entry into the group, and serves as a bridge for the member to enter into relationships with other members. It is especially desirable to have the person who will be the group's practitioner conduct the interview.

Preparatory interviews are essential in arriving at an accurate preliminary assessment of the member. Understanding the member's goals, perceptions of self in relation to group membership, and expectations of self and others assist the worker in deciding about the suitability of the particular group for the person and assessing the possible influence of the member on the group. Making a decision about the fit between a person and a group requires knowledge about prior group experiences, feelings about participation, and the nature and intensity of needs and problems. A two-way process is operating here. The worker is learning about the potential group member and deciding about that person's suitability for the group. The potential group member is learning about the worker and the group and deciding whether or not to participate.

Understanding the nature of the group and the worker's role in it is a necessary condition if the person is to make a fairly realistic decision about group membership. A direct statement about the group and why a person is thought to be a good candidate for membership needs to be made clearly and reactions to the information secured. Even young children and seriously disturbed people can usually understand a simple, nonthreatening explanation.

When an interviewee's initial ideas about the group and its expectations are clarified, his initial anxiety and uncertainty are lessened, and thus positive motivation is enhanced and resistance is reduced. Most new group members have apprehensions, fantasies, and fears about membership in groups.[26] The members may fear that the group will make unrealistic demands on them for instant intimacy. They may have pervasive dread of forced self-disclosure, fearing that they will be forced to confess shameful transgressions and thoughts; may fear emotional contagion—that they will catch the problems of others or be sicker by association with others, especially when the group is composed of physically or mentally ill clients; or may believe that groups are second-rate forms of help. They may doubt that they can be helped by anyone other than an expert or that their individual concerns will not get attention in a group. They may fear that they will be excluded or rejected by other members or by the practitioner; that their privacy will be invaded and that "the whole world will know how weak they are"; that the pressures toward conformity will make them lose their individuality; and that, in the group atmosphere, they will lose control of their feelings and behavior in the presence of others who will ridicule them. The interviewer needs to explore the prospective member's ideas, accept the feelings, and provide reassurance about the naturalness of these fears.

In pregroup interviews, the worker can instill hope through offering reassurance about the benefits of group experience. There is evidence from research that instillation of hope during initial interviews is a factor in continuance of treatment.[27]

Research findings indicate that there are important benefits of pregroup interviews. In a controlled experiment comparing sixteen groups whose members had interviews with an equal number without interviews, Meadow concluded that the pregroup interview is a useful tool in facilitating attendance and developing clarity of purpose and expectations. It does not, however, enhance risk-taking behaviors and cohesion. After all, she says, it is the worker's skills in influencing the group process through which these benefits accrue rather than through one-to-one contacts.[28] From his own research and a review of studies on the subject, Yalom concluded that evidence from a compelling body of research demonstrates that systematic preparation of patients for group therapy facilitates the patients' course in that therapy and supports the efficacy of advance preparation of the group.[29]

Illustration of an Interview. The following illustration presents excerpts from a taped interview with a recently discharged patient from a mental hospital. The patient was referred to a group in a community setting by her psychiatrist, who had talked with the group worker and provided her with information about the patient's schizophrenia and current state of psychosocial functioning. She needed to break out of her social isolation, enhance her self-esteem, and develop skills in relating to other people.

Mrs. M. arrived early for her appointment with the social worker, who greeted her, invited her to take off her coat, and find a comfortable chair. The worker said she understood that Mrs. M. was here to learn about the mental health group and decide whether or not she wanted to become a member. Mrs. M. responded with "uh-uh-yes." The worker gave information briefly about the purpose, composition, and content of the group, stopping frequently to ask Mrs. M. if she understood. The response was always "uh-huh." She listened intently, with nonverbal gestures indicating extreme anxiety.

WORKER: Sometimes people feel uncomfortable about being interviewed.

MRS. M: (laughing): That's me.

WORKER: Yes, most people do at first. Could you tell me what you think of your doctor's suggestion about the group?

MRS. M: Well (pause) I just came here because the doctor arranged the interview, so I'm here . . .

WORKER: Uh-huh. . .

MRS. M: And I do want him to think I'm trying.

WORKER: Well, I know that he thinks that the group would help you and that being with other people will improve your health.

MRS. M: That's what he told me.

WORKER: But, you're not sure you want to try it.

MRS. M: Well . . . when you tell me about the group, it makes me feel a little dazed . . . (silence)

WORKER: A little dazed?

MRS. M: Yes—that's how I think I feel.

WORKER: Can you tell me more about that feeling?

MRS. M: I'll try. What will happen to me in the group? It'll be so confusing—so strange—all so new.

WORKER: It will feel that way at first all right—but I'll be there to help you feel more comfortable.

MRS. M: Like here today?

WORKER: Yes—you're not as anxious now as when you first came in, are you?

MRS. M: No. No. Could you tell me again what we'll be doing in the group—what it will be like?

WORKER: Certainly. (W explains what the purpose of the group is, how it can help, who will be in it, and what the content of the sessions will be).

MRS. M: So, we'll hash over each others' problems?

WORKER: Well—yes. But not only that. It's also what's going on in your daily lives—how you can get along living in the community—and learning social skills.

MRS. M: I guess I need that. There are no lectures, then?

WORKER: No, but what do you think about that?

MRS. M: Well—if there were, I could just listen—I wouldn't have to talk.

WORKER: You won't be forced to talk until you're ready.

MRS. M: (sigh of relief)

(Mrs. M. asked questions about when the group would meet, whether there would be a fee, how many members there would be, whether the group would do other things, to which questions the worker gave answers and tried to determine the meaning of the questions to Mrs. M.)

MRS. M: Well, yes, I just don't know. It seems rather . . . (inaudible)—just to be around people who are sick like me—it'll be almost like being back in the hospital again. That's scary.

WORKER: I think I know how scary that feeling can be.

MRS. M: Yeh, it's really scary.

WORKER: It's true that all members of the group have been in mental hospitals, but that does not mean they do not have many abilities and good qualities. They all want to make it in the community and they're in the group because we think they can make it in the community—and the group can help them with that.

MRS. M: Well--I want to make it, too.

WORKER: That's something you have in common with the others. The group can help you to enjoy being with other people and getting along well with them. That's what it's for.

MRS. M: When your whole life has been disrupted like mine has been, I just don't feel any satisfaction with anything or anybody.

WORKER: Would you like to?

MRS. M: Oh, yes, I would, but it seems so hopeless.

WORKER: Hopeless—that's a scary feeling.

MRS. M: Yes. (silence) Could the group help?

WORKER: I feel quite sure that it can and your doctor feels it can, too.

MRS. M: That's what he said.

WORKER: But you still feel unsure about it.

MRS. M: Well—it's so scary to have to meet new people.

WORKER: Yes, it is. But you'll have help with that. You'll be surprised how helpful members can be to each other.

MRS. M: I've always been shy about meeting people.

WORKER: And that's what the group is for . . .

MRS. M: Maybe I should try it—all my life—getting out and making friends—I haven't been able to—I haven't been able to.

WORKER: Would you like to learn to do that?

MRS. M: (Sigh) You think I could?

WORKER: Yes, I do—in the group.

MRS. M: Well, I'll give it a try.

WORKER: Good. (Then W gives information about the importance of not just dropping out after first meetings and of giving the group a real try for at least two months and answers more questions about the conduct of the group and other members.)

MRS. M: If you think I should come next Tuesday, I'll be here. Both you and my doctor seem to want me in the program.

WORKER: And I hope you'll soon feel that you really want to be in it, too.

MRS. M: Well, I do want to come, but I know I'll feel like a sore thumb sticking out all over.

WORKER: That's not a pleasant feeling, but you're not like a sore thumb with me.

MRS. M: It's not so hard to talk with you now (smiling).

WORKER: You're not nearly as anxious as when you first came in here, and after you get used to the group, you won't be so anxious there either.

MRS. M: I will come to the group on Tuesday. (There followed discussion of transportation; a visit to the meeting room; an introduction to the receptionist; an invitation to call the worker if Mrs. M. had any more questions that need answering.)

MRS. M: Goodbye and thank you. I'll see you Tuesday.

In this situation, the social worker agreed with the psychiatrist's judgment that Mrs. M. could make appropriate use of a particular group. There are instances, however, in which the decision is that any group, or a particular group, is inappropriate for the client at this time. When the interviewer has doubts about the group's suitability, he shares these doubts directly with the person. For example, in the case of Mrs. M., a simple "maybe you are not ready for the group now" or "I think I see that you need something different from what the group could offer" may suffice, and then the interviewer follows up with eliciting the responses to such a statement. The response would tend to confirm or disconfirm the worker's judgment. When the decision is not to admit a person to the group, the worker sensitively, with empathy, explores and responds to the person's feelings about the decision, whether or not it is jointly made. The important point is that an alternative be offered—the search for a more appropriate group, or an offer of individual or family help, or a different type of service through referral within the agency or elsewhere.

EXPECTATIONS AND WORKING AGREEMENT

The outcome of pregroup interviews should be a preliminary working agreement or contract, covering the general purpose of the group, the needs or problems to be addressed, the reciprocal role of worker and members, and mutual expectations. Introduced into group work by Schwartz in 1961, the concept of contract now has general acceptance.[30] Such mutual agreements are fundamental in determining the direction, structure, and nature of service. But flexibility is necessary if working agreements are to be tools in treatment. It needs to be recognized, for example, that some mental patients or young children will be extremely limited in their ability to participate verbally in such an interview, but they can at least understand a simplified explanation of what the purpose of the group is, how the group can benefit them, and what will be expected of them.

John Dewey warned that aims cannot be completely formed in advance:

> The aim as it first emerges is a mere tentative sketch. The act of striving to realize it tests its worth. If it suffices to direct activity successfully, nothing more is required, since its whole function is to set a mark in advance, and at times a mere hint may suffice. But usually—at least in complicated situations—acting upon it brings to light conditions which had been overlooked. This calls for revision of the original aim; it has to be added to or subtracted from. An aim must, then, be flexible; it must be capable of alteration to meet circumstances.[31]

Flexibility makes it possible to redirect efforts, as appropriate to the needs of clients or according to changing circumstances. Beall shows that there is a danger that if an initial contract is formal and explicit, it can become a "corrupt one," as when the initially stated goals of clients are specified in the contract and conceal more important unavowed ones.[32]

A tentative working agreement is derived from shared experience in exploring the potential members' needs and situations. Its major values are that it gives both parties a sense of involvement and participation and signifies mutual commitment and responsibility. It provides a common frame of reference for the participants so that each one is clear about what is expected. It provides a foundation for periodic review of progress and next steps. Congruence among worker and member contributes to effective functioning, and lack of congruence promotes maladaptation and hinders directed activity.[33] Congruence allows a worker and individual or worker and group to establish a working alliance.

Working agreements with persons who are to become members of the group are crucial to its success. Too often neglected, however, is the work with other personnel in the organization who have power over the group. Since the organization is an important social context, an agreement needs to be negotiated with appropriate personnel to achieve congruence about the group's purpose, mutual expectations, appropriate structural arrangements for the group, and the way staff will work together to assure the quality of the experience for the members and for the benefit also of the organization. Organizational sanction for the plan for the group, based on adequate knowledge about it, can do much to assure its success.[34] In a sense, then, the worker develops two contracts—one with the members and the other with appropriate persons in the organization.

In developing a plan for the selection and preparation of members for a group, several matters are crucial to the success of the group. The worker makes decisions concerning these questions:

1. How will potential members apply for group membership or be recruited for a particular group?

2. How and by whom will the potential members be oriented to the services available and prepared for entry into a particular group?
3. What will be the major themes of content for pregroup interviews with members and other persons in their behalf?
4. How will the guidelines for assessment be adapted for use in a particular situation?
5. What criteria will be used to determine the person's suitability for participation in a particular group? If an applicant is not suitable, how is that decision shared with the applicant and what alternative help is offered?
6. Are contacts to be made with referral sources or relevant persons in the member's social network and, if so, for what particular purpose?
7. What will be the form and content of the initial worker-member agreement or contract?

An effective plan for the selection and preparation of members for entry into a group requires decision making based on sound use of knowledge within a theoretical perspective.

8

Group Development

It takes time for a collection of people to develop into a group that becomes an instrument through which positive gains may be achieved by its members. Gradually, from a collection of individuals, a group emerges. As a group develops, noticeable differences occur in the behavior of the members and in the structure and functioning of the group. Although change in any group is a continuous, dynamic process, it is useful to think of a group as moving through a number of stages characteristic of its life cycle. The identification of stages in a group's development provides clues for assessing individual and group functioning and for selecting appropriate content and interventions. This enables a worker to ascertain where a given group is in its development and then plan what needs to be done to help it move forward toward the achievement of its purpose.

STUDIES OF GROUP DEVELOPMENT

The first major study of group development was published by Tuckman, who derived a model from a comprehensive review of fifty publications dealing with stages of group development in training, therapy, task-oriented, and laboratory groups.[1] Using Bales' concept of socioemotional and instrumental or task realms,[2] he concluded that four analogous stages occur within each realm. The stages that occur in all groups are:

1. Forming. This stage is characterized by the members' dependency on their leaders and other members or on preexisting standards and by orientation and testing to define boundaries of both interpersonal and task behaviors.
2. Storming. This stage is characterized by conflict and polarization around interpersonal issues, with concomitant emotional responses in the task area.
3. Norming. The resistances during the storming period tend to be overcome in the process of developing norms. Group feelings develop, new standards evolve, and roles are adopted. In the task realm, intimate and personal opinions are more often expressed.

4. Performing. Flexible and functional roles have emerged that contribute to the achievement of the group's tasks. Structural issues have been resolved and the group's interpersonal climate and structure become supportive of task performance.

5. Adjourning. This stage was not in the original formulation in 1965 but was added by Tuckman and Jensen in 1977.[3]

A more recent study in 1980 by Lacoursiere reviewed slightly more than one hundred studies of group development, again covering varied types of groups.[4] Lacoursiere concluded that there are five developmental stages, which he labeled orientation, dissatisfaction, resolution, production, and termination. There is a period of assessment or orientation to the experience when the members are concerned about what it will be like to be in the group. Then there is dissatisfaction when members realize the reality that seldom lives up to their hopes and fantasies. If the members are to remain in the group and learn from the experience, the conflicts need to be resolved. The group reaches a more productive period characterized by mutuality, enthusiasm, learning, and working toward goals. Then the group faces termination, with a sense of loss over the anticipated end of the group. The orientation, dissatisfaction, and resolution of conflict stages may be brief or prolonged, depending upon the characteristics of the members and the nature of the group. In task-centered groups, for example, interpersonal relationship processes may be less significant than in counseling and therapy groups. Positive expectations for the group predominate in most groups, but there may be a negative, resistant orientation stage in some groups, particularly when membership is compulsory.

In Lacoursiere's study, the authors whose works were included in the study delineated different numbers of stages. Lacoursiere concluded that when only two or three stages are formulated, some important distinctions are lost: on the other hand if too many divisions are made, it is difficult to generalize the findings and replicate the work. He concluded that his findings essentially support the earlier work of Tuckman, even though he gave different names to the stages. The group forms (Tuckman) through a process of orientation (Lacoursiere); dissatisfaction (Lacoursiere) is reflected in conflict (Tuckman's storming); resolution of dissatisfaction (Lacoursiere) is brought about largely through the adoption of norms (Tuckman); productivity (Lacoursiere) results from performing (Tuckman); and termination (Lacoursiere) is a process that leads to adjournment (Tuckman and Jensen).

Whittaker compared formulations of development in growth-oriented groups that had been proposed by social workers.[5] He concluded that the model by Garland, Jones, and Kolodny represented "the most complete statement to date on the subject and contains within its stages the basic elements of the models proposed by other contributors."[6] The model consists of five stages of development: its major focus is on the socio-emotional issues facing the members; less attention is given to the realm of tasks.[7] The stages are the following.

stages

1. Preaffiliation. In this stage, the members become familiar with one another and with the situation. They are anxious and ambivalent about involvement. The characteristic patterns of behavior are approach and avoidance in determining whether or not the group will be safe and rewarding.
2. Power and control. The problem of status, communication, decision making, and influence come to the fore. There is considerable testing of the worker and other members in an attempt to define and formalize relationships and to create a status hierarchy. Dysfunctional roles may develop. The behavior of members reflects the ambiguity and turmoil occasioned by change from a nonintimate to an intimate system of relationships. The basic issues to be coped with are rebellion against the leader, individual and group autonomy, acceptable norms, protection, and support. The clarification of power issues gives the members freedom for autonomy and readiness to move toward intimacy.
3. Intimacy. There is intensification of personal involvement in the group and of self-disclosure and striving to satisfy dependency needs. There occur a growing awareness and mutual recognition of the meaning of the group experience in terms of personality growth and change.
4. Differentiation. Acceptance of others as distinct persons occurs. Mutual acceptance of varied personal needs brings freedom and ability to differentiate and to evaluate relationships and events in the group on a reality basis. Mutuality and interdependence predominate. There is strong cohesion accompanied by a respect for individual autonomy. There is a heightened sense of both individual and group identity. Relationships with other groups and the community become more natural and comfortable.
5. Separation. Members begin to move apart and find new resources for meeting needs. There may be some regression and recapitulation of former group experiences and patterns of relationships. A number of emotional reactions are set off that are reminiscent of the approach-avoidance maneuvers of the first stage. The anxiety now is around separation. Various defensive and coping devices are used to avoid and forestall termination and to face and accomplish it.

The model was developed inductively from analysis of records of practice with therapeutic club-type groups of children and adolescents. It was later found to be applicable for work with groups of adult patients in mental hospitals but with many variations in behavior and a greatly prolonged time in the first two stages.[8] The central theme of the model is closeness. The authors recognize that other themes, such as cooperation, might also be important, but they think that "closeness conveys best the sense that the group experience involves social beings and human emotions."[9]

OTHER SOCIAL WORK PERSPECTIVES

Since Whittaker reviewed the social work literature on group development in 1970, almost all writers have given attention to developmental aspects of groups. Northen's was the first book to conceptualize theory and practice within a developmental framework.[10] Two years later, Hartford proposed a model consisting of the following stages: (1–3) three pregroup stages; (4) group formation; (5) integration, disintegration, and conflict and reintegration; (6) group functioning and maintenance; and (7) termination.[11] She states that this scheme is consistent in many respects to the one developed by Northen: a pregroup stage; orientation; testing-conflict; problem solving; and termination. She viewed the formulation also as consistent with the earlier work of Garland, Kolodny, and Jones and with the work of Sarri and Galinsky.[12]

More recent writers have consistently paid attention to one or more pregroup stages of development. In this book, planning, selecting and recruiting members, and preparing members for group experiences have already been discussed. What happens in these processes has great influence on how a group will emerge and develop. Planning and pregroup contacts are a necessary prelude to the emergence of a group, but a group does not begin to develop until members meet each other.

Group development is viewed in a multiplicity of ways by writers, depending at least partially upon the purpose, composition, and structure of the group. It depends also on the theoretical stance of the social worker. For example, relationship and process-oriented approaches—as in this book—put more emphasis on the socioemotional dynamics than behavioral and strictly cognitive approaches do. The number of stages described by social work authors, excluding a preplanning or pregroup one, range from three to six. Any division of group life into stages is somewhat arbitrary, for indeed there is a continuous flow of interaction that shifts and changes throughout the group's duration. Just as one stops the camera to take a still picture, it is evident that a group is different at that moment from what it was earlier. The group has changed.

Three stages of group development have been used by several authors, referred to simply as beginning, middle, and ending stages.[13] The rationale for a three-stage model is that there is greater agreement on the issues to be addressed at the beginning and ending of a group than there is in intermediate stages. On the other hand, some authors assert that two- or three-stage concepts are oversimplified. Cohen and Smith argue that: "This reduction of a highly complex process of group interaction to two or three phases, as reflected in the literature, may be due to an inability to deal with group phenomena because of inadequate methodology. However, oversimplification represents a disservice."[14] They based their judgment on an analysis of one hundred forty four characteristics of member behaviors, taken from critical incidents throughout the life of the group.

Several social work writers who have conceptualized four stages of development add a stage of dissatisfaction or interpersonal conflict between the beginning stage and the one in which a cohesive group comes into being.[15] When a fifth stage is added, further distinctions are made between the stage of dissatisfaction or conflict and the most advanced group level, as when Garland and associates distinguish between a stage of intimacy and one of differentiation, when Klein adds a stage of negotiation before intimacy is achieved, or when Anderson has a stage of closeness between autonomy and interdependence.[16] Henry has both a convening and a formative stage toward the group's beginning, preceding a conflict stage.[17] Two formulations of group development include a pregroup stage, plus six other stages. Trecker conceptualizes stages primarily in terms of the development and decline of group feeling or cohesion.[18] Sarri and Galinsky relate their material primarily to changes in the emergence and development of group purpose, structure and cohesion; challenges to those processes; and movement toward higher levels of stability, integration, and goal-directed activity.[19]

Each social work author has selected similar, although somewhat different, formulations of stages of group development beyond one or more stages of planning and preparation that precede the coming together of prospective members. Table 8.1 presents the stages of each author, as they may be fitted into a four-stage model. Six of the authors describe only three stages; four present four stages; four, five stages; and two, six stages.

A MODEL OF GROUP DEVELOPMENT

To develop a useful model of group development, several facets need to be taken into account: (1) the predominant patterns of behavior related to socioemotional issues; (2) the typical patterns of behavior related to tasks; (3) and typical characteristics of group structure and process. Each stage has its own developmental issues that must be attended to and at least partially resolved before the group can move into the next stage. What happens in a particular stage influences the processes and content of the next one. Although there is always some distortion of reality in attempts to integrate and combine findings from diverse sources, certain trends seem to emerge from the major studies of the literature. Because of the complexity of the problem and variations in types of groups,

Table 8.1. Stages of Group Development, by Date and Author

Author & Date	*Stage I*	*Stage II*	*Stage III*	*Stage IV*
Garland, Jones, Kolodny, 1965	Preaffiliation	Power & control	(3) Intimacy (4) Differentiation	(5) Separation
Northen, 1969	Orientation	Exploration testing	Problem solving	Termination
Hartford, 1971	Convening	Integration-disintegration, conflict-reintegration	Group functioning & maintenance	Termination— (4) Pretermination (6) Posttermination
Klein, A. F., 1972	Orientation	(1) Resistance (3) Negotiation	(4) Intimacy	(5) Termination
Trecker, 1973	Beginning	(2) Emergence of group feeling (3) Development of bond, purpose, cohesion	(4) Strong group feeling (5) Decline in group feeling	(7) Ending
Sarri, Galinsky, 1974	Formation	(2) Intermediate (3) Revision (4) Intermediate II	(5) Maturation	(6) Termination
Schwartz, 1976	Beginnings	- - - - - - - - - - - - - - - Middles	- - - - - - - - - - - - - - -	Endings & transitions
Tropp, 1976	Beginning	- - - - - - - - - - - - - - - Middle	- - - - - - - - - - - - - - -	Ending
Levine, 1979	Parallel relations	Inclusion	Mutuality	Termination-separation

O'Connor, 1980	Emergence	Exploration & Revision	Work	- - - - - - - - - - - - -
Garvin, 1987	Beginnings	- - - - - - - - - - - - - - Middles	- - - - - - - - - - - - - -	Endings
Henry, 1981	(1) Convening (2) Forming	(3) Conflict	(4) Maintenance	(5) Termination
Balgopal, Vassil, 1983	Exploration, involvement	- - - - - - - - - - - - Middle-Work	- - - - - - - - - - - - -	Endings & transitions
Toseland, Rivas, 1984	Beginning	- - - - - - - - - - - - - - Middle	- - - - - - - - - - - - - - -	End
Anderson, 1984	Trust	Autonomy	(3) Closeness, (4) Interdependence	(5) Termination

NOTE: Numbers indicate when title represents a separate stage.

a four-stage model seems adequate if short-term, as well as longer term, groups are to be taken into consideration.

Orientation-Inclusion. The title of this stage conveys the socioemotional and task issues that concern members of the group. Other titles given to this stage of development include preaffiliation, convening, emergence, beginning, trust, and parallel relations—each indicating an aspect of the behavior of members or the task to be achieved. The predominant socioemotional themes are inclusion and dependency. The typical patterns of behavior are those of approach-avoidance, reflecting ambivalence about becoming a part of or included in the group's membership. Relationships are basically parallel; trust has not developed; and discussion tends to be scattered, self-centered, and rather superficial. Members feel some anxiety and confusion about inclusion and acceptance, but overt interpersonal and intragroup conflict tends to be minimal.

In the task area, the members become oriented to the group through receiving and seeking information from the worker and searching for the common ground and the meaning of the group to them. The task is to become oriented to the new situation, including the group's purpose, roles of workers and members, and mutual expectations. The initial purpose, structure, roles, and rules are those tentatively predetermined by the practitioner and the organization that sponsors the group. To use the group well, the members need to come to an agreement on initial goals and expectations.

Members are usually motivated positively toward group membership. These predominant themes are modified in some groups that have what Lacoursiere has identified as a negative orientation stage, usually occurring in groups in which membership is compulsory.[20] Although some ambivalence is typical in almost all groups, resistance to inclusion and to the perceived power of the worker may predominate in youth gangs or other groups in which members have little or no choice about attendance and in which there is great distrust of the leader or the organization.

Regardless of the theoretical differences reflected in the literature of social work, psychotherapy, and the social sciences, there is common recognition that there is a point of initial formation when members come into face-to-face communication. Both the practitioner and members deal with socioemotional and task issues.

Stage II—Dissatisfaction and Power Conflict. The title of this stage indicates that members become disatisfied with and test out certain aspects of the group's operation and engage in a conflict over who has power to do what. Other titles for this stage are storming, exploration and testing, integration-reintegration, negotiation, hostility, conflict, power struggle, and power and control. These words convey some of the flavor of this crucial stage of group life. But as the members deal with these feelings and conflicts, the transition to a working group occurs.

Before a number of people can use a group for their mutual benefit, Balgopal and Vassil note that there needs to be a group culture of

> normative sets, which typically refer to implied or explicit agreements among the group members. Common agreements in groups are acquired through the processes of opinion exchange, discussion, conflict resolution, decision making, and interpretation of others' comments which incorporate both covert and overt aspects of communication.[21]

Through such means, a unique group develops that becomes both the means and the social context for treatment. Uncertainty, dissatisfaction, and conflict contribute to, rather than detract from, the development of a cohesive group.

The predominant socioemotional theme is dissatisfaction with the perceived structure and expectations of the group, particularly in relation to the worker's authority and the distribution of power and control among the members; the solution of the issue leads to an increase in autonomy for the members. The typical patterns of socioemotional behavior are expressions of frustration, competition for status, disappointment, anger, discouragement, and anxiety about mutual acceptance and group identity. Exploration of the reality of the situation in respect to its hoped for benefits, testing of the worker's acceptance and authority, and challenges to the existing structure occur.

The primary task is the development of realistic mutual expectations and interpersonal relationships based on mutual trust and acceptance. As a result of the exploration and testing, the group's purpose and individualized goals become clarified, an acceptable structure of roles and subgroups emerges, norms are clarified and modified and become major sources of support and guidance, and interpersonal and intragroup conflicts about power and autonomy are lessened. Working through the conflicts results in considerable cohesion. The pattern of communication gradually shifts from being scattered and self-centered to one of free and open communications with the worker and among the members by the close of this stage.

The position of social workers in the organization and in the group gives them certain authority to influence the members toward changes in attitudes and behavior and to influence the structure and processes of the group itself. The manner in which group leaders exert their authority is crucial. The authority is effective only to the degree that the members permit the worker to influence them. In this stage of development, that is a primary issue: how much power will the members grant the worker; what power will the members have; and how will the worker use his legitimate power?

With some types of groups, this stage might be divided into one primarily dealing with expressions of dissatisfaction and conflict and a second one dealing with the resolution of these group problems. In many instances, however, these seem to go on simultaneously around particular problems and issues. One issue becomes prominent, at least a partial solution is achieved, then another issue emerges and is worked on, and so forth in an evolving process.

Stage III—Mutuality-Work. The title given to this stage indicates that the predominant socioemotional theme is interdependence and the task theme is work toward goal achievement. Other titles given this stage are intimacy, problem solving, group functioning and maintenance, strong group feeling, affection, mutuality, and middle stage.

The typical socioemotional patterns of behavior are intensification of personal involvement, seeking or avoiding intimacy, and enhancing personal identity along with group identity. Members tend to cooperate and participate actively in the group's work. Mutual aid is at its peak. The major task is to maintain and further enhance the group as a means of goal achievement and to use appropriate ways to resolve problems, enhance understanding of self and others, and develop social competence. Members are generally committed to the group's purpose and the achievement of each one's goals, which provide a focus for the group's work. Communication is open; norms and roles are flexible; subgroups are functional; interpersonal relations are usually characterized by mutual acceptance, self-disclosure, empathy, and respect for differences; conflict tends to be recognized and dealt with in functional ways; and the group is an appropriately cohesive one that allows for differentiation, as well as integration.

This stage would be divided by some writers into a stage in which issues concerning intimacy predominate, followed by a fourth stage of differentiation that precedes separation.

Stage IV—Separation-Termination. This title indicates that the predominant social-emotional issue is separation, and the task is to leave the group and make transitions to other activities. Other titles given to this stage include endings, transition, and adjourning. The members are ambivalent about separation from the worker, the group, and other members.

The predominant behavior patterns tend to be the mobilization of defenses against ending, feelings of loss of relationships, regression, reenactment of earlier experiences, and uncertainty about ability to function without the group. The major tasks are to complete unfinished business, review and evaluate the experience, and stabilize gains that have been made and transfer them into situations in the community. Cohesion lessens as the members find more satisfactions in the community; the strength of interpersonal relationships may weaken; norms and roles are flexible; and conflict centers around the reality of termination and perceptions of abandonment by the worker. Plans are made about post-termination activities or services for members of the group.

This stage may be divided, as suggested by Hartford, into three sub-stages: pretermination, termination, and posttermination.[22]

RECURRENT ISSUES AND VARIATIONS

Within the stages of group development or as transitions between stages, some authors have proposed that there are issues in interpersonal relationships that recur, but in different ways, throughout the duration of the group. These are often referred to as phases to distinguish them from stages. Levine, for example, points out that authority, intimacy, and separation are recurring issues.[23] The initial resolution of these issues represents points of change in the direction and emotional quality of relationships, especially in long-term treatment. As an example, he says that:

> the initial shift of power from the therapist to the members may be sufficient for group members to take some control of their group and vie for that control but it requires many more shifts of power for the members, many of whom are perhaps rendered powerless by their life experiences, to gain sufficient feelings of power to cope with their outside environment.[24]

Glassman and Kates point out that two mutually inclusive themes—power and intimacy—run through all stages.[25] Bennis and Shepard also make this point.[26] Schutz views the interpersonal issues of inclusion, control, and affection as recurrent cycles in groups.[27] O'Connor asserts that there is a continual interplay of two sets of forces—integration and differentiation. Integrative forces foster interdependence, drawing the members together, leading to cohesion. Differentiating forces tend to separate and distinguish various aspects of the group, promoting autonomy of the parts. These forces occur simultaneously: they counterbalance each other, preventing the group from deterioration or, in systems terms, from entropy.[28]

The model of stages described earlier does not deny the presence of these recurrent issues. They are often evident in the dynamic interactions of members as the group moves toward a new stage. The concept of stages emphasizes the points at which a particular issue predominates. These formulations of recurrent issues are indications of the complexity of the group process.

The social context influences the particular ways that each group develops in terms of the duration of each stage and the specific issues addressed at a given time. When groups are composed of nonvoluntary clients or severely disordered mental patients, the initial stage is apt to be prolonged owing to resistance or deficits in capacity to develop relationships and to communicate effectively. With such groups, the dissatisfaction stage will also be prolonged because it will take some time for the members to explore, test out, and accept the group's purpose and ways of work. A group whose primary purpose is psychosocial education may have a much shorter period of dissatisfaction, with fewer overt conflicts because the focus of the group may be primarily on personal learning rather than learning through interaction with other members.

Groups that are part of an intensive treatment program, as in hospitals and institutions, are influenced by the combinations of treatment received by a given client and the priority accorded to social work with groups in the hierarchy of services. The members' engagement in the group is affected by what is going on elsewhere. Such changes in motivation, in turn, influence the particular socioemotional and task issues to be dealt with and the rate of group development.

Many conditions have an impact on the rate of the group's development and the particular issues that predominate. No particular group exactly fits the model. Different groups proceed through the stages at different rates of speed. Groups with closed memberships, voluntary participants, clear goals, and clients without major socioemotional problems may move into the work stage very rapidly. Groups of acting-out delinquent boys or of withdrawn, regressed adult mentally ill patients will move much more slowly than a group of fairly adequate adolescents with a need to work out a problem of Jewish identity will or a group of mothers whose primary concern is with their behavior in relation to their young children. A group is composed of individuals, each unique in some ways. People progress at different rates, in different ways, and in relation to different needs. A group tends to move irregularly, not uniformly, on all the relevant dimensions of group structure and process. That does not deny the fact, however, that there is a fundamental core of movement, with variations along both individual and group dimensions, that can be thought of as the development of a group.

9

Stage I: Orientation-Inclusion

Before a viable group develops as a means through which its members grow and change, a complex process of group formation begins at the time of planning for a new group and continues until a group emerges. For, according to Coyle, "collective behavior is something more than and different from the sum of the individuals who produce it."[1] As members interact, a new entity is created: a group is born. This "groupness" occurs as a result of a process of orientation and a subsequent one of testing out and achieving commonality of perception of purpose, relationships, and structure. The primary task of the social worker during the initial stage is to help a group to form—a group that will be beneficial to its members.

CHARACTERISTICS OF THE GROUP

Considerable consensus exists among writers that the stage is characterized by initial anxiety on the part of the members toward the unknown situation. Members enter into the group with feelings and behavior characterized by uncertainty, anxiety, and tension and by self-conscious and noncommittal behavior. The relationship of the members with the leader is often one of dependency. As members become acquainted with each other and oriented to the situation, there emerges a pattern of interpersonal relations, values and norms, and communication. Relationships of members with each other evolve out of the efforts to adapt to the expectations for the role of members in the particular group.

When a collection of persons comes together for the first time, a group does not yet exist. Likewise, when a natural group meets with a social worker for the first time, a group for social work purposes has not evolved. The aggregate tends to be a collection of individuals with the center of attention on selves rather than on others. There is a lack of congruence among members and with the worker about the purpose and more specific goals. Membership is not yet determined; there is often lack of knowledge about the criteria for inclusion in the group. In formed groups, the structure is the one established initially by the social worker. In natural groups, there is lack of clarity about how the existing group structure will be modified to include the worker and meet the requirements of the organization that sanctions the group. In either instance, there is a lack of clarity about the interacting roles of client-member and worker. Except in natural groups, subgroup structure has not developed. Members of formed groups have not developed relationships with each other or with the worker. In the case of natural groups, not only is there not an established relationship with the worker, but also relationships among the members will become modified in unknown ways as the members engage in a new enterprise.

The members bring their own social and emotional needs into the group. The activation of these needs depends upon the group structure, initial feelings about the worker and other members, and the motivation of the members to join the group. If a group is to survive, it has to meet the needs of each member, even though these needs are incongruent with those of other members. The members bring their own norms of behavior, based on their values, to the group. The worker has his own norms as a person, as a representative of an organization, and as a member of the social work profession. There is lack of knowledge about each other's values and norms, with lack of mutuality around this aspect of group process. Established patterns of verbal communication have not yet emerged so that discussion is apt to be self-centered, scattered, diffuse, and lacking in continuity. Similarly, attention to any activity may be short-lived. There is lack of clarity about and acceptance of the boundaries to the group's power to make decisions. There is often a fear of self-disclosure and a tendency to deny problems or project them on to others. Cohesiveness is indeed weak, for there is little common basis for members' attraction to the group.

If a social work group is to form, the major task for the members is to become oriented to the situation and to decide to become included in the group's membership. Initial working relationships with each other and with the leader are established around these tasks. During pregroup contacts, some orientation to the group experience occurred, yet such preparation is not enough. The principal orientation remains to be done in the group. A decision to be included in a group cannot be a sound one unless a person has adequate information about the experience. The major tasks for the practitioner are to take leadership in the establishment of relationships, the enhancement of motivation, the development of a group culture, and the achievement of an initial working agreement.

At the point of entry into a new group, there is co-presence among the members, but psychological bonds are not present, unless members have known each other previously. Coming together psychologically is accomplished through social exchange among the members. Someone makes an overture and, according to Goffman, the "adaptive line of action attempted by one will be insightfully facilitated by the other or insightfully countered, or both."[2] Thus a pattern of affective ties and communication emerges. It cannot be known in advance what the configuration will be, for that depends upon the interaction among many individual, group, and environmental factors. The first tie is to the worker, who usually has had one or more interviews with the members before the first meeting. The members still have concerns, however: will the worker like me, be interested in me, compare me favorably against others, and accept me as a member of the group?

The predominant socioemotional issue for the members is inclusion. The members decided earlier that they wished to belong to the group or at least give the group a try, but they also have many doubts about the appropriateness of the group for meeting their needs. The members' inner, if not avowed, questions tend to be: what am I here for, what is expected of me, who are the other members, how will I measure up to them, do I really want to get acquainted with them, and will I find a place for myself in the group?

When people enter a new group, they scan the situation for signals that indicate to what extent they are welcome. They may be especially sensitive to those signals that indicate aloofness, arrogance, indifference, or mild hostility as these are communicated through tone of voice, facial expressions, or gestures. Such messages are often more potent than verbalized ones are. They may communicate warnings to be wary, retreat, wait and see, avoid others, or reach out to others. People may perceive the signals fairly accurately or may distort and misinterpret them. People tend to have highly selective awareness of others, predominantly unconscious, so that they see and hear only certain things. Such distortions interfere with effective entry into new groups. In their efforts to cope with the new situation, certain members may have positive feelings of interest, hope, trust, pleasure, curiosity, friendliness, or satisfaction. Negative feelings may run a gamut of insecurity, anxiety, distrust, rejection, doubt, confusion, discomfort, disinterest, self-consciousness, resentment, or disappointment. Combinations of positive and negative feelings seem to be quite universal. They seem to be as prevalent with members of groups in youth service agencies in which membership is thought of as desirable and voluntary as with members in hospitals or correctional institutions.

Most people are threatened by groups if they are expected to discuss personal problems in the presence of strangers whose reactions cannot be predicted. They often fear criticism, ridicule, rejection, inability to meet expectations, or being made anxious by the worries and unacceptable behavior of others. At the same time, they may want to be in the group and participate whole-heartedly in its events. Whitaker refers to this ambivalence as the initial focal conflict in the group.[3]

During this early stage, the social worker's stance is an active one. He is the central person in the group who carries a role of professional authority, responsible for getting the group off to a good start.

PREPARING FOR FIRST MEETINGS

In preparing for the first meeting, the practitioner reviews the plan for the group and makes a preliminary assessment of the members. But something more is needed. It is what Schwartz refers to as "tuning in," which involves reflecting about the group, moving into the meeting with confidence and competence, and engaging in anticipatory empathy.[4]

Self-awareness is essential to the task of helping a group to form. Even experienced workers continue to have some fearful fantasies about entering a new group.[5] They share anxieties similar to those of the members about how they will be received by the members. Since each group is like all others in some ways, but unique in other ways, the workers often anticipate what might go wrong. The questions they ask of themselves and worry about are varied: what if the members are very resistant, what if I lose control of the group, what if hostility breaks out, what if no one talks, what if they make overwhelming dependency demands on me, what if they don't like me, or perhaps the most anxiety-provoking of all, what if nobody comes? Awareness of these doubts and fears may free workers to move from preoccupation with self to reflective consideration of the needs, capacities, and initial anxieties of the members. As they try to feel what it would be like to be in the members' situations, their capacity for empathy is enhanced. Self-awareness is also crucial in relation to accepting professional authority for the conduct of the group. The members rightly look to the worker for guidance and direction. The worker's role is not as a client-member but as a member with the role of responsible professional practitioner. The active role does not violate the principle of client self-determination or autonomy, because people cannot make wise choices without the necessary orientation to and knowledge of the new and often strange situation of being in a group developed for social work purposes. Within the role, of course, the worker's responsibility is to enable members to participate actively in the tasks essential at the time of a group's beginning.

Workers engage in other forms of preparation also. Knowing who the members will be, they review their knowledge about the particular characteristics, needs, and situations of members and use literature and other resources to increase their knowledge. For example, Mrs. K. was to work for the first time with a group of patients who had been diagnosed as borderline. She reviewed, therefore, the most up-to-date knowledge about that syndrome and clarified its implications for her work with the group. Workers also set the stage for the first meeting, on the basis of knowledge of the meaning of space to people, and make sure that necessary supplies are available.

DEVELOPMENT OF RELATIONSHIPS

The social worker uses understanding of the meaning of the new experience to the members of the group to develop an initial working relationship that will sustain the members through the period of initial uncertainty and anxiety and serve as a catalyst for promoting the development of relationships among members. In each new situation, an individual faces, to some extent, a renewal of the basic conflict of a sense of trust versus distrust and the need for synthesis of these polarities.[6] Achievement of trust is relatively easy or hard, depending upon the extent to which members have previously developed a basic sense of trust. If members have not worked through, in a fairly satisfactory way, the basic issue of trust versus distrust, they repeat feelings of being unloved or rejected; they are often suspicious of other people; and they lack confidence in themselves and others. The extent to which a person has achieved a basic sense of trust influences the amount and duration of uncertainty and anxiety that is typical of encounters with new situations. Each new experience offers some occasion for mistrust until the unknown becomes familiar. Until members can come to trust the people involved and the situation, they cannot participate in truly interdependent relationships with others.

Social workers convey trust by modeling, through their own attitudes and behavior, the qualities of acceptance, empathy, and genuineness, which are components of a professional relationship. They help members relate to each other through the small courtesies that indicate interest in one's comfort and that acquaint members with each other. They help members express their feelings of doubt about whether or not they can trust the worker and the group. In one example:

> In a first meeting of a group of fifth-grade boys, the worker recognized that they were suspicious about the group. The worker said, therefore, that maybe he should explain to them what the group was about and how they had gotten into it. He shared with them the information that he had met with the vice-principal, who had thought these boys could do better in school if they were in a group. The boys looked skeptical, and when they did not respond to his request for responses, he went on to say that he and the principal thought that the group would be a safe place in which they could talk about some of the troubles kids often have and do things that might help them get along better. Then he added, "Some of you seem to feel the group

is some kind of punishment." The boys were verbally silent, but a couple started to giggle. The worker added, "Perhaps you don't think you can trust me." The comment identified the boy's feelings accurately. First one, then others asked such questions as: well, are you connected with the police; will you squeal to the vice-principal on us; will you squeal to my mother; and, if I mess up here, will you kick me out of the group? Facing these doubts and finding acceptance from the worker began a gradual change from active resistance to positive motivation to be in the group.

Recognizing with the members that the experience is a new one, that it is natural to feel uncertain, and that the group experience will be a valuable one for the members is a specific means of developing an atmosphere of mutual trust. With the necessary amount of support, members of groups who have a basic sense of trust will move rather quickly into fuller exploration of the potentials and demands in the group experience. In groups composed of such members, an initial working relationship with the worker and one another develops fairly quickly. An example is a group of parents who voluntarily joined a parent education group to learn how to understand their teenaged children. With a minimum of anxiety and basically positive motivations toward the service, the period of inclusion-orientation was achieved within the first session.

Many persons lack a basic sense of trust in others and in their own ability to cope with situations. For some, the symptoms will be withdrawal and fearful responses to efforts to engage their participation. With severely disturbed mental patients, for example, work usually involves a prolonged period in which the worker nurtures and develops the capacity for trust. This may be done through providing opportunity for members to be somewhat dependent on the worker and engaging them in a variety of simple activities that are clearly within their capacities and that focus on individual or parallel participation but that also can be done cooperatively. The members may be encouraged, but with a minimum of pressure, to discuss everyday events and common experiences and may be provided with some gratification in the form of food or concrete achievements. Within a protective and permissive environment, members gradually become able to express their feelings, ideas, and goals. It may take a period of many weeks before a relationship of trust in the worker and each other is established. The process is somewhat similar to that used with very shy and fearful young children.

Personal characteristics and qualities of the practitioner influence the development of the worker-group relationship. It is desirable that the members feel accepted by and respect the worker. Initially, some members of groups assume correctly that the worker has professional competence on which they can depend, but they also need to feel accepted. Other people, especially children, tend to respond initially in terms of the worker's personal qualities. Such persons need to feel that they know and like the worker as a person as a basis for using him for help with their problems. Spergel emphasizes that in street gang work, it is essential that the worker "achieve a specific person identity in his role rather than an abstract identity with an agency."[7]

The members may inquire about the worker's background, experiences, and values in an effort to find out what she is like and what motivates her to work with them; this often arises out of an unexpressed desire to get psychologically closer. It is often difficult to deal with personal questions relating to age, race, education, or marital status because these questions are mistakenly perceived as threats to professional competence. Such potential difficulties require that workers have self-understanding and an ability to recognize the meaning of these reactions for their work with groups. They can learn to replace these nonhelpful reactions with acceptance and empathy, which helps the members and reduces the worker's discomfort and anxiety in relation to them. The worker answers the questions simply and honestly but also explores the members' motivation for asking them.

Frank cites some evidence from research suggesting that mental patients tended to remain in groups when practitioners interacted freely with them and that they dropped out when practitioners were enigmas to them. Further, there is evidence that there was a higher improvement rate when practitioners showed active personal participation with them than when they showed a less personal and less understanding attitude.[8] An informal atmosphere is usually conducive to the development of trust in the worker and to the development of relationships among members. If appropriate to the members' preferences and the purpose of the group, an informal action-oriented experience, even as simple as sharing coffee, touring the facilities, or making name tags may facilitate the development of relationships. With some groups, such devices are unnecessary.

Through their own attitudes and behavior, social workers try to convey acceptance, accurate empathy, and genuineness. They face numerous challenges to their skills in facilitating the development of relationships that will further the members' goals. To develop an effective working relationship, they need to be sensitive to their own interpersonal needs. They learn to recognize that each member has a particular psychological meaning for them. They may react with fear, hostility, affection, or overprotection: some members trigger these reactions. A clinging, dependent person, for example, may reactivate a worker's unresolved dependency need. An elderly client may stir up feelings of inadequacy or fear of aging or death. A person who complains continuously about other people may stir up feelings of impatience. It is hard for some workers to accept conflicts as constructive and useful in problem solving, so they tend to deny the conflict, which only erupts later in less constructive ways.

Lacking faith in the group process, some social workers have difficulty in relating to the relationships among members as distinct from relating to each member as an individual. They need to be able to express empathy with all members of a group and with the group as a whole. But they may identify with children against their parents or with shy, conforming members more than with outwardly aggressive ones. Fearing the relinquishment of some of their authority, they may take over parental roles rather then help parents learn to be more effective. They may have difficulty in feeling comfortable with rambling discussions, provocative questions or comments, or disruptive activities. They may find it challenging to help members to bridge the differences among them when groups are composed of members from more than one ethnic category, social class, or religion.

An important step in becoming able to develop effective relationships with members is to recognize one's own difficulties but then to move from self-awareness to self-control; that is, as Solomon said, "the ability to control heretofore unconscious aspects of one's personality which have served as an obstacle to establishing warm, genuine, and empathic relationships with certain kinds of people."[9] As practitioners become more able to recognize and then control their difficulties, they become able to enhance the development of a sense of cohesion or group bond, which is the result of the degree to which members have achieved psychosocial closeness to each other. This bond, in turn, provides a strong motivation for members to continue in the group.

Ethnicity and social class influence the development of effective working relationships. Characteristics of the worker interact with those of the other participants in the process. Depending upon past experiences with people of other races or nationalities, a quality of mutual strangeness may pervade the initial meeting. Both parties to the relationship feel uncertain about the other's feelings and expectations, with accompanying suspicion or fear. Each person, worker and member alike, often unconsciously tends to evaluate the other in terms of certain stereotypes based on ignorance or preconceptions about differences between them and on prior experiences with apparently similar people.

Stereotyping is a major deterrent to developing and sustaining effective relationships. Some practitioners are not able to respond to a member of a different ethnic group as a unique person, instead of as a symbol of a particular category of people. It is imperative that cultural differences be recognized and respected and that ethnic identity be fostered. Attention to culture should not, however, be at the cost of individualization. Cooper indicates that if ethnicity is overemphasized, clients tend to "lose their individual richness and complexity: there is the danger of no longer treating people—only culture carriers."[10] Workers may emphasize ethnic factors to such an extent that individual needs and solutions to problems become obscured. The point is important, but lack of emphasis on culture may also oversimplify the member's situation. Cultural factors need to be viewed as they interact with psychological and environmental ones in a particular situation.

People from minority groups have valid reasons for initial distrust of white practitioners because many white people are prejudiced and discriminate against nonwhite people in many subtle and overt ways. Barriers between workers and clients of different races and among members need to be recognized and dealt with early in a relationship. It is easy for workers to avoid color differences. If, however workers are able to communicate their awareness of the ethnic difference in a sensitive manner, the potential for developing a helping relationship is enhanced. Workers begin to bring differences into the group discussion by introducing the subject at an appropriate time and then responding sensitively to the responses of the members.

People who have experienced discrimination are often particularly sensitive to the social worker's attitudes in the initial contact. They value being treated with respect, but often they have not been so treated. Effective work with groups requires that practitioners observe those formalities that are overt indications of respect, such as proper introductions, use of titles and surnames, and shaking hands. Such formalities are important to black clients who have been denied these symbols of courtesy. They are important to people of other cultures also. An example is given by Velasquez and associates, who point out that the Spanish language includes two terms for use in adddressing another person, depending upon that person's status in terms of both age and social role. Addressing a person who is older or in a position of authority by his first name is perceived, not as a friendly gesture, but as lack of respect; social workers are in positions of authority and should, therefore, be addressed by their surnames and titles. It is a sign of disrespect for a Hispanic client to disagree with a person in a position of authority. If unaware of this cultural norm, workers may misinterpret silence or acquiescence as resistance, which militates against developing a relationship characterized by mutual trust.[11]

Along with the need for symbols of courtesy and respect, Aguilar notes that in the Mexican-American culture, it is the custom to have an informal and personalized conversation before entering into a business transaction.[12] An example is of a group of women in a community mental health center that serves a multiethnic population.

> An elementary school principal became aware of the need for some of the Spanish-speaking mothers to understand how they might become supportive of their children's education. Accordingly, a group was formed through referrals from the school, composed of seven women between the ages of twenty-four and thirty, who spoke little English but recently enrolled in an English as a second-language class.

All were born in Mexico and got their education there. A Spanish-speaking social worker was assigned to the group. The stated purpose of the group was to help the members to be able to support their children's education in this country, where the expectations are quite different from those in Mexico. Since education is highly valued, the mothers shared a desire to help their children to succeed in school.

In the first meeting of the group, the bilingual worker expressed pleasure that these women had desired to be in the group. She invited them to have coffee and get acquainted with each other. They chose to tell each other about their children. They addressed each other and the worker by the form "usted," which persisted for several sessions, after which they moved to the informal "tu." Although given consent to use the informal form of address and first name by the worker, the formal term continued to be used. During the first meeting, the formality extended into topics of group discussion and a tendency to agree with the worker. The orientation and goal-setting process could not, therefore, be completed in the first meeting. The members were reserved about sharing feelings and difficulties. During the meeting, it became evident that they lacked self-esteem and felt devalued by Americans. The worker decided to introduce some of the arts of Mexico as a tool for bridging the two cultures.

After preliminary greetings and sharing of refreshments, the second session began with the worker informally showing the members a small porcelain mouse from Tonola in Mexico, which was admired by all. Mrs. R. said she had seen one of these in a friend's house. She said she has something just as cute from Oaxaca and offered to bring it next time. The worker asked if the others might have something of beauty to share with the group. Mrs. M. asked if it could be a lace shawl instead of an art object. She was assured about this, and slowly then, other members said they could find something of which they were proud. From there, Mrs. R. said that maybe they could teach their children to take pride in their heritage. Through such a seemingly simple act by the worker, a bridge was built between the two cultures, which contributed in a small way to the group's purpose and to the development of shared relationships among the members so that they were then ready to share some of the problems they were having with the children and engage in setting goals.

The importance of informality and personalized contacts is not unique to Hispanic cultures. Hammond emphasizes its importance in establishing relationships with native Americans.[13] Within some Asian cultures there is a similar expectation that time will be taken for social amenities and for getting to know a person. The offering and accepting of a cup of tea aids in setting a climate that will be comfortable for the discussion of problems. In some Asian cultures, as well as Hispanic ones, respect for authority is important. For example, for persons reared in traditional Japanese families, it may be exceedingly difficult to disagree with someone in a position of authority. In such situations, the worker does not press the members for agreement or a decision before the members become somewhat comfortable about expressing difference. It is important that the worker pose options rather than assume that the first "yes" signifies agreement or support of an idea. Etiquette may dictate agreement when an expert makes a suggestion. In many Chinese families, saving face or preserving the dignity of the family takes precedence over open communication, and signs of affection may not be demonstrated directly. The social worker's task is to develop a supportive climate in which it is safe to allow for expression of feelings rather than the enactment of expected role behavior.[14]

When a worker and members share a similar ethnic background, it is often easier for the worker to accept and empathize with the members. Similarity may provide the member with a positive model of ethnicity. Matching worker and client in regard to ethnicity has the advantage of fostering a sense of comfort in sharing certain identifiable physical and social characteristics and of understanding the culture into which both were socialized. It is, however, easy to overemphasize the similarities within a category and to fail to take into account the many individual and family differences. It has been noted, for example, that in black client-black practitioner relationships, problems often develop. The practitioner may either deny the common tie to the members or overidentify with them. In spite of sharing a common racial experience, unless workers can recognize their own countertransference reactions and learn to control them, it is unlikely that an effective working relationship will develop.

Working across ethnic lines has both positive and negative implications. It is possible to capitalize on the values that come from learning about and facing differences, as well as from learning about and facing similarities. Social distance between people can be reduced. In Kadushin's words:

> If the worker's professional training enhances the ability to empathize with and understand different groups and provides the knowledge base for such understanding, the social and psychological distance between worker and client can be reduced. If the gap is sufficiently reduced, clients perceive workers as being capable of understanding them, even though they are the product of a different life experience.[15]

Similarly, Solomon emphasizes that one of the characteristics of nonracist practitioner is the ability to feel warmth, genuine concern, and empathy for people regardless of their race, color, or ethnic background. A further skill is the ability to confront members when they distort or misinterpret the positive feelings that the worker has for them. When workers are too threatened to open up the issue, "the client is denied an opportunity to learn something about himself and how he relates to others."[16] The worker's failure to explore the issue with the member interferes with the development of relationships.

Ethnicity interacts with social class, contributing to potential barriers to effective worker-group relationships. Social class differences largely determine the people with whom one associates and with whom one feels comfortable.

That social class differences are one of the more important influences of clients' expectations about help has been suggested by a number of studies.[17] Clients from middle-class orientations tend to expect that value will be placed on introspective and reflective discussion and on verbal sophistication, that the helper's role will be a relatively inactive one, that other family members may be involved in treatment, and that treatment will be prolonged. Clients from less advantaged socioeconomic backgrounds, on the other hand, tend to expect that the practitioner will be direct, supportive, and active; that "cure" will occur more rapidly; and that the practitioner will do something in an immediate, tangible way to relieve discomfort. They may be confused by the demand for verbalization as contrasted with action. Too often it has been assumed that the reluctance of these clients to question the expectations and their passive compliance with the worker's definition of roles are due to lack of motivation. Rather, such behaviors may be a sign of confusion and uncertainty. Unless workers appreciate the importance of money and other material resources in relating to people, they are apt to interpret certain problems as internal to the person when the problem is a societal one. Stereotypes about a culture of poverty or of the limited potentials of poor people interfere with developing truly helping relationships that build on strengths and hopes for a better future.

Questions are raised about the influence of the gender of the worker on the development of relationships. Many women are concerned that counselors and therapists tend to perpetuate sex-role stereotypes and that this "may harm rather than help their patients by training them to conform to narrowly defined roles and adjust to unhealthy life situations."[18] From a review of research on psychotherapy and behavior change, Parloff, Waskow, and Wolfe concluded that the effect of the practitioner's gender on outcome has not been confirmed.[19] Nevertheless, as with ethnic and social class differences, social workers need self-awareness and sensitivity to issues of gender. It is probable that the attitudes and values of the practitioner, rather than gender per se, are of primary importance in the development of a worker-group relationship.

Social workers feel, it is hoped, some eagerness and zest as they become involved with a group. When this is so, they can convey to the members their willingness to involve themselves openly and spontaneously within their roles as helping persons. Inasmuch as the core of work with groups is the alleviation of obstacles that prevent gratifying relationships and productive interaction, it is essential that workers be able to interact freely in this, a relationship with other human beings.

HOPE AND MOTIVATION

Initial motivation is influenced by the personal and social characteristics of members, the adequacy of members' psychosocial functioning, the social agency and its place in the community, the extent of support from significant persons in the environment, and cultural factors that influence attitudes toward and the use of institutional resources. These are, in turn, often related to the initial application or referral, whether initiated by the group member or someone else in his behalf and the extent to which membership in the group is voluntary. But even voluntary attendance does not imply eagerness and motivation to become a part of a group. Most people come to a new experience both wanting it and fearing it. As Osborn has said vividly:

> Just as we must remind ourselves that there are many shades of grey between black and white, so we must recognize that all voluntary affiliations are not equally fervid. Joining is more like a five to three vote than the miniature landslide we might prefer.[20]

Whatever the initial motivation, it is modified as a person has experiences in the group. The fact that most people want the goals of improved personal adequacy and social functioning for themselves is an ally to the social worker in his efforts to support the initial motivation of members. Another ally is the powerful fact that all people have potential for growth and development. Yet most people also have some resistance to involving themselves in a group. Resistance is a trend of forces against using the help that is offered. It consists of those attitudes and behaviors that interfere with making progress. Resistance is not necessarily negative. Indeed, it is often a sign of good ego strength to be able to resist the advice and suggestions of others, including the worker, when such ideas go against one's own realistic understanding of one's situation and the consequences of following the advice. Change means discomfort or disequilibrium, for it means giving up the comfort of the familiar present for an unknown future. There may be a sense of hopelessness about oneself and one's situation. Some persons may be reluctant to admit they need help. If they value independence more than interdependence, they believe they should be able to "pull themselves up by their own bootstraps." Some associate the present experience with similar past experiences that were unpleasant.

The worker's own value system, in part, determines her skill in this important area. A belief in the potential for change in each human being tends to be communicated nonverbally to the group. If this feeling is picked up by one or more members of the group, such members may in turn influence others toward hoping for something better for themselves. What the social worker strives for is to motivate the members to select one or more specific goals toward which they may work.

Within some of the common reactions to becoming involved in a group, there are striking differences in initial motivation. Sometimes, there is eager anticipation of belonging. In a children's hospital, for example, a group was initiated for five- and six-year-old girls and boys. Its purpose was to help the children to understand the varied treatment procedures and develop relationships with other children that might sustain them through the difficult period of hospitalization. When the social worker entered the ward to invite the children to come to the group, she found poignant desire combined with apprehension about exclusion. One little boy in a wheelchair asked, "Do you want me?" in a tone that expressed both wonder and fear. A girl tugged at the worker's skirt and in a high pitched voice, asked, "Me, too—me, too?" The oldest boy asked, "Is there room for one more—is there room for me?" How different this initial behavior is from the hostile reactions of adolescent boys who were referred by a judge with the admonition to: "Be in this man's group or go to Juvenile Hall," hardly a positive motivation toward the service. Such differences in motivation are reflected in the members' feelings about and reactions to the social worker.

An example of strong initial resistance that changed into positive motivation is of a group of five boys, aged eleven to thirteen, sponsored by a child welfare agency. In late September, reports had come to the social worker that five of the boys in AFDC families were engaged in early delinquent behavior. As a small gang, they had raided neighborhood fruit trees, stolen from the variety store, stayed out after curfew, and were often truant from school.

The social worker approached the mothers of the boys to secure their permission for the boys to be in a small group. The mothers agreed to have their sons come to a meeting at the school on Friday afternoon. They were advised to tell the boys that the worker would sponsor them as a club whose purpose would be to provide interesting social experiences for them and to help them with their personal and school problems.

> *First Meeting.* I looked up to see George standing in the doorway of the meeting room. He was dressed in clean but worn clothing. He was a short and stocky youngster, had a deep voice, and his whiskers were starting to grow. He had the manner of an old man, with deep concerns. I invited him into the meeting room and asked if he knew whether or not the other boys would be coming. He evaded answering and

asked me "What is this all about?" I said that I had offered to sponsor the boys as a club. He asked why. I told him that the school, the juvenile police officer, and the mothers had told me that he and his four friends had been in some trouble and that I could help them do better—so I wanted to help them out. He then asked me a number of direct questions—what did I mean they had been in trouble; who was it that snitched on them; what made me think they needed an adult sponsor for a club? I responded to these questions directly and honestly. I listened as George blasted the school for sticking its nose into their business and expressed many complaints about the school. I said I certainly couldn't promise to solve the problems about school, but I could make things better for them outside of school. George wanted to know exactly how.

I talked about the idea of forming a club and suggested a number of possible things they might do. George listened with interest but was skeptical. He told me that they already had a leader—he was the leader of the gang. I sensed that I was threatening his role and explained that he could continue to be the leader—that a sponsor was something different. He wanted me to spell out the difference. He then asked me if the school had "planted" me to do this job. I again told him that I was a child welfare social worker, but both the school and the police had informed me that he and his gang were getting into trouble and thought they needed help with things that might be "bugging" them. George then admitted they were all "bugged about a lot of things."

I suggested that George take my offer back to the gang so that the boys might decide whether or not they wanted me to work with them. He jumped out of his chair, ran to the window, lifted the shade, and signaled with his hand. Almost immediately, four faces appeared at the window and George directed them to come into the room. I was somewhat surprised that George formally introduced me as each one entered the room. When all were seated, I offered to serve them some cookies and coke. Their faces lighted up. I noticed that four of them gobbled down their food.

When we finished eating, I asked George to tell the other boys about our discussion. This he did in a businesslike manner and was completely accurate in describing my proposal, even emphasizing that I'd help them with what they were "all bugged up about." Steve and Bill immediately said they liked the idea. Wendell and Bruce waited for George to say he thought they should do it. I suggested that they did not need to decide today: they could tell me whenever they are ready. They began to talk about what they could do if they became a club.

As the boys left, George told me that they had all decided to take me up on my offer. I said I was pleased and they could come to the same place on Friday. He said they'd all be there.

In this first session, the social worker demonstrated the skills essential to reducing resistance to an offer of help. Observation of appearance and behavior gave clues about how to approach the leader of the natural group. He displayed acceptance through welcoming first the indigenous leader and then the other boys, making them feel comfortable and lessening anxiety and hostility. He made it clear that he would not usurp the indigenous leader's power. He conveyed an attitude of genuineness by answering questions honestly and without becoming defensive. He listened in a nonjudgmental way to complaints.

The social worker provided support through the relationship, offering reassurance about roles, and securing the support of parents for the boys belonging to the group. He encouraged the exploration of feelings and the possibilities for the group's content. He gave essential information to both the group and the parents and gave advice to the parents concerning the boys' membership in the group. He made appropriate suggestions concerning possible activities and discussion. He confronted George, in a gentle way, with the fact that the boys were in trouble with the school and the police. He clarified the purpose of the group, the reasons for referral to the group, the roles of social worker and indigenous leader, and the group's right to make the decision about whether or not to accept the offer.

Clients need support from significant people in order to be motivated to use a service. The group is a major source of support, but it may not be sufficient. The social worker needs to take into account the extent to which the environment provides support for the members. Studies show that both continuance in treatment and outcome are related to the availability of environmental supports.[21] Thus, a frequent task for the group's worker is to seek support from significant others in enhancing the motivation of clients in the use of service. When a child is the member, the minimal involvement of the parents or guardian is that of granting informed consent for the child to have help for a particular purpose.

THE WORKING AGREEMENT

Orientation to the worker, other members, and the plans for the use of the group is necessary to reduce some of the uncertainty and anxiety, to enhance the potential value of the group for its members, and to motivate the members to use the group for meeting their needs.

Purpose. The purpose of the group needs to become explicit if the group is to be of optimum benefit to its members. The group purpose consists of a statement of the general hoped-for outcomes of group membership, as perceived initially by the worker and accepted by the members in the pregroup interviews and later in the group's deliberation concerning the fit of individual goals within the group purpose. The members of the group are most receptive to change when their goals and aspirations are similar and are meshed with the social worker's purpose.

When members of groups are not clear about the motives of the social worker, they tend to become confused and distrustful. To say, "I'm here to help," without indicating for what purpose, implies that the worker is omnipotent and the members are dependent upon him. In her research, Hartford found that workers frequently failed to make explicit the purposes, or they intervened inappropriately in the process of goal formulation. In such instances, there was a tendency for the group not to form.[22] This finding supports the principle that it is the worker's responsibility to help the group become aware of its reason for being in terms of both the general purpose and the members' goals for themselves. Yet workers often find it difficult to express clearly, simply, and explicitly their perceptions of the social work focus of the group. Or they find it difficult to use activity-oriented devices to help groups of nonverbal members to play out the purpose. They often avoid encouraging the members to react to the stated purpose with varied degrees of positive and negative expressions and to relate the general purpose to their own goals. Even though the initial purpose of the group as perceived by the organization and the worker was explained to members during pregroup interviews, it is still important that the members hear it and have an opportunity to react to the worker's explanation, discuss it, and make it their own.

To present the purpose in positive terms of what members can expect to achieve through the group, as contrasted with a focus on the problems of members, connects the purpose to the positive motivations of members. To express hope that members will be able to "get along better with others," "be able to understand and bring up your children better," "find out how you might be able to complete high school," or "get the health services you need" does not deny the need for help but does tend to enhance motivation toward change. It is important that the members express, as best they are able, what they hope will happen and what they hope can be achieved in the group. An example from a group of severely disordered hospitalized patients with diagnoses of schizophrenia follows:

First Meeting: Present were Mr. R, Mr. M, Mr. K, Mr. D., Mr. N.

The technician escorted the members to the meeting room. When all were present, I began the meeting by reviewing my name and reminding them that I had told them I was the social worker who would be meeting with them in the group. I said that I would introduce them and they could call each other whichever name they pleased. I then looked at each one as I said both his first and surname. After introducing them, several began talking at once, and there seemed to be an air of urgency to get all the things that were bothering them out in the open. They were all tense, moving in their chairs restlessly and lighting cigarettes. Mr. M. and Mr. R. both offered me a cigarette, which I declined.

After listening to the flow of conversation that was confused and lacking in focus, I asked if they were ready to listen to one person talk at a time. Mr. R. started by saying that what he wanted was to get out of here. There was a general nodding of heads. I said, "some of you seem to feel as Mr. R. does." "Yes," said Mr. K. in such a low voice that it could barely be heard. Mr. R. responded that he guessed that no one would disagree, would they? I said I thought most of them wanted to get out of the hospital as soon as possible and that here we could work on how that could happen. Mr. M. said that what he wanted was to find his wife and find out if she had signed him into the hospital. This led to a flood of conversation about not wanting to be in the hospital and not thinking they should have to stay here.

When there was a brief pause, I suggested they might be willing to tell each other what things they would like the group to help them with. Mr. D. who is the most disturbed member, said that what he wanted was a drink—a real one. Mr. K. and Mr. M. laughed. Mr. N. told him he couldn't drink here, but they could get tea and coffee. I told them that we had some here on the side table and asked if anyone could help me serve it, but no one offered to help. Mr. M. said he did not care to discuss his business but asked what he could do about his wife. I took this opportunity to again define my role with them—I could not help Mr. M. to find his wife. I would be working with them in this group. They each had another social worker who would help them with other things. As I had told them in our interviews, this group could help them to talk with others and learn to have good relationships with other people. Did they understand that? Mr. M. said they did, and there were general nods from the others.

Mr. M. immediately talked about how he had been ill before and had been in other hospitals and how badly he wants to stay out next time. He used to blame other people for his illness, but he doesn't do that as much now. I said that was an example of how the group could help. Mr. K. said he didn't feel exactly like that, but he was sometimes unable to talk so others could understand him; things just buzz around in his head.

Mr. R. said that one doctor used one kind of treatment and another said he wasn't responding to that and would change it. I said that must seem pretty confusing, to which there was a strong response of "you said it" from Mr. M., echoed by the others. Each member then mentioned the kinds of treatment he had had. I said that a group such as this one was another form of therapy—that it was not a physical treatment like the others but was more a social and emotional therapy. It would help them to learn to express themselves more clearly, to be less afraid of other people, and to be able to enjoy being with others: did they understand what I meant? All, except Mr. D. nodded affirmatively. Mr. R. said that he knows the group will help him—that's why he came today. Mr. M. said, "the same for me."

I said that we would have to stop for today but that I would meet with them on Monday and Thursday at one o'clock and would probably see them on the ward in between times. Mr. R. asked me my name again and I repeated it. He then said it over and over again. Mr. M. and Mr. N. said they would remember my name. I said that I would remember all of their names and I would remember them. I'd see them all next week here.

From a therapeutic standpoint, the process of goal formulation is to bring to the awareness of all participants the direction in which they are moving. In the initial stage, this is done in accordance with the worker's judgment of what the members can take hold of at a given time.

There is skill in stating a purpose with both sufficient breadth and explicitness that, within the generalization, the members can begin to formulate their own purposes. The difficulty is greater in those instances in which the recipients of service do not apply voluntarily but are referred to a group or for whom a group is prescribed. With some prospective members, the worker and the members may be far apart in their perceptions of mutually agreed-upon goals. For example, inmates in correctional institutions want nothing but to get out. The worker perceives the need for changes in their behavior. He, too, wants them released as soon as possible, but only after they have made sufficient progress in improving their attitudes and behavior to be able to live in the open community. The worker can thus begin by defining the conditions under which release can take place.

A professional relationship is developed through activity that is related to the purpose, not through subterfuge, as when a worker offers a recreational activity without clarifying her purpose and role. This subterfuge leads to confusion about the role of the worker and to further difficulty in achieving congruence of social work purpose. Hidden agendas are not congruent with empathy, acceptance, and genuineness: they violate trust, respect for members, and honesty. Rather, a clear and simple presentation of who the worker is, how she sees the purpose of the group, and why the group or an individual was referred to the agency is effective. The worker makes it clear that she is interested in the members' views about their aspirations, goals, problems, and possible solutions.

Even young, disturbed children accept an explanation of the reason for the group and can express their feelings about membership and their concepts about help. As the worker gets started with a group of children, a simple statement introducing himself and explaining what they will be doing together tends to reduce anxiety and prepare the child for his part in the process. As the worker senses evidences of anxiety, he can universalize the experience by saying that this is a place where lots of children come to get over their troubles and that, when they first come, many don't know what will happen and that feels scary to them. Exploring for, recognizing, and responding to the child's concerns is crucial. Inviting the child to ask questions about the worker's initial statement of purpose often leads to personal questions about the worker's status and interests. The worker usually gives the sought-for information directly and briefly instead of requesting reasons for the question or turning it back to the child. Children want to know and need to know something about the worker if they are to admit him into their lives.

When the children become aware of their need for help, they are able to share many feelings and problems in the group. When this happens, there is less tension, and evasion is reduced. Listening and reacting verbally to the explanation by the worker may be supplemented with play, through which the children dramatize their views of the situation. The worker seeks to find the common threads of purpose that seem to underlie differences in goals. It is her task to seek compatibility between her view of what the group needs and the composite of members' motives.

Levinson, having reviewed sixty-one articles on social work with groups, found that when the purposes of members and workers were in accord, the groups tended to operate optimally to achieve their purposes. When the worker described the purposes for the group, these tended to be rejected by the members, leading to dissolution of the group.[23] The development of a group purpose is a process—not a simple single event. This is illustrated by Lee's record of a group of homeless women living in a shelter.[24]

After an initial period of getting acquainted, the social worker said that maybe she could help the members to help each other.

> This group, if they wanted to become one, would be a place to talk about making this place better and about getting out and back on your feet again. I didn't need to ask what they thought because they were telling me as I spoke by saying "yeah" and "right on." I asked for their concerns and they began. In a steady stream, Iris, Jean, and Carla shared what the problems were. Ana and Dora agreed with all that was said by nodding. They went on with a list of fifteen grievances. All of this was said with much feeling of anger, depression, and desperation, and I related to these feelings with empathy as the process unfolded.
>
> (Later in the meeting). Carla said, "We're all treated like we're crazy

or in prison. It's hard enough to be down and out, but to be treated like dirt gets us desperate." Then Jean said, "This place is so tense, it's going to explode." Everyone agreed. I said I understood how angry they were. Jean said she'd sum it up for us. "There is lack of compassion here. Everything is hard and tough and soon you become hard and tough. You get treated like dirt, so you feel like dirt. To be treated like a criminal is the worst part of the pain. You already hate yourself for messing up and landing here. Where is the compassion?" It was a moving moment. I said that I agreed and everyone nodded, solemnly. I said I saw today that they cared about each other. I suggested they could become a group here with me and we could worry about taking care of each other. I honestly didn't know how much I could do about the shelter system. I would be pleased to try.

(Later in the meeting). I then said I'd like to have the group be about getting back and on your feet and out of here, not just changing it here. What did they think about that? There was 100 percent agreement. They said they want "to get back out there" and "make it in the world." At the worker's suggestion, the members shared some of their life experiences, how they got into the shelter, and what some of their goals were. Many depressed and angry feelings were expressed as the members told their stories. The worker acknowledged the feelings and named them. In ending the meeting, the worker accredited their work, giving them hope of accomplishing their goals and also recognizing their strengths.

During this meeting, the members came to an initial agreement about the dual purpose of the group—getting out of the shelter and addressing grievances through social action, with the worker as mediator. The record indicates that goal setting is a process: goals become clear as the members develop purposeful working relationships with the worker and each other, explore needs and concerns, open up communication about things that matter, ventilate their feelings about themselves and their situations, discover areas of common concern, develop hope that things can be better, and come to an agreement about the purpose and the initial structure of the group. In this group, as in most groups it will take more than one session for these young women to work on particular personal and social change within the agreed-upon purpose. The time it will take depends upon the state of the members' psychosocial functioning, their sense of urgency about having something be better, the sense of a common plight, and the internal and external resources that can be mobilized.

Structure and Membership of the Group. The social worker provides direction for the initial organizational structure of the group. Although the degree of her activity may vary somewhat according to the group, it is usually more apparent during this stage than at any other point in the group's development. It is the worker's responsibility to orient the group to the agency's rationale for the particular form of organization and for the decisions concerning time, place, frequency, and content of meetings. The members' reactions to these plans are sought and modifications made when appropriate to the members' needs and within the governing policies. The members have a right to know the source of authority for establishing and changing procedures, including the part they have in this process.

Uncertainty and anxiety about the basis of membership in a group is usually present in formed groups. In natural groups, the concern tends to be one of ambivalence about the inclusion of a social worker in the group. Questions from members about the reason why they were referred to or selected for the group need to be responded to with brevity and honesty. Later, there can be clarification of the members' questions and concerns about this matter. Even in groups in which the members have sought a place, the provision of information about the major criteria for group composition may enable members to feel some sense of commonality, a necessary first step toward identification with the group. Similarly, sharing with them information about anticipated changes in membership helps to provide a sense of security. Members need to know if there are expectations that they be prompt and attend regularly. They need to know under what circumstances others will be added or they will be terminated from the group.

The Emergence of Norms. If the potentially dynamic forces in the group are to operate, a system of norms needs to emerge that is appropriate to the particular purpose of the group and the characteristics of the members. In this respect, Yalom refers to the practitioner's role as that of culture builder.[25] A commonly accepted set of norms provides support and security for the members and contributes to the development of cohesion.

Persons often come to social work situations ignorant of what particular behaviors will be expected of them. They bring their own norms with them into the group, but if this is a first experience with a social worker, they have no experiential base for knowing what to expect of the worker and what is expected of them. An illustration is of a group composed of eleven- and twelve-year-old boys who were making a poor adjustment in school and had been referred to a group for help with their problems.

> The worker sensed the members' discomfort about the silence that followed his suggestions that the members talk about what they might discuss or do in the group. He then repeated an earlier explanation that the purpose of the group was to help them get along better in

> school and added that he knew it could be very hard to do well in school. One member then told a story about a new boy in school who was "teased by the kids and given a rough time by the teacher." A silence followed. The leader interrupted, saying that he knew it would be hard for the new boy in school; that they were in a somewhat similar situation, coming to a new group and not knowing what to expect from the worker and maybe from each other, too. "Yeah, that's exactly it," was the boy's response. The worker then clarified his role and how this group was different from classes and other school activities.

A worker's sensitivity and appropriate response to indirect forms of communication facilitate the members' orientation to the group.

There may be wide disparity between the expectations that the worker has for the members and those of the members themselves, or there may be wide disparities among the members of the group. If they are to make good use of the group, the members need to know what rights and responsibilities they have in relation to each other and to the worker and what the basic rules are that govern their relationships with each other. An unequal power distribution is inherent in the differences between roles of members and workers. The members' perceptions may, however, exaggerate the extent or the facets of the worker's power. Clarification of expectations helps members to understand and assume the rights and responsibilities that are theirs. The worker likewise needs to be sure that her expectations are relevant to the capacities and sociocultural milieu of the members.

Members often come to groups with some fear of the worker. One common fear is that the worker will violate the members' right to privacy by revealing to others what he knows about them and that these revelations will be to the detriment of the members. Hence, dealing with these fears in the initial interviews is essential but needs to be repeated now so that all members have a common understanding. A direct statement that this group is one in which the worker respects the right of the members to express what they feel and think without fear that he will talk about them outside the group, unless he tells them about it first, usually suffices for a first meeting. The worker's sensitivity to the reactions of the members is a clue about whether or not this theme needs to be pursued further. Confidentiality, though, is not limited to the worker, for members acquire information about each other. The worker serves as a model for the members in this respect, and in addition, he expresses the hope that they will not share information about each other outside the group.

Children are often reluctant to discuss difficulties at home or at school, because they are dependent upon their parents, guardians, or school personnel. They fear that what the worker shares with other adults will be used against them: they fear collusion between the worker and other adults. Work with children almost always involves work with the significant adults in their lives. Full confidentiality cannot be promised, but it is reassuring to the child to be told that the leader will be talking with certain adults, what the reasons are for doing so, and what kind of information will be shared and what will not be shared.

Members of groups have a right to expect that, when it is desirable, the worker will use information constructively in their behalf. Pertinent information may be shared with appropriate persons in order that the best possible service may be given. The agency is responsible to the client and also to the community that supports it and makes its services possible. This dual responsibility may create problems in applying the principle of confidentiality to specific situations. Mutual trust will be developed between the worker and the group as varied situations occur that are of concern to the members and as the worker deals with these in the person's best interests without violating the community's interest.

The norms that facilitate the progress of the members and the development of the group include, but are not limited to, the following: (1) mutual aid and mutual support; (2) flexibility and experimentation, which promotes the idea that it is good to try out new things and new ways; (3) the ideas that differences are normal and acceptable, that members can learn from them, and that conflict can be constructive; (4) the assumption that participation is expected according to capacity; (5) the concept that self-disclosure is not dangerous and privacy is respected; (6) the expectation that members should assume increasing responsibility for their own functioning as time goes on, participating in decision-making and evaluation processes; (7) a communication network that emphasizes interchange among the members; (8) a commitment to the group as an important event in the lives of the members; and (9) procedural norms about attendance, fees, confidentiality, space, seating, and so forth that are appropriate to a particular group. These are not rules that the worker enforces: indeed, they cannot be enforced. They represent desirable conditions, based on values, through which the group can facilitate the growth and development of its members.

The worker strives to develop agreement about expectations. Similarities of expectations tend to create both stability and progress in therapeutic social systems. When asymmetry of expectations occurs, strain in communication is likely to follow. One manifestation is apt to be withdrawal of members from the group. Periodic stress is bound to occur and is essential to progress. But when it is too severe in initial meetings, it is more likely to be disruptive to what is still a tenuous connection among the members. To resolve the problem of what a person may expect and what may be expected of him appears to be an indispensable requisite for maintaining the mutual aid system. Without some resolution of the problem of discrepancy in expectations, continuation in the group becomes doubtful.

In the first one or two meetings, much of the content concerns mutual expectations. In a study, Brown found that discussion of expectations leads to congruence between worker and members on their attitudes toward the group.[26] They share similar perceptions concerning the experience. Workers of groups in which agreement was highest initiated the discussion of expectations in the first meeting. These workers helped the members stay with the topic and dealt with their resistance to clarifying expectations. They were able to pick up and respond to nonverbal cues indicating that a member might be ready to react to something said earlier. They were able to recognize and encourage expressions of feelings about the experience. In contrast, in those groups in which agreement was low, the workers were less likely to initiate the topic and to deal with it in early sessions. In one group of parents, for example, it was never clarified whether the group would focus on personal or family problems of members or engage in social action. The major conclusion of Brown's study was that developing mutual expectations as early as possible is significantly related to the effectiveness of group functioning and member satisfaction.

Clarity and consensus about expectations not only prevent discontinuance but also have a positive effect on progress in problem solving. In his study, Garvin found that when the worker accurately perceived the expectations of members, his responses tended to be more appropriate and there was significantly greater movement in problem solving than in instances in which the worker did not perceive the members' expectations correctly.[27] From a survey of research in the field of family service, Briar concluded that "there is strong evidence, both from casework and psychotherapy research, that clients are more apt to continue in treatment when they and their therapists share similar expectations."[28]

Clarifying expectations occurs through a process of verbal interchange among the members. Even relatively nonverbal clients can participate if the worker uses activity-oriented experiences through which members may express themselves and through which their capacities for verbally expressing their feelings and attitudes may be increased. The skills of the worker include the appropriate use of all of the techniques of help: supporting the members in their discussions, structuring the situation in ways that facilitate the expression of norms, clarifying norms, gently confronting members when they violate the accepted norms, and selecting appropriate content. But, as Schein points out, there are also special mechanisms for the creation and enforcement of norms.[29] The members are likely to develop and act in accordance with the norms if the worker systematically pays attention to certain messages that are communicated and ignores others, for example, by verbally supporting appropriate self-disclosure and efforts to try out new experiences; commenting on the extent to which there has been a spread of participation in discussion; or noting the absence of a member. Casual remarks or questions consistently geared to a certain area convey clear messages to members about the behavior expected of them

The way in which workers react to critical incidents and conflicts is another primary means of embedding culture. If, for example, a worker shuts off heated discussion of differences by changing the subject, she conveys a message that it is dangerous to express differences. If, for example, she states that she believes the group is very important to the members' welfare, the members will get that message. Such an example comes from a group of young children in a hospital when a physician entered the meeting room and announced that he was ready to give a test to Jimmy. The worker said she knew it was important for Jimmy to have the test, but so was it important for him to remain in the group. The group would be over in fifteen minutes—could he wait until then? The doctor agreed that he could wait and apologized for interrupting. By such action, the worker confirmed the importance of group attendance to the youngsters and also to a colleague.

Another way in which norms are transmitted is through direct teaching. The quality of a worker's relationships with the members serves as a model that members gradually come to emulate. By teaching the members how to listen and respond to each other, he supports the expectation that members will become able to communicate with each other. Still another mechanism for developing a group with therapeutic norms is the allocation of status and rewards. By the kind of activities he proposes, for example, the worker has an opportunity to stress cooperation rather than competition and success for all rather than success for some and failure for others.

Children want to set rules for their groups, sometimes more rigid ones than they are able to follow and sometimes quite realistic ones. In a group of six fifth-grade girls in a school, the worker explained the purpose of the group and engaged the members in playing a name game to get acquainted. After all of the girls had been introduced by a partner, the worker said,

> My name is Mrs. C. The important thing about me that I think you would want to know is that I'm not a teacher. I'm a social worker and I'm going to be your group leader as I told you before.

MICHELLE: May I ask if you're a social worker, why are you here? A social worker gives mothers a check.

KATHY: No, stupid. That's not what a social worker does.

MICHELLE: You're wrong.

KATHY: No, I'm not.

WORKER: Well, sometimes social workers do help a family to get a check, but they do many other things, too. Did you have another idea, Kathy?

KATHY: Yeh, you can call a social worker if your check doesn't come and it has something to do with the county. But, another thing—if my brother was in trouble, my mother could ask the social worker to come and help her with the problem.

JEANINE: Does your mother have a social worker?

KATHY: (loudly and facing the worker) Last Christmas my mother fell in the garage and was knocked out all day. She's never been out that long before and the social worker came to help.

KIM: How long can we stay here?

WORKER: Until ten minutes after 1:00.

KATHY: I wish we could stay here all day.

KIM: Me, too.

WORKER: Do you want to continue to talk about social workers or—

BETTY: A social worker . . .

KATHY: My brother-in-law—

JEANINE: My mother had a social worker—

KATHY: I want to tell you about my brother-in-law.

WORKER: Kathy, could you please let Betty or Jeanine finish what they want to say? Could we listen to each other and let each one have a chance to talk?

JEANINE: (walking to the chalk board, she wrote: Our Rules: 1. Listen to each other. 2. Give everyone a turn. 3. Say please, like Mrs. C. did. Kim went to the board and added: 4. Say please be quiet instead of shut up. Jeanine said:) Please add be friendly to others, and Betty said, and add we can have fun talking here.

Through limiting Kathy's monopolizing behavior and suggesting a norm, the worker stimulated the group to respond to the worker's intervention and, in a sense, made the worker's suggestions about shared communication their own. Although the members called them rules, they obviously are not regulations that can be enforced but rather statements about desired ways of behaving. Members of children's groups often set rules that are rigid and enforced through punitive means. Such rules have little place in social work. When they are proposed by members, the worker needs to comment on their inappropriateness to the group's purpose, explore with the members what they hope to accomplish through such rules, identify the underlying problems masked by rules, and work toward alternative solutions to the revealed problems.

In another group of depressed adolescent girls in foster homes, a norm of self-disclosure was established in the initial session.[30] Lee and Park report:

> Pat asked, "What do we do here anyway?" I said the group was offered so they could discuss things that bother them as teenagers and as foster children. . . . I asked how that sounded to them. Pat said angrily, "I don't like that foster children part—neither the foster nor the children." I said, "Good—tell us more." She did, and the girls went into their reactions to the word *foster*—it means being on welfare and being unwanted—we're not on welfare and we're wanted. . . . Glenda said thoughtfully, "Being foster is like being some kind of new and strange race—nobody knows what to do with it." Serious nods. "Except to hide it," I said. "Yeah," and relieved laughter. I said "Here you don't have to hide it and you can share what makes you mad about it." "Right on," Kenya said. . . .

In response, the girls shared more about their experiences with foster and natural parents and learned it was safe to disclose their feelings, established commonality, and related the content of the group to its purpose.

Content. The selection of content is a process that relates what is done to the needs of members. The major content of the initial stage concerns orientation to the worker, each other, and the group's purpose, structure, and norms. At the very beginning, topics introduced by members tend to be superficial and restricted. The members share demographic information, symptoms, or prior experiences with groups as a means of getting acquainted and learning what they have in common. Such a process reduces the sense of uniqueness and stigma associated with some problems and creates one of the first bonds among the members. When problems are mentioned, the members are often quick to give advice, which is the way they interpret the meaning of mutual aid or helping each other. They try to provide practical solutions to identified problems.

Exploration with members about what they prefer to discuss or to do provides a natural base for understanding their primary concerns and their readiness to deal with particular issues. Rosen and Lieberman studied the relevance of content to the experiences of clients.[31] The major finding was that a clear mutual orientation between worker and client to the purpose of the session assists the worker in keeping the focus on relevant content. Thus, content becomes directly related to purpose.

In a study of two groups of adoptive parents by Gentry, discussion of preferences for content led to a consensus that the members wanted to deal with legal procedures in adoption, knowledge about parent-child relationships, the process of informing a child that he was adopted, and the reasons for placing a particular child with particular parents. The findings supported the importance of the worker's initiation and maintenance of an appropriate focus on topics that members felt to be important. Attrition is often related to the extent to which the member's expectations about content are met.[32] Sufficient commonalities among members are a requisite for continuing interaction over a period of time. Exploration is the primary set of techniques used to discover the common ground for discussion or activity-oriented experiences. The worker carries responsibility for assuring that the content selected will be such that the goals can be achieved.

THE SOCIAL WORKER'S ROLE IN GROUP INTERACTION

As members come into the first meeting, the worker's responsibility is to support each member's entry into the group. Attending to the members' comfort, calling them by name, introducing himself and members to each other, and suggesting ways for members to initiate interpersonal exchange are simple everyday courtesies but important ones. It is usually appropriate for the worker to review briefly what he understands the members have already been told about the reason for the new group or the group's referral for service. He tells them briefly what the nature of his participation will be. He presents the essential facts simply and succinctly in an informal manner. He notices the nonverbal responses to these statements and invites verbal responses, giving each member an opportunity to comment and ask questions. What happens next depends upon the type of group, the individuals who comprise it, and the specific responses of the members to the introductory comments. Whatever his next act and regardless of whether the content is talk or activity, however, he attempts to set up a pattern of participation that gives encouragement to each member's efforts and facilitates communication among the members, according to the readiness of particular members. Some members may be silent owing to uncertainty about what to say or how others will respond to them. A simple acknowledgment of this will help. The worker may request, either through words or nonverbal signals, that the members respond to each other's suggestions and reactions, but he usually does not pressure them to do so. He may make comments that connect the contribution of one member to that of another. In such ways, he makes clear that one aspect of his role is to help the members to interact with each other.

In her participation in the group, the social worker selects and uses specific techniques within the major categories of support, structuring, exploration, and information-education. Clarification tends to be limited to concerns about the properties of the group, the members' roles and expectations, and common interests and concerns. Confrontation is used more in the form of gentle requests but rarely in ways that seriously upset the members. Within the general categories of intervention some specific acts are more appropriate during the early stage and some are less appropriate. Although there are common elements in all groups, the worker's particular focus and activity are different with every group. Two examples from practice may clarify the similarities and differences in the worker's participation in group interaction during first meetings.

> Ten seven- and eight-year-old girls came into a first meeting, excited about the invitation to be in a group, whose purpose was to help the members to succeed in school. The girls had been referred to the group because they were naughty in school, their academic work was unsatisfactory, and they were economically and socially disadvantaged.
>
> Initially, the children were exceedingly quiet and conforming. I introduced myself, explaining in simple words what the group was for. I said, "Your teachers told me that you wanted to be in this group so you could learn to do better in school. Do you think this is what you heard?" There was no verbal response but positive nodding of heads. I continued, "Your parents gave permission for you to come. Here we'll do things and talk about things that will help you get along better in school. How does that sound to you?" The girls looked intently at me but were silent until one girl raised her hand and asked, "Do we all get to come teacher—is it for sure?" I reassured the girls about this, told them that I was not a teacher but a school social worker, and reviewed my name for them and wrote it on the board. Since there were no other comments or questions, I suggested that they get acquainted by playing a game. All enjoyed this game, so another one was introduced to help the girls to learn each other's and my name. The girls had difficulty following directions, so I simplified both the directions and the game itself. Some members enjoyed this and succeeded in it, but others gave up quickly when they could not remember a name. Two girls became restless and roamed around the room investigating the equipment but came back to the group when I announced that it was time for refreshments. In closing this short meeting, the girls were told about the schedule of twice weekly meetings, but it was apparent that they had no idea when Thursday would be. I said they need not worry about the day, for I would make plans with their teachers to remind them of the next meeting.

In such a group, it will take many sessions before the members become a working group.

A second example is of a group of six mothers of preschool children that was organized in a child development center for the purpose of helping the mothers to become more effective in dealing with their young children. Through an application and study process, the women had become well acquainted with the clinic's purpose and procedures and had had several interviews with staff concerning the treatment plan for their children and the nature of their expected participation in the plan. Basic orientation to the group had been done through interviews. Furthermore, the women had all seen each other before as they waited for their children, who were in the same therapy group. These facts did not, however, mean that orientation in the group was not necessary.

> In the first meeting, the worker was able rather quickly to review the purpose and plan for the group with the mothers and to engage them in some discussion of the group. She said, "You agreed to come to this group because each of you brought children to the clinic who are having emotional problems. The group can help you to relate better to your children and to learn how to help them get over their difficulties." With agreement to this statement, she asked the members to share with each other the reasons for coming and what they hoped to get from attendance here. Although each member differed in her pattern of participation, there was a general tendency to direct statements to the worker rather than to each other; to take turns in reporting, in a restrained manner with little expression of affect, on the symptoms of their children that brought them to the clinic; to look to the worker for approval of their comments; and to express their goals in terms of knowledge about children rather than of changes in their own attitudes and behavior. There was little spontaneous interaction. From here on, the major tasks for the worker were to elicit the expression of feelings about the situations that brought them to the clinic, to search for the common ground underlying seemingly different problems and goals, to establish a network of spontaneous communication among the members themselves rather than perpetuate the individual to-worker-and-back interactions, and to discover some preliminary focus for their work together.

During the first meetings, the worker needs to be supportive. She does not withhold information or support when the group needs it. She provides whatever information is relevant to the situation. Turning questions back to a group when the members simply do not have the necessary information is not helpful. Knowing when to give information directly to members and when to help them to use resources to find out the facts for themselves is an essential skill.

One of the most crucial skills is exploring, and responding sensitively to, the feelings of members. As the worker observes the members and listens to them, he becomes able to recognize their feelings. He does this through observation of nonverbal cues such as facial expression, body posture, and gestures, as well as through the verbalized content. He understands the members' uncertainty and ambivalence and the meaning of some of their defensive maneuvers. As feelings are expressed, he meets them with a feeling response rather than an intellectual one. The principle is to respond to a feeling with a feeling response. Certain types of activity facilitate the expression of feelings; others inhibit such expression. Some forms of communication seem to be more effective than others. One effective technique is to show genuine interest in individuals, through giving special attention or recognition. Through attending, the worker communicates that he is taking in the uniqueness of a person and is paying attention to him. Another type of comment conveys acceptance of a member's feelings, particularly those that express doubt, hostility, or distrust. Whether or not the members can yet trust the worker's responses, they come to feel his acceptance and understanding and to begin to grasp what is expected of them.

The free but protected atmosphere of the group may be a new experience for many members. Particularly during a first session, the worker avoids asking questions concerning the members' reasons for feeling or behaving in certain ways. Asking why tends to elicit defensive responses, instead of releasing feelings and setting a problem-solving process to work. Such questions may be perceived as reprimands or be confusing to members who do not know what kind of answer is expected. A restatement of the feelings expressed by members can be effective if the worker puts into words the feelings she senses the members are trying to express or restates them in a way that they are named and hence recognized. Often, the simplest responses are the most effective. To bring a feeling into the common ground of group experience, the worker may test with the group whether or not the acknowledged feeling is shared by others. To be able to respond to the underlying meaning of the members' requests, challenges, or comments is an important skill. Within a climate that supports the expression of feelings, the worker tries not to stir up feelings that cannot be dealt with during the session. She may make mental note of sensitive areas but hold them for discussion until the person or the group is ready to focus on them. If a worker really desires to be helpful to the members and is sensitive to their feelings, her responses are likely to be appropriate.

Contagion of feelings from members to members and to the group as a whole seems to occur very infrequently in initial meetings of groups. Rather, the feelings tend to be idiosyncratic to individual needs and reactions to the new situation. With some exceptions, there is usually not yet mutual identification or much expression of empathy. The worker takes, therefore, responsibility for assessing the flow of feelings and for noting the common elements within the myriad of individual responses.

Six recently discharged patients from a state hospital were living in a board and care facility in a large urban city. In the first meeting there had been considerable mistrust of the social worker and his role, several members expressing the fear that the worker would send them back to the hospital. There was, at the same time, a genuine reaching out or wanting to be included in the group. The worker records:

I had begun the second meeting by asking the members what they thought we might do to make our group a useful one for them. After several minutes of discussion, it seemed that learning to communicate better was a dominant theme. I said, "Well, it seems that we would like to try to understand better what each of us is trying to say—it can be very difficult sometimes to get across a simple message." The members picked up on this comment and talked about how hard it is for them to say what they want to say.

One member, who thus far had given the impression of taking the group as a joke, became very serious and said, "I been in lots of groups. Who knows which way the wind blows? There's too much hate in this room. It might kill us like it did the beautiful people. I feel the edge of pain and the what of sane." There was absolute silence. After waiting for some response, I said "Mark, I'm confused about what you want to tell us. I gather you have fears about being in this group." Mark did not reply, but Bob said, "That's the way Mark always talks—he says a lot of poetic bullshit that always turns me off." Shirley said, "That's what he's trying to do—get you to leave him alone." I asked, "Mark do you want us to leave you alone or were you trying to tell us something else?" He replied, "I just dig weird language." Minnie said, "He's always talking that way when he wants to fox us." Mark then responded to my earlier statement, ignoring Minnie's remark. "I try to say what I mean—what I feel inside—but most of the time I can't do that so I talk in images." I would have supported Mark at this point, but several members started grumbling, telling me all at the same time about Mark's refusal to talk to people directly. I wondered, "Can you talk to Mark directly instead of talking about him to me?" There was surprised silence. Minnie said, "Mark, I think you're playing games with us." Bob said, "I don't know about that—are you scared to say what you mean?" Mark responded, "I guess it's true. Talking to people scares me so I guess I try to throw them off balance by making myself hard to understand." The members responded to this statement with considerable approval, culminating in the statement by one withdrawn girl, Cindy, who said, "I know how it feels to be scared, but it feels even worse to be lonely." I said that I understood it could be very painful to feel scared or lonely or both scared and lonely. Mark said, "Yeah, I'm both." I said that other members might have some fears, too. There was strong nodding of heads as Bob said, "You've said it directly to us all." I said the group could help them with these feelings as we learn how to talk more clearly to each other about things that matter to us.

In making his contribution to the group interaction, the worker needs to follow the manifest content of the conversation at the same time that he seeks to understand the latent content. The manifest content consists of the literal and obvious meanings of the verbal messages; the latent content is what is below the threshold of superficial observation. It may be just before the level of awareness, subject to ready recall, or it may be at the unconscious level. The latent content may extend and add meaning to the manifest content or may contradict it. If the former, the process of communication is enhanced; if the latter, mutual understanding is hampered.

To make sense out of the often apparent unrelated contributions of the members, the worker searches for the underlying common threads of feelings and meaning and responses to these. She tries to discover how a succession of comments and questions by members are linked together around an underlying concern common to a number of members. For example, a common concern in first meetings is often that of inclusion—whether the members really want to belong and feel others want to include them. This concern is seldom expressed directly, but the sensitive worker makes the inference from her observation of the verbal and nonverbal cues provided in subtle ways during the meeting.

The social worker needs to follow the interaction process itself. The process is transactional because of the reciprocal influence of people on each other as they participate in the conversation. The practitioner's concern is with the nature and spread of feelings, opinions, and ideas; who interacts with whom; who initiates behaviors; and who follows the initiator. He is interested in discovering the factors that create a beginning sense of mutuality among the members and, on the other hand, with the sources of tension and conflict in the group.

To open up communication among members, the worker seeks out the blocks to communication in the group that may be due to interpersonal hostilities or to differences in culture, knowledge, or values. She assesses each member's ability to listen, to observe, and to respond to the message of others with or without distortion of those messages.

Young children need to learn to communicate with the worker, often in new ways. Many children are expected to listen and to obey adults and to respond only to specific questions asked them. Often they are not expected to enter into discussions with adults present—to give, as well as take, in reciprocal verbal communication. The worker needs to develop interest in the children's viewpoints and to be able to enter into the world of childhood so that she and they can talk with each other. To talk with children in language suitable to the children's level of understanding without talking down to them is a precious attribute in a worker. Children are not as nonverbal as is often assumed. The clue, to a large extent, is in the adult who is able to listen, to enter into the child's world, and to talk simply and concretely with the appropriate amount of seriousness or playfulness as indicated by the child's mood. Adults, too, have their troubles in listening and talking. Observations of the capacities for communication of the members are used by the worker in making a professional judgment about when to enter the conversation, when to intervene in an activity for a particular reason, and when to support silently the interacting processes within the group.

In the early period of group life, it is desirable to focus on shared experiences as a basis for the development of motivation. Members usually behave in compliant ways in order to protect themselves from feeling different and from being rejected by others. Initially, discussion or activity should provide for some immediate sense of learning something that is valued or that brings gratification. Early discussion, though scattered, tends to promote a feeling of belonging and reduces the members' anxious feelings. At any one time, there are diverse topics available for consideration by the group, from which a selection is made, either by formal decision or through the influence of a central theme that underlies free-flowing discussion. Although there is a model for stages in the process of decision making that is useful for purposes of analysis, in reality, each group is different.

It is not easy to get started with a new group. The social worker cannot really know the members well enough for an accurate assessment of their goals, expectations, problems, and capacities. The worker, as well as the members, feels anxious with a new group. She is uncertain of the responses of the members to her. If she is not comfortable, she may overdirect or underdirect the group. She may present introductory material in such a didactic manner that members tend toward passive agreement. She may become anxious over silence and enter into the discussion prematurely or may tend to answer questions or make comments when turning them back to the group would be beneficial. A worker who is too passive usually makes a group restless and insecure. In such cases, the members often leave a meeting feeling that they have been let down and that nothing has been accomplished. A worker must give direction and simultaneously allow for freedom of expression and self-direction.

MOTIVATION TO CONTINUE IN THE GROUP

Hope is a powerful motivating force. Before the group's closing, the social worker often gives a brief summary of what has happened in the group thus far. He makes sure that the members understand the arrangements for meetings in terms of time and place and explores any concerns or problems about such matters. He engages the members in a decision to try out the group a little longer. He elicits from members, or suggests, some immediate goals to be worked on in the next session. He creates a bridge to the next meeting. It is hoped that, during the meeting, he has provided a fair test of what it will be like to be in the group through the provision of some immediate satisfactions in doing something together, identifying interests and concerns, and making some satisfying personal or corporate decisions.

The social worker hopes that the experience each member has had in the first meeting will be such that he will want to continue. Far too often, persons drop out before they have had sufficient experience for making wise decisions for themselves. A number of studies have reported that difficulties in communication and lack of understanding between the worker and client are factors related to unplanned discontinuance after the first session.[33] In a study of adult clients' reactions to initial interviews, it was learned that a client's willingness to commit himself to a relationship with a helping person was related to two goals: the achievement of some progress in the solution of a problem and a degree of social satisfaction from the relationship with the helping person.[34] In another study, the willingness of adolescents to see a helping person again was positively associated with a perception of the practitioner's desire to help and his ability to understand.[35] It is likely that these same conditions would hold for work with groups, with the added complexity of the nature of the members' interactions with each other. Factors in the social environment also influence continuation. When there are readily available alternative resources for service or relevant other persons who do not support the person's quest for professional help, the client is more likely to discontinue.[36]

The members are ready to move into the next stage when a tentative agreement has been reached between the worker and the members concerning (1) the purpose of the group and the ways in which individuals' goals can be met within it; (2) the expectations for the roles of worker and member and the major rules that govern behavior; (3) and the major means of determining content. It is generally agreed that mutual agreement is fundamental in determining the direction, quality, and content of the group experience. The values of such a working agreement or contract, according to Maluccio and Marlow, are as follows: (1) it is derived from shared experience in exploring all aspects of the agreement; (2) it gives both worker and members a sense of involvement and participation and signifies mutual commitment and readiness to assume responsibility; and (3) it provides a baseline for periodic review of accomplishments, assessment of progress, and examination of the conditions of the agreement.[37] The working agreement at this stage is a very partial and tentative one, based on enough agreement between the worker and group for the members to want to continue in the group.

The conclusion is that it is likely that a member of a group will continue beyond the first one or two meetings if he feels that the worker has recognized him, is interested in him, and was able to be helpful; that he felt recognized by other members and had something in common with them; that something happened in the first meeting that was useful to him in the way of a relationship, an attitude of hopefulness, a concrete experience, or an idea; and finally, that he has some sense of knowing what to expect next time; that he knows in a very general way what the group is for and what he might hope to get from it. If other significant persons in his milieu support his decision to join the group, his own positive attitudes toward it will be reinforced. He will be ready to engage himself in an active process of further exploring and testing out the potential in the group for meeting his needs.

10

Stage II: Dissatisfaction and Power Conflict

Involvement of members in a group does not occur during a brief period of orientation. Following the initial stage, there follows a period of dissatisfaction and conflict over power. Through engaging in a process of testing the issues of power and control, the members become committed to the group. As conflicts over power are resolved, the satisfaction of the members is enhanced and the members are freed to work together on other problems, which further the group's transition into the next stage.

CHARACTERISTICS OF THE GROUP

The first core concern of members of the group was inclusion, directly related to feelings of accepting and being accepted by others. The shift in focus is now to preoccupation with the need for power and control. Garland and associates identify three major issues.[1] The first is autonomy and rebellion. At least some members rebel against the great power they perceive the leader to have over them. They are concerned about how the leader will use that power—will he permit the members to question his power and share it with the members so they gain autonomy over their own affairs within appropriate limits? The second issue is a normative crisis occasioned by the unfamiliar standards in regard to permission and limits, as the members are given considerable freedom to express their feelings and ideas. Traditional patterns of norms break down, resulting in some degree of ambiguity and tension among the members. The third issue is one of protection and support. To survive the ambiguity and conflict, the members need to feel that they have a reasonable degree of safety from attack by others and support toward self-control.

The conflict over power and control is to be regarded—not as an obstacle to be overcome—but as behavior consistent with the democratic values of social work in enabling people to participate effectively in the group, with the accompanying power inherent in it. Power may indeed be a force used against other people. But, according to Solomon, power is the ability to mobilize internal and external resources to achieve some desired goal.[2] It need not reside in one or a few but can be broadly distributed. The other major source of conflict is over acceptance of members, one for the other.

The emergence of conflict is inevitable, often taking the form of hostility toward the worker. The hostility may be overt or subtle and suppressed, expressed indirectly through complaints about other people or the organization. Members tend to imbue the worker with unrealistic attributes: if expectations are too high, disappointment is inevitable. The members have their own needs, which they seek to satisfy. The worker cannot meet all of the members' dependency needs, their desires to be the one and only, to be loved by everyone, or to succeed in all things. Nor does the worker fulfill the traditional authority roles of teachers, parents, and employers. The members, instead, are expected to share with others and seek their own solutions to problems. The needs and dissatisfactions are varied, but they are concerned with relationships among people.

Members have varied behavioral responses to the tension and conflict. They form alliances with other members in pairs or larger subgroups; they participate actively in the conflict situation; or they maintain aloofness, suppress hostility, or leave the group. These are what Bion refers to as flocking, fighting, and flight responses.[3] Working through the struggle for power and acceptance is essential. Through the shift of some power from the worker to the members, the members gain a sense of power to cope with their own personal and environmental problems. Authority issues will recur throughout the life of the group, but if the first one is satisfactorily resolved, power no longer tends to be the major issue. Working through the power struggle leads to mutual acceptance among the members and mutual attraction of the members to the group.

During this stage of group development, the members interact with the worker and each other to test out the meaning of the group experience for them and to determine their roles and status in the group. The members begin to examine themselves in relation to the group. They explore the views of each other in relation to the group; as they do so, their awareness of similarities and differences among them becomes acute, resulting in considerable ambiguity and tension. Through dynamic decision-making processes, the members modify their original perceptions of the group and try to change it so that it will feel like their own group with which they identify and which becomes an important reference group for them. In order for this to happen, the major tasks of the leader are to (1) further develop understanding of the members and of the group as a social system; (2) strengthen relationships between the worker and among the members through working out authority conflicts; (3) enhance positive motivation and reduce resistance; (4) support the members in their exploration of the group's purpose and their goals; (5) stabilize membership; (6) develop a flexible structure of status and roles; (7) work toward resolution of conflict and tension; and (8) engage in activities beyond the group in behalf of members. These tasks are essential to the development of a viable working agreement and a cohesive group.

UNDERSTANDING THE GROUP

Crucial to the worker's success in helping members use this stage of group life toward the achievement of individual and group purposes is acumen in assessment. During the planning stage, attention was given to the process of assessment and to certain knowledge about people requisite to determining group composition, eligibility for service, and placement in a particular group. During the inclusion-orientation stage, the leader derived additional understanding of the members as he talked with them and observed their behavior in a variety of situations. Now he continues to review and organize the facts about each member and the group's structure and process, ascertain the meaning of the facts, and evaluate each member's problems and potentials as these relate to the group. Understanding of groups goes hand in hand with assessment of individuals. Similarities and differences among members in relation to their goals, motivations, capacities, and problems need to be assessed. The impact of the individual on the group, members on each other, and the group on individuals is to be considered.

The social worker assesses the current state of the group at a given time. She considers whether it is in a state of dynamic balance, in severe upset, or in a state so fixed and static that it is unable to cope with change. She evaluates the nature and severity of the stresses and strains within the group and the group's interaction with other systems. She seeks to understand the interpersonal relations among members: presence or lack of mutual acceptance and affection; the group's need to isolate, scapegoat, demean, or glorify one or more of its members; and conflicting loyalties among members of the group and significant persons in the environment. She seeks to understand the amount of congruence among the members and between herself and the members, concerning goals, values, and expectations. She evaluates whether the composition of the group and its organizational structure are faulty or functional to the system; ascertains the meaning of the pattern of statuses and roles that emerge out of group interaction, both to the individuals and to the development of the group; ascertains how open or closed are the channels for communication and the nature of the blocks to more effective communication; evaluates the nature and effectiveness of the decision-making process, the personal and impersonal controls within the group, and the relationship of the group to other systems in terms of conformity to, or deviance from, the norms of the community; and assesses the varied facets of group structure and process in order to discover the common ground among the members that can be built on to develop cohesion and plan for her interventions in the group and its environment and to identify problems and help the members work toward their resolution.

STRENGTHEN RELATIONSHIPS

The social worker is an authority figure, with professional power. Most people come to a group with some attitudes toward and problems with authority. Often they have had little prior experience with social workers and hence have to learn what to expect from them. Their expectations tend to be colored by experiences with other authority roles. They may become bewildered and confused when the worker does not live up to their expectations concerning power and control; may use certain devices to learn about the worker's role and expectations; and may test the worker in subtle or obvious ways. The testing may last for only a brief period. It may be prolonged if the worker has difficulty in understanding and accepting the members, if he is inconsistent in his responses to them, or if he is ambiguous about expectations, the purpose of the group, its operating procedures, and the roles of worker and member. Or it may be prolonged if he is authoritarian in his use of power or if he has made unrealistic promises to the members. If a worker has a need to avoid or deny conflict, it will be enacted in more subtle ways or displaced elsewhere. It will be prolonged also in groups composed of persons who have had prior unsatisfactory or disturbed relationships, particularly with persons in positions of authority. The tension and ambivalence about the members' relationships with the worker have their roots in both reality and transferred reactions.

Members of groups commonly test the use the worker will make of her authority to limit and control them. They may provoke her to use her power; may compare her unfavorably with other leaders of groups they have known to learn whether or not she will become defensive or retaliate; may make comments about the worker's race, age, status, or physical appearance; and often test how far the worker will permit them to break rules, behave in unacceptable ways, or hurt themselves before intervening. In such ways, they seek for proof that the worker will protect them against their own and each other's hostile impulses. Such maneuvers also serve as means of discovering the boundaries to the right to self-determination of individuals and autonomy of the group.

In natural groups particularly, some of the behavior of the members may be with the intent of testing out whether or not the worker will usurp the role of the group's elected officials or of its indigenous leaders.

The worker makes explicit the safeguards that will be provided so that the group can take responsibility for itself as soon as possible. The safeguard for self-responsibility is usually the democratic process itself. The right of the group to make its own decisions whenever possible is based on the principles that it is important for people in this society to learn to govern their own lives and that growth is more likely to occur when the change is felt to be self-initiated rather than authoritatively imposed. Therefore, the active and central role of the social worker essential in the initial stage must not continue indefinitely. The worker must release responsibility to the members as they become able to assume it: some power must shift from the worker to the members.

Being in a position of power is often an issue for social workers. They may deny that they do have authority and its concomitant responsibility for the welfare of the group. The worker's feelings about power and about sharing it are tested. Workers may have had negative experiences with figures of authority and be uncomfortable with the role. They want to be liked by the members, to be thought of as a friend, and to be democratic. They confuse democracy with laissez-faire leadership. They may deal with their feelings by abdicating the role or becoming authoritarian. Such behaviors tend to provoke severe testing by the members, who expect the worker to give professional opinions and take appropriate action in the group, while always respecting the members' right to question these opinions and actions.

Clearly tied to the conflict over the worker's power and the way he exerts it are the members' continual concerns about their status and power in the group, combined with ongoing concerns about trust and acceptance. Members of groups often need to determine whether or not they can trust the worker and each other with feelings of hurt and anger and whether or not they accept each other. They gradually become more able to express their feelings and concerns. Thompson and Kahn point out that the process that operates is based on the use of two types of information.[4] Each member hears about the feelings and ideas of others and also perceives the reactions to the messages sent by him. Each disclosure stimulates the members, leading to another comment until more and more information is disclosed. The members learn that the feared consequences of sharing do not happen.

Underlying the conflicts over power and control, according to Levine, is a quest for acceptance as full-fledged members of the group, with some degree of influence or power in it.[5] It is natural to be uncertain and ambivalent until trust is established. In most groups, the members seek proof that the worker accepts and cares about them. Being absent may be a test of whether or not the worker missed a member. A request for a special favor from the worker or an offer of gifts to the worker may serve the purpose. Learning how the worker reacts to a range of behavioral patterns may be a means of testing acceptance. The members may behave in ways they feel might be disapproved of by the worker in order to test the limits of his acceptance.

A group of adolescent girls, for example, asked permission to comb their hair. When told they could do this, the girls tried out every bizarre hair style to test the worker's reactions to styles that are forbidden by school authorities. They also tested the worker by using foul language. When the worker commented that these words did not shock her or make her angry, the behavior stopped. Such nonjudgmental behavior can be more effective than trying to impose rules. A similar maneuver by members is to confess to feelings or behavior that might bring disapproval. When a worker is able to clarify with the members the fact that she is not interested in placing blame and that her acceptance is not dependent upon conforming behavior, the testing is reduced or stopped.

This example from a third meeting of a group of depressed adolescent girls in foster care, reported by Lee and Park, illustrates the challenges to social workers in this stage of development.[6]

> After some talk about boy friends, there was a silence. I waited. Pat then wanted to know why social workers care and why they come around anyway. I sat silently; then said, "It is rough when you don't live with your natural parents; you have to go through a lot of change." Cherise said sadly that she doesn't think that anyone loves you like your natural mother who "birthed" you. Some of the others agreed and each shared her fantasy around how easy and beautiful life would be with her natural mother. Cherise added, "Social workers are all alike; they say, oh how sad, how can I help you? But they can't do anything unless they can bring my mother back." Silence. Then Pat said to me, "Well, what do you think of that?" I had trouble answering, so I asked what they thought, but Cherise asked me again. I then said, "No one can bring a mother or father back and I can hear you are angry about that. You are also wondering what life would have been like with your parents. You hope it would be better than you have now." There were nods and comments of agreement. I said that it is rough but maybe this group can help to make things better for you by helping you to deal with the things on your mind and the way things are for you now. We shared a thoughtful silence and they began to clean the room.

In analyzing the situation, the worker said she responded to Pat's question by ignoring the hostility and responding instead with an empathic response, based on understanding the members' situations, which brought out Cherise's anger and sense of hopelessness and Pat's subsequent challenge to the worker. She shared her recognition of what the members were feeling, provided strong support, and gently offered some hope for change. It is important that the girls deal directly with issues of foster care and express their feelings freely; acceptance of the feelings is a step toward help. In such a situation, assessment of individuals, as well as of the group process, is crucial; for example, knowing that Cherise is the only member whose birth mother is dead helps the worker to understand the depth of Cherise's depression.

There are groups in which one or more members are extremely dependent upon the worker. Such members expect the worker to fulfill the role of a parent figure; they show their feelings through making exaggerated efforts to please him, seeking his exclusive attention, being rivalrous with other members for his love and attention, seeking praise or reproof for their actions, or commenting unrealistically, "You never think I can do anything right." They may seek a close relationship with the worker but become frightened by the feelings of closeness; may fear they will be hurt; may try to withdraw from the group or provoke rejection; or may make unreasonable demands on the worker and then feel rejected when these cannot be met.

Distrust of a practitioner may be tied to stereotyped perceptions of differences between the worker and members. Differences between a worker and a group on any characteristic that tends to create or maintain social distance are initially bars to mutual acceptance. The distrust is often aggravated when there are efforts to avoid facing or denying the difference. Some examples are a group of aged clients with a young worker, a black worker with a group of white adults or vice versa; or a nonhandicapped worker with a group of orthopedically handicapped patients. One example is of a socialization group of black girls between the ages of eleven and thirteen. The worker is black also but of a lighter complexion and different texture of hair than the girls.

> Marcia was a new member and was with us for the first time. I asked the group to clue her in on some of the things that we had been doing. Frances and Susan responded, telling her about the group's activities. Marcia seemed preoccupied, however. When the girls finished telling her about the group, she looked at me directly and asked, "Why do you have to have all the good hair—why couldn't I have it?" Before I could respond, the other members chimed in with such statements as: "Yea, you make us sick. All light skinned people think they're cute. Yea, just like this girl in school." This led to talking about the girl in school. After a while, I interrupted by saying, "I can see that you have certain ideas about me. Maybe we should take the time to talk about them." Frances said that so far as she was concerned there was nothing to talk about—this is how they felt. The others expressed strong agreement. Attempts to engage them further were fruitless: they became absorbed in the project they were working on. The crucial issues were lack of self-esteem and the impact of color on people. My own discomfort with the issue of color led me to go along with the

members' avoidance of it, rather than help the girls to understand and face the differences.

Open recognition of such differences may not only break down barriers to communication but also lead to enhancement of a positive sense of identity. One example is a group of seven adolescent black girls whose members had been adjudicated as delinquents and assigned to a white worker for help with improving their socially unacceptable behavior. For the fourth meeting of the group, the leader had invited the members to a neighborhood center for a swim. She knew that the girls loved to swim, but she also knew that the obvious differences in physical characteristics would be accentuated in this situation. As one girl groaned over the problems of straightening her hair, the worker used this opportunity to acknowledge the outward differences between the races and to comment on how this might make it hard for them to trust her and work with her in the group. This comment led into a discussion of the girls' feelings about their race and their troubles with white people. This activity, designed with a particular purpose, marked the turning point in the group's relationship with the worker.

An illustration of perceived social distance due to differences in age is of a group in a senior center. The men and women members average more than seventy-five years; the male worker is thirty. The following excerpts are taken from a group record.

RALPH: There's no way a young person like you could really understand or help somebody my age. Not that there's anything wrong with that, I mean, how could you?

(The other members jumped to my defense, as in Hilde's remark, "Oh, no, I don't think that's true at all.")

WORKER: Hold on a second. I've often thought about this matter. How do you think I'm unable to help you, Ralph?

(Ralph talked about being eighty-six years old, having physical problems he never dreamed of when he was the worker's age, and having had more experiences and lived longer. The other members talked about friends who are younger and their feelings that there are no reasons why younger people should want to understand them. Others commented that age has nothing to do with an ability to understand others. After listening to these views, the worker said,)

WORKER: But, you see, I do want to understand you and I believe I can. Not everything about you, but some things. I think there's a common ground where we can talk to each other. (The members agreed with this, but I felt that Ralph did not really accept the idea. So, I said lightly,) It may be true, but I don't think you really believe that.

RALPH: Well, no, to some extent, but it's like this . . . when I see someone my own age or in a somewhat similar dismal health, we exchange a knowing glance and in that look, there's an understanding that you just can't talk about.

GRETA: I think that what Ralph is saying is true, but you can go too far with it.

(The members then returned to their earlier conversation about whether or not age makes a big difference in understanding others.)

(At the next meeting,)

HILDE: You know, Ralph, I was thinking about what you said about young people and I want to tell you about an experience I had.

(She spoke of how she went to see her ophthalmologist, a thirty-three year-old woman. She told her doctor that her failing vision was so depressing to her. The doctor chastised her and gave her a pep talk. She now agreed with Ralph that younger people can't really understand the aged.)

WORKER: Wait a second. I'm guilty without a trial. I agree that your doctor showed a real lack of empathy, but she is just one person.

RALPH: No, that's really the way it is.

In evaluating the meeting, the worker recognized that he had personalized the issue and become defensive: he felt uncomfortable about the age difference. He said that he should have engaged all the members in sharing their feelings, exploring the issues, and then examining the implications for his work with the group.

Simple acknowledgment of differences often leads to further exploration of them. The worker facilitates the exploration of the meaning of differences and the members' expression of feeling about such differences. That contributes to a reduction in distortions of perception of others occasioned by feelings about such differences. The need to accept difference is accompanied by a need to identify and express whatever will tend to further a sense of unity between the worker and members.

Recognition of the group's various forms of dissatisfaction is important in establishing and continuing a purposeful, working relationship with the group. To pass these tests, the worker needs to assess accurately the meaning of the words or actions of individuals and the level of the group's development at a given time. She needs to be sufficiently secure to be able to accept expressions of indifference or hostility without retaliation. This is not always easy. She needs to support the ventilation of feelings and concerns, unless contraindicated. Communication of feelings may be indirect. An example is of a natural group of children in which members talked to the worker through each other. In complaining about each other, the real target of communication was the worker. The members of this group also asked questions such as: "Why does teacher always meddle with us?" when feelings were those toward the worker. The worker can often assess the real target of the communication through the tone of voice used, the direction of eye movements, or the accompanying gestures. Likewise, members may talk with each other indirectly.

An awareness and acceptance of his own feelings toward the testing maneuvers is an important prelude to an ability to understand the members' use of the testing process and to respond in appropriate ways. Owing to preoccupation with problems in relationships, a worker might well remember the need for expression and acceptance of positive feelings. Indeed, he welcomes and encourages instances of affection. He assures the members of his interest in them and of his desire to support them in their efforts.

A major task for the worker is to strengthen relationships among the members. He does not just establish his own relationship with individuals and then focus on group relationships, but rather simultaneously works on both. The members not only test the worker; they also test each other, using essentially similar devices as in testing the worker. The worker perceives and helps the group not only to identify positive ties as they develop but also to recognize difficulties and tensions. Recognition of differences brings them into the arena of the problem-solving processes of the group. Through exploration of differences, the members may come to understand that negative feelings exist side by side with more comfortable ones. The leader needs to reach out and give to members in appropriate ways. He identifies and expresses his awareness of common interests, concerns, and feelings as these develop in the group. He suggests ways in which members can be helpful to each other. What needs to get worked through in this stage is not only ambivalence toward the worker as a person and the power he has in his professional role but also feelings of competitiveness and rivalry among the members for status and acceptance. The effective practitioner recognizes that,

> working on problems of relationships to each other often precedes working on other problems. With each experience in trying to work it out, the members become increasingly able to recognize and handle conflict. It is how the worker helps them to handle these conflicts which determines whether the group bond will become sufficiently strong so that the members can use the group more intensively for help with other problems.[7]

ENHANCE POSITIVE MOTIVATION—REDUCE RESISTANCE

An integral part of the work in this stage is to enhance positive motivation and reduce resistance. The purposes of resistance are several. Resistance preserves the steady state or existing equilibrium. Any major change disturbs the existing balance of forces, and fear of change may be greater than the discomfort felt from the problem is. Resistance is a means of warding off anxiety, protecting the personality from hurt and preserving the immature satisfactions and secondary gains that accompany a particular kind of relationship or problem.

The members provide clues that resistance is operating. Being resistant is seldom a conscious process. A person does not say, "I'm going to resist the efforts to help me"; rather the resistant behaviors are at the preconscious or unconscious levels of experience. The clues are numerous. One clue is the way time is used—coming late, leaving early, or being absent. Another indication consists of maneuvers to control the situation so as to avoid facing issues. Examples are complaining, verbosity or monopolization, repetitive discussion, silence, intellectualization, rationalization, arguing to prove that others are wrong rather than to find answers, or prolonged joking or laughing. Other behaviors to avoid facing issues are changing the subject, minimizing issues, denying, forgetting, withholding facts, talking about the past in order to avoid dealing with the present, quickly confessing or admitting guilt to ward off the need to explore the situation, or being unwilling to consider suggestions made by the worker or other members. Many interpersonal responses are largely colored by transference reactions, such as dependency, flattery, seduction, berating others, questioning the competence of others, subtle insults, anger that is not realistic to the situation, or open or overt hostility. Such barriers to the effective use of the group experience are built out of the multiple stresses in the lives of members.

CLARIFY PURPOSE

Explanation and clarification of purpose is not a task to be completed in one or two sessions. It is rather a continuous process of definition and redefinition of both the long-range and immediate purposes as these become more specific and as they undergo gradual changes. In this stage, as members interact around the primary issues of authority and control, their capacities and needs become known to themselves and the worker, making possible the development of realistic goals. This can be a tremendous relief to the members. The worker's verbal recognition of the commonality of their situations tends to strengthen motivation to use the group for goal achievement. People hear selectively so that, being preoccupied with other concerns in the orientation stage, they take in only part of the explanation and discussion of purpose. Later, they are eager to explore and clarify the purpose for the group and its meaning to them.

In one group of thirteen- and fourteen-year-old boys, for example, this event did not occur until the fourth meeting.

> One member commented that here he was again, but he didn't even know how he happened to be in the group. The worker explained that

> perhaps others wondered about this, too. When he got confirmation of this concern from others, the worker explained that they had been referred by the vice-principal of the school. Another boy said he guessed that meant they were the worst kids in the whole school. Following a spontaneous period of complaining about the vice-principal, the worker explained that all of them were in trouble in school and that, through the group, it was hoped that they could talk about some of these troubles and do things together that would make it possible for them to get along better. He added that he remembered that one of them had said that being sent to the group meant they were the worst boys in the school; this was not so, and he did not feel that way about them. Other questions then poured from the boys: Was the worker connected with the police? Would he squeal on them? What would he tell the school and their parents about them? Would he kick them out of the group if they messed up here, too? Feeling accepted by the worker, the members were ready to listen to an explanation and to discuss the purpose for the group and their reactions to the group.

To be noted is the social worker's use of many categories of skills. Within an accepting relationship, the worker offered support in the form of sensitive listening, reassurance, and hope; he structured the situation by focusing the flow of communication; he explored for feelings and opinions; he encouraged the ventilation of complaints and concerns; he provided information; and he clarified the purpose of the group and reasons for referral. He facilitated the group process by seeking responses from the members and by identifying commonalities.

Adults, too, often have doubts about what the worker sees as the real purpose of the group. The following excerpt is taken from a meeting of a group of mothers in a mental health clinic.

> Mrs. D. asked if the clinic had planned this group because the staff felt the mothers had the problems or was it planned so that the child would be given help. Mrs. B. thought we are here because the clinic thinks that we are to blame for the kids' problems. "Well, I certainly don't agree with that," said Mrs. P. Mrs. J. asked if the group might be set up for both purposes. The worker asked if she could explain what she meant by that. She said she thought that we do have some problems and by meeting together we would be helped and, in turn, the child would be helped. Mrs. O. turned directly to me and said, "I guess you're the only one who knows why we are here." I said I would review with them the original purpose for the group, but I wondered if first they would make some comments about how they see the reasons for meeting. Each of the members responded, some of them mentioning that they had already seen improvement in their children; some saying they wanted to get ideas from others; two saying they found

they were not all alone; and one commenting that this was different somehow from just talking to her neighbor about the child. They shared some of their feelings of being different from other members because of the age of the child, their marital status, and their work. Mrs. K. said that she thought all the mothers were learning how to relieve their own irritation at the child, which makes it easier for them and is also helpful to the child. All of them said they agreed with Mrs. K. and gave examples of what they had learned in the preceding meeting.

I pulled together some of the comments the members had made about the reasons for these meetings. I noted that it was true that they would not all benefit in the same way and that I was pleased they could express how they felt. I restated the purpose of the group as explained in the first meeting: it was to help them to become better able to help their children. We are not blaming them for their children's difficulties. That means that, as one of them said earlier, it is to help both mothers and children. The help given to the children here is important, but more important is the parents' understanding and ability to help the child. Mrs. K. said that she liked that idea—if we could learn to be better parents our children would benefit. All of the members seemed relieved to have clarified the group's purpose in relation to their own goals.

Motivation for change is related to the extent to which there are shared perceptions by members of the need for change. As the members recognize that the group's purpose is related to the shared needs of the members, a sense of some pressure toward change develops. An individual's recognition that his own goals can be met within the group, when these are not in conflict with the general purpose of the group, provides strong motivation toward more involvement in and effective use of the group. Not only does the worker encourage questions and reactions to the purpose for the group, but also he works toward the recognition and elaboration of objectives of individuals and toward discussion of how one member's goals are similar to those of others or how different goals can be accommodated within the group. He recognizes the varied ways by which members make requests for help. A comment by a member, "I'll drop by your office," or "I want to go home last," or a nonverbal request in the form of lingering after other members leave often signifies readiness to share concerns and goals with the worker. The worker usually meets these requests but often clarifies also how the group may be used for help and how the individual's concern, even if unique, can be related in some way to the concerns of others. He takes advantage of opportunities to relate the concerns of one of those of others. Mutuality of goals is not necessarily achieved through talk alone. Activity-oriented experiences may be used to identify problems and hoped-for outcomes. An illustration is of a group of young boys and girls on a pediatrics ward in which the worker engaged them in playing doctor and patient in order to identify for them some of their feelings and concerns about being in a hospital and to relate the problems of one child to those of others and to the purposeful use of the group.

When social work service is expected to continue beyond several sessions, it tends to be focused on a constellation of goals, as contrasted with the single purpose typical of brief service. Clarity about goals on the worker's part and the members' part and, more important, congruence between the two perceptions are not achieved in one or two meetings. One outcome of the second stage of group development is that members come to perceive with greater clarity what they want to achieve for themselves through the use of group experience.

A group of mental patients had been unable to participate verbally in formal discussion of the group's purpose until the twelfth session of the group.[8] An excerpt from this meeting follows:

VICTOR: What did you say this group is for?

ELAINE: To help with what's troubling us and to help us stay out of the hospital.

VICTOR: Sounds like group therapy to me.

ELAINE: Well that's what it is.

VICTOR: Not to me—group therapy is so boring.

ELAINE: Well, it would make me happy if we could agree that this is group therapy. O.K. Tell us what this group is, Victor.

VICTOR: It is a semisocial self-help group.

JONATHON: Why do you call it that?

ELAINE: You said social?

VICTOR: Sure. I don't know what I'd do with my Thursday nights if I didn't come here.

JONATHON: I don't get that and I don't get the self-help idea.

ELAINE: Yeh, you said self-help?

VICTOR: Uh, huh . . . by talking we might help ourselves to learn about our problems and . . .uh, uh, well and to overcome them.

ELAINE: Well, that is almost like what I said the group is—and that's therapy.

VICTOR: (laughing) Well, all right, but we don't have to call it that.

WORKER: Maybe we ought to hear what the rest of you think because no matter how it was explained when you first came here, the group has a different meaning to you after you've been here awhile.

VICTOR: To me, it's a step to help you.

JONATHON: Oh, ahh. . .

VICTOR: To help you get out and socialize.

JONATHON: You mean to help you mingle with other people until you get enough confidence to be with other people—other than those of us who were in hospitals.

VICTOR: You said it—that's it.

JONATHON: Ah . . . Ah . . . the idea is to be able to have good relations with other people—at home and even with a girl friend.

VICTOR: Yeh, I used to get in a lot of fights. I used to mess up with people even if I wanted them for friends.

DONALD: It's not comfortable any place but here . . . I mean it.

WORKER: Well, how is that?

DONALD: Oh, ah, oh . . . I can't say it.

VICTOR: 'Cause here is no pretense. We don't have to be on our guard. Everybody knows you've been nuts, you know. (Starts to laugh in a nervous manner.)

JEROME: Yeh, we trust each other here.

WORKER: Donald, can you try now to tell us what you wanted to say earlier?

DONALD: Ah . . .no. (Silence) I'm not scared here anymore.

ELAINE: And we are getting better—we're not nuts now.

JEROME: I'd like to have some real friends—I think the group is helping me.

ELAINE: Yeh, that's group therapy.

JONATHON: This group is to help us be more comfortable with others—but that means working on our problems.

ELAINE: Yes, Yes.

The worker summarized what the members had been saying about the purpose of the group and then led them into talking about her role with them. The skill of the worker is demonstrated through her ability to support the group by remaining silent when the members were interacting productively and encouraging the participation of all members and by requesting clarification of feelings.

Through research, both Clemenger and Main learned that the worker's ability to perceive accurately the members' own goals and to formulate treatment goals and plans varied for different members of the group. Clemenger found that a tendency on the part of a worker to stereotype, in a negative way, certain members of a group was related to lack of skill in assessing the members' perceptions of their roles and the group's structure and functioning.[9] Main found that treatment goals and plans for individuals tended to be more fully developed when the worker had made a complete diagnosis of the individual, an assessment of the individual's own goals, and a diagnostic statement of the group's functioning and used himself appropriately with the group. She found that workers tended to develop goals and treatment plans during the first five meetings for those members who had roles that were regarded as important to the group and that they tended to overlook isolates and other less active members of the group.[10]

These findings point up the difficulty, yet the necessity, of focusing on each individual, as well as on the developing group system. The overall purpose for the group, being related to individual and group goals, cannot be furthered fully unless each person's needs are understood.

Some social workers have assumed that a client's right to determine his own goals is limited if the worker has professional goals for individuals and the group and shares these with them. There is evidence, however, that lack of clarity about the worker's goals introduces confusion into the client's perception of what the worker is trying to do. Indeed, Schmidt found that the presence of explicit aims on the part of workers did not deter clients from developing their own objectives. During the sessions, the objectives of each person are communicated to and perceived by the other.[11] In a group, a worker's purpose for individuals and the group is reformulated on the basis of his perceptions of needs, capacities, goals, and environmental circumstances of individuals and those of the group as a unit. The focus of the group experience revolves around a purpose recognized and at least partially accepted by all participants in the process. Members of groups are able to perceive clearly the way in which the worker communicates the purpose of the group to them. Workers are able to develop a high degree of skill in assessing the members' perceptions of the purpose of the group, as it has evolved through group discussion.

STABILIZE MEMBERSHIP

From an aggregate of individuals who lack clarity about who does and who does not belong to the group and who may or may not be admitted to membership, stabilization of membership gradually occurs. In the case of natural groups, the problem is that of inclusion of the worker. Promptness of arrival and regular attendance is important, yet it may take some time to stabilize these patterns. When there is irregularity of attendance, the composition of the group is different each time, and therefore, the group itself is different. The worker's task is to recognize with the members the difference that these factors make. Their individual and group decisions about these matters are important.

The consequences of changes in membership are that the group's progression is decelerated. Paradise asserts that a new member is likely to add to the existing frustrations of the members that are typical of this stage.[12] When possible, it is desirable to delay changes in membership until the struggles for power and control have been addressed. When there are new members, time is taken to orient them to the members and to the group. In addition, they bring their own sets of needs and values into the group, which may be in harmony or conflict with those of the other members. Time must be taken to attempt to integrate them into the group's purpose and culture.

Members who did not attend earlier meetings may have problems about becoming involved in a group. For example, in a group of mothers in a child guidance clinic, Mrs. B. had missed the first two meetings and come late to the third meeting. This interrupted the group's discussion. The worker introduced Mrs. B. to the members and told them that she had prepared Mrs. B. for the group but knows that it always feels uncomfortable to come into an ongoing group. She reviewed how the members had shared with each other their reasons for coming to the clinic. Mrs. B. quickly replied, "But first I have to know why you are all here. You look so normal," with a sigh of relief. The other members took this lightly. One said, "Oh, we found out that we all have our troubles but that doesn't mean we're crazy." Another member added that Mrs. B. looked perfectly normal, too. The worker emphasized that it was true that coming here did not mean that they were abnormal: indeed, to come was a sign of wanting something better for their families and themselves. The feeling of shame and stigma connected with having a child with social and emotional problems runs deep with some parents and they need realistic assurance. Other clients may have similar feelings; often this is true of the mentally ill or physically handicapped, for example. In addition to helping Mrs. B. enter the group, the members were reassured about their strengths and offered hope. Through helping the new member, the purpose of the group became more clear to all of the members.

Stabilization of membership is partly the product of the resolution of problems of ambivalence and resistance on the part of members. Partly, it is the result of greater clarity about the purpose of the group and the organization's policies and procedures concerning membership. Partly, it is sensitivity to cultural values on the part of the worker or some members. In a parent education group, for example, Mrs. G. mentioned that her sons had collected some old aluminum cans. They used the money to buy shoes for school. Last week they made several dollars, which Mrs. G. divided equally between the boys and herself. The worker commented that Mrs. G. might be expecting too much of the boys by expecting them to give her half of their earnings—since they were saving for shoes for school, particularly. Mrs. G. did not respond, and she did not come to the next meeting.

Lasater and Montalvo report that the dropout was occasioned by a clash of cultural values unrecognized by the worker. The comments made by the worker reflected his—not the members' value orientation. Mrs. G. was trying to teach her sons a basic cultural value: in the Mexican-American community, children are taught that sharing, mutual aid, and reciprocity strengthen family relationships and contribute to respect for and dedication to the family. The worker saw the behavior as discouraging the children's independence and exploiting their achievement. Mrs. G. did not make the worker aware of her feelings, choosing instead to withdraw from the group. In her culture, it is as important to respect individual's feelings as it is to express deference to the worker's opinions. The worker should, however, recognize that there are differences in the extent to which people of a particular ethnic group embrace traditional values.[13]

A distinction needs to be made between a person's initial attraction to the group and his continuation after the first one or two meetings. Uncertainty about involvement, if not worked through, often leads to withdrawal from the group.

In all forms of treatment, there is considerable discontinuance against the judgment of the practitioner. If a group is to benefit its members, they must remain in it long enough to be influenced by it. Some of the reasons for discontinuance are lack of clarity about the purpose and means to be used in working toward it, problems of inclusion and acceptance, deviation from the group in some important way, cultural dissonance, complications arising out of subgroup formation, early provocateurs, inability to share the practitioner, and inadequate orientation to the situation.[14] Other reasons for discontinuance are environmental obstacles such as lack of transportation or child care, work schedules that interfere with the time of the sessions, and lack of material resources. Thus, it is crucial that the worker take sufficient time to explore the meaning of membership through discussions within the group or, in some instances, through interviews with individuals outside the group.

The social worker does many small things to stabilize membership. She helps members to know who belongs, follows up on absences, works separately with some members around their ambivalence toward continuation at times when such help does not seem appropriate in the group, and discusses openly some of the members' attitudes toward each other and their effect on group belongingness. Lonergan has elaborated on many techniques that can be used to encourage attendance.[15] These include using relationship, emphasizing the special ways the group can help, taking the person's reluctance seriously and discussing it, reaching out to members who are absent, expressing pleasure when members tell the worker something positive, encouraging them to bring problems into the group, and expecting people to attend, emphasizing that attendance will help them.

In natural groups, the worker engages the members in a problem-solving process concerning the inclusion and exclusion of members, making clear the organization's values and procedures about this matter. In all groups, he continues to get facts about and evaluate the impact of individuals on each other and on the development of the group. There may be instances in which, in spite of every effort, the composition of the group is faulty and some decision about changing the membership should be made, through the addition of new members or the withdrawal of old members. In some groups, there is a difficult combination of people with personality patterns who cannot be helped to fit together or in which membership is too heterogeneous for compatibility. In other instances, there are competing subgroups that cannot develop a working relationship and become part of the group. Decisions to add or drop members in order to correct faulty composition need to be based on accurate assessment and thoughtful planning, rather than on the operation of the acceptance-rejection process in an unacknowledged way.

INFLUENCE STATUS AND ROLES

During this stage of group development, the structure of interpersonal relationships emerges. Out of the process of ranking, described earlier, leadership emerges in the group. Certain members exert more than average influence upon the purpose and activities of the group. Leadership changes dynamically with the changing needs and conditions of the group. All members can be ranked in terms of the degree of influence they exert upon the activities of the group. All things being equal, leadership tends to be situational; that is, it tends to alter according to changing individual and group needs. Leadership is usually a shared phenomenon, rather than a constant role of a particular member. Even so, some members will have more influence than others will. Influence is power; that conflict and competition for power will exist among the members is to be expected, just as conflict will exist about the worker's power. There is some correlation between individual factors that enable a person to exert influence and group factors that acknowledge, recognize, or tolerate that influence. Some members may do little but follow others. Certain indigenous leadership roles may become relatively stable in certain members, or they may be performed by different members of the group at different times, as the members expect certain attitudes and behaviors from them.

The reciprocal roles of initiator and follower are especially puzzling in relation to contagion, a particular type of social interaction marked by the spontaneous imitation by other members of a feeling or behavior initiated by one member of the group. The initiator, without conscious intent, starts the ball rolling, or a pattern of action simply seems to "spread like wildfire." In their research, Polansky, Lippitt, and Redl found that the initiator of the action has a status in the group that makes other members susceptible to his influence. In this particular form of influence, the recipient's behavior changes to become more like that of the initiator, even though the initiator does not overtly communicate his intent to evoke such a change.[16] The susceptible members often perform in ways they would ordinarily resist quite easily; an unconscious process of identification seems to be operating. The followers, who imitate the behavior patterns, have identified with the initiator. The basis for identification may be similar etiologic needs or a response to latent emotional tensions. It is difficult for an individual to be immune to an emotional infection when the content or cause is antithetic to the individual's intellectual convictions. In addition to the status of the initiator, other factors seem to influence contagion: the affinity of the behavior to the group's norms; the commonality of the basic expressional trend; the size, structure, organization, and content of the group; and the cohesiveness and climate of the group.

Two major types of roles emerge in groups—task roles and socioemotional roles. Task roles contribute to the achievement of the group's agreed-upon goals. Some socioemotional roles contribute to the development of positive relationships among the members; others place certain members in precarious positions in the group and detract from the group's effectiveness in moving toward its goals.

Many patterns of behavior, often referred to as task roles, have been identified by Bales and Slater, Benne and Sheats, and Coyle.[17] The task may be personal problem solving or decision making for corporate action. Each group varies in the particular ways that contributions are made toward achieving a task. An information or opinion seeker asks for information pertinent to the situation and for clarification of suggestions and opinions. An opposite role is that of the information or opinion giver who offers facts, generalizations, experiences, or opinions pertinent to the experience in which the group is engaged. A particular member may be able to express feelings that stimulate others to do likewise or seek out the feelings of others in the group. Another member may typically initiate or suggest a new activity, issue, or means of working on a problem. An elaborator is one who develops further the feelings expressed or the suggestions of others, in terms of examples, meanings, or consequences of a proposal. A coordinator reconciles the various points of view or coordinates the activities of subgroups. A critic forms and expresses judgments of other members, things, or the group functioning; or he may question or evaluate the logic or feasibility of a proposal. Other such patterns of behavior may be specified such as the teacher or demonstrator of activities, the spokesman for the group, the procedures technician, and the recorder.

These patterns of behavior may or may not stabilize into roles in the sense that the particular members are expected to behave in this way regularly. Variability, not consistency, is the rule. Remember that individuals have many different interchanges with other people each day, and it is only when a person seems routinely and consistently to behave in a way toward others, and others toward him, that a role relationship can be said to exist. Even within institutional role arrangements, there is usually much room for flexibility in meeting the expectations.

Other role behaviors are oriented toward the socioemotional needs of the members of the group. There may be an encourager who praises, gives support, reassurance, or acceptance of the contributions of others. A harmonizer senses the differences between members, attempts to reconcile disagreements, and relieves tension in difficult situations. A member may tend to go along with the group, passively accepting and using the ideas of others and quietly supporting other members of the group. In a good-humored way, the tension releaser jokes, laughs, and shows enthusiasm for the group and its activities. The ego-ideal, who embodies the group's values, becomes an object for identification.

Perhaps more fascinating and more perplexing are the varied role behaviors that members assume or those that they are forced to adopt, which are related to the satisfaction of the participant's or the group's particular, often unconscious, needs. In some of these situations, the role is assumed by a person, predominantly as an expression of his own emotional needs. It is necessary to keep in mind, however, that there is always some interaction between individual and group needs in the creation and persistence of such role behaviors.

Among the patterns of role behaviors that develop in a group, Konopka describes the isolate as one that is of special concern to the social worker.[18] An isolate is one who lacks bonds with fellow human beings; isolation is a relative concept, for it is impossible to be completely separate from other human beings. All isolates are not the same or in similar positions in a group. Isolation may be temporary or lasting, forced or voluntary. When one is a stranger in a new group, temporary isolation is normal and to be expected, for there is always some ambivalence about joining a group and some toward newcomers on the part of older members. Some people can develop bonds with others in new situations much more easily and rapidly than others can. Another type of isolation is psychological withdrawal from the group. Instead of finding a place in the group, some members withdraw, owing perhaps to lack of interest but often owing to fear of the group.

Some persons are isolates because the group makes them so by rejecting them. One reason might be that an isolate deviates so far from the values of the group that members cannot understand him. An example would be that of a boy who was a model and an intellectual in a group of nonconformists and nonachievers in school. Another reason might be that an isolate may attempt to break through the usual initial isolation in ways that are inappropriate. With the rejected isolate, a vicious cycle is set up. He usually wants and needs affection; because he fails to receive it, he becomes troubled and hostile, he feels guilty because of his hostility, and he experiences a great sense of insecurity about his position in the group. The members do not give him the positive responses he hopes for; in a psychological sense, he does not become a member of the group.

Few members of a group are in such desperate situations as the rejected isolate is, and yet others may not truly belong to the group. Some members are fringers or near isolates who feel some minimum acceptance and desire to belong, yet are not quite of the group. They often, however, need the group so badly that they do not seek to withdraw from it.

The role of scapegoat is one that causes distress to the person in the role and to the worker confronted with such a phenomenon in the group. Scapegoating involves the simultaneous infliction of pain on its victims and a threat to the group's morale.[19] The members turn their aggression onto another member who becomes a symbol of some tendency or characteristic they dislike in themselves and on whom they project their hositilty and thus protect themselves from recognizing their own unacceptable tendencies and freeing themselves from guilty feelings. It is one way to avoid conflict. When a group has a scapegoat, a relatively stable equilibrium is achieved. The scapegoat performs a valuable function in channeling group tensions and in providing a basis for group solidarity. The fact that a scapegoat is not necessarily present continuously suggests that his presence bears a relation to the sense of security of the members. The scapegoat is usually one from whom the others do not fear retaliation.

At a third meeting of a group of early adolescent girls, the following incident occurred.

> After Jean and Johanna expressed their likes and dislikes, Jean instructed Gloria to speak next. She said, "My name is Gloria S. I'm not too tall." Johanna interrupted by laughing loudly. I told Johanna that she had had her turn—now it was Gloria's turn. Gloria continued, "I have black hair, I wear glasses, I'm kinda fat." Jean and Johanna laughed in unison. Johanna said, "kinda fat—you're real fat." Gloria joined in with the laughter. I intervened ineffectively by suggesting that Gloria would look strange if she were as tall as she is now, but as thin as you are, Johanna. Johanna was offended. Gloria continued to tell us about herself. Johanna rudely interjected, "And what size shoes do you wear?" Gloria answered, "size 9." Johanna yelled, "You got big feet!" "I can't help it," answered Gloria, laughing. Jean and Johanna are close friends, who have serious problems in relationships, lack self-esteem, and tend to project their own feelings onto others. Their dominance, combined with Gloria's needs to agree and laugh at their hostile statements, set the stage for Gloria to become the group's scapegoat.

When there is a scapegoat, a two-way transactional etiology is seen, at both individual and group levels. The scapegoat adapts to the situation through defensive maneuvers: the primary dynamic is often, however, the group's need to place a person in such a role.

Still other role behaviors seem to be clearly directed toward meeting the emotional needs of a particular member of a group in a way that is not helpful to the group, either in maintaining itself or in accomplishing its purpose. These patterns of behavior are varied, according to the needs and problems of the members of the group.

There is often a clown, who seeks acceptance by offering himself up to be laughed at. The main purpose of clowning seems to be to relieve one's own tensions by breaking the tension of others and getting their amused attention. There is usually, however, an undercurrent of contempt for oneself and for the other members.

The monopolizer is another dysfunctional role common in group situations. The monopolizer feels compelled to hold the center of the stage, becoming anxious when anyone else is the center of attention. The pattern tends to be self-perpetuating since the more the monopolist talks, the more he senses the irritation of others. This makes him talk all the more. He is afraid to stop for fear that other members will attack him. Unconsciously he hopes that by continuing to talk he can appease or divert the group. Members often react through silence.

A person in the role of aggressor may be present in some groups. He may work in many ways to deflate the status of others or to attack the group or its efforts toward achievement. Members may also have other roles referred to by such labels as gossip or bully. Once a member is selected as a deviant, there tends to be a circular reaction that perpetuates the role assignment, and a vicious circle is thus set in motion.

What the social worker does in supporting or influencing a change in roles depends upon his evaluation of the meaning of the role to the individual and to the group. Generally, he promotes flexibility in role structure so that members may experience varied ways of contributing to the group and testing out their capacities. His supportive comments and actions are directed toward encouraging members to try out new ways of communicating more effectively with others or toward recognizing and modifying inappropriate patterns of behavior. Usually his activities are directed both to the person in the role and to the group. The development of basic trust, through acceptance and empathy, is essential.

With a fearful and shy isolate, great gentleness is required in efforts to involve him with the group. Since behavioral patterns often become stable quite early and other members tend to respond in stereotyped ways, efforts need to be made to secure early involvement. Discovering some interest of the isolate, recognizing his feelings, guiding the discussion or activity so that success is probable, and avoiding questions that tend to elicit defensiveness are examples of techniques to be tried. Sometimes a period of focus on a simple activity that provides for freedom of expression and that stimulates undemanding relationships with others is useful. Preparation of refreshments, hand arts, and noncompetitive games are other examples.

Involvement of an isolate in role playing may be the key that unlocks spontaneity and brings him into participation with others, as in the example reported by Ganter.

> An illustration is a group of boys and girls in a child guidance center. For the first two sessions, one eight-year-old boy, Jimmy, did not talk or enter into the activities of the group, in spite of the worker's efforts to help him to do so. During the third session, the children were playing school. Tommy had mentioned that he was in a sight-saving class, and the others wondered what that was like. The children were playing school, with Tommy as the teacher. He wanted Jimmy to play, because Jimmy was the only other member who wore glasses. The worker suggested that Tommy make Jimmy a pupil, even though he stayed across the room. In the role of teacher, Tommy asked Jimmy a question. When Jimmy did not answer, the other children became impatient. One boy said that Jimmy was "dumb." All eyes turned toward Jimmy. The worker went over to Jimmy, took him by the hand, and brought him into the group. All the other children watched, quietly. Tommy resumed the class. He soon came around again to Jimmy, who looked down at the floor. Kenny called him "dumb" again. The children looked at Jimmy, and in the silence that followed, Jimmy made the first break in his withdrawal. He began to cry. The worker put her arm around Jimmy, comforted him, and told him that he was coming here to get help with the things that made him cry. She asked the other children if they would take time out from playing school to talk to Jimmy. In the ensuing discussion of the things that hurt them, Jimmy was able to stay with the group.[20]

When the developing role behavior is destructive to the group, as well as to the individual, as in the case of a monopolizer, early efforts of the worker may be directed toward encouraging spread of participation among all the members through stating this pattern as an expectation, requesting that members take turns, giving nonverbal encouragement to others to enter the discussion or activity, or using comments that summarize so as to encourage others to enter into the conversation. At the same time, the worker accepts the monopolizer. Since talking is often an attempt to deal with anxiety, the anxiety rises if the person is attacked by others, which sets in motion a cycle of increased talking. If the worker can convey interest in the monopolizer, attend to him, and suggest how he can participate effectively, the cycle might be broken.

Often limits need to be set in a supportive way, through requests to give others a chance to participate or to wait until others have expressed themselves. If the pattern becomes established, the worker may then use direct means to clarify what the problem is, what its meaning is to the person and the group, what members do to perpetuate the situation, and how they might work it out together. He engages the group in discussion to illuminate the process going on among the members.

With a scapegoat, the worker uses herself in similar ways, first indirectly to avoid getting members trapped into roles. Then, if the role becomes stereotyped, she works directly toward clarification of the conditions that led to scapegoating, analysis of the stresses in the group that result in this projection of hostilities onto a particular member, and isolation of the actions the scapegoat performs to provoke it. She makes use of the procedure of illumination of the group process. Often, the more supportive interventions are used first, for the members may not yet be ready to work toward clarification of the meaning of such behavior. Later, attention can be given to motivational factors.

In intervening to change roles that are painful to a member or that threaten the stability and progress of the group, the worker needs to check his own responses to the situation. He may come to recognize that he has strong countertransference reactions. In scapegoating, for example, he may feel strongly that injustice has been inflicted on a weak victim by cruel aggressors so that he defends and protects the scapegoat. He may align himself with the scapegoat against the group and be unable, therefore, to accept and empathize with those members and serve as a mediator. Or if a worker is identified with the group and its anger toward the scapegoat, he may support the group in its attack on the individual. Shulman puts it this way: the worker needs "to be with both clients at precisely the same time . . . the anger directed toward the scapegoat is often a signal of the hurt and confusion felt by the group members."[21] To remember that the scapegoat symbolizes some of the attacking members' problems with self-esteem, identity, and displaced anger helps the worker to focus his interventions. As in any dysfunctional role, the problem is a result of the interaction between the person in the role and the needs of the group. The worker needs to be able to accept and empathize with all members and to focus on the common feelings and problems. As members are ready to do so, he helps them to recognize the patterns of behavior and their common and divergent feelings and assists them to find ways of problem solving.

When members become stereotyped into a role, they tend to become known by the label given them, and other contributions they might make to the group are ignored. Regardless of their desires, such persons become typed and stuck in a particular role. The role into which they are cast affects their perceptions of what they can and connot do and, thus, their self-esteem. Hartford suggests that the role of the worker may be "to reinforce these roles which are consistent with group organization and the pursuit of group goals, and to discourage those which are hindering individual and group development for the benefit of each.[22]

In whatever the dysfunctional role, a worker may use two major types of intervention, depending upon how well established the role. When the role is not yet firmly established, the worker may use indirect means to help the member not to get stuck in the role and to help the other members not to trap that person into a negative role. These techniques include the strong use of support, including encouraging participation of all in discussion or activity, approving a norm of acceptance and concern for each member, and using activities that involve the threatened member in positive ways. Once a member has become stereotyped into a negative role, however, such interventions are insufficient. The worker needs to become active in directly confronting the group with the situation and moving the discussion toward clarifying the process that led to the establishment of such a role. Roles are reciprocal: the worker needs to assess and attend to both the person in the role and the other members; both individual and group play a part in creating and maintaining the situation. The group needs, therefore, to examine its own process in efforts to change the attitudes and patterns of behavior of all the members.

In the initial stage, the norms of the group were primarily those initiated by the worker and reinforced by his interventions. Now, a primary task is to develop a group culture that will transform a collectivity into a growth-promoting social system. The group needs to develop its own norms. As the members interact over the issues of power and acceptance, a code of norms develops. As this happens, the members move toward self-control and sharing responsibility for their group: they acquire power. The desired norms are those that make it possible for the dynamic positive forces to operate. As was noted in the last chapter, those norms include freedom of expression, an open structure of communication, mutual acceptance and mutual aid, and motivation for goal achievement.

The social worker influences the development of norms primarily as a model-setting participant who demonstrates empathy, a search for understanding of what is going on, and confidence in the group process. She also influences norms by supporting certain behaviors and withholding support for other behaviors, making suggestions, pointing out that a norm has been developed, and engaging the group in problem-solving processes concerning how certain conflicts should be resolved.

Interventions of the worker may be directed toward helping the group itself to recognize norms as these become evident. The worker may do this in a variety of ways: by calling the members' attention to the fact that they are doing things in a certain way or that they now seem to have agreed upon a norm, for example, about confidentiality. He may raise questions that help the members to decide upon norms for the group. Such simple questions as "Do we want to cut off discussion like that?" and "Did you intend to suggest that we do it this way?" or "Is there a better way to work on this?" help to clarify norms of behavior. Gradual clarification of differences in expectations for the group as different from those of other groups to which members belong is often crucial. Adaptation requires that a person be able to distinguish the norms suitable in one situation from those suitable elsewhere. Members may often be confused about conflicting expectations. A common example is that of a norm that encourages the expression of angry feelings in a social work group and the expectation that these be suppressed at school or at work. Difficulties occur when the members fail to distinguish between what is appropriate in the group and what is appropriate in other situations.

Interventions of the worker may focus on teaching the members how to find better ways of relating to each other through setting limits and giving information. An example is of a group of girls who lack tolerance for frustration. Limits were necessary because the girls often got into situations in which they could injure themselves or other people. In one early session, the members fought over scissors that needed to be shared. "They kicked each other, spat, cursed, and behaved in almost ungovernable fashion." The worker did not lecture about breaking a rule, almost universally ineffective. Rather she stopped the group's activity, said she recognized their angry feelings, and when the members had quieted down, said she would like to tell them what some children do when they want to use the same scissors. She described such alternatives as drawing straws, working in pairs, taking turns, or talking about the problem and making a decision they could all live with. The girls said they would draw straws now. The worker used this approach repeatedly until the girls learned to plan ahead to make decisions.

Development of norms about the distribution of power and control is essential to the group's further development. When desirable, the worker tries to influence the modification of agency rules that affect the group adversely. Hartford found that overly restrictive regulations often contributed to the failure of a group to form.[23] The worker permits the testing of rules and policies, recognizing that as a right of the members, but he also maintains appropriate limits on behavior. Members learn to take control as the worker turns issues back to the group and clarifies their right to determine certain matters.

At the sixth meeting of a group of adults coping with the demands of community living following hospitalization for mental disorders, all the members came early, with the exception of Mrs. J.

> I opened the meeting by saying, "I made a mistake last week." The response was "What mistake?" "What do you mean?" I explained, "Last

> week I told you that the group could decide whether you wanted to meet at 6:30 or at 7:00 o'clock. All of you wanted to begin at 6:30, except for Mrs. J., who wanted to begin at 7:00. I said that then we would begin at 6:45. I took the decision away from you, didn't I?" Mr. G. gave me a knowing smile and said, "Oh, that's all right." Miss L. said, "That's just how it happened. I don't mind." I said, "but you have a right to mind." Mrs. J. said that the extra fifteen minutes made so much difference to her in getting here on time. Mr. P. said, with a grin, "I kind of thought that's how it was." In the guise of good humor and tolerance, the members continued to talk about their annoyance. They wanted to hear me say over and over again that they could be angry with me and that I had made a mistake in not really letting them decide when the group would meet.

The worker explained that she wanted to make her statement very positively because most of the members have been afraid to express feelings and differences, yet they have covert anger directed at Mrs. J. because she has maneuvered decisions and monopolized the discussion. Some of the subtle anger was directed at the worker for falling in with Mrs. J.'s maneuvers to get the time changed. Through bringing this matter into the group, the worker supported the norm that the members have power to make certain decisions, to be open with each other, and to be free to express feelings and concerns.

Groups need to establish norms that deal with differences in values concerning what proper behavior is. At the beginning, the tendency is to seek commonality and avoid facing differences. True acceptance from others comes, however, from recognition of both similarities and differences. In a group of older adults,

> Mrs. P. vividly described her visit to a nursing home. The conditions were disgusting. The patients were lying in their own feces. She would never place her husband in a nursing home no matter what. Mrs. S., who had been checking nursing homes for her husband, looked panicked. The worker said that social workers are available to help with placements and that, while we are all aware of some horror stories, there are some good nursing homes. Mrs. N. said that she was determined to take her husband home, virtually at any cost. The members kept trying to establish the norm that "virtuous people took their relatives home": people who did not do so were bad.[24]

In such instances, the worker needs to engage the members in further work to accept the norm that what is a good decision for one member may not be for another—that different situations require different solutions. He does this through supporting differences, providing information, problem solving, and using such environmental resources as visits to rest homes.

Conflicts about norms often deal with whether expression is preferable to inhibition of feelings and experiences and whether only positive expression is allowable instead of free expression of hostilities and differences. When a group code develops, it takes over to some extent the internalization of standards of behavior. Members test and come to trust that they can express their feelings and bring problems into the group without suffering rejection, punishment, or other severe consequences. In a group of adolescent girls in a residential setting, the girls confessed that they had violated a strict rule. The worker listened to the full story and then responded in a nonpunitive manner, which led to discussion of the rule and consensus that the particular rule was necessary for the protection of the girls themselves. The organization's rule became a group norm.

Through the interaction of members, influenced by certain actions by the worker, norms develop in the group. Through a process of negotiation, a unique normative system develops. Norms, initially specified and supported by the worker, have become internalized. A culture has been created that is unique to the particular group.

RESOLVE CONFLICT

Differences among members in their need to defend themselves from facing their problems, or in their uncertainty about the means through which the group can be helpful, may lead to conflict in the group. Some members will be ready to move into the use of the group for focused problem solving earlier than others will. An illustration is taken from a record of a third meeting of a group of adult men in a hospital.

> For the first time, there was expression of deep feeling by Mr. B. and Mr. P. concerning their inability to return to full-time employment owing to physical handicaps. Mr. C. and Mr. S., with more optimistic prognoses for work, empathized with them. Another severely handicapped patient, Mr. M., became restless and then wise cracked, "Who wants to work anyway—only fools, not me." And Mr. D. quipped, "Yeh, a life of Riley's what I want." The four men who had been discussing seriously what it means to a man to be unable to work, looked taken aback. Mr. B., who had emerged as a leader in this group, told Mr. M. and Mr. D. to: "Cut out the wisecracks. You know this is no joke," but the two men continued their behavior. The atmosphere became heated. Mr. D. challenged, "Who are you to tell me what to do?" Mr. M. echoed the challenge. I said that we seem to be fighting about who has the power now. There was a silence: all eyes were riveted on

> me. I commented that perhaps it was hard to talk about what their lives might be like when they leave the hospital. Most members seemed ready to do this: could the others give them a chance? The facetious remarks stopped, but it took some time before Mr. M. and Mr. D. were able to verbalize some of their fears and problems about illness and return to their families and communities. The group was then able to make a decision about a few problems that seemed most pressing to all of them and to use the group for working on these concerns. This meeting marked a transition for this group into the next stage of development.

The social worker facilitated the use of group processes by supporting expressions of empathy, feelings, and concerns among the members. Although recognizing the need of some members to defend themselves from facing their physical limitations, he allowed one member to confront the disturbing behavior of two others, allowing conflict to emerge in the open. He interpreted the basis for the differences as a power conflict and then moved to universalize the fears that interfered with some members' readiness to move into working on the group's task. A suggestion that all members try to focus on the problem led the group into productive decision making.

In work with disturbed children, discussion is difficult because they lack the requisite skills and are well defended against looking at their own involvement in situations. They tend to react to discussion of their part in situations as an attack on them. They use denial, conscious lying, distortion, and projection when they attempt to discuss what happened. They often get into physical fights with each other. An example is of an activity therapy group of six boys, aged eight to eleven, whose members share similar behavioral problems. They have low tolerance for frustration, act impulsively, have unreliable controls, and use action as a dominant means of communication. They live in a poverty-stricken community where deprivation and crime pervade all aspects of life. All of them have been subjected to inconsistent child-parent relationships in families in which parents have been unable to provide essential material resources, guidance, and protection. They experience marked deprivation at all levels; the harsh handling and brutality they experience at home are reinforced in the streets and, to a lesser extent, in their schools. The group worker has an assistant, Ramiro.

> The worker records. Darrell was acting out continuously. He accidentally hit Larry in the eye. Larry started to cry. Ramiro and I ran to him and Ramiro took him out to get a cold compress. When they returned, Larry was angry and wanted to fight Darrell. I pulled them apart and told them they could fight with words—not with their fists. Larry began to attack me and everyone else, through angry words. I

guided him to a chair and told him to sit and rest. He came grudgingly. I gently told him that when he gets angry he loses sight of the reason and begins attacking everyone. He was listening, as were most of the other members. I told him that I know it is hard when he feels angry and hurt and wants to hurt back, but that doesn't make it better and I would like to help him find a better way. He did not respond.

Later, Gregg accidentally knocked into Larry. Larry smacked him, and Gregg cried. Ramiro and I called all of the boys over and asked how we could help Gregg and Larry. There was no response. I wondered if they could say what was bothering them today. The members accused Ramiro and me of being late for the meeting. We said that was true and it was O.K. to be angry with us, but why take it out on each other. I clarified, "If you get angry that's all right, but you need to fight with words—not fists." Joseph said, "o.k., mother fucker." The boys were silently waiting for my response. I asked calmly, "What's not so good about that name, mother fucker?" The boys seemed shocked that I repeated the words but did not respond verbally. Although I wanted them to discuss the matter, it was time for the meeting to end, so I said, "Curse words don't help express what you're feeling; they don't say what's wrong." I told them we would return to talking about how we express anger next time.

In this record, the social worker accepted expressions of anger and also placed firm limits on destructive behavior, distinguishing between verbal expression and action. He avoided taking sides in the conflict, encouraged particular members and the group to evaluate their own behavior, gave advice about better ways to deal with anger, offered clarifications of the nature of the behavior, and interpreted its meaning. He fostered a norm of mutual aid by requesting that the group help two of its members, a suggestion for which the members were not ready. Although several interventions were directed to one or two members, there was clear recognition of the responses of all to the content. Very slowly do such members take the step of substituting angry verbal outbursts for physical action, and it is only much later that talking becomes a tool for problem solving.

Early detection of uncertainty and stress makes it possible for the worker to help members to acknowledge and deal with the differences among them before a crisis occurs. The worker's comments and questions may be directed toward the ventilation of feelings, full exploration of the sources of conflict and different views about how the conflict developed, and parceling of the issues to make solutions possible. Rather than take sides, the worker supports all factions by giving concrete assistance in finding means of exploring and resolving the differences. By finding some rationale for the various views expressed, he is more likely to help each side communicate with each other. Open communication often leads from accusatory comments such as "You did so say that" to "What was it you meant to say?"

The worker steps in to regulate conflict when it is too threatening to one or more members of the group or when it threatens the very continuance of the group itself. She may do this through placing a direct limit on a member or the group. She may point out the self-defeating aspects of behavior. Without being punitive and by conveying empathic understanding, she may confront the members involved with the unacceptability of the behavior and the need to stop it. Attention to supporting the group in its efforts to deal with conflict and to accrediting each bit of progress in working through the testing of relationships and use of the group is essential. Continuous evaluation of the members' capacity to handle conflict and acting on the basis of this evaluation are not easy, but there really are no easy answers.

Conflict is an important ingredient in development and change. It can indeed be destructive in its impact on oneself, other members of the group, or the organization. Yet, it can also be a constructive building force in groups. Conflict, if worked through, may lead to enhanced understanding and consequent strengthening of relationships among members because differences are aired and not allowed to remain irritatingly below the surface. It provides stimulation toward new ways of thinking and feeling. Only as areas of disagreement are explored do areas of agreement also become clarified. Efforts to deny differences and to suppress conflicts are unsuccessful over the long run; such devices lead to stagnation, dysfunction, or disintegration of the system. Unity in diversity is a value that recognizes differences, uses them to strengthen the group, and makes it possible for conflicts to be resolved through democratic processes. Mutual acceptance, open communication, and respect for differences enable members to deal with the conflicts so characteristic of the human condition.

All is not seriousness in a group: moments of fun and spontaneity contribute to the development of relationships and cohesion. A simple example is of an outpatient therapy group in the psychiatric unit of a medical center.

> The members were coming into the room and beginning to sit down. As usual, I waited a little before taking my seat so that members could have some choice of seating. The last member to enter, Mr. G., said, "Here we are sitting in the same chairs," I suddenly said, "Yes, . . . the same chairs . . . why don't we just all change chairs?" Everybody smiled and started crossing back and forth between the chairs—it was like children playing upset the fruit basket. There was a lighthearted feeling; the members all looked around the circle and smiled; and it was as though they had laid down their troubles and felt their burden lightened.

This brief activity, directed to the entire group, produced a multiplicity of little changes. All of a sudden, people seemed more relaxed; there was more interaction in that meeting than ever before. Toward the end of the meeting, several members commented on how much we had accomplished after changing chairs. The incident certainly facilitated interaction among the members, but it also demonstrated to these mentally ill adults that they can learn to enjoy other people. As Maier has pointed out, "in moments of playfulness, clients find an added capacity to deal with heretofore unmanageable events."[25]

While recognizing with the members some of their interpersonal conflicts, the worker guides discussion and other activity toward some strong common interests or concerns. She emphasizes similarities and positives, as well as differences and negatives. She has a responsibility to provide new opportunities for participating in experiences that have the potential for testing and strengthening relationships, identifying common concerns and capacities, or affirming preferences and making decisions. The use of activity-oriented experiences, as well as discussion, will have much merit with some groups. For members to explore capacities and relationships, test out the authority of the worker, and identify common and divergent norms, there must be a real situation in which the persons can be truly ego-involved and act out the meaning of these objectives. The action is upon a stage where the chips are not down, where a mistake can be retrieved, where amends can be made.

WORK BEYOND THE GROUP

Conferences with individuals are an integral part of the social worker's practice with groups. The worker's use of himself in interaction with the group is, in one sense, the essence of social work practice with groups. Yet the worker is extremely limited if he views this as the only means of treatment. He often works directly, on a one-to-one basis, with some members or with a parent, spouse, or other person of importance in the life of the member.

There are brief interviews between the worker and a member within the life space of the group, which Redl refers to as life space interviews.[26] Such interviews are held immediately before, after, or even during a group session. The member may seek out the worker or the conference may be initiated by the worker, usually when his particular concern about a member is not likely to be brought into the orbit of the group session itself.

Sometimes conflict between a member and other members of the group becomes so intense and the group is so unready to handle it that private conferences may be necessary.

In one group in a community center, for example, Janice complained about the recreational staff; she thought they picked on her, disliked her, and blamed her for things that were not her fault. Kathy criticized Janice for not being able to say anything good about anybody, and other members agreed with Kathy. Janice angrily turned her chair to the wall, sat there for awhile, and then left the room, slamming the door behind her. The other members were very upset. The worker acknowledged with them some of their feelings. She suggested the group continue its planning with the assistant leader while she went to see if Janice was still in the building so she could talk with her and help her return to the group. She found Janice sitting in the lobby, crying. In a brief conference, the worker said she knew that Janice was troubled about the number of things that seemed to make it hard for her to get along in the group. After some discussion, Janice responded to the worker's suggestion that she return to the group to try to work things out there. This was done.

The important skill is to use such brief interviews to meet the immediate needs of the person, yet not detract from the group itself as the primary means of service. A great deal of analytical judgment is necessary to decide wisely whether to deal with the concern privately with the member or to encourage the person to bring the concern into the group. The skilled worker can often find ways to relate what seems like a unique problem to the concerns of the group, through searching for likeness in seemingly unlike situations.

Interviews with members of the group, or other persons in their behalf, often take place in privacy, usually by appointment. Such interviews are used for several purposes. One is to orient and prepare new members for making a satisfactory initial entry into an open-ended group. Another purpose is to help a member to cope more effectively with a pressing problem that seems unsuitable for discussion within the group at a particular time, owing either to the situation in the group or to the fact that, at the time, the person cannot bear to express feelings and thoughts or to present a problem to the group. A conference may enable the person to bring it into the group or may indicate that individual or family treatment is necessary. In groups in which certain responsibilities have been assigned to officers or committees, a conference may be used to aid such persons to fulfill their responsibilities as effectively as possible.

Another common purpose of the interview is to refer a member to another service in the community for forms of assistance that cannot be provided through the group or the agency or to provide special support to a member as she gets connected with a special service. Knowledge of social, health, and educational organizations in the community is necessary for effective referrals—knowledge of their functions, auspices, concepts of service, and interrelationshsips. Referrals to employment services, social clubs, work training programs, health and medical care, or religious organizations should be part of treatment if members are to be helped to function at or nearer to their full capacities. When the member has enough confidence and skill to handle the situation herself, the worker supports her in doing this, for the principle is that the worker supports the person's ego functioning by strengthening her ability to handle her own affairs. Sometimes the worker needs to mediate between the client and the desired service so that the client does not get lost between slots of agency functions and policies. It may mean explaining the member's goals, problems, capacities, and special needs to appropriate staff in the new organization. It may mean giving considerable assistance to help a member to understand the intake procedures and to make concrete plans for the first encounter. Successful referral involves clarification of the specific needs or problems, motivation to initiate an application, and follow-through procedures.

Lack of resources and conditions in the community often make it difficult for clients to function effectively. Some persons need to be taught to use available resources. The lack of use of resources is sometimes striking: a group of mothers never thought of using a park within walking distance of their housing project; an adolescent with an infected finger did not think of going to a nearby clinic; a mother had not thought of applying for a special nutrition program for her children. Such failures to use resources may stem from lack of knowledge about the resources and how to use them or from fear and distrust.

The social worker may help groups to take direct action in behalf of their members when this is appropriate to the purpose of the group and is within the function of the agency. Although the focus is on action that will directly benefit the members themselves, broader social change may also be the outcome of such efforts. Practitioners also have a responsibility to note facts about policies and conditions that need to be changed and to report these facts to appropriate persons within the agency, the professional organization, or community planning and action bodies.

Social workers need to remind themselves that a group does not exist in a vacuum, that it is part of a larger social system encompassing the agency, the families of the members, and the community. The means of achieving improved psychosocial functioning are indeed partly with the individuals and group interaction. But working with the environment is crucial also, for the environment supports or impedes the person's or family's efforts. Concrete needs of members must often be met; relatives must often be involved in appropriate ways. A family- and neighborhood-centered approach is preferable, wherever possible.[27] A social worker serves as a bridge between the members, their families, and the community. He may refer members to other resources; then he may participate with other organizations serving the family to ensure that all efforts in behalf of the family are meshed for its benefit. He may make use of his observations of unmet needs in calling these to the attention of appropriate social planning and action bodies. He may actively participate in community efforts to make the environment work for people.

A COHESIVE GROUP EMERGES

If all has gone well, a social worker has a group with the characteristics that make it a potent force in the lives of its members. The members have delineated goals for themselves that are in harmony with the group purposes. They have come to accept each other sufficiently to want to continue together. They have given up some of their earlier self-centered attitudes and behavior, or overdependency on the worker, and moved into a relationship of interdependence. They have developed some understanding and acceptance of the worker's role in relation to their roles in the group. They have accepted a norm of experimentation and flexibility and of responsibility for both supporting each other and stimulating each other toward the achievement of individual and group goals. They have come to some acceptance of a set of norms through which necessary control is effectuated within a general climate of acceptance of difference.

Essentially, what has emerged is what Henry calls a group with a contract, in which the agreements about the group hold among all of the members with each other and with the worker.[28] Considerable evidence from research exists to demonstrate the importance of such agreement. Garvin has reported that "the existence of the 'contract'. . . is an important correlate of worker activity and group movement."[29] Brown found that early attention by the worker to the problem of mutual expectations seems to produce reductions in the amount of time spent in testing, allowing the groups to move to their work more rapidly.[30] And, from a review of research, Yalom concluded that "anxiety stemming from unclarity of the group task, process, and role expectations in the early meetings of the group may, in fact, be a deterrent to effective therapy."[31]

A major outcome of the process of exploration and testing is that considerable congruence is achieved between each member's perception of the group and the worker's perception of it. Members of groups usually have come to perceive quite clearly the activities of the worker in contributing to the members and the group as a whole. The analytic skills of the worker have been translated into accurate judgments about the perceptions that members have of the functioning of the group and the worker's role in it. Group cohesiveness has developed, defined most simply as attraction to the group, referring to the forces binding members of a group to each other and to the group.[32] In a cohesive group, the dynamic therapeutic forces are free to operate so that the members use the group for more intensive work on their needs and problems in psychosocial functioning.

11

Stage III: Mutuality and Work

IN the third stage of group development, the group is a cohesive one in which the members engage in a process of mutual aid and use that process as a vehicle for work on personal, interpersonal, and environmental problems. The predominant socioemotional issues are no longer those of power and control but of intimacy and differentiation. The predominant task issues are finding ways to solve the problems of the members. Groups, as described in chapter 1, are ideal social contexts for coping with difficulties in social relationships, resolving crises, and enhancing social competence. One or more of these goals become the focus of the group sessions during this stage of development.

CHARACTERISTICS OF THE GROUP

A group, in which members basically accept and help each other, has emerged. Through the development of a working agreement in the preceding stage, the members are now fairly clear about their goals as these relate to the general purpose of the group. Most members have found an acceptable niche in the group but need to confront the demands for intimacy and differentiation. Membership has stabilized, most members being committed to continuing in the group. As the group enhances its cohesiveness, the sense of belonging may be threatened by the entry of new members. Motivation is generally strong but with episodes of ambivalence and resistance as the group moves more deeply into facing and working on problems. The group now has a set of guiding norms; roles tend to be flexible and functional; communication is generally open and participation is widespread; and interpersonal, group, and environmental conflicts are acknowledged and worked on. Differences among members are accepted and used for collaborative work toward the achievement of agreed-upon individual and group goals. Actually, no group moves along in an orderly sequence, but progress is made unevenly with steps forward and back and then ahead to a new level of accomplishment. Most groups are in transition somewhere between identifiable stages of development. The social worker's major focus is to maintain and further enhance the group as a growth-promoting modality, so that increasingly the members learn to help each other. He supplements what the members themselves are able to do.

MAINTAIN AND STRENGTHEN THE GROUP

Relationships. The predominant qualities of relationships in this stage are trust, acceptance, and a search for intimacy and differentiation. There are a noticeable decrease in the ambivalence of members toward the worker and each other and an increase in ability to empathize with each other. Within the positive climate of trust and acceptance, the members display both realistic and unrealistic and both positive and negative attitudes and behaviors. Their perceptions may be distorted. There may be multiple transferences, often below the conscious level of awareness, as evidenced by such comments as "You're just like my father," "She's your favorite," "Johnny never did like me," or "I want to stay here forever."

The relationship with the worker is predominantly positive, characterized by less dependence, less struggle against his authority, and more reliance on each other, combined with a realistic dependence at times when help is necessary. Members often develop strong positive feelings expressed in a desire to have the worker to oneself, difficulty in sharing, strong overidentification, or unrealistic dependence. In a group of mentally ill young women being prepared for leaving a hospital, for example, the worker took the members on a shopping trip. As she took them to a coffee shop for lunch, the members were necessarily dependent upon her for guidance and concrete help. Later, as she helped the members to select and buy small articles in a nearby store, one member said, "Come on, mommy, we want to show you what we want to buy." More often, this type of transference occurs in groups of young children, as illustrated by a social worker's visit to a member of her group who was to have surgery the next day.

> When I entered the room, Catherine saw me and burst into tears. I approached her with a smile but with concern, too. I put my hand gently on her shoulder. She looked up and said tearfully, "I'm going to surgery tomorrow." I said that I knew and that she is worried about it. She started to shake her head negatively but then slowly changed and said, "Yes, I am." I asked if she wanted to tell me about it. She said, "There's a sticker up my spine and it hurts a whole lot." I said I knew it hurt and asked if she was afraid of what would happen tomorrow. She nodded her head. There was silence, during which time she stared intently at my earrings. She asked, "May I see your earrings?" I took one off and gave it to her. She patted it very lovingly

> and said, "My mother has a lot of earrings." This was the first time she had ever mentioned her mother. I said it must be hard for her not to be able to have her mother here when she goes into surgery. She agreed but said she understood. Then she asked if she could touch the pretty buttons on my blouse. She touched them slowly, each one. I knew she was grasping on to every bit of security she could find and that I was in a mother role with her.
>
> While she was playing with my buttons, she began to cry again softly and said, "I can't be in the play group any more." I said she certainly could. She couldn't be there tomorrow or perhaps for several days, but then she'd be able to come. She said she really could not come, because she would have to be lying on her bed. I said I knew that, but it didn't matter because we could move her bed or have the meeting around her bed. This pleased her very much and she relaxed visibly.

During this stage of group development, the members tend to identify with the worker. They may begin to dress like the worker or imitate some aspect of his appearance or mannerisms. They may comment that they try to think about how the worker would handle a particular situation and copy his behavior. They may comment that they did something to please the worker. Through such means, they incorporate some part of the worker into themselves. Such identifications occur also among members of the group. They enhance the sense of relatedness and, in addition, lead to changes in attitudes and behaviors. The worker, while fostering positive identifications, also helps the members to move to an enhanced sense of their own identities.

Within the general atmosphere of acceptance and trust, negative feelings may occur. The worker analyzes whether the feeling about her is limited to one or two members or is widely shared and, if the latter, the extent to which contagion has occurred. Some hostile reactions toward the worker are very natural reactions to realistic situations, in which instances the involved members have every right to be angry with the worker, as for example, when the worker does not follow through on a promise or does not notify the members about an absence. In other instances, hostility toward the worker may be a defense against involvement, or feelings may be displaced or projected onto the worker from other life experiences. Facing things in herself that she finds difficult to tolerate may anger a member and cause her to project the reason for her discomfort onto the worker. Hostility may be expressed against the worker, who represents to her a parent or other person she feels is against her. Even though such transference reactions stem from feelings that were realistic in the past, the irrational elements should not be continued in the present if the member is to cope with such experiences constructively. Such strong feelings toward the worker are more noticeable in therapy and socialization groups of children than in educational or behavioral groups because the former place more emphasis on self-understanding and affect than the latter do.

Members develop positive and negative feelings and reactions to each other similar to those they develop with the worker. For example,

> In a group of women, Mrs. J. glowered at Mrs. P. when the worker asked Mrs. J. to wait until Mrs. P. had a chance to speak. Mrs. P. asked Mrs. J. why she was angry with her. Mrs. J. looked startled and then said, "Well, I've a right to be angry—you cut me off." Mrs. B. said, "But the rest of us have a right to talk, too." Mrs. P. said she could not understand why Mrs. J. acted so strongly against her. Mrs. J. did not reply. There was a silence, which I did not interrupt. Mrs. J. broke the silence, saying that she did react too strongly; Mrs. P. had done nothing to her. I commented that I was the one who had requested that Mrs. P. be given a chance to speak. Mrs. B. asked Mrs. J. if she might be jealous of Mrs. P. because the worker had turned her attention away from Mrs. J. and toward Mrs. P. Mrs. W. said she agreed with that idea, commenting that it was natural to be jealous of the attention that another member receives "just like children who want the mother's attention all to themselves." The members all laughed at this, including Mrs. J. Mrs. W., in a light manner, said that the group sometimes acted like a family of kids who get jealous of each other. Mrs. J. thought it was natural for kids to feel this way but not for adults. The members continued to talk about the incident and reassured Mrs. J. that other adults often reacted as she had done.

This example is but one of the many ways in which member-to-member rivalries may be expressed in the group and of how the group process can be used to help members understand themselves better. Note that the predominant social climate was one of mutual acceptance and support, allowing for the expression of negative and positive feelings, and that the worker was comfortable in setting a limit, using silence to stimulate reflective discussion, clarifying her part in the process, and trusting the group process. Note, too, that the members of the group explore the problem, offer interpretations of behavior while simultaneously providing support, and then universalize the situation.

The development of intimacy began in the preceding stage of development as the members came to know each other better, worked out certain conflicts, and learned to trust the worker and each other. Mutual acceptance and shared self-disclosure are essential ingredients of intimacy. In this stage, the members come to share more and more of themselves in the group, but they often reflect ambivalence about the search for intimacy. Derlega points out that there are realistic risks to full disclosure.[1] Members may fear that others will discover all that is wrong with them and abandon them. They may fear that confidentiality will be violated; that what they say will be used against them; that they will lose control of their own destructive impulses as these come to awareness; that they will lose their individuality; or that they will become engulfed by or enmeshed with other members. The ability to develop intimacy is essential to effective adult psychosocial functioning. Horowitz reports that failure to develop intimate relationships has been found to be the most common reason for seeking outpatient psychotherapy.[2] Without intimate relationships, people feel lonely, isolated, and alienated. The group modality has the potential for the achievement of desired intimacy.

Membership. Usually, members have become invested in the group: they feel that belonging is important to them and they know who belongs. The social worker has a responsibility to maintain members in the group when the group can be beneficial to them; this is done through follow-up of absences and provision of encouragement and support when resistance or ambivalence recurs. Members tend to feel threatened by the entry of newcomers to the group but are generally able to face and work through the problem. The newcomer upsets the steady state, including the norms and patterns of relationships. Addition of new members to an ongoing group dilutes and interferes with the progressive deepening of feelings among the members until the newcomer is accepted by the group.

Membership turnover influences orderly movement. A new member needs to become oriented to the group, develop relationships with other members, and test the mutuality of perceptions of goals and expectations; he is in the initial phase of treatment. The older members need to adapt their roles and contributions to the group to take into account the needs of the newcomer who may have difficulty in accepting other members or the group's norms and process. When intimate relationships have been achieved, a newcomer can feel great discomfort in trying to become a part of the group. The usual anxieties about entering a new situation are aggravated by the sense of intruding into an existing system of relationships.

The newcomer to a cohesive group is in a difficult position. She has the feelings typical of entry into any new group situation, but in addition she needs to become socialized into the member role in a group that has developed its own patterns of goals, relationships, communication, and norms. In many cases, the new member is left with the responsibility of finding her place in the group; the old members may not willingly share responsibility with her. One example of the difficulty for an individual and a group in adapting to a new member concerns a young adult therapy group in which most members had been together for several months. No members had been added since the end of the first few sessions. The group had developed a sense of togetherness and had been engaged in discussions of intimate relationships.

> One afternoon, just as the group was beginning, a stranger arrived, saying she had been referred to this group. The worker entered the group at about the same time the stranger appeared. She had not prepared the group for this event but welcomed Genevieve and introduced her to each member. The members were polite and made efforts to orient her to the discussion. At the worker's suggestion, they returned to the discussion that had been started earlier, but the content was superficial and there was almost no sharing of deep concerns.
>
> Genevieve attempted to give advice to the others about their problems, which is typical behavior for the first stage. After the session ended, Genevieve left but the other members lingered. When the worker indicated that they might be upset about the new member, each one expressed much anger toward the worker for having permitted this to happen and for not letting them participate in making the decision. Jack said, with sadness, that it had taken them so long to be able to trust the worker and themselves. Sallie agreed and said it would be hard for her to really share herself again. The worker said she had no idea they would feel this way; she just thought that a group experience would be good for Genevieve. She thought the group was ready and should be able to work it out. The members left, without saying goodbye. In a conference with Genevieve, the worker learned that it had been a devastating experience for her. She felt the members' great discomfort and hostility and just couldn't seem to fit into what was going on.

Such experiences are not uncommon when there has been inadequate preparation of both the newcomer and the group and when the timing of entry is inappropriate. They can be used for the benefit of all concerned, but that requires great sensitivity to the emotional interplay among the members and the readiness of people to learn from them.

Assimilation into the group is dependent upon learning to take roles, to perceive oneself in relation to others, and to acquire the commonly shared frames of reference. The nucleus group already has a culture of norms that may, however, have become so much a part of the members that they cannot readily be verbalized.[3] The new person needs to discover these and test them out before he finds a place in the group. In the case of disturbed persons, the process may be prolonged and fraught with hesitating and belabored efforts to find acceptance.

Preparation of the group for the arrival of a new member helps the group to maintain its cohesion even while adapting to a new person. Through discussion of changes in membership, some members may recall their own feelings concerning entering the group and generalize about what makes it easy or difficult to find one's place in a group. Assimilation of new members seems to be easier in open groups with frequent turnover of members than in relatively closed ones, but it should be remembered that the developmental process in open groups tends to be slower. The timing of the entry of a newcomer is important. He may at one time bring in a desirable new stimulation. At other times, he may seriously disrupt the stability of the group. Although there are no clear rules, the best time to admit members is usually after the group has worked through a conflict or completed its work on a particular task or issue and is ready to move on to a new topic or activity. It is also necessary at times to admit a new member when someone drops out, in order to maintain a sufficient number of members in the group. Changes in membership provide opportunities for bringing new inputs into the group and for solving problems of acculturating new members, breaking affectional ties with departing members, and realigning roles and friendship alliances. It is the worker's responsibility to prepare the group for the entry of new members, as well as to prepare the newcomer for the group. She prepares the group by informing the members that a new person has been referred to the group; seeks the response to this announcement; answers appropriate questions about the entry of a new person. She asks the members to recall some of their own feelings and experiences in their first meeting and what they think can be done to help the newcomer.

When members have been prepared for a new member, they can be very helpful to that person. An example of the successful entry of a new member took place on a ward of a mental hospital in which the group had been meeting for three months.

> I went to the ward to gather up the group and introduced Betty, a new member, to each of the members. They had been prepared for her coming in the preceding two meetings. When I introduced Betty to Martha, Martha smiled and said, "Oh, I know Betty; she eats at my table with me." As we walked off the ward, Martha walked with Betty arm in arm. Martha and Sarah are the two most verbal members of the group.
>
> As we walked to the store, Martha told me that she had seen Joan, a former member, at the laundry. Jane interrupted Martha to tell me that she didn't go to the dance last night. When Martha asked why not, Jane said, "I just decided not to." Sarah said she wanted to get the next issue of a magazine she was carrying with her. She's reading a continued story and "just can't wait to see how it ends." She asked Betty if she ever read stories that she enjoyed. Betty said she hadn't read for a long time, but she'd like to try. Then she began asking questions about the group, which Sarah and Martha answered very ac-

curately, a sign of their great progress. Betty asked me about my age, marital status, and other personal questions. Before I had a chance to answer, Sarah said, "Betty, there are some things that people just don't tell and we don't ask Miss J. such personal questions." I smiled at Sarah and she smiled back. Betty said she was sorry. I said that it was perfectly all right and natural that she should want to know something about me and things about the other members and the group, too. Joan said, "Yes, you can ask her." I added that we would all try to help her fit into the group. She said, "You have already and so has Martha and Sarah—and all of you."

Discontinuance of members from closed or semiclosed groups is not frequent during this stage. Some members cannot, however, accept the increasing demands of the group for give and take, or they cannot tolerate dealing with the subject matter of the group. They become anxious and resistant. Feelings about exposure of self in the group may recur as its content touches upon more areas of the life experiences of its members. It is crucial that the person come to "have confidence that his real self can be understood and accepted by others in the group."[4] Until the point is reached in which there is openness and acceptance of self and others, some members may seek to withdraw from the group. The worker needs to support such a person in staying, through making very clear that he wants him to remain in the group. It is hoped that the other members can reassure him that he has a place in the group and can put gentle pressure on him to continue. Departure of a member stirs up varied reactions: a sense of loss, fear that the group will disintegrate, or ambivalence about wanting the person in the group, with accompanying guilty feelings.

Positive Motivation and Resistance. Identification with the social worker and feelings of trust and mutual acceptance provide powerful motivation for continuing in the group. In such an atmosphere, anxieties and fears are lessened and hopefulness is increased. People are not likely to remain in groups if they believe that some positive changes in themselves or their situations are not possible. They need to have and to believe that they have the power to achieve some change. In an earlier chapter, it was noted that there must be hope that relief from discomfort, pain, or dissatisfaction with the current situation can occur. There must be enough discomfort with what is for a person to desire some further development or change in the situation. Thus, the worker needs to work to maintain a balance between discomfort and hope as the members try to change in some way. Mastery of skills and situations strengthens the ego and suuccess tends to build on success. What might have been a vicious cycle of hopelessness-failure-greater hopelessness gets replaced with a cycle of hopelessness-success-hopefulness.[5]

Even within a general atmosphere in which individual and group motivation is high, there will be times when apathy or discouragement sets in. Particular members resist efforts by the worker or by other members to help them work on difficulties or obstacles to goal achievement. In this stage of group development, resistance is often mobilized by anxiety about the helping process itself. As the demands for work increase, members may find it difficult to participate in the give and take of group life. They may fear disclosing certain secrets or highly charged experiences or become aware of feelings and ideas that have been suppressed as these break into consciousness. Facing things in themselves that they find difficult to accept upsets the steady state. When anxiety increases beyond a tolerable level, the person defends himself: he resists. During this stage, resistance often represents an effort to hold on to the familiar, fears of intimacy, and fears of trying out alternative ways of feeling, thinking, and doing. According to Ackerman, "it reflects the patient's need to place a fence around the most vulnerable areas of self in an attempt to immunize the self against the danger of reopening old psychic wounds."[6] But resistance does not occur only because of the feelings and needs of the members. It may be a reasonable response to the worker's part in the process, as when he is late to meetings, when he confronts members in a punitive manner and without conveying empathy, or when his interpretations are too many and too threatening. The resistance of some members may also be due to their interactions with other members when they are attacked or devalued or when member-to-member confrontations and interpretations are inappropriate.

The following example is taken from the record of a group of adult men and women with problems in social relationships in an adult psychiatric clinic.

> About halfway through the tenth session, the subject turned to religion. The discussion was more of a social conversation than an application to the members' problems. There was very little personal investment in the subject by any of the members, and it seemed to be a device to avoid talking about their fears. After a while, I said, "You've been talking about religion; does that help you to work on your difficulties?" Joe said he was just interested in making a philosophical point—he enjoys talking about philosophy. I asked, "Do you remember that, in our last meeting, you shifted away from talking about yourselves to talking about general things that didn't really seem to involve you much: aren't you starting to do the same thing again today?" There was an uncomfortable silence.
>
> I said, "It's been different in this group for the last two sessions." There was another uncomfortable silence. Allen broke the silence. "Who's holding back?" Everyone laughed.
>
> Shirley said she came to this group because she was putting all her

own problems on her children. I said, "Yes, and you and the others have not been working on those kinds of problems recently. What accounts for that?" There was another uncomfortable silence.

Shirley broke the silence. "You don't want to bring out the real, deep problems that are bothering you."

Leon: "It's hard to even put your finger on the real problem—I'm mixed up about that." Allen: "It's easier to talk about religion than about what I really feel. I guess it's a cover up."

Leon cracked a joke and the mood changed. The other members laughed and Leon told another joke.

I said, "Let's look at what's been going on right now. Shirley said it's hard to share the real problems; Leon, that he's not sure what these are; Allen, that he needs a cover up for what he really feels; and Susan, Barbara, and Carl haven't said a thing. Some of you were just getting close to talking about things that matter when Leon cracked a joke to take the focus off yourselves. It may feel scary to delve deeper into the feelings and relationships that contribute to your troubles."

Shirley said, "I have to agree with that." Susan said, "Me, too, what will happen to me if I tell too much? But, I'm willing to try."

The major principle to guide the worker is that she respects the members' need to protect themselves and does not arouse more anxiety than can be dealt with at a given time. Certain actions of the worker or other members often arouse anxiety. To advance expectations and achieve certain gains, it is necessary that some anxiety be felt; the crucial factor is whether the members have the ego capacities to cope with the disturbed feelings. Confrontation is used quite frequently in this stage, but it tends to arouse anxiety and hence resistance. What is to be conveyed is not condemnation or withholding of acceptance but a direct sharing with the group that the worker is aware that something is going on that prevents moving ahead. There is an obstacle to work. Such challenges bring the obstacle into the conscious awareness of the members and make it possible for them to express their concerns and move ahead in problem-solving activities. Confrontation that strips defenses is harmful; the worker needs to allow time to provide support to the members as they try to take in the confrontive message and then to work it through.

Interpretation often follows confrontation. Such statements about the meaning of behavior may be resisted, or they may be readily accepted. They may be resisted because the worker has expressed a truth that the member is not yet ready to recognize or because the worker has misunderstood the meaning of the situation and the interpretation is inaccurate. It is hard for anyone to face the intensity of deep feelings, and it is no wonder that members defend themselves against such understanding until they have developed enough self-esteem to accept these aspects of themselves. Secrecy leads to resistance. When a member keeps a secret from the group, she is making it impossible for others to help. When a worker withholds information from a group, the members are deprived of a source of help. In therapeutic groups, Balgopal and Hull explain how resistance often occurs because there are secrets between one or more members and the worker that are not revealed or discussed in group sessions. These areas of secrecy create barriers.[7]

The specific interventions of the social worker in overcoming resistance are as varied as the reasons for the resistance. But, to be worked with, the members must be supported as the resistance is acknowledged and brought to the group's attention. The worker may comment that she has noticed a particular thing has happened. She brings to conscious awareness the expectations, disappointments, or anxieties that work against continuation of effort. Her next move depends upon the response from one or more members. She may invite ventilation of the feelings of anxiety, hopelessness, or fear that create the stalemate; provide support in the form of realistic reassurance to reduce threat; universalize the problem, acknowledging that it is natural to be uncertain about the consequences of efforts toward change or that distrust is often realistic owing to times when trust has not been earned; engage the individual or group in exploration of the situation; and, at times, use confrontation to disrupt the steady state in order to overcome apathy, denial, or avoidance of a particular issue. She may offer facts that have not been recognized or encourage the members to search for facts on which to base a decision about moving into a feared area, through the use of process illumination techniques. When the worker feels secure in her interpretation of what the problem is and how it developed, she can share these observations with the group in a way that invites their responses to them.

Roles and Subgroups. During the preceding stages, the members assumed or were assigned to roles in the group, and a leading task for both the worker and the members was to identify and work through dysfunctional roles. Some stereotyping of members may continue that prevents the use of the group in a flexible manner, according to the needs of the members. A norm of flexibility and experimentation is crucial in making possible changes of maladaptive role behavior.

Subgroups can generally be accommodated by the group and can contribute to the group as a whole. This does not mean that no subgroups will be inimical to the welfare of individuals and the group. Indeed, unhealthy pair relations may develop or continue from the earlier stages, that indicate problems in interpersonal relationships, and their modification becomes an important goal for those members. It is natural that transitory negative relationships will develop within the group as the members try to solve the many individual and group problems.

Norms. A group code was developed in the last stage, consisting of norms that are recognized, understood, and generally accepted by the members. The worker's efforts were directed toward influencing the nature of the code. If this has been successful, differences are now perceived as being potentially useful, although they may create discomfort. Individual differences and talents are acknowledged, used, and viewed as valuable. As Balgopal and Vassil have said, "An overriding principle is that the potential for change in groups is enhanced when differences are harnessed for work through interdependent efforts. Individual differences are not lost in the process but are expanded to the end that the members' goals have been reached."[8] Prestige is now attached to a person's efforts to express himself and to work on problems. The members recognize that conflict can be used constructively toward the achievement of purposes.

During this stage of group development, the worker continues to help members to recall and act in accordance with the norms in the group and some of the underlying values. He accredits and supports the norms that are positive to the achievement of goals; openly questions changes that are negative in the influence they have on the group; encourages the examination of existing norms and the consideration of alternative ones; and continues to help the group to find an appropriate balance between control and freedom in feeling and behaving. It is a temptation for a practitioner to overstress group loyalty and group standards to strengthen the impact of the group on its members; the crucial consideration is that the code of standards approve and support flexibility, experimentation, and individuation. Schein says that, otherwise, there is danger that the group will become "so stable in its approach to its environment that it loses its ability to adapt, innovate, and grow."[9]

Behavior that deviates from the norms of the group poses a threat to the stability of the group. The other members tend to respond with efforts to control the deviator. The deviator's failure to conform to the group's expectations makes life difficult for all concerned. An example is of an activity group for older adults in a community center. The activity is cake baking. The group had established a particular structure for working together in triads, with each person responsible for some part of the whole, and had established rules for sharing equipment and ingredients. During the midstage of the group, a new member, Helen, entered the group on an informal basis. Unfortunately, she had not had adequate pregroup preparation, and the group had not been prepared for her entry. Helen was an excellent baker and a hard worker, but her interactions with the old members have been stormy. Her efforts to help others resulted in rejection, partly because of her controlling manner and negative attitudes toward others and partly because of the rigidity of the group's system of work. As time went on, Helen became more angry and upset with the others and they with her, as indicated by the following excerpt from the group record.

> Helen said to Dorothea, "What are you doing there? That's all wrong. Let me show you." Sally said, "Dorothea's doing all right." Helen said, "No, it's not mixing—what's the matter—she doesn't hear me." Dorothea said, "I hear you, but this is my job. You don't have to tell me." Helen took the sugar before Dorothea had a chance to measure out what she needed. Dorothea said, "You're grabbing things before any one else has a chance to finish. Stop that." Sally said to Sue, "See, Helen thinks she knows everything." Anger was mounting. I said, "Ok., time out. I'm wondering what's going on among you."

The other members cannot count on the deviator—in this case, a newcomer—so they tend to respond by penalizing her in order to influence her toward conformity to the expectations of the group. This is essential to the group's ability to continue its activities. But the deviator has expectations, too, which need to be taken into account, and by doing so, the group may find better ways of accomplishing its tasks. The worker's task is to assess the contributions that all members make to the conflict and to work toward mutuality of understanding. The major set of techniques in such situations is illumination of the group process.

Communication and Conflict. Patterns of communication appropriate to the purpose of the group were established earlier. There is now greater ease in communication about feelings, problems, and opinions and greater spread of communication among the members. Conflict continues, however, to be present and serves as a dynamic for change. Many intrapersonal and intragroup conflicts concerning power and acceptance were worked out during the preceding stage. But resolution of major interpersonal and intrapersonal conflicts usually cannot occur until the group has developed a basic consensus that provides strength to face and weather serious differences. The conflict now seldom takes the form of physical fighting, as might have been true in children's groups earlier. When the social climate of the group is marked by mutual acceptance and support, members are more willing to risk exposure of themselves and their ideas than in the earlier stages when they were more uncertain of their acceptance and the consequences of self-expression. They recognize that expression of difference need not mark the end of the relationship. In the words of Simmel:

> It is by no means the sign of the most genuine and deep affection never to yield to occasions for conflict. . . . On the contrary, this behavior often characterizes attitudes which lack the ultimate unconditional devotion. . . . The felt insecurity concerning the basis of such relations often moves us to the

> avoidance of every possible conflict. Where, on the other hand, we are certain of the irrevocability and unreservedness of our feeling, such peace at any price is not necessary. We know that no crisis can penetrate to the foundation of the relationship.[10]

There are numerous sources of conflict. Conflict often has its source in the intrapersonal drives and needs of the members—their differential needs for control, affection, and inclusion as these interact with the needs of other members. Intrapsychic conflicts often get displaced onto the group. Members work out their sibling rivalries and relationships with parents and others within the arena of the group. Members bring with them into the group the values and norms from their primary reference groups. Many subcultural and idiosyncratic differences within American culture influence the way people shape their goals, perceive other people, and influence their attitudes toward the process and content of the group. As these differences become acknowledged, people become defensive and tend to promulgate their own points of view. Or they have different knowledge about and experiences with issues. The external situation and differential perceptions of that situation are another frequent source of conflict. For example, awareness of ethnic and political differences is very intense at times, and different population groups vary in regard to how they view the services of community organizations. It is not one of these, but the interaction among them, that creates conflict.

Generally, the group has developed means for the resolution and management of conflict that are appropriate to the members' capacities. More frequently, conflict is resolved through means of consensus, acknowledgment of the right to differ, or integration, rather than elimination of some members or subjugation of some by others.

Cohesion. Cohesion is generally present to a great extent in that the members are mutually attracted to each other and to the group. The degree of cohesion is, however, relative. It is dependent upon the members' common interests and goals and their abilities to enter into collaborative and intimate relations with others. It is unlikely, for example, that very sick mental patients will develop into as cohesive a group as persons with greater competence in interpersonal relations might. But the group has come to have meaning to the members. As the members become more secure in their own relationships and in the identity of their group, they become more able to relate to other groups in an effective manner. The worker continues to pay attention to the development of the dimensions of group structure and process in order to maintain the group as a viable modality for the achievement of the goals of its members.

In this stage of development, groups exert their greatest influence on the members, owing at least in part to the fact that the group has become attractive to its members. It is sufficiently cohesive that the mutual aid process predominates, even though some members are more attracted to the group than are others. Yalom has summarized the evidence from research on the importance of a high degree of cohesion in the interpersonal learning process.[11] He reports that findings from seven studies support the proposition that group cohesion is an important determinant of positive outcome, both in encounter and therapy groups. Cohesive groups are characterized by mutual trust and acceptance. They also permit greater development and expression of hostility and conflict. When unexpressed hostility and hidden conflicts exist, open and honest communication is impossible. When members of groups have come to mean enough to each other, their relationships are not permanently disrupted, and they can, with help, work through the conflict. Highly cohesive groups also have better attendance and less turnover of membership than those with low degrees of cohesion do.[12]

WORK TOWARD GOAL ACHIEVEMENT

During this stage, the predominant focus of the content is on the problematic situations of the members, as these are connected with those of others and with the general purpose of the group. This emphasis does not mean that the earlier stages were devoid of problem-solving activities. By the time an integrated group emerges, members have made some modifications in their attitudes, relationships, and skills. The early changes tend to be in their abilities to adapt to a new situation, to relate more effectively with a professional person, to resolve problems of inclusion and power, and to identify and begin to explore individual and group problems. Now there is a greater focus on working through the identified problems, and members are more effective in helping each other. The particular problems that become the focus of the group's discussion and activity-oriented experiences are those that are primary concerns of the members at a given time. Successful outcome usually involves work toward (1) some degree of improvement in affective and cognitive understanding of oneself in relation to others, (2) enhancement of capacities to cope with personal or group crises, and (3) achievement of the social skills essential to the performance of vital social roles.

Interpersonal Understanding. Acquisition of more accurate perception of self in relation to other people and to the demands of the environment is a frequent task of this stage. Striving for self-understanding is based on the theoretical assumption that if people can understand how the values, emotions, patterns of behavior, and prior experiences have contributed to the current problems, they become able to distinguish which attitudes and behaviors best serve their goals. It is assumed that the more accurate the perception of inner and outer reality, the firmer the foundation for effective social functioning. More accurate perception of other significant persons may lead to changes in attitudes and behavior toward them. In the group, it must be remembered that interaction among the members is the primary instrument of change. Mutual aid is a powerful means of influencing changes in feelings, thought, and action. As members interact with each other, they become aware of themselves in their relationships with others. They can test out their assumptions not only against those of a professional helper, but also and more important, against those of their peers. They not only develop cognitive understanding but also integrate that with their feelings and learn about the effects on their behavior. They develop explanations to account for the particular patterns of behavior. They may come to a better understanding of their feelings and attitudes, their patterns of behavior in relation to what they are doing with other people, the reasons for the behavior, and, in some instances, the influence of the past on current functioning.

When people are anxious, they tend to cling to the familiar and avoid risking further upsets in the steady state. Change is threatening, resulting in the use of maladaptive coping strategies. What is required is that the group leader use supportive techniques and adequate exploration of the situation to assist the members to enter into reflective discussion of the situation and their parts in it. Acquiring self-understanding requires that persons disclose aspects of self that may be frightening and painful and that they fear will be unacceptable to the leader and to other members as well. Some members can, however, gain a great deal from listening to others and silently integrating the knowledge. But they do not gain the benefits from receiving feedback on their own feelings and ideas. The leader needs to differentiate between a healthy need for private contemplation and compulsive secrecy. Some members, on the other hand, reveal too much too soon. Experimentation with different ways of behaving requires wading in unknown waters. To venture into this arena requires that a relationship of trust has been developed among the participants. Research indicates that an adequate amount of self-disclosure is positively related to successful outcomes in various forms of groups.[13]

The attitudes toward the self with which the worker deals most frequently are the closely interrelated ones of identity and self-esteem. Erikson has pointed out that "a common feeling of having a personal identity is based on two simultaneous observations: the immediate perception of one's self sameness and continuity in time; and simultaneous perception of the fact that others recognize one's sameness and continuity."[14] This sense of identity involves knowledge about and acceptance of oneself. As it develops through the life cycle, it incorporates more broadly and fully many aspects that define who a person is, what he can do, and what he will become. Often, members of groups feel stigmatized by the nature of their illnesses or handicapping conditions, for example, mental illness, mental retardation, cancer, AIDS, delinquency, or even the "bad mother" or "bad child" label. Feelings that people have about their sociocultural backgrounds often interfere with the development of a positive self-image. This was brought out in work with a group of seven-year-old girls during a game in which the members were parading in front of a mirror. One child said, "Look, how much darker I am than you are: guess I'm badder." A sense of self-esteem is closely related to, indeed, may be a part of, identity.

Certain events threaten the self-esteem of even healthy egos. Report cards, civil service examinations, work evaluations, or comparisons of development between children arouse fears of failure and worries about adequacy. These events force the person to find out how her performance stands in relation to her own expectations and in relation to others. Sexual adequacy is a recurrent theme in groups of adolescents and adults, related to the underlying theme of sexual identity. For aged persons, forced retirement and loss of relatives and friends through death are threats to their identity and self-esteem. Conflicts in identity also often come to the fore with clarity as members come to feel some success in their achievements. One typical example is the delinquent adolescent's struggle as he realizes that, in order to achieve certain goals, he needs to give up his identification with his gang or friendship group. Whether members approach an experience with competence and hope or a devastating sense of inadequacy with its accompanying hopelessness is of deep concern to the social worker.

In interpersonal learning, observation and clarification of nonverbal behavior is an essential skill of the social worker. An example is of a group of parents in a child guidance clinic. The meeting opened with listening to a tape on parent-child relationships.

> During the time the tape was being played, Mr. D. appeared to be fully involved. Hands, eyes, posture, body movement, and absence of whispering to others reflected his involvement. Since he had not been this intense before the tape, something was affecting him deeply. When the tape was over, he sat back for only a second, but it was long enough for a discussion to get going about children's problems. Every time he tried to get into the discussion, someone else got in first. His finger tapping, leg crossing, and squirming seemed to indicate growing anxiety. By the time he got into the discussion, the topic was only distantly related to the tape.
>
> Mr. and Mrs. A. were talking about their nephew's difficulty in cub scouts. Mr. D. stated that, since he is a den master, he could help the boy if they would like. After some further discussion of children's problems in clubs, I said to Mr. D. "I bet you really enjoy helping the cub scouts—it does seem to strengthen parent-child relations . . . but you know what? I have a feeling you would like to talk about something else and just haven't been able to get it into the discussion. It

seemed like parts of that tape had a lot of meaning for you." Everyone perked up when Mr. D. said, "Yes, they did. There was a lot of me in that tape. I could see myself in it." All of a sudden, the members seemed to realize that, in their excitement to talk about how the tape related to their children, they overlooked how the content might relate directly to themselves. The members were very supportive of Mr. D. as he shared some emotionally powerful experiences. That, in turn, led to discussion of other members' parts in the problems of relationships in their families.

The skills in practice reflected in this brief excerpt include sensitive observation of nonverbal, as well as verbal, behavior; support of Mr. D's positive abilities in Boy Scouting; the nonthreatening use of interpretation based on observation and sensitive listening; demonstration of an empathic response to anxiety; and a refocusing of the content to the primary needs of the members. With a worker who supports the group process, the ventilation and discussion of feelings by one member evoke greater self-disclosure on the part of the others also.

Adequate exploration of the person-group-situation configuration is an essential foundation for reflective discussion used to enhance understanding of self in interaction with varied situations. Adequate ventilation and sharing of feelings to ascertain the similar and different ones among the members are often essential, too. One example is taken from Lee and Park's record of a group of adolescent girls in foster homes.[15] Considerable time was spent in exploring their feelings about being foster children, requiring support and empathy from the worker in sharing such feelings as "being foster is like being a piece of garbage" or "you're just something somebody tossed out."

Carin, who had been reading, lifted her head, put her hands flat on the table, and said, "I got one for the group—what would you do if you thought you were going crazy?" There was a silence, and the members looked at one another. I asked Carin if she was talking about herself. She said yes, and the girls appeared to freeze. I asked if she could tell us what this going crazy feeling feels like. After thinking, she said seriously, "It feels like nothing matters to me anymore." Kenya asked her what about school, and she unfolded her story. I let them know it wasn't so crazy to feel that way with a life like Carin's.

In this and other situations, as feelings and experiences are revealed and understood by self and others, the members can move next to desired changes in feelings, relationships, and behavior. It is necessary to state the reality that a person like Carin is not mentally ill, in spite of the feelings, and to offer realistic hope that things will get better.

The group process can be very effective in helping members acknowledge feelings and problems in relationships. A short-term group of young adults in a psychiatric clinic had as its purpose the improvement of interpersonal relationships, primarily with members of their families. Joseph, aged twenty-four, tended to deny his mixed feelings toward his wife's parents. Marjorie, aged twenty-three, has expressed anger at her mother's need to control her. The following interchange occurred in the fifth meeting.

MARJORIE: I am afraid mother will collapse if I disagree with her. The few times I did express myself, she acted oh so hurt. It just made me feel very guilty.

JOSEPH: You feel mortgaged?

MARJORIE (acknowledges Joseph's insight): When I go home for the weekends, mother treats me like a special guest. But when we discuss almost anything, I just have to restrain myself from saying anything, since our values are so far apart. And I mean far apart. (She makes further comments and several members point to difficulties with their parents, also.)

WORKER: You seem to be listening intently Joseph.

JOSEPH: Yes . . . (silence) I'm really with what Marge says.

MARJORIE: How?

JOSEPH: Well—it's just like me and my in-laws. They give us all kinds of material goods, but if I don't think like them—wow! I get so upset. I feel trapped.

WORKER: Trapped? Feeling mortgaged as you thought Marjorie felt?

JOSEPH: Absolutely.

MARJORIE: Like me! Definitely.

JOSEPH: (Goes on to explain situation. He often gets angry with his in-laws, with whom he lives. After a pause, he said, "but angry with myself, too.")

KEVIN: Yeh, I'll bet you feel guilty like Marge said she did and asked. Is there nothing we can do to not feel so mortgaged at home?

The members had become able to express empathy for each other and identify with the common underlying feelings in spite of different family situations. The movement is from ventilating feelings, recognizing their nature, blaming others, and beginning to want to make some changes.

Sharing of feelings often produces mitigation of fear, guilt, hopelessness, or other strong emotions. Members often talk about situations in which they have been unable to express their feelings because they didn't have the words to symbolize the feelings, were afraid of offending other persons, felt guilty about the feelings, or were fearful of the consequences of acknowledging the feelings. The ventilation and discussion of feelings by some members evoke similar or different responses from the other members. The following incident occurred in a group of parents in a child guidance clinic. The purpose of the group is to help the members to cope more effectively with their emotionally disturbed children who are enrolled in the clinic's pregrade school. Most of the parents are not emotionally disturbed, but two members, one of them Mrs. J., have been diagnosed as borderline cases. Mrs. J. has been in the group for five months. She was divorced shortly after the birth of her only child, Jonathon, who is now five years old. She is head of the household, has a meager income, and is the sole support of herself and her son. The case study gives evidence that Mrs. J. is very dependent on the child for love and support, but she has not previously revealed the extent of her dependence on the boy.

> During one session, the members were discussing how angry and disgusted they felt about being parents of disturbed children. Mrs. S. said, "Sometimes I feel like I could just give Tommy away—get rid of him—because he isn't getting any better." Mrs. J. responded loudly, "Oh No! I could never give my Jonathon away because he is my life —he is my life. If I did not have Jonathon I would have had a nervous breakdown." There was silence. The members' eyes were riveted on me. I responded, "I think those must be painful feelings—can you tell us more about the feelings, Mrs. J?" She said, "They are terrible and terrifying." Mrs. B. nodded and said she guessed they had all had some terrifying feelings. Mr. P. said, "You're suffering—but I'm curious about what makes you feel you could have a nervous breakdown." The tears came to Mrs. J's eyes as she said simply, "I just know it—Jonathon means everything to me." Her voice began to crack and there were facial twitches as she continued, "I'm afraid to be without him—I'd feel so all alone." One member, feeling uncomfortable, changed the subject. I said, "It's hard for some of you to listen to Mrs. J., isn't it, but could we stick with the subject a while longer?" Mrs. J. became calmer and the tears stopped. She asked, "Have none of you ever felt so all alone that you thought you'd go crazy?" Mrs. B. said, "I really think I know the feeling." That remark led to a new level of sharing feelings about their relationships with their children and a desire to understand these feelings.

Members of groups often need assistance in disclosing information about themselves. When members find it difficult to express their concerns, comments from the leader or another member that mention the universality of certain feelings and problems often release inhibitions. Examples would be a statement that it is normal to feel unhappy about being a foster child, for teenagers to feel rebellious against their parents at times, or to have frightening feelings about sex. Those things that people are often ashamed of, or are embarrassed about, are also of deep concern to them, for example, sexual attitudes and experiences, racial differences, failures at school or work, and fear of permanent disability or even death.

> In a group of fifteen- or sixteen-year-old girls, when Ernestine was absent, the worker asked about her. Her older sister, Verna, obviously embarrassed, said she'd be back in a few months. The other girls looked knowingly at each other. The leader said she thought she understood. Verna, after a long pause, said, "Yeah, I think you do. She got herself mixed up with a fellow—she's pregnant," and then hurriedly walked away. The worker said that it was all right for the girls to talk about this and that Ernestine was still welcome in the group. The girls could hardly believe it and required reassurance from the worker that she really meant it.

This interchange opened up discussion of feelings about pregnancy, unmarried motherhood, and means of dealing with sexual feelings. In such ways, permission is given to open topics that have previously been taboo. Naming the taboo subject makes it a normal concern and tends to enhance readiness to deal with it. The skill is in being able to stay with the members' feelings and thinking, rather than veer away from such subjects. Along with permission to explore and work on such topics is the explicit understanding that such discussions rest on mutual trust and confidentiality.

Confrontation. Sometimes inability to perceive reality is an obstacle to the group's progress. The social worker then needs to gently confront the members with the irrationality of their thinking, the destructive use of defenses, the unacceptability of their behavior, or their lack of progress. Under such circumstances, Schwartz points out that "a force is needed within the learning group system that will challenge the obstacles as they appear by calling attention to their existence and asking the group to come to grips with them."[16] The worker may use confronting questions or comments with the intent of interrupting the process to encourage the members to face and work on such problems. To confront people enables them to face the reality of a feeling, act, or situation. In order to use confrontation effectively, the worker's assessment of the situation must be sound. The confrontation must be accompanied by empathy, with "an arm around the shoulder." There is support from empirical research for the view that when it is accompanied by a high degree of empathy, confrontation is an effective therapeutic ingredient. When employed by practitioners with little empathy, it is not.[17]

The worker's attitude and choice of words make a vast difference in the extent to which the members will feel attacked, and retreat from facing reality, or will be enabled to move into coping with it. For example, "I know you're lying," or "Don't you dare deny it," sounds far different from, "Sometimes it's hard to say what really happened; let's try to look at that." When they are not able to do so themselves, the members need a worker who can face them with some of the feelings, ways of thinking, and behavior that are destructive and thus free them to move forward constructively. The worker may directly share his feelings about a member's behavior in order to face him with it and then help him. One example would be sharing with a father who covered up for his son's stealing, "I feel angry with you because you say you want to help your son, but you really are contributing to his delinquency instead of helping him to get along better." Confrontation is not synonymous with demolishment of someone. Its focus is on one aspect of a person—not the total personality.

Supportive techniques accompany confronting ones. An example is that of a worker's use of herself with a group of black girls, all with problems in high school and from low-income families. Frequent topics of discussion were feelings of being discriminated against and feelings of prejudice toward others. The sensitivity of these girls created frequent outbreaks of emotion in the group.

> At first, the worker supported the expression of feelings about the girls' race and toward others, then gradually worked toward clarification of what part was the reality and what was displacement and projection of feelings onto others. When a teacher, also black, asked the girls to be less noisy, one member screamed, "Oh, I hate her; she is just prejudiced. She doesn't even stick up for her own race." Others joined in the ventilation of feelings against teachers and white students, who were perceived as being discriminatory. Gross distortions were evident, one complaint being that no black student had ever been an officer of the student organization.
>
> When the worker expressed understanding of the members' feelings but confronted them with the reality of the situation, including the fact that the president of the student organization was a black boy, the girls stopped to ponder the statement. One grudgingly admitted, "That's true, but I just hate white kids." Later, the worker commented that the members seemed to feel at one about this. All agreed. The worker asked, "and there are no exceptions?" Two teachers were mentioned as being all right, but the expressions of hatred continued. To the two girls who expressed most of the feelings, the worker commented, "You seem to be full of hate today." The response was, "Well, yes, we've a right to." The worker acknowledged that sometimes there were reasons to feel hatred. Gradually, the members themselves began to confront each other with the facts. One girl said, "After all, Mrs. G. (the worker) is white, too." The most vociferous of the members looked startled, and said, "Oh no," and broke into tears, then added, "But, but, I like you." From that point, the girls began to in-

dividualize people, with more realistic evaluation of people and situations.

Social workers need to remember that one of the characteristics of a nonracist practitioner is the ability to confront members when they distort the intentions and behavior of others.[18]

When members confront each other, the worker needs to understand whether the intent of the confronter was to hurt or to help, the influence of the confrontation on the members toward whom it was directed and on the other members, and the needs and readiness of the group to use it. An example of a group's confrontation of one of its members occurred in a group of couples with marital problems.

One couple was engaged in unproductive and prolonged accusations of each other's part in threatening the marriage. The worker confronted them with the observation that, although both of them had said they wanted to make the marriage work, they had not yet tried to make it work. The husband, Ben, said he was willing to open up communication with Alice, his wife. Then, he said angrily, "But will you promise to do that, too?" Alice's response was to leap from the chair, hysterically shouting that she saw no point in staying here to be the object of abuse and insensitivity from Ben—she was leaving. Tom said quickly and sternly, "Don't leave, Alice. I have something to say to you both." Alice didn't sit down, but remained in the room, leaning her arms against the back of her chair. Tom said that both of them should stop fighting right now. Both looked taken aback. Tom told them they were acting like two children, just like the kids that he works with at school. He related an episode of a fight between two kids, neither of whom would admit what happened and each blaming the other for the fight. He said that's exactly what Alice and Ben were doing. Each blamed the other, and neither would tell each other what it was all about. He went on to explain the relationship as he saw it. There was a dead silence in the room. Ben said, "Well, I'm willing to try," but then asked Alice in an angry way. "Are you willing, too?" Jane shouted, "My God, Ben, you didn't take in a single thing that Tom was telling you." Steve said, "For God's sake, Ben, what's the matter with you?" Elaine shouted, "There you go again." Ben was silent, looking as if he had been hit. I wondered what message Ben got from the group. He said, "I got the word clearly, and I will try." This time he did not add angrily that Alice should do this, too.

When it was time to end the meeting, I commented that the free expression of conflict had been hard for all—especially for Alice and Ben. Elaine said, "You can say that again, but we learned through it." She got up from her chair, and the others followed. Ben went over to Alice and helped her to put her coat on. As they were leaving, Tom said to Alice, "you and Ben are coming for coffee, aren't you?" They said they would like to do that.

On the basis of an on-the-spot assessment of the situation, the worker supports or does not support the efforts of the confronter, encourages the members to continue dealing with the issue, and works with them to summarize the learnings and generalize from a particular situation. Gradually, the members become more able to empathize with each other and thereby become more helpful than hurtful in the intent and nature of their confronting comments.

Clarification. According to her understanding of the needs of the members and their motivation and capacity to deal with personal and interpersonal problems, the worker helps the group to focus on clarification of patterns of behavior that are helpful or destructive to them. There seems to be a natural progression from recognition of the behavior in the situation to elaboration of the situation more fully in its many facets—the feelings about it, the behavior patterns and the situations in which they occur, and the consequences of the behavior. In some situations, such understanding is sufficient; in others, further work is desirable in order to clarify the meaning of the situation or behavior.

The social worker's major efforts build on and support the use of the members' positive motivations and capacities and encourage members to support or to question the comments and behavior of each other. For example, in a group of adolescent boys, one member asked Pete directly about school. Pete, aged seventeen, replied that he had quit. One member said it was stupid to have done that. The other members agreed. One member commented, "We'd better stop jumping Pete and find out what happened." Here, the worker supported, through purposeful silence, the group's work in understanding one of its members and then helping him to face his behavior more realistically.

Within the protection of the group, the worker may create an awareness among members of the discrepancy between their private attitudes and behavior and their earlier statements to the group. He may do this by encouraging a member with high status in the group to tell the group about his feelings and behavior that deviate from his earlier public expressions. One example is of a group in which a high-status older adolescent revealed that his earlier exaggerations concerning his sexual conquests and his sexual security were not true; that he really felt very uncomfortable with girls. Following their expressions of surprise at this admission, the other members openly expressed their fears and anxieties. The facade of sexual adequacy gave way to efforts to achieve more adequate masculine identification. Thus, instead of continuing to support each other's denials, the members could move toward support of efforts to change attitudes and behavior. Blum says that, when possible, the selection of a member with high status is deliberate; if such revelation emanates from a member with low status, there is danger that he will become a scapegoat. Such a member is also less likely to be able to influence the behavior of the other members.[19]

Irrational beliefs about oneself are forms of lack of self-knowledge. A low self-image or lack of positive identity leads many clients to deprecate themselves and engage in self-defeating patterns of behavior. "I am not loved"; "I'm really ugly"; "If you really knew me, you'd know how rotten I am" are messages that often convey irrational beliefs about oneself. Such beliefs about who one is develop through relationships and experiences with other people who confirm or contradict the beliefs. Responses from others interact with one's own perceptions.

> In a group of hospitalized mental patients, Mr. M. started a discussion of the possibility of getting a job when he is ready to go home. Mr. R., the newest member of the group, mentioned his fears about being able to get a job, and all of the members, except Mr. D., who is still not able to participate very much, laughed and said they all had those fears. After further discussion, I said that it really was a worry not to be sure about a job, wasn't it? Mr. M. and Mr. R. both said I was right, and other members seemed to agree through nonverbal nods. Mr. R. then said that was not his biggest worry: he had a really big worry, but he did not want the members to know about it. He asked me if I knew what it was. I said I knew whatever was in his record. I reassured the members that they could express whatever they wanted to in this group, but they did not have to talk about things until they were ready to do so. Mr. M. said that the group is here for us to talk about our problems. Mr. R. then started to talk in a very general way about sex, but it was difficult to follow what he was saying. The others listened quietly to his efforts. I said that if he could try to be a little more specific, perhaps other members could help him with the problem. Mr. R. asked if I would explain his "big problem" to the others. I merely said in a questioning way, "You want me to tell the group for you?" He nodded. Mr. M. said he gathered that the problem had to do with sex. Mr. R. said that was it and thanked him for saying it.
>
> Mr. M. said, "Well, go ahead and discuss it; that is what the group is for—to talk about problems like that." Mr. R. looked at me, and I assured him that it was all right to talk about those things. He said then that his problem was that he was in love with somebody. Finally, Mr. M. asked him if he were talking about women, and Mr. R. said he was not. Mr. M. then said, "Oh, you're talking about being gay then." Mr. R. said that was it—he didn't want people to know about it, but he thought they could tell just by looking at him. The other members assured him that this was not so. Mr. R. then said he guessed

he should talk about this with me alone, because I had training and understood these things. Mr. M. supported this proposal. I said that I needed to disagree; it would be better for them to work on such problems here in the group. I said I thought other members had their own feelings about this subject and perhaps we could work on those, too. Mr. M. and Mr. O. said they were gay, too. I said we could talk about that next time.

It was almost time to close the meeting and Mr. R. said, "You can tell me to get out of this group and not come back." I said he must be afraid that we would kick him out because we thought that being gay was bad. He said, "How did you know?" and added that was exactly what he was feeling. First Mr. M. and then each other member said something to reassure him that they did not think worse of him for what he had shared here. I asked if he wanted to tell us anything else about his feelings about sharing with us. He said that part of a big load was off his mind, but he had another one now, knowing that others also shared his problem. I hoped his fears would not get so bad that he would not want to come back to the group. He said firmly, "Oh, no—I will be here." I said I would be on the ward tomorrow morning so any of them could see me if they wanted to. After the meeting, Mr. R. shook hands with me and thanked me for helping him to tell the group about himself.

In this example, the newest member opened up a subject that the group had avoided but was almost ready to discuss. In light of the reality that many people have homophobic attitudes, Mr. R. was appropriately cautious of and fearful about the responses to the self-disclosure. He tested the assumption that if the members knew about his sexual orientation, they would reject him. In the group, however, a process of mutual acceptance and capacity for empathy was operating that made it possible for Mr. R. to share his deep concern with the others and open up a hitherto taboo topic.

The social worker can provide conditions, through the relationship, that allow clients to test the validity of their beliefs about their worth and identity. When possible, a worker can use external realities to correct distortions in perception of self. In a group of married couples, for example, the leader said to a wife, "John just said that he loves you very much—didn't you hear him say that?" John said, "And I meant it—I do love you and want us to be happy together." Another member said, "And I think he really means it." Others nodded in agreement. Groups offer a broader arena for such testing than is true of one-worker–one-client relationships.

Activities may often be used for the express purpose of stimulating reflection on feelings and concerns. Many children will pour out their feelings and ideas on toy telephones, tape recorders, role playing, or through puppets, for such communication is one step removed from face-to-face communication with the leader and other members. As members progress in treatment, the nonverbal behavior becomes less prominent, and there is more moving back and forth between action and talking. In work with adults, movies, tape recordings, books, and pictures are often used to stimulate discussion of the event and then to move to discussion of how it is related to the experiences of the members.

The major skills used to achieve clarification of feelings, relationships, and behavior are numerous. The worker supports the members in ventilating feelings and then recognizing them by name. He contributes facts and ideas that are not otherwise available to the members; encourages appropriate self-disclosure, opening up frightening subjects for reflective discussion; and stays with the feelings rather than veers away from them. He uses confrontation selectively to interrupt nonproductive behavior and thus challenges obstacles to progress. He engages the members in reflective discussion of patterns of behavior as exhibited by individuals or the group. Through rephrasing statements, a member might modify her view of the problem or situation. He offers statements that connect two or more events; states clearly what he has observed and encourages members to check out these observations against their own; discloses his own feeling or reactions when he judges that will help the group—not to meet his own needs; asks the members to respond to each other's words and actions so as to maximize the value of feedback through using group processes in testing the validity of impressions and beliefs; and uses silence to promote time for reflective thinking. As members present their views, he searches for the common ground that often underlies differences. He uses activity-oriented experiences, as well as words, to help the members perceive themselves and situations more accurately. In whatever he says or does, he conveys strong support for the members' efforts to learn and conveys acceptance, empathy, and genuineness in relationships with them.

Many of the skills are used to illuminate the process that is going on in the group at a given time. The worker asks the members to reflect on what has happened in their relationships with each other in order to understand their patterns of feeling, thinking, and doing. She asks them to reflect on the consequences that the behavior has for them and for others and to discover discrepancies between attitudes and behavior or between past and present experiences. To help members examine their own process, the worker has to assess the process and request that the members look at what has been going on among them: what happened in what order, what they were thinking and feeling about what happened, and what alternative explanations they can give about the process. There may be initial resistance to a request to work on understanding the process. Examination of the behavior of self in relation to others may create anxiety because it reminds them of earlier comments about their behavior; such discussions are usually taboo in most social situations: there may be fears of retaliation for feelings expressed toward another or fear of disrupting the existing power structure. Once the members find acceptance for their thoughts and feelings, however, they become able to engage in such discussion and find it helpful. These discussions are a form of reflective thinking about the process going on among the members at a given time, which Yalom refers to as process illumination.[20]

A number of principles govern the use of techniques aimed at clarification.

1. Clarifying techniques should be based on sound assessment, yet offered in a tentative manner so that the worker can check his observation against the members' own views and invite feedback from the group. The worker shares the basis for reaching a particular generalization.
2. Usually, the briefer and more concise the comments, the better. It is important to present only one fact or thought at a time and to express oneself clearly, simply, and directly.
3. The worker needs to follow through with considerable exploration of the reactions of the member who is the target of a particular intervention and of the other members to the clarifying message. Furthermore, whatever understanding has developed needs to be repeated in different forms over a period of time if it is to result in more adaptive behavior.
4. The worker finds the thread of connections between one individual's need and the needs of others. There is a tendency to direct clarifying statements to individuals rather than to the group system. If more ascriptions are directed to the group, it is likely that a greater sense of relatedness and cohesiveness will develop.
5. The worker needs to pay attention to the group process—the continuity of content, communicative abilities and patterns, emotional ties, and roles of worker and members. Clarifications may be directed to an individual, but only when that will not detract from the group's progress. Individual reflection and introspection are pursued when they can be connected to the needs of other members and the readiness of the group at a given time.

To carry understanding further, when the worker judges it to be desirable, interpretation of the underlying meaning of behavior or its roots in the past may be used. Assessment of each member deals with the nature of the obstacles and the capacities of the ego to use such explanations. The worker considers the readiness of the members to participate, in relation to the nature of the common and unique needs in the group, mutuality of empathy, and potential effect on each member. It is futile and may be hurtful to present information about the underlying meaning of behavior before it can be comprehended or related to the current situation. Working toward such understanding should be a natural process, with members participating and the worker supplementing or affirming what the members are able to do.

> An illustration is from a group of patients in a mental hospital. One member, Mrs. J., was hiding under a blanket. The worker commented on this, saying that the members might like to discuss the idea of using physical hiding to shut out reality. One member suggested that Mrs. J. was hiding behind the blanket so she would not need to admit that she was daydreaming. Mrs. J. came out from under the blanket. She said she wanted to shut out her problems from the view of others. The worker said, "I wonder if you might want to shut out problems from your own view, too." Mrs. J. did not respond verbally, but other members acknowledged that this could be so. Two members gave examples from their own experiences. At the next meeting, Mrs. J. freely brought out deep feelings of hurt and said she no longer needed to hide behind her blanket.

Seeking for the meaning of behavior or underlying emotions may help persons to make connections between various aspects of problems, as they appear in current functioning, or to make connections between the past and the present. The focus is on bringing to conscious awareness such feelings and experiences that are not readily verbalized and acknowledged but that can be recalled, verbalized, and acknowledged with some assistance from others. At times, the past must be dealt with. As Konopka said "This does not mean that the past serves as an excuse, but even Freud never thought of it that way, nor that it suffices to dwell on the past. Looking at the past may help to work through present problems and to prepare for the future."[21] Many members of groups suffer from the memories of earlier traumatic experiences such as the Holocaust, rape, sexual molestation, parental divorce, or a murder or suicide in a family. The ghosts of the past must often be brought into the present and coped with.

The worker may ask the group to consider connections between feelings, behavior, or events. She may point up the consequences of behavior. When members or the worker suggest explanations, these are related to the particular situation, not generalized to the total personality. There is general agreement with Coyle's view that the worker refrains from "interpretations of unconscious mechanisms to individuals in the group, although he may help group members to deal with conscious or preconscious material."[22] Probes for connections and interpretations of meaning are likely to be more effective with clientele who have fairly good ego integration than with clients who are more emotionally disturbed.[23] Explanations and interpretations must be attuned to the particular perspectives of the members and timed in accordance with their readiness. That is a general principle, applicable to all groups.

An example of the use of interpretation is taken from Lee and Parks' record of a group of depressed adolescents in foster care.[24] Cherise is the member of the group with the most severe depression.

> After a round of work on accepting natural mothers for what they were, Cherise said her foster mother was old and didn't care much about her. She felt she had no family to talk about here. Her natural mother is dead, they don't know where her natural father is, she's never met her brother, and on top of all that, she doesn't feel she belongs in her foster family. The other girls were overwhelmed by this and saddened. They looked at me. I said that Cherise feels that everything has gone wrong for her. Let's help her to take one part at a time. The members asked different questions about what she had said. After Cherise told her story, I said that I think she feels particularly upset today because each of you has a living mother to talk about. She feels left out. (Interpreting and pinpointing the immediate provocation for her depression.) Cherise nodded in agreement. The girls were very supportive, but Leticia added, "Yeah, but with or without mothers, dead or alive, we all wound up in the same boat anyway—foster care, and none of us got fathers." They all laughed lightly, including Cherise. The work continued on a new level about foster families, and Cherise was with it.

All the principles used in clarification of members in their situations are used when interpretations of the meaning of behavior are made, but there are some additional principles.

1. In interpreting meaning, the worker usually offers his comments as impressions, suggestions, or opinions. He encourages the members to test out the applicability of the comments to their situations and to respond to them.
2. The worker avoids generalizations that deal with the total person. Rather, he partializes them to a particular feeling, behavioral pattern, or situation.
3. Interpretations are usually directed to the conscious or preconscious levels of personality. Usually the focus is on the present. Recall of the past is facilitated and past events are interpreted when such recall helps the person and other participants to cope with the past as it has an impact on the present.
4. Offering interpretations that explain the underlying meaning of behavior may threaten the ego's defenses; children and adults with weak egos need considerable support and empathy as they attempt to deal with understanding and coping with their difficulties.

5. The worker's aim, as with any other technique, is to help the members do as much as possible for themselves. Hence, questions that help members to explain feelings, behavior, and situations may be more effective than interpretations given by the worker because those contribute to a sense of power over their own lives. But when meaning eludes members and is considered by the worker to be important to progress, the worker's interpretations may be very useful and sometimes essential.

6. A special characteristic of the use of interpretation in a group is that, to be useful, it need not be directed specifically to a person. During a period when a problematic situation develops, various members may present experiences, feelings, and make relevant comments. To the extent that the underlying theme of the content is relevant to a particular person's concerns, he may derive understanding of himself and his experiences. Often when feelings or explanations are universalized, they touch closely on some members' particular concerns. This dynamic is what Konopka refers to as anonymity of insight.[25]

Whatever the major purpose of the group, some work on enhancing understanding of self, other people, and social situations is relevant. Skills are used differentially according to the major goals of the group and the needs of the members. In counseling and therapy groups, particularly, there is greater focus on interpretation than is usually true for groups in which the greatest emphasis is on cognitive learning, behavioral modification, or social action.

CRISIS RESOLUTION

Some groups are established for the primary purpose of helping individuals or families to resolve crises in their lives. But, in addition, crises are bound to occur in any group. Crises faced by members outside the group may be brought into the content of the group. The group, with its potential for support and stimulation, may be an effective aid in helping the person resolve the problem. Some crises, such as death of a loved one or attempted suicide, may require an individual service first, followed by membership in a crisis group.

Members of some groups are faced with crises over and over again, precipitated by lack of water and heat due to nonpayment of bills, suspensions from school, arrests, interpersonal violence, and illness. This is particularly true of low-income families with multiple situational problems and of persons with character disorders. Crises may occur also within the internal system of the group. The absence of a worker from a group of severely disturbed children, the transfer of the group to another worker, the death of a member, or any other sudden change in the group may be perceived as a crisis by the members. Such situations may stir up suppressed feelings about prior separations, so that the event itself is magnified beyond the reality of the situation. Within the climate of acceptance that tends to pervade the group during this stage, conflict between members or subgroups may be severe enough to constitute a crisis for the group.

A crisis is precipitated by a hazardous event, such as more than usual difficulties in making transitions to new roles, or by such circumstances as loss of health, death of a loved one, or traumatic experiences such as rape or physical assault. Or they may be precipitated by community disruptions or natural disasters such as riots, floods, and earthquakes. When people are in a state of crisis, they are especially susceptible to well-timed and well-focused help. The intensification of stress often enhances motivation to find new ways of coping with the problem. Two major goals of crisis intervention are to relieve anxiety and other symptoms of distress and to mobilize capacities for coping adaptively with the effects of stress on the person, family, or group.[26]

Crises that are most amenable to treatment through groups seem to be those in which members share the same precipitating event. The sense of a common fate is a strong force for mutual identification, support, and mutual aid in finding effective means of coping with the problem. An example is taken from the record of a rape survivors' group.

> Sara, twenty-five years old from a working class family, was the most troubled of the group of six survivors of rape. Her symptoms were the most severe: she was extremely fearful, nervous, and depressed. Having been, according to her own account, a sociable person, she was now leading a lonely, isolated life. She was able to work only part time and was angry with her parents who were divorced, paid no attention to her, blamed her, and offered no emotional support. The violent attack haunted her day and night. She was at work alone in the evening when two men broke into the office; they taped her face and arms; ransacked the office; and then took her into the bathroom, where each one raped her before locking her in. She had managed to get out eventually, called the police, who treated her politely but who were never able to find and arrest the men.

At this time, all members had attended at least three prior sessions. They had described and achieved some understanding of the nature of the rape, ventilated their feelings, and discussed the positive and negative reactions of families and friends to the event. The content of the group was now on how members were coping with their feelings and with other people, making efforts to find acceptance and understanding from families and friends. Sara was presenting information about the fact that she is alienated from her family. She kept repeating her story, with the result that several members became impatient.

> Recognizing her great sense of loneliness, I said, "Sara, it seems to me, as I have listened to you, that I hear something from you that I don't hear so much from the others. The other members seem to have found friends and family to confide in, but you seem to have few people just now to whom you can turn. Do you feel that you are very much alone with your fears and troubles?"
>
> Sara was silent for a moment and there were tears in her eyes as she replied that she was lonely and that, except for the group, there was no one to turn to. At this point, other members turned to Sara and assured her of their concern for her. Then Ellen questioned her about her reluctance to turn to anyone for comfort and company. Lois said that Sara seems so independent, but she needs help now. Sara replied, "I can't ask people. I can't do that. I don't want to be a little girl again. I've always been able to tough it out and that's what I want to do this time." Kathy said, "But, Sara, it doesn't mean you're weak because you ask other people for help." When there was a pause, I said, "You know, maybe you are ashamed to let anyone outside of this group see that you feel badly and need help."
>
> Lois picked this up and said that, until she had broken down with some of her friends, none of them had been able—or had dared—to offer help. Esther told the group how she had suffered after her father died, and the rape brought up a lot of those painful memories. But she has learned to challenge her mother and stepfather when they hurt her, and they are more respectful of her as a result. Alicia, a nun, said she had begun to discover new friends in her order, to whom she was beginning to open up about the rape and in whom she was learning to trust. Turning to Sara, she said, "I want you to listen to me. My dearest friend and I had a long talk about what had happened to me. It took me a long time to tell her because, as you know, I'm not a blabber mouth about myself. Anne said to me afterward that she was happy that I had confided in her and that she was able to help. I'm much stronger now because I know I can depend on someone else without giving up my integrity." Others shared their experiences in confiding in friends. Sara explained why she couldn't do that. She had told one old friend about the assault recently, but "I can't wake her up at two in the morning, when I feel most depressed." Esther said, "You're not listening to us: you can call me and any of us any time." Sara gulped and nodded. There was an exchange of phone numbers, and Lois asked, "Why didn't we think of this before? We can call each other." I said I was very glad they thought of this idea, and then asked Sara, "Do you know now that you have a good circle of supporters here?" She answered, "I do know that now."

The group is a temporary support system, but people in a state of crisis need to find others in the wider environment who will not blame them, who will listen to them, and who will provide opportunities to develop or reestablish relationships that have been cut off. In a research study, two thirds of the rape victims who were interviewed listed the need for support and understanding as most important.[27] The victim must deal not only with her own emotions and reactions but also with the reactions of other people, who, too often, blame the victim. Thus, the victim's efforts to cope are compounded by the reactions of others.

Working with people in a state of crisis makes full use of the problem-solving process in a time-limited treatment. It requires rapid assessment of the extent of the stress, the impact of the hazardous event on the person or group, the emotional reactions to the event, the coping devices that have been tried, the person's adaptive capacities, and available external sources of support. Within a climate of support and accepting relationships, the major interventions in this stage are intended to encourage ventilation and identification of the emotional reactions to the hazardous event as a means of relieving anxiety, to use clarifying techniques to achieve cognitive understanding of the event and its meaning to the person, to explore and evaluate coping mechanisms previously used that did not reduce the stress, to consider alternative solutions and select one or more that might best fit the person's needs and situation, and to test the appropriateness of the solutions to the situation. In the group, the members, as well as the worker, are expected to provide support, sensitive listening, suggestions for alternative means of problem solving, and hope that comes from perceiving that others have successfully risked new ways of coping and changing. Through such means, stress is reduced and social functioning is restored.

COMPETENCE IN ROLE FUNCTIONING

In this stage of development, many opportunities arise to help the members to learn adaptive behavior in carrying their social roles. The skills acquired in the group are then tested out in the community, which, after all, is the real proof of changes in adaptive capacity. Adaptation is a dynamic process that involves mastery of tasks and situations, as well as appropriate use of defenses and coping efforts. Mastery is successful performance in meeting the requirements of social roles. To become competent, people need considerable understanding of themselves and others and a network of skills, knowledge, and talents that enable them to interact effectively with their environments.

Knowledge about the tasks typical of stages of development in the life cycle, as described by such writers as Erikson and Maas, is useful to the practitioner in locating common needs and concerns, provided that the worker assesses individual differences and group deviations from such norms.[28] Unresolved problems from earlier stages may be brought into the group. Differences in life style concerning such matters as orientation to time, patterns of child rearing, gender role typing, group associational patterns, and educational and vocational aspirations need to be included in the worker's assessment of the adequacy of the members' performance of roles. The fact that most members have achieved satisfaction in their roles as members of the group enhances their readiness to examine their performance in other roles in which they have difficulty or the variables that seem to account for greater success in one role than in others.

Effective communication is one of the most important social skills. During earlier meetings, in order for the group to have formed, some satisfactory channels for communication were developed, and communication among members was adequate to achieve the tasks typical of those stages. The members now tend to use the group for help in working through problems in communication with such persons as their parents, children, siblings, employers, teachers, or colleagues.

> An example concerns Chata, aged fifteen, who announced that she had been "kicked out of school." The worker suggested that this was a good place to talk about it. Chata replied, "Oh, no, I never could." There followed considerable ventilation of negative feelings about school and empathy with Chata. But when she felt the worker's and the group's acceptance, she told the group about the situation. When another member asked if the suspension were final, it developed that Chata could be reinstated only if her mother would go to school. Her mother had refused to do this when her brother had been in similar trouble. Chata brought out much anger toward school and a feeling of hopelessness about her mother's lack of cooperation. Another member said, "Then there's just nothing that can be done." The worker said she did not think the situation was hopeless and suggested that the group could act out the situation to try to find ways that Chata might talk to her mother. She knew that the members were ready and able to help with the problem and that, as they worked on it, they would also learn more effective ways of communicating with their own parents.

One frequent type of competence is successful decision making. Members often have difficulty in making, evaluating, and implementing decisions. In social work practice with groups, the worker's emphasis is on helping the members to learn how to use a problem-solving process in arriving at decisions. The decision may focus on resolving a problem of a member or a problem in the group structure and interaction.

As the group progresses through time, its decisions now extend from those about the group's purpose, structure, norms, and process to those about the life of its members outside the group. The worker helps the group work toward decisions applicable to the life situations of the members. It is not realistic to hope that, if members learn how to make decisions about their group life, this ability can be transferred automatically to other situations. The members need to recognize the carryover to other areas of social functioning. Thus, the focus on problems in the interaction between individuals and the social environment needs to be maintained. It is important that the participants experience the relevance between what they do in the group and what they can do in the community.

Participation in planning and decision-making processes is often a means through which members of groups gain in social competence. How difficult this is for some people is often underemphasized.

> For example, during the sixth month of service to a group of very disturbed boys, aged twelve to fourteen, in a residential treatment center, the boys requested a trip to an amusement park. The worker, assessing that the boys were ready for it, engaged them in detailed planning for the trip. One of the first steps was to consider the nature of the decisions to be made: where to go, how to get there, how much money was needed, what to bring, and so forth. The tension became almost unbearable as the group decided that Billy, one of the oldest members, should make a phone call to get information about the amusement park. All of the boys tried to instruct Billy on how to use the phone and what questions to ask. None really knew how to do this. What a great sense of accomplishment the boys had when Billy was able to get at least some of the desired information.

Arriving at a decision is in and of itself not necessarily helpful. It is crucial that alternative solutions be considered and the consequences of each alternative explored thoroughly. To look at alternative modes of behavior and act on the basis of such examinations tends to enhance social competence.

> In a group of delinquent boys on probation, John exploded that his father was angry and had had enough of him. Tom asked about the trouble. John said he had been forbidden to use the car, but some of his friends insisted, so he gave in. Later that evening he was arrested for speeding. Then he grumbled about his father for a long time. Brian said, "But you're in double trouble—with the cops and with your dad." Tom said, "You sure messed up." The worker commented that John seemed caught between two pulls: his father and his friends. He suggested that the members go back to the time when John made the decision to take his father's car and think about other ways that John might have dealt with the problem.

In the discussion that followed, the worker helped the boys to understand conflicting desires and pressures, weigh circumstances, and make decisions based on what solutions bring satisfaction and have utility. Then, the group content turned to what John could do now. This decision-making process focused on one member, yet it provided a valuable experience for the others as well. It contributed to enhanced understanding of themselves in relation to situations. As they learn to be helpful to each other, people become more confident in their own capacities to face issues and make decisions.

Once implemented, decisions need to be reviewed, evaluated, and often modified on the basis of experience. Thus, there is a recurrent cycle of problem identification, decision making, and action on the part of an individual or of the group as a unit. Such problem-solving activities can enhance the members' general competence to make decisions that are based on understanding of one's own motives and the demands of the situation.

A variety of activity-oriented experiences, as well as discussion, may be used to enhance decision-making capacities. As part of the problem-solving process, members may be helped to carry out decisions through rehearsal. Rehearsal is useful in work with certain persons, regardless of their age, to clarify situations and plan how to face difficult situations. How to tell the teacher that one needs help, apply for a job, communicate effectively with parents or spouse, talk with a probation officer or employer, or behave when challenged to fight are common situations that can be discussed and rehearsed in the group. Follow-up of what happened when efforts were made to apply learning from the group to situations outside the group provides opportunity for evaluation and, when necessary, stimulates further efforts to solve the problem.

The problem-solving process can be used to help members with problems in their functioning in particular roles. Members can be encouraged to report incidents of problematic situations, explore the situation, and consider alternative means of dealing with the situation more effectively. Other members who have observed or been involved in similar situations can be effective in correcting each other's false perceptions of the situation or of their own behavior and in proposing alternative coping methods. When decisions have been made about the modes of behavior and means of achieving desired objectives, the worker suggests ways they can be put into practice between meetings. Through such means, persons can learn that new efforts are worthwhile, and progress becomes more rapid. Role playing may be used to recreate the stressful encounters and to test out alternative solutions. As new roles are explored, the members gain experience with different attitudes and a clearer perception of both the dynamics behind the action and the ways in which others perceive them. Such activities may be effective as practice for reality.

Movement toward more focused discussion of the members' own functioning in their roles may take different routes. In earlier stages, for example, there may have been concern with concrete problems that impede effective performance of roles, such as environmental stresses or lack of opportunities for education, job training, child care, and so forth. When such stresses are relieved, or opportunities provided, there is often consideration of attitudes and behavior that limit effectiveness of functioning and efforts to cope more effectively. In other groups, progression may be from concern about the behavior of others to concern about one's own behavior.

The development of skills necessary for improved performance in selected roles may comprise a considerable portion of the content of the group. Using communication skills, rehearsing behavior, preparing budgets, practicing ways to make friends, and learning activities that are expected of a person of a given age and gender are but a few examples of specific content in this area. Reports of progress or successes in meeting expectations of roles outside the group become more frequent as the group progresses. The worker's focus is not limited to the content of specific roles but is also on the development of affective and cognitive styles or processes of acquiring mastery over oneself and the environment.

To become competent in the performance of social roles requires that a person have knowledge about and ability to use resources and supportive networks. Depending upon the purpose of the group and the members' situations, the content of the group may include information about and skills in identifying and using resources through discussion, sharing of experiences, bringing resource persons into the group, and referrals. The members of groups are thereby linked to other people and services in the community in a manner that enhances their self-esteem, as well as their problem-solving capacities. The members' participation in the process is extensive; the leader offers his knowledge and expertise to them.

Altruism is a dynamic positive force for change. Concern with dependency-interdependency conflicts and the concomitant need to both give and take are prevalent with many members of groups. With people in hospitals and other residential settings, particularly, there is necessary dependence on many staff members. A sign of maturity in relationships is to be able to give, as well as to receive. The group itself fosters interdependency among members, but often a need also exists to give to others outside the group, within the institution or the wider community. The ego-enhancing opportunities to give to others, in terms of contributions of time, ideas, or material things, should not be underestimated.

A group of mothers of hospitalized children, toward the end of their experience in a group, used the last session to plan and carry out special holiday programs for all the children and staff in the hospital. A group of physically handicapped children were enthralled when, instead of only being entertained and given to at a community party, the members could contribute cookies and take responsibility for registering guests. A group composed of mentally ill patients sent representatives to a meeting that was held to plan a community action program on mental health. A group of black adolescent girls, following discussion of their own feelings about experiences with discrimination, initiated and participated responsibly in a social action project directed toward making a recreational activity available to people of all races. A parent education group, in cooperation with a church, developed a playground for young children and volunteered to supervise it. Low-income parents, previously fearful of approaching school personnel, became active in a parent-teachers association and thereby helped to achieve a school lunch program.[29] Interdependence, then, is important, not only within the group, but also between the group and the community.

The worker progressively extends the experience of the members to other areas of community life. Expectations for members are raised gradually as they show the capacity to achieve certain tasks and as they indicate readiness for more complex activities. Through broadening the experience of members and evaluating with them their responses to new situations, members become able to handle a greater variety of experiences in an adequate manner. Soon they will become ready to leave the group.

12

Stage IV: Separation, Termination, Transition

Termination is a dynamic and vital process in social work. It is more than a symbol of the end of treatment: it is an integral part of the process. If properly understood and managed, it becomes an important force in integrating changes in feeling, thinking, and doing. These changes, though, are of little value to the clients until they can apply the benefits gained from the group experience to everyday relationships and achievements.

Social work services are always time limited. "The goal of treatment," said Hamilton, "is always to help the person return as soon as possible to natural channels of activity with strengthened relationships."[1] Professional help beyond the point that the person's natural growth can be resumed may interfere with the natural potential for growth and lead to continuing dependency. If a member is helped to face the meaning of the group experience and to leave it with a sense of achievement, she should be able to use what she has learned in her relationships and roles in the community. She may be more able to cope with other separations that occur throughout her life. As Yalom says, "termination is thus more than an extraneous event in the group; it is the microcosmic representation of some of the most crucial and painful issues of all."[2]

Ending an experience needs to be done in such a way that social work values are implemented. Ideally, a person belonged to a group in which he has been helped to achieve his goals, has felt that he had been treated with acceptance and respect, and has been encouraged to participate actively in the process, with due regard for the welfare of self and others. A somewhat interdependent and intimate relationship has been achieved with the leader and other members of the group. The members have found mutual acceptance and respect and have participated actively in a process of mutual aid. Now the termination of a member or the breaking up of a group needs to be done in such a way that the ending becomes a dynamic growth-producing experience.

The decision to terminate and the process of ending make use of the knowledge essential to effective practice. A group has been formed and sustained for achieving particular goals. Now, the knowledge about biopsychosocial functioning is used to help the members to leave the worker and each other. Particularly useful are perspectives on growth and development that incorporate the concepts of loss and separation related to the significance of social relationships to people in each phase of development and that explain the ways the ego defends itself against, copes with, and masters the experience. Erikson, Maas, and Shapiro have such a perspective.[3] When faced with loss or separation, the steady state is upset. The members react with a variety of emotional and behavioral reactions to the loss of a member or worker and to the threat of group termination. The nature and intensity of the reactions to termination depend upon many circumstances, such as the structure of the group, the length of service, reasons for termination, past experiences with losses and separations, and the extent of meaningful relationships and supports in the environment.

CHARACTERISTICS OF THE GROUP

Balgopal and Vassil point out that the termination stage is marked by a

> transition from the rhythm of work to disengagement and preparation for the future. Earlier themes of loss, dependency, and ambivalence are revisited and co-exist with feelings of satisfaction and recognition of limited but worthy accomplishments. As members look backward and forward, the group experience is memorialized and affirmed as a reference point for negotiating the future.[4]

As the group moves toward readiness for termination, the socioemotional issues become separation and coming to terms with the meaning that the group experience has had for the members. The members exhibit anxiety about separation and ambivalence about the loss of relationships with the social worker and other members. They mobilize their defenses against facing termination. Although they accept each other, there is a movement toward the breaking of interpersonal ties as members find satisfaction in relationships outside the group. Exceptions are in work with family units or peer groups that will continue to meet after the ending of the social work service.

The goals that members have for themselves and for each other have been partially achieved, although movement in the group may have been faster for some than for others, and some may be more satisfied with the progress made than others are. Members generally talk about some of the changes that have taken place in themselves and in the group. Future plans become prominent topics of discussion, and there is greater readiness for new relationships and experiences in the community. Attendance may become irregular unless the worker makes special efforts to motivate members to continue until the final session. Some members may feel ready to terminate before the time set for the group; others may want to drop out owing to insecurity, feeling they have been left behind by members who have made more rapid progress. The structure tends to become more flexible, for example, by the giving up of official roles within the membership or by changes in time, place, and frequency of meetings. The norms of members have become more nearly in harmony with those of appropriate socially desirable segments of the community where the members live or of which they are a part. The members' norms evidence some degree of confidence in the future. Communication tends to be free and easy, although sometimes obstacles to open communication arise. Group controls are lessened, and a greater increase in inner controls occurs on the part of the members. Cohesion weakens as the members begin to find satisfactions and new relationships outside the group.

TERMINATION OF INDIVIDUALS

Termination occurs for a number of reasons, some of them planned as an integral part of service, and some of them unplanned or unanticipated. Ideally, termination occurs when the members no longer need the professional service. The social worker is required to make a judgment that there has been sufficient progress to enable the person to continue to consolidate the gains he has made without the help of the worker and often also without the group. All people have problems, but usually they can cope with them with the support and help of families, friends, and nonprofessional community resources. It is unrealistic to continue service until the members have achieved their fullest potential; the question rather is whether or not there has been sufficient progress to assume that the members can continue to improve without the group.

Too often, termination occurs that is not the natural outcome of a plan for one or more members of the group. Changes in the interests and situations of members often result in premature termination from a group, for example, a move away from the locale in which the group meets, a change in the work or school schedule of a member, an illness, the removal of a child from a group by the parent, lack of continued eligibility for public assistance, or other situations over which the worker has no control. Whenever a member drops out, both the member who leaves and the remaining members have varied feelings about the event. Here is an example of a group in which one member discloses that he is going to leave the group.

The members of the group have severe coronary artery disease and are in different stages of recovery. The goals of the group were to enhance the members' understanding of their condition, reduce the isolation they all felt, lessen anxiety through the ventilation of feelings, reduce reliance on unhealthy defenses, develop an awareness of the patterns of behavior that influence health, and deal with the practical realities of daily living. The group had been meeting for several months when faced with the loss of one of its members, Ben. Seven members were present.

> Ben was very quiet throughout the meeting. When there was a pause in the discussion, he announced that this would be his last time in the group. He was moving up North to a new home. He invited the members to visit him there when he got settled. He wrote down the address and phone number so that the members could copy it. He said he was sad to leave in a way: he did not think he could have made it without the group. He said this feeling was a dramatic change from the beginning when he really did not think the group would be worth much, but he learned differently.
>
> It was very quiet. All the members sat with arms crossed and heads down. I said that I would miss Ben. I appreciated his openness and friendliness. Ed looked up and said he would miss him, too. He said he had always felt comfortable with Ben. Jerry just shook his head, unable to say anything. Gloria made light of it, saying in a teasing way, "If I come to see you, do I have to bring my husband?" Ben joked with her about this, but there was a sense of mutual caring in the banter. Jim said he admired Ben for all he had done and wished him the best—he wished he had the guts to do what Ben had done. Jerry got up, went over to Ben, and said, "We've been here since the group started—both of us—it's hard to see you go." Mary said she never dreamed he would leave like this, and Janet looked sad but said nothing.
>
> Ben told of leaving the group in a calm and gentle manner, but the group felt betrayed and let down. Although he had mentioned his intention to move much earlier, the group thought he meant some time in the distant future, and none of the members were prepared for his leaving now.

The group was able to make use of the group process to express their feelings about one member leaving; the worker intervened actively only to open up discussion through sharing his own feelings about the loss and through nonverbal support of the members' interactions.

Another major reason for early termination is the dropout's problems in group participation. When members drop out, they tend not to share their intention to do so with the worker or the other members. They stop coming to the meetings. The stress of belonging to the group is too much for them. They fear intimacy or the demands for self-disclosure, they are unable to share with others, they get inadequate support, they lack a sense of compatibility with others, or they do not see the group's purpose and procedures as relevant to their particular needs and situations. These problems in participation often result from errors in the planning process or in inadequate preparation for the group experience.[5]

Other dropouts are due to lack of skill on the part of the social worker. The dropouts are dissatisfied with the worker or the group in some way, and the worker has not helped them to explore these dissatisfactions. The worker or other members may have threatened their defenses, so they cope by fleeing the group. The worker may not have given adequate attention to helping the person find solutions to the problems of group participation to enable the members to remain in the group.

Follow-up of absences is essential in order to understand the reason for withdrawal, to assess the member's needs and situation, and, when indicated, to help the person to return to the group. After all, people cannot be helped if they do not come. Some highly competent practitioners almost never have dropouts, because they have skill in the planning process and in preparing prospective members for the group; they also have confidence about the value of the group, and this gets transmitted to the members. They have skill in selecting and using the appropriate supportive or challenging techniques at a given time.

In many groups, the plan is that members may terminate at different times. In open-ended groups, a member leaves a group that is going to continue without him. Even in relatively closed membership groups, some members may be ready to leave before the termination of the group itself. The termination of one member poses both special problems and opportunities for the worker and the members. In some instances, the fact that a member is ready for termination provides both hope and stimulation toward change for the other members. In other instances, it points up the slower progress of the others and is reacted to with a sense of failure or discouragement. It may arouse feelings of rivalry and competition among the members. Those members who remain may feel apprehensive about what new members will come to fill the place of the departing one. They have to adapt to a changed group. When a new person enters the group, both the old members and the newcomer worry about whether they will be acceptable to each other. If these feelings are not recognized and dealt with, the old members tend to project onto the new arrival the anger left over from the experience of losing a valued member of the group.

Time needs to be devoted to preparing an individual for termination and to helping the remaining members with their reactions to the person who is leaving and to the change in the composition and dynamics of the group occasioned thereby. The worker tries to use this change for the benefit of all. If the members do not bring up the subject of the loss of a member, a collective denial may be operating. The worker needs to introduce the subject and explore its meaning to the members. A universalizing comment is often effective, for example, that people usually feel sad when someone is leaving, followed by asking the members to discuss this topic. Usually, members are relieved when the issue is brought out into the open. Such discussion is invaluable to the terminating member, who perceives the meaning her leaving has for her and for others. Some members with long histories of damaged self-esteem find it difficult to imagine they have really helped other members and contributed to the group. The painful disruption of relationships during termination is eased for such a person when she understands not only that she is ready to leave but also that she will be missed.

TERMINATION OF WORKER

The social worker may be the person who terminates his relationship with a group, particularly in groups that meet for many months as contrasted with short-term groups. Too often, the worker leaves when the group is in the early part of the work stage. The members have developed trust in and affection for the worker and may be in the very midst of working on interpersonal problems. The reasons for the worker's termination tend to be such situational factors as a change in work assignments, a long illness, change of job, or the planned end of an assignment, as when interns complete their field work. When a worker leaves before the group is ready to terminate, the desirable situation is a planned transfer to another worker. The amount of time it takes to accomplish a successful transfer depends upon the nature of the group.

One example of a transfer of a group to a new worker is taken from the record of a group of fourteen- and fifteen-year-old girls who had been referred by their school to a community agency that specializes in services to adolescents with severe problems in school and in the community. The worker, a second-year student in a graduate school of social work, was to complete her assignment at the time of graduation. The group was well into the work stage of development. She introduced the topic of her leaving several weeks before the event.

> In the next meeting, Sally asked if I meant it when I said I would be leaving them in June. Opal protested that she still needed me "real badly," and Sally said, "We all do, honestly." I said I thought I understood that they really wanted me to stay with the group, but I could not do so. I had to leave because I was completing my internship—I was taking a full time job—but another social worker from our agency would meet with them for another six months. Ann said, "That's not the same," and the others nodded agreement with her. I acknowledged that it would not be the same but that I felt confident the group could continue and have a good experience with another worker. Opal

said she didn't want "a fat social worker from the welfare department." I said it would be one of the workers from this agency and helped them to express some of their fears about what the new worker would be like.

Next meeting. Jan said that all this talking made her hungry and wondered if we could go to the hot dog stand in the station wagon. I asked if the others wanted to do this, and they all agreed they did. On the way, we talked again about my leaving. I said we had four more meetings and the last meeting would be on June 14. Sally protested that she didn't realize it would be so soon. The others echoed this statement. Ann said she wanted to cry because she did not want me to leave. Jan said she guessed they would all cry when I left. I told the girls that it would be hard for me to leave them also. When they asked who the new social worker would be, I said I would give them a definite answer next week.

Next meeting. As we were driving in the station wagon, I said that I wanted to tell them that Mrs. D. would be their new social worker. They said it would be hard to get used to somebody new—just as they got used to somebody, she left them. I said I guessed it felt as if I were deserting them. Opal said that "That's exactly it—you are." Most of the girls then expressed a little anger at me. Opal wanted to know if Mrs. D. were Causasian or black. I said she was Caucasian but wondered why she asked that question. Opal said they just wanted to know. I wondered what they would prefer. Ann asked, "What are you?" I said I was Caucasian, and Opal said, "Then, that's what we want." Sally said she didn't care what color the new worker was, whether she was pink, purple, yellow, white, or black so long as she was someone they could get along with. I asked what she meant by "get along with." She said someone who could understand them and was kind and considerate. Ann added, "someone we can talk to and won't try to tell us what to do." When Gladys said, "and someone who can help us with our problems like you do," Ann said, "we'll all buy that." And Kay added, "but not too serious—we need some fun, too."

I said that, although it would be hard at first, I'm sure they will become able to get along well with Mrs. D. I said that Mrs. D. had asked me to ask them what meeting she should come to before I leave so that they could become acquainted. After some discussion and further protest of the fact that the end would come too soon, they agreed she should come to the next-to-the-last meeting. They wanted to be able to tell me if they liked her at the last meeting.

Back in the Center, as the girls were eating corn chips and cookies, Opal brought up the question of Jenny's infection: they expressed concern about her. Opal asked what it meant if you had a discharge. I said it could mean different things, ranging from something very minor to something quite serious. Opal said she guessed they all better go back to the V.D. clinic. We talked about their experiences at the clinic. Opal and Kay said their reports were negative. Helen said that her and Mary's reports had been positive until last time, which was a great relief. The discussion turned quite naturally to the subject of pregnancy. I answered their questions and said they seemed to have deep concerns about the matter. They said they did. I said this was one thing we could work on in the remaining time we had together, and then Mrs. D. could also work with them on their concerns if even more help was needed. I said I had told Mrs. D. about each of them and about what the group had been doing. They said they were glad that I had done that—it would make it easier for them to get acquainted with her.

Next meeting. The girls expressed concern about whether Mrs. D. would let them be noisy at times and smoke as I had. I said I was sure she would understand that there were times when they needed to blow off a little steam, and although we wish they didn't smoke, the agency does not forbid them from doing it. Again, we talked about their fear of having a new worker, and I repeated exactly how we would work out the transfer of leadership. They seemed to take some comfort from knowing what would happen and that I would be present when they meet Mrs. D.

Next-to-the-last meeting. Mrs. D. and I arrived at the Center a little early. All of the girls were already there, dressed in their best clothes. There was an air of excitement in the room. At my suggestion, the members all participated in telling Mrs. D. something about the group. I shared what the members had told me about what they wanted in their next worker, asking them if I had got it right. They nodded their approval. Mrs. D. said they expected a lot from her, but she would do her best in working with them. There was a very positive tone, until Mrs. D. said she was sure they could work out some of the problems they had mentioned before the group would end in December. Although I had told them twice that we thought the group would be continued for six months more, the girls became very resistant and defensive, saying that if we really cared about them we would not throw them out like that. Sally said she didn't expect her problems to be gone by December, and besides, "we like the group." The other members supported Sally by grumbling assent to her remarks, although they became silent and sullen for most of the meeting.

Mrs. D. left about 5:30, and the rest of the meeting was spent in helping the girls to express their feelings of hostility and frustration. They questioned whether they even wanted to continue in the group. I said this was certainly their choice to make and I thought they probably had mixed feelings about it. Opal commented that Mrs. D. was "too serious" for us. Ann said this was probably because she was "nervous." I suggested that they might also have felt nervous. This met with an emphatic positive response. They said they had wanted to make a good impression on Mrs. D. and wanted her to like them. I expressed my confidence in their ability to get along with her and in her ability to like and care for them. I reminded them that the decision to plan for the group to last for six more months resulted from the progress they had made and that they should feel pride in the fact that we think they can get along without therapy after that time. Mrs. D. can help them find other groups to which they would like to belong or interests they would like to pursue in the community. They will not have to give up the friendships they have made in the group. They seemed to take some comfort from these comments and even began to talk about how different they were now than when they first came to the group.

Last meeting. The girls had planned a surprise party for me and took a great deal of pride in what they had done. They were pleased with my surprise and delight in the party. There was some discussion of the next week and their relationship with Mrs. D. It was much more positive than last week. Sally was able to say she was looking forward to getting to know Mrs. D., and the other girls seemed to support this idea.

Toward the end of the meeting, I asked them to share their impressions of how each of them had made progress this year, and I shared my own impressions with them. I mentioned that we had worked on many individual and shared problems and that they could continue to help each other and get help from Mrs. D. with those that were still most troublesome. I let them know that it was difficult for me to have to say goodbye to them, for they had taught me how to be a better social worker, and I liked and cared about each of them. There was a thoughtful silence, broken by Sally's saying, "We'll sure miss you," echoed by the others.

I took pictures of each girl with my Polaroid camera and also gave each girl a turn at deciding what kind of picture of the group she wanted. Giving the pictures to the girls served as a fitting closing ritual. I drove each of the girls home and went to say goodbye to the families and to each girl in turn.

Note that the social worker had established a close relationship with the members and they with her and with each other. She accepted and clarified the girls' feelings about her leaving and the new worker's coming. She gave the members accurate information, reviewed and supported the progress they had made, engaged them in making decisions about priorities for work during the remaining time together, prepared them for the next experience with a new worker, supported their efforts to cope with the situation, and ended her relationship with them. She did not forget the importance of the girls' families to the success of the group and took time to terminate with them.

The loss of a worker, especially in groups of persons with serious psychosocial problems, may be a traumatic event unless handled with empathy and skill. Successful working through of separation from workers can have beneficial outcomes in the members' learning to cope more effectively with the many separations that people face in their lives. But, too often, the termination of a worker unnecessarily disrupts progress toward the agreed-upon goals for each member and the group as a whole. Inadequate time is given to preparation and consideration of the consequences of the loss of a worker to the group. Too often, the too early loss of a worker occurs in groups led by students who are on an academic year calendar, which often does not coincide with the needs of clients. If initial planning for groups were more thorough, these situations could be anticipated and means developed to minimize the negative consequences of worker turnover. A planned duration for a group that coincides with the planned time available for the practitioner may be an effective alternative to continuous groups with frequent changes of workers and members. The goals would be sufficiently specific and clear that the members could feel satisfaction in their progress in the group. When such help was insufficient, the members could be assigned to new groups with revised goals to meet their specific needs. The existing group could be reorganized with some new and some old members and a new worker but with a new working agreement. In light of the evidence from research that services of planned and fairly limited duration are at least as effective as long-term help is, there should be compelling reasons for continuing groups from month to month or from year to year.[6] Social workers have a responsibility to make efforts to change organizational policies and procedures that create obstacles to the successful termination of individuals and the group.

TERMINATION OF GROUPS

The purposeful nature of social work implies that from time to time it is necessary to assess the desirability of continuing the group. One criterion for termination is that progress toward the achievement of goals has been sufficient and further help is not necessary, so the group should be terminated. In addition to the achievement of specific goals, there should be an expectation that the members will be able to function without the group but will use appropriate resources in the community for meeting their needs. The worker has anticipated termination from the beginning of her work with the group and has clarified with the members its possible duration, so that the goals and the means of achieving them have been related to plans for both individuals and the group. Sometimes the nature of the service itself determines the approximate number of sessions, planned and understood from the beginning. That form of termination is typical of family life education groups, task-centered practice, crisis intervention, and services to patients who are hospitalized for a fairly predictable period of time.

When the members have made little progress and there seems to be little potential for changing the situation, the service may need to be terminated. But every effort should be made then to find a more suitable form of service for the members. There are times, too, when entropy takes over; the group disintegrates owing to the loss of members or unresolvable problems in the relationships among the members or in the group's structure and processes. In such instances, the social work goals have not been achieved. If it is too late for the worker to help the members to work through the problems, then there is no choice but to terminate the group. Mayadas and Glasser postulate that neither task nor treatment groups will survive unless there is a high level of both task interdependence and socioemotional attraction among the members.[7] Attraction to both the tasks and to the relationships results in the members' satisfaction with the group.

Some groups are established for a particular period of time, and the members have known this fact since the time of the initial interview. Ideally, planning for the length of service was related to the agency's purpose of offering the group service. Knowledge about the duration of the group has been an important factor in the determination of specific goals by the members and of the content and focus of the group.

Some groups of predetermined duration are time-limited ones, consisting of from one to approximately sixteen sessions. They are used for such purposes as orientation, preparation for a new experience, coping with crises, support during a period of transition, or the resolution of specific situational problems. The limited duration of the group does not mean that it has been less meaningful to its members than if it had been of longer duration. The greater specficity of the shared problems or the crisis situations may indeed have influenced the development of intensive relationships among the members and with the worker and a deep sense of accomplishment. A short-term group moves through all the stages of development but in a condensed manner. Knowledge of the duration of the group has, to some extent, eased the trauma of leaving a meaningful experience. But the members of such a group still have many ambivalent reactions to the reality of the group's termination similar to those of members of continued service groups.

In groups without a preset date for termination, there is a tendency to delay making decisions about the group's ending. The worker needs to search for clues that the group should be terminated. The initial clues often come from the members themselves. The content of the group tends to include more reports from members about their successful efforts to try new things or to modify their patterns of behavior outside the group. The worker is alert to such a development in the group. He responds to these cues, if his own evaluation of progress confirms the members' views, by introducing the possibility of termination of the group in the near future. The responses of the members indicate whether or not he should pursue the subject further or await developments. But the practitioner cannot wait for the group to introduce the matter of termination and to make a decision about it. When it does not come from the group, he is responsible for introducing the reality of termination and for shifting toward preparing the members for it.

A short-term group without a preset duration was started for assisting severely disabled women patients to accept and plan for their discharge from a rehabilitation hospital. During the past two months, the group had made great progress and become very cohesive. The first few meetings were devoted to clarifying group purpose, developing mutual expectations, and ventilating hostility toward being discharged. Then the group considered what alternatives were available to them for future living and made some realistic decisions and plans. The group members became able to help each other a great deal and had changed from narcissistic attitudes to mutual concern for each other.

The worker opened this meeting by stating that the group would soon end, as all of them would be moving into nursing homes of their choice. She said that each one had made progress and had been able to help others, too. She then asked if the members would like to discuss their progress. One by one, the women reported how much they felt they had accomplished. It was obvious that the group had been a meaningful experience for each of them. The worker encouraged and supported each in her evaluation of the group meetings. Then, the focus was on the dates when the members would leave the hospital.

MRS. G.: I don't care when they set the date for me to leave. If I have to leave, I'll just go on and leave. I don't want to be in anybody's way. If the doctors are through with me here, and there's nothing else they can do for me, and if they don't want me here, then I'll just go ahead and leave. But they promised me an electric wheelchair, and as soon as I get my chair, I'll just go on and go.

WORKER: You feel they don't want you here?

MRS. G.: Well, they must not—they're sending us out.

WORKER: Does anyone want to respond to Mrs. G.'s feelings about being set out? (No response.) Do any of the rest of you have feelings like that?

MRS. C.: All I want is for them to give me time to have my sister come out and help me get my things together. But, I still have some problems getting my shoes on—maybe that swelling will hold me back.

MRS. A.: (Started to say something when interrupted by Mrs. T.)

MRS. T.: I don't want to go—I want to stay here—but they won't let me.

WORKER: It's not easy to leave a place where you have lived for so long, is it?

MRS. T.: (looked wistfully and said softly) "No."

MRS. C.: It won't be easy—I'll feel very sad, but I'm ready.

WORKER: Mrs. A., you seem to have wanted to say something earlier but didn't have a chance.

MRS. A.: The way I feel about it is that since we have had these wonderful meetings, it has brought out many things and thoughts we wanted to express. You've all done wonderful work with us. I don't believe, like Mrs. G. said, that they don't want us here. It's just that there are new patients coming in every day and this is rehabilitation. After they have done all they can for us, they are trying to find us a better place to go if we don't have a home to go to.

MRS. G.: I didn't mean that they don't want us here, but rather that they are ready for us to go, and they have done all they can for us. I'm sure they would want us here if they could do more for us. We just have to go where we can be peaceful, and I think the doctor does want us to go where we can get the care we need.

MRS. C.: We really have been treated well here, and you (looking at the worker) have helped us so much.

WORKER: The group seems to have had a lot of meaning for many of you.

She then turned the discussion toward how the group could help them until they leave the hospital. The discussion focused primarily on the choice of nursing homes and the things they could do for themselves now.

In the last two meetings, there were further discussions of sadness at leaving the worker, each other, and the hospital and still some anger about being pushed out. The predominant feelings, however, were those of pride in having made enough progress to leave and to prepare for a new life in a nursing home.

The need for termination should be discussed well in advance of the termination date to allow sufficient time to make of it a positive experience for the members. But if termination is discussed too early, anxiety and hostility may be aroused that detract from motivation to use the group fully toward goal achievement. The time span between the initial information about termination and the final meeting of the group will vary with many factors, including the group's purpose, the length of time that members have been together, the problems and progress of the members, their anticipated reactions to termination, and the press of environmental circumstances on them. If a tentative date for termination is set, work can proceed with that time in mind, yet it is hoped there can be flexibility in changing the date if circumstances warrant it.

REACTIONS OF MEMBERS TO TERMINATION

A group experience may feel so good and be so gratifying to the members that they want to continue, even though they have made many positive gains and could probably maintain these in the community. The conflict between the acknowledgment of improvement and movement away from social work help, and the fear of the loss of the worker's special attention and the support of the group, lead to varied reactions to termination on the part of members.[8] In groups in which intimacy and interdependence have been prominent and in which members have disclosed their feelings and problems, the members need help to work through their ambivalence about termination. The major theme is separation and loss.[9]

The theme is addressed both in terms of feelings among the members and in terms of opportunities to work on old conflicts about loss and separation. As Bywaters says, "closure is an opportunity to choose, face, and accept separation and to experience the survival of loss and evidence of new strength and mastery."[10] The desire for dependency is reactivated, and there is a need to retest relationships, as was done in earlier stages. To the extent that a worker or a member of a group becomes loved and valued by one of the members, that member will feel a deep sense of loss and will need to mourn the loss. Thus, as Bowlby indicates, "separation anxiety is the inescapable corollary of attachment behavior."[11] When members face the reality of their feelings about the loss that is inherent in termination, they react with expressions of sadness and engage in reflective thinking about the situation. Such reflective thinking and acceptance of the separation are major sources of therapeutic gain. The learned capacity to deal with separation and other aspects of the group experience may be carried over to more effective coping with later losses in life.[12]

When members of groups have achieved a sense of closeness, termination is especially difficult, as exemplified by a therapy group in an adult psychiatric clinic in which the members had been together weekly for six months to work on their maladaptive patterns of interpersonal relationships. About halfway through the session, the focus shifted from discussion of sexual matters to termination.

Shirley said she thought the group really understood her situation. Maria casually commented that now that she finally felt understood by us, the group is going to finish. She added that when this group finishes, she is going to have to go back to something stronger. What will we do?

WORKER: What about when this group finishes? (Response is confusion.)

SAM: I wanted to ask about that.

SHEILA: Do we get thrown out with the garbage?

WORKER: Thrown out with the garbage? That's how you feel about terminating?

SHEILA: I feel, yeah, like where do I turn? Cause I look forward to it so much all week. To me, this is my everything. And to think by next month, you know, I don't know what happens. What will happen then?

MARIA: That's what I was trying to ask.

WORKER: Might we talk now about what's going on with us in thinking about parting. What are you feeling now?

SHEILA: It's been on my mind for some time. You said something about next month being the end and that's been bothering me ever since. (After some other discussion.)

MARIE: I think we are getting closer. I think everyone feels like they want more, and then all of a sudden, there's nothing to get together.

SHIRLEY: Even if we find another group, it won't be the same. (Each member of the group expressed similar feelings of regret about the end of the group, and Maria reiterated, "And just as we're really getting close!")

WORKER: It may be that what Maria is talking about is really what is happening. Somehow, in spite of all our fighting and carrying on back and forth, there is a feeling of closeness.

MARIA: Yes, we know each other.

WORKER: And the feeling that something has happened here.

TERRY: Yes, yes.

SHEILA: Yes, definitely. And it feels so good.

WORKER: Is closeness not the heart of the problem? Everybody needs to be close to people, and yet you fight against it all the time. And suddenly the thought that whatever you're sharing here is blowing apart makes you feel terrible.

SHEILA: That's right—definitely! I've been thinking. What am I going to do?

SAM: I had that feeling before, when a worker at the child agency left. She left.

WORKER: What's the feeling when a person gets left?

SAM: You feel lost . . . or . . . well, that's the way I felt.

SHIRLEY: I remember the feeling, but I can't put it into words.
SAM: The feeling is lost.
SHEILA: And frightened.
SHIRLEY: And, oh, so lonely
SHEILA: All of these—lost, frightened, lonely.
TERRY: That's it. All of them.

Terry shared an experience when he felt lost and lonely, followed by stories from several other members. The group continued with this level of intensity for the remainder of the session. I shared my feelings of loss regarding termination, also. There was a reluctance to end the session when the time was up. I said that we still had two more weeks together and we can try to make the most of them.

The worker recognized that she needed to encourage ventilation of the ambivalent feelings, clarify them, and connect the feelings to the issue of intimacy and other losses in the members' lives. The interacting skills are primarily support, exploration, and clarification.

Termination is viewed with ambivalence by almost all members of groups and by the social worker, for that matter. In another group of adult women, the worker commented that people usually have mixed feelings about ending with a group and asked if some of them could express their feelings about termination. Mrs. B. spoke up, saying that she knows she still needs to come—she is not ready to leave. The worker wondered if she were feeling pushed out, to which Mrs. B. replied, "That's exactly what I feel," and elaborated on these feelings. Mrs. T. and Mrs. G. said they also felt that way. Mrs. J. said she would miss the group, but she would feel good to be able to manage on her own. Mrs. T. said that she was being pushed out too soon; then, after a silence, "but I feel I've gained a lot, too."

Expression of ambivalent feelings about termination makes it more possible for the members to evaluate the experience realistically, rather than have it clouded by unrecognized feelings. If ambivalence is worked through, the members' ego capacities are released for other purposes. Doubt, hesitancy, and unresolved tugs between positive and negative feelings are characteristic of this stage of development. Members recognize the progress they have made and want to move on to new relationships and new activities, yet they also want to continue to receive the gratifications provided by the worker and the sense of belonging to the group. They may mobilize a variety of defenses to cope with the ambivalence. The strength of the dependency needs, the nature of the relationships in the group, and the amount of improvement that has been made will influence how a particular member will respond. The diversity of reactions set off by the confrontation that the group will definitely terminate is reminiscent of the range of maneuvers displayed during the time when the group was forming. Anxiety similar to that experienced over coming together is felt now in relation to moving apart and breaking the bonds that have been formed. Some members do not know their feelings and are bewildered by them. Garland, Jones, and Kolodny point out that many maneuvers are employed by the members both to avoid and to forestall termination and to face and accomplish it.[13]

It is certainly natural to feel sad when one has completed an experience and is separating from others if the experience has had deep meaning for the person. The sadness is aggravated by the fact that one separation often reactivates feelings of loss from other life experiences. When members face the reality of their feelings about the loss that is inherent in termination, they react with expressions of sadness and engage in reflective thinking about the situation.

Although anxiety is often directed toward the loss of the worker, a study by Scheidlinger and Holden found that the major separation anxiety was expressed in regard to the threatened loss of the group as an entity, rather than to the loss of the worker.[14] As one member of a prerelease group in a mental hospital expressed it, "I came to say good-bye to you [the worker] again. It's hard to do this and hard to leave the hospital after such a long time. But leaving our group is the hardest of all." Then, following the workers comment, "Yes, I know," the patient continued, "But it's easier knowing others are facing the same thing, trying to make a go of life outside." A member of a group of adults in a family service agency said it this way, "I feel that the group is the family I never had," associating separation from the group with the family situation. The group that is being dissolved is usually a meaningful reference group and a vehicle for social gratifications for the members, which fact creates additional anxieties and resistances concerning termination.

Members resist termination in numerous ways. Denial that the group is terminating is one typical reaction. Denial serves as a defense against facing the impending separation and the feelings of loss and anxiety associated with it. The members refuse to accept the notion of termination, behave as though it were not going to happen, and forget that the worker has explained the plan for the duration of the group and its termination. Sometimes denial is more subtle. Some evidences of denial may be long atypical silences when termination is mentioned, numerous references to loss scattered throughout the discussion, or changing the subject when the worker tries to explore the meaning of separation with the members. A variation of the usual denial maneuvers may be exaggerated independence that is not an accurate reflection of the person's level of functioning. A person may act stoical and need to appear strong when confronted with the loss. The denial may also be expressed through superficially greater cohesiveness than before: the group strengthens its bonds against the threat of the worker or agency.

Angry reactions often overlap with denial. Clients may react with anger to what they perceive as abandonment, rejection, or punishment. There may be what Schiff calls the "unspoken rebuke" aimed at the worker for leaving.[15] Anger may be expressed in such phrases as: "so, you're kicking us out," "I guess you never did care," "it doesn't matter," "the group is no good anyhow," or a simple, "so what?" An example is from a group of young children, reflecting the depth of their feelings.

> Toward the end of the meeting, the worker said she wanted to bring something up for the members to think about so they can talk about it more fully at the next meeting. Jane asked, "What is it?" "Yes, what is it?" asked Johnny. The worker said, "I think we should talk about the group ending when school vacation begins." Jane asked, with distress in her voice, "b-b-but—why?" All of the children were very quiet. The worker said thay had been talking about how much better things were for all of them now—they'll soon be able to get along fine without the group. "Oh, no" screamed John. "No," added Jane, and then, after a silence, "So—you're just like everyone else after all." And Johnny said, "You, you—you're no good for us any way." Then Jane said, "To think I thought you really cared." Then, she cried.

The expression of anger may often begin with indirect or displaced expressions directed toward the worker, each other, or people outside the group. Members may talk about their anger at other people who have disappointed them, such as parents, teachers, employers, friends, or lovers. This ventilation of anger serves as a catharsis and needs to be accepted by the worker for a time. If the worker recognizes these expressions as symbolic of the member's feelings and accepts them, he may then move to making comments or asking questions that connect these expressions of hostility to the group's termination.

Apparent regression is another frequent response to the need to terminate: the members return to earlier patterns of behavior. These actions may be in the form of inability to cope with situations and tasks that had apparently been mastered earlier or in the reactivation of conflicts among members. The members may become increasingly dependent on the worker's leadership and on routines. They may repeat earlier patterns of scapegoating, susceptibility to contagion, and impulsivity. Sometimes the members behave in ways that are dramatically reminiscent of earlier developmental phases, reflecting a desire to begin all over again. It is not unusual for a group to face the fact of termination in an explosion of behavior that says, in effect, "You thought we were better or more able, but you were wrong. We really are not. We still need you and the group." There is an increase in bringing up problems that were previously worked on.

> In an open-ended couples group in a family service agency, Walt and Jane announced that they had been getting along very well for the past few weeks. As they described how they had handled some upheavals in their lives, it appeared that they had developed ways of coping with their conflicts and also were able to enjoy intimacy with each other. The other members and the worker expressed their feelings and reactions to the prospect of Walt and Jane's leaving the group. Walt and Jane then decided they would come to two more sessions just to make sure they were ready to get along without the group. When they returned the next week, they said things were very bad; they were back to where they were at the beginning; they had not made any positive changes after all. Several members commented that Jane and Walt were certainly not ready to leave. The worker explored with them what the major problems were and recalled their prior experiences with similar problems. In the ensuing discussion, Walt and Jane were able to cope with the problem with a minimum of help from the worker and other members. The worker then suggested that last week the focus had been on their readiness to leave, but they had not dealt with their mixed feelings about the group and what it meant to them. Walt and Jane decided to come back twice more to talk about this matter. By that time, they were really ready to leave.

It is important that the worker not interpret these incidents as actual regression or agree that the members are back at the beginning. Rather, it is necessary to understand the acts as the members' ways of coping with ambivalence about ending. In some instances, the negative behavior expresses anxiety that the worker will put the members out before they are ready to leave. The flare-up may be an indication of difficulty in leaving relationships and experiences that have been important. Such members need the worker's assurance that they will not leave until they are ready.

Flight is another pattern of behavior. A group member may be so fearful of being left that she is compelled to break off the relationship precipitously, as if to say, "I'll leave you before you leave me." People who have never experienced much trust in parents and others in positions of authority are particularly fearful of the intimacy of the social work relationship. Through the many hurts of their life experiences, they are easily triggered to withdraw if they have a glimmer that they might be hurt again and fearful that they will not be able to deal with the actual separation. The impulse to flee from the warm group climate may be great. With such a problem, the worker's activities need to be geared to helping the members to stay in the group until its official ending or until a member has been prepared for termination.

Feeling rejected by the social worker is another typical reaction to termination. The feelings of rejection are often accompanied with anger. As aptly put by Schiff, "The therapist has been a big liar. What good parent would throw his child out?"[16] Or, as members of one group said, "Why don't you just drive us back to the housing project and forget you ever knew us?" Some members may react through denying the positive meaning of the experience for them to prove that the worker never really did care for them. Some may feel that the group is terminating as a punishment for their unacceptable behavior. To this end, the members exhibit a variety of rejecting and rejection-provoking behavior toward the worker. They may be absent, leave the group, or express verbally their feelings of being rejected by the worker or of rejecting her.

Not all reactions to the group's termination are related to inability to accept it. Another set is concerned with accepting and making constructive moves toward separating from the worker and often from the other members, too.

The literature places heavy emphasis on the painful feelings and problematic behavior that tend to accompany work toward termination. There is always, perhaps, some sense of loss in leaving an experience that has been helpful in important ways or to which a person has contributed much of himself and his skills. Schwartz has suggested that, in groups, "the resistance to endings seems to be marked by a general reluctance to tear down a social structure built with such difficulties, and to give up intimacies so hard to achieve."[17] It is to be remembered that there is also the positive side of the ambivalence and that this side predominates in some situations.[18] There may be happy anticipation of the ending, as is true of certain other experiences in life such as graduation or leaving the parental home. Some members have highly positive reactions to termination, such as "I really feel I'm ready," "I never thought a group could be so great—I'll miss you all—but I'm ready to try on my own." There may be high motivation to use the remaining sessions to complete unfinished business. Feeling competent to cope more effectively with life's challenges and having confidence in one's ability to do so are richly rewarding and are accompanied by feelings of satisfaction and hope. These feelings and reactions are often the outcome of having achieved the goals, accepting the positive and negative feelings about ending, and making constructive moves toward new experiences and relationships. Realizing that the positive changes have come from a process of mutual aid—the dynamic force of altruism—gives the members a sense of pride in having helped themselves and others as well.

A combination of varied reactions tends to occur, with modifications in tendency and duration, in most groups that have continued with sustained attendance over a significant period of time. There is a tendency for reactions to occur in flashes and in clusters, even within the space of a single session. Over a period of time, there seems to be a certain progression in rationality among the reactions, for example, from denial or reactivation of symptoms to review and evaluation. Nevertheless, the actual emergence is not always in sequence. It is not uncommon for members to evaluate their experience together in a reflective manner and later explode into mutual recriminations over responsibility for unacceptable behavior that occurred some time ago.

VARIATIONS IN REACTIONS

It was noted earlier that feelings and reactions toward termination vary from person to person, depending upon the intensity of the relationships among the members and the members' prior experiences with separation. Germain and Gitterman note that "the intensity of feeling associated with a relationship and with its ending depends upon its duration and its quality of mutual regard, respect, and reciprocity."[19] The termination process has been described as especially intense and prolonged in groups of elderly patients in nursing homes, in groups of adolescents in residential treatment, and in groups of hard-to-reach adolescents in community agencies.[20]

Other factors also influence the termination process. One is the purpose of the service. Therapeutic services are apt to be more intense and more permeated with problems in relationships than educational services are or those that aim to enhance the social competence of people who do not usually have serious problems. In the latter instances, members are more able to anticipate and work through termination without intense emotion and with fewer negative reactions. In task-oriented groups, the fact that the participants are there to work toward some defined tasks that are achieved outside the group means that somewhat less emphasis is placed on the socioemotional dynamics of the experience.[21] This does not mean that there is not a sense of loss of relationships at ending such an endeavor. It does not mean that feelings of satisfaction or dissatisfaction are not stirred up, including the possibility of anger at the worker or group that more was not accomplished.

In some models of social work practice with groups, the focus is limited to the acquisition of particular tasks or changes in overt behavior. The practice is behavioral or cognitively oriented, instead of psychosocial, which takes into account socioemotional, as well as cognitive and behavioral issues. Mayadas and Glasser, for example, regard some models of practice as focused too much on "sentimental nostalgia," rather than on highlighting satisfactory learning and as a point of reference for the initiation and assessment of other challenges.[22] If groups have not developed close relationships and worked on problems of interpersonal and group relationships, reactions to termination may be less intense.

General agreement is found in the literature on both socialization and psychosocial treatment groups that emotional reactions to termination occur. The findings come from analysis of process records or tape recordings of practice. Research was conducted by Lewis, who studied fourteen treatment and ten socialization groups, predominantly of adolescents but also including a fewer number of groups for children and adults. The groups met weekly for an average of one year and were led by social workers with graduate degrees. The purpose of the study was to test the characteristics of the termination stage as formulated by Garland and associates. The study confirmed the presence of the major categories of emotional reactions in the groups, although not all groups were characterized by all reactions.[23] In another research study, Lackey also confirmed the presence of multiple emotional reactions to termination.[24]

The duration of the service influences the content of the ending process to some extent. Generally, short-term services of up to three months are offered to persons whose problems are less chronic than the problems of clients are who are offered long-term treatment. Hence, the impact of termination will usually be less upsetting to these members than to those in longer term treatment. In crisis intervention, which is by definition a brief service, the resolution of the crisis or at least a return to a previous state of functioning provides a natural time for termination, which has been built in from the beginning. Little attention has been given by writers to the ending phase of crisis intervention. Rapoport, however, emphasizes that "in brief treatment, termination needs to be dealt with explicitly."[25] Since the length of treatment is discussed in the initial interview, the ending process is anticipated from the beginning. Because of the partialized and specifically defined goals and the assumption that the state of crisis is a time-limited phenomenon, the minimum goal is achieved within a period of several weeks. It must be remembered, however, that clients in an acute state of crisis do not always grasp the idea of brief service. A person is bound to have feelings toward a worker and members of a group who have helped him to overcome unbearable anxiety, confusion, and uncertainty. An example is from the record of a crisis intervention group in a community mental health agency. The six members of the group are between the ages of nineteen and twenty-three and are middle-class white women. The group is open ended; members attend for six or seven sessions.

> Sara, age twenty, came to the clinic with an unwanted pregnancy, resolving the immediate crisis by planning for and obtaining an abortion, which, in turn, engendered another crisis. In addition, she resolved the masochistic relationship with the child's father by ending

it and thus creating another loss. During the period of treatment, she gained some understanding of the dynamics that led to the presenting crisis, namely, a six-month self-destructive and chaotic period following the simultaneous loss of her fiance and rejection by her parents. She has now established a new and more healthy relationship with her parents.

Individual treatment supplemented the group modality because it was necessary to connect Sara up with other resources. Brief interviews and telephone consultations were frequent. Sara became very dependent on me, since we had developed a more intense relationship than is usual with group members. As termination approached, Sara denied the impending separation and reached out to me for more, rather than less, individual attention. During the last week, she telephoned me twice, insisting that she would "crack up" if I did not have another interview with her. I saw her but used the interview to remind her of the impending separation from me and the group and the importance of new ways of dealing with loss, but her denial continued. She did not want to attend the group meeting or acknowledge her investment in the group. I worked with her to help her understand that really dealing with saying goodbye to the group was essential if she wanted to maintain the gains she had made with us and if she was to be free to enter into a new therapeutic relationship. She finally accepted this and agreed to come to the group, but she had not yet accepted her ambivalent feelings.

Hoping to see me alone before the group, Sara arrived early. Since the receptionist did not inform me of her presence, I saw Sara only briefly before the meeting. After my cotherapist had worked on some other matters in the group session, I suggested that Sara might want to say goodbye to the group. Earlier in the meeting, she had seemed calm and participated only minimally. In response to my comment, she seemed stunned, gazed at me for a moment with a strained expression on her face, and then burst into tears, her face in her hands. One of the members handed her the tissue box, a symbol of support and concern when a member is having a hard time. Sara accepted the tissue, fiddled with it for a moment as she still looked down; then looked at me and in a broken voice said how much I had helped her, how she felt she would never again find anyone who would care so much about her. Then she turned toward the other members and said, "and you've helped me, also." Leaning forward in my chair, I said softly that she had made a great many gains in our time together, but she had done much of the growing herself. The group and I had helped her to help herself. I then said, "It's hard to leave people you're grown close to, isn't it?", to which comment she replied, "It sure is," with more tears.

The members of the group had been very quiet and listened intently to our conversation. I asked if they could respond to Sara. Each, in a different way, said she felt close to her and would miss her in the next meeting. Greta said she thought the group was helping them to get in touch with their feelings and that seemed to help. Sara had helped her to do this. There was nodding of heads all around. Sara said it was hard to talk about how you felt inside, but now that it was over, it didn't feel so scary. Then she said, "Mrs. G. did help me enormously, but you in the group will never know how much you helped, too." There was a warm feeling in the room. I said that we had gone way overtime today, but I thought it had been important to do so. All agreed, either verbally or through nods. I said I thought we should still take time to say goodbye to Sara and for Sara to say goodbye to us. As the group ended, I put my hand on Sara's shoulder, and we said goodbye to each other.

One of the powerful dynamics in crisis intervention is the experience that there are people available—a professional worker and a group—who reach out to help at a time when one's own coping capacities are inadequate. Thus, the relationships between worker and member and member and member are very meaningful. Since many crises, as with Sara, involved loss of some kind, it is essential that members learn better ways to handle the loss of the worker and the group. Working through the difficulties of terminating can thus contribute to competence in facing and coping with future losses.

It has been suggested that in open-ended groups in which membership changes frequently, intensity of relationships and strong cohesion tend not to develop. If this be true, then it would be expected that termination would be less imbued with strong emotions in open than in closed groups. Crisis intervention groups are certainly exceptions to that generalization. The important point is that social workers have the sensitivity and the knowledge to make an accurate judgment about the meaning of endings to the members and the group and that they use this understanding in the termination process, whether the service has been brief or long or in an open-ended or closed group.

INTERVENTIONS OF THE SOCIAL WORKER

Self-awareness on the part of the social worker and an ability to control emotional reactions are essential. The social worker is not immune from feelings about terminating with members of the group. It is natural that a worker will often feel pleased about the progress of the group and her part in it. It is natural, too, that she will feel some sense of loss. It is essential that she be able to share these feelings with the members. The feelings expressed must be genuine, not phony. An example follows:

> Four weeks before the planned termination day, the worker reminded a group of high school girls that there were only two more meetings before school was out and the group would end. The members protested that they did not know time would go so fast—they wanted to continue. After the meeting closed, the girls insisted upon staying. They gathered in a corner of the hall. Later, they went to the worker's office to give her a letter in which they expressed their feelings about leaving her. The worker read it and said she was very touched by it and commented that it would be hard for her to leave them also. One girl asked, "You really mean it?" The worker assured them that she really did mean it; she would miss each of them and miss working with the group. Betty exclaimed, "She really means it—I can tell." Clarise said, "See we like her and she likes us—we'll never forget what she did for us." The girls all clapped spontaneously. The worker reminded them that they would still be together for two more meetings and engaged the girls in making decisions about priorities for those meetings.

It is natural that a social worker will have strong emotional reactions to the feelings expressed by the members. When the members express hostility toward or rejection of her, the worker may take those statements personally rather than accept them as part of the process. She may react with anger, may respond to apparently regressive behavior by agreeing that the members really are back at the beginning and that no progress has been made and by feeling that she is a failure, or may resist termination by forgetting to remind the group of the approaching deadline or by continuing discussions or activities as though the group would go on forever. When one is in the midst of a group process in which there is anger and reactivation of unacceptable behavior, it is easy to forget that these behaviors are typical of the ending phase and blame oneself for creating the chaos or hostility.

If a group has been particularly difficult for a worker, there may be a great sense of relief that it is ending. As one inexperienced male student exclaimed, "Thank God, it's over—I never thought I'd see the day." On further reflection, however, he realized how much he had learned from the experience and could observe quite realistically that every member had made some progress. Some workers may expect perfection of their clients and be dissatisfied with their progress. Or they may feel that surely their clients cannot live without them; they get overattached to some of the members, so they cannot support them in going on to new experiences without them. Termination also stirs up feelings about the quality of the worker's performance, for example, certain guilt feelings for not having had the time or the skill to have been more helpful to more members. The worker may have doubts about the nature and permanence of the gains made by the members, leading to a desire to hang on to the group. If he is to use his own feelings in a helpful, rather than a hurtful way, the worker needs to acknowledge them and to renew his faith in the members' capacities to continue to grow after his relationship with them is terminated.

Preparatory to working with the members on issues of termination, the social worker needs to make a decision concerning when to initiate the process. The goals, preferably clear and mutually agreed upon, serve as a basis for the decision. The worker needs to be clear about what criteria are being used for initiating a termination process: preset time limits for the duration of the group, the achievement of goals, or forced termination due to an unforeseen circumstance. Once the group has been informed of the impending end, the worker's efforts become centered on helping the members to cope with the stressful situation of ending.

If termination is to be a growth-producing experience, the social worker has a number of important instrumental goals to achieve during the final stage of service. These are to help the members to: (1) explore and clarify their feelings about termination and resolve the ambivalence about leaving the worker and, except for natural groups, the others members as well; (2) review, evaluate, and support the progress the members have made, acknowledge the realistic gains, identify the needs that still exist, and evaluate the effectiveness of the group; (3) set priorities for work on unfinished problems or tasks that are clearly relevant to the members' progress and work toward stabilizing and generalizing from the gains that have been made; (4) make transitions toward new experiences, such as follow-up sessions or referrals, as indicated.[26]

The social worker uses all the categories of skills in carrying out these tasks to help the members work toward successful termination.

Resolution of Ambivalence. Once the social worker has reminded the group of the impending end, his efforts become centered on helping the members cope with the stressful situation. The worker faces a complexity of feelings: the separate reactions of each individual, which may be like or different from those of the other members. But, through mutual influence, a group feeling or mood emerges to which he needs to address his attention. He uses supportive techniques in facilitating the ventilation of ambivalent feelings toward termination, conveys acceptance of the feelings, universalizes them to the extent possible, and communicates empathy. If a reaction is one of feeling abandoned or rejected, additional support is needed. At times, the worker needs to help the members identify and understand their feelings. He may need to interpret how the present reactions are similar to modes of dealing with other problematic situations in order to help members to understand and modify them. He may reach out to confront gently those members who attempt to flee, requesting that they try to work out their feelings in the group rather than run away from them. He recognizes that, unless the group is to continue as a unit, the feelings tend to revolve around the loss of the group, as well as the loss of the worker.

Acknowledging Progress. Members need to have ample time to ventilate and come to understand their feelings about termination. But one important task for the social worker is to move the members from prolonged preoccupation with feelings to a recognition that they are approaching the completion of a group experience through which at least some of their goals have been achieved. While missing the group, they are ready to find new satisfactions in the community. Their feelings often get in the way of recognizing positive gains that have been made. In a last group session, for example, one man said, "I'd rather not stop, it's hard for me to let go, to end things. I just want to stay there, stay there, stay there. Each session that we've gotten together has become more profitable—my feeling is that it's getting better and better. I'm worried about ending." He has moved from expression of feelings toward evaluation.

Evaluation. The appraisal of the quality of the service and of the members' use of it is an ongoing process. It involves a capacity to make sound judgments in relation to the agreed-upon goals. The ultimate test of the effectiveness of social work practice is the extent to which the persons who were served have made positive changes toward the goals set with them. The progress or regression of a member is appropriately made in relation to her particular characteristics, background, problems, and needs, rather than in relation to fixed or uniform standards. This view is in opposition to some evaluative research studies that have used the same tests or measurements to evaluate the success or failure of a given service, regardless of the differences in the conditions of clients or environments, type of service provided, and agreed-upon goals. In some instances, notably work with families or other groups that will continue to exist when social work service is terminated, the concern is with changes in the structure and interacting processes of the group, as well as with the individuals who comprise it. If goals for each member and the group have been developed, evaluated, and modified periodically, they naturally become the criteria against which progress is measured.

Evaluation of the progress of members is made more precise and easier for the worker if some plan is developed for periodically tracing changes in attitudes, relationships, and behavior as they relate to goals. Minimally, summary reports should be made at the end of the pregroup interviews, toward the end of the second stage, and when termination is being considered. As changes occur, they can be noted from week to week or periodically. These changes are usually those in attitudes toward self and others, the quality and range of social relationships, problematic behaviors, and social competence. Necessary data are then available to the worker for use in evaluating the nature and extent of the changes made. The movement of each individual is evaluated in relation to the trend of changes in the group and the impact of environmental influences on it. According to Chin: "evaluation studies of goal achievement or outcome are of limited importance unless the evaluation study also tries to pinpoint the components which 'cause' the degree of attainment or hindrance of goals."[27] Thus, both progress and process must be studied, as must changes in the client's external relationships and conditions. The worker's own evaluation is not sufficient. He also engages the members in a mutual process of review of the working agreement and evaluation of the members' views of whether and, if so, to what extent they have reached their goals.

One common focus during the last meetings is a review with the members of the group's purpose and individual goals and the extent to which the members perceive the achievement of these goals. The social worker accepts differences in progress made. She may need to work with the group to help bring about acceptance of differences or give special help to a particular member of the group who feels disappointed that he has not made as much progress as he had hoped for. She has a responsibility to share her observations of progress and her confidence in the growing ability of the members to get along without her and usually also without the group. As the group evaluates its experience together, the worker needs to be secure enough to accept and elicit evaluations of things that could have been done differently, as well as of those things that she did that were most useful and satisfying to the members. She seeks to learn to which aspects of the group the members attribute the satisfactions and gains that have been made; which of the dynamic change mechanisms seemed most important to the members; and what they liked and did not like about the group.

Assessment of the performance of the social worker, as well as of the progress of members, is a means for advancing the quality of service given to other groups. The following guidelines are offered for the worker's self-evaluation of the group and her participation in it.

1. *Planning*

What needs did the members have that would suggest the group as the modality of choice?

What did you want to help the members to achieve? Were your goals and the members' goals congruent? Were the goals revised, if and when this seemed to be indicated by the situation?

To what extent was the composition of the group functional or dysfunctional to the achievement of goals?

How suitable was the structure of the group to the needs of the members?

To what extent did you create a social environment that was maximally therapeutic?

What norms developed in the group and what did you do to influence their development?

What type of authority seemed to be required of you (permissive, laissez-faire, democratic-facilitative, directive-authoritative, flexible)? How did you help this authority to change during the life of the group?

To what extent did the members understand what was expected of them?

Did the content of the initial meetings seem appropriate to the needs of the group?

2. *Ongoing Assessment of Individuals and Group*

To what extent did you demonstrate ongoing understanding of each members' needs and problems?

How aware were you of problems in the functioning of the group as a system?

To what extent did you take into account environmental influences on each member's progress and that of the group?

To what extent did you make appropriate use of cutural values and norms as they influence individuals and the group?

3. *Use of Relationship*

What seems to be the nature and quality of your relationship with each member? Consider the qualities of empathy, acceptance, genuineness; adherence to ethical principles; ability to accept and respond to positive and negative feelings expressed toward you and among the members; and transference and countertransference reactions that are evident.

To what extent have you been able to facilitate interpersonal relationships among the members, appropriate to each stage of group development?

4. *Use of Categories of Intervention*

To what extent did you select and use appropriately the major skills of intervention, keeping in mind the needs and readiness of each member and the group? Consider support, structuring, exploration, education, clarification, confrontation, and interpretation.

5. *Effective Use of Group Structure and Interactional Processes*

How successful were you in helping members to participate?

To what extent did you help the members use norms for participation related to the dynamic forces in groups?

To what extent were you alert to opportunities to give individuals and the group as much power as possible to make choices, within their capacities?

To what extent were you able to help the members search for and find common ground, when approopriate, to tie needs and contributions of one individual to those of others?

When giving suggestions, information, explanations, or interpretations to one member or a subgroup, were you able to help others make connections to the content?

How successful were you in dealing with problems in the functioning of the group, such as difficulties in communication, resistance, dysfunctional member roles, instability of membership, maladaptive self-disclosure, interpersonal and group conflict, or malfunctioning decision-making processes?

To what extent were you able to promote a sense of continuity and sequence appropriate to the needs of the members?

To what extent did you help the members to select and use appropriate activity-oriented experiences and discussion to achieve the goals?

6. *Evaluation of Service and Termination*

To what extent were you able to help members to evaluate the experience and progress made?

To what extent were you aware of the movement of each member and the group as a whole through the major stages of development?

To what extent did you adequately prepare each member and the group as a whole for termination?

Competence is the performance of roles with integrity, knowledge, and skill. In Hearn's words,

> To act with professional integrity is to act consistently within a framework of values, a framework that is shared generally by members of the profession; to act with knowledge is to act with an awareness of the rationale for and probable consequences of our actions; and to act with skill is to exercise such control that our actions more closely approximate our intentions.[28]

The use of guidelines for the analysis of skill can be useful in helping workers assess their own competence and then use supervision, consultation, and study to further enhance their skill.

Setting Priorities and Stabilizing Gains. Once the worker has engaged the members in an evaluation of their progress and of the group's effectiveness, he anticipates and plans for making use of the remaining sessions. An important challenge is to keep the members working toward goal achievement, even as they deal with the issue of separation. Otherwise, the group will lose its effectiveness too early, and the last meetings will not be productive. As the members engage in a preliminary evaluation process, they tend to identify needs still unmet. The worker can use this review to help the members set priorities for what they still want to work on during the time that remains. Awareness of a limited amount of time may enhance motivation to use that time effectively. But the worker needs to beware of the danger of trying to get everything possible accomplished at the last minute. The priorities set should be realistic in terms of the members' capacities and readiness and the constraints of time. The major priorities are often to engage in talk and activities that test out the skills that have been learned, first in different situations in the group and then in situations in the community. In these ways, the skills are stabilized and generalized to new situations. These activities are a natural progression from those in the preceding stage of development. They tend to be oriented to the community, as for example, in visits to schools or employment offices or participation in sophisticated social experiences that test the members' capacities for adaptive behavior in relevant situations. Sometimes, the members desire to repeat earlier experiences, either those that were gratifying or those in which they failed in some way. Through such repetition, the members confirm their judgment that they are more able to deal with problematic situations now than previously. They have developed competence.

The social worker supports the members' efforts to move away from the group, to develop new relationships outside the group, and to find their place in the usual activities of the community. The worker's activity is pinpointed on helping the members transfer the skills learned in the group to other experiences; she thereby instills hope for future satisfactory performance. She helps them develop their own identity apart from the group, a natural extension of earlier work on problems of identity and differentiation. For the members need now to be able to get along without the group, to have further help in integrating the gains, and to make decisions about their own futures. She accredits the members' developing interests in other things and is pleased when other interests come to take precedence over group meetings. Hamilton said it this way: "The painful aspects of terminating a helpful relationship are diminished by the clients' own growing sense of strength" as he is able to extend his interests and social relationships into the community.[29]

The social worker facilitates the members' consideration of and use of health, welfare, and educational resources in the agency or elsewhere in the community. All members can benefit from information about and discussion of how to seek additional services if they should be needed. They can benefit, too, from knowledge of community resources for the enrichment of their lives, including other forms of social support, informal educational groups, and opportunities to develop hobbies or occupational skills. Some members may need referral for help with psychosocial problems that were not addressed adequately in the group. The worker needs also to indicate and clarify the nature of any continuing relationship she may have with individuals, their families, or with the group. When feasible, she makes plans to be available to the members if problems are encountered, to follow up with interviews for the purpose of evaluating how members are getting along later, or to have reunions with the group. It is the social worker's ethical responsibility to ensure, to the extent possible, that members are not left to fend for themselves when they clearly need additional help.

In time-limited groups, a decision may be made to continue the group for an additional period of time or to reorganize it to meet new or continuing needs of members. Although most members may be ready to leave, others should continue. In such instances, a new working agreement needs to be negotiated about the plan, with clarity about the goals to be sought and the duration of the reorganized group.

The tasks of facilitating the expression of feeling and resolving the ambivalence about ending, continuing work on unresolved problems, stabilizing changes, evaluating progress and process, and making transitions to new experiences seldom occur in that order but are interwoven into the last meetings of the group. One example is of a group of couples with serious marital conflicts that threatened the continuation of their marriages. It was a planned time-limited group of four months' duration. In the next to the last session, the members had worked toward stabilizing gains they had made in communicating with each other and with other family members and in making important decisions that affected their marital relationships and families. They had considered what they would try to do to make further gains before the final session. They had been reminded of the reality of the group's ending, with a tendency to deny it or to express mild feelings of sadness and unreadiness to give up the group. They had been given information about the agency's crisis intervention services that would be available to them if they should require them and about resources in the community to meet some of the members' or their children's needs for vocational testing, tutoring, family planning, and recreation.

> Members of the group had earlier ventilated many feelings about ending. Now they were engaged in evaluating the progress they had made. While they recognized gains, they also identified unresolved problems. As Katherine told about a recent fight with her husband, she blurted out, "The trouble with this whole therapy is just that it isn't long enough. Why in hell can't these sessions go on: here we are right in the midst of our problems and the whole thing is going to end soon." I said that Katherine was certainly feeling that she was not ready for the group to end and that she is still very angry about it and asked how the others felt. All said, in different ways, that I just did not care about helping them any more. I said that most of them seemed to feel I was abandoning them in their time of need. "I sure do," and "that's what you are doing," were typical responses. I said that I, too, wished the group could meet for a little longer, but that is not possible. I reminded them that we had agreed to meet for fifteen sessions, and that time is up next week. There was silence. I also reviewed briefly what each had said earlier about how things were bet-

ter for them now and said I had confidence that they could continue to work on their problems outside the group. What they had learned here could be carried over to their discussions with each other and with their families.

Esther changed the mood with a statement that while she still has a long ways to go, this group had helped her and her husband more than earlier therapy had. When Katherine asked her about this, she replied, "Well, it's something when six people land on you at one time; boy, that really made an impression on me; it was a painful process and I wouldn't want to go through it again. But I lived through it because you all seemed to like me and care about me." Her husband said that he agreed—it was good to be able to talk things over with people who had marital problems, too, even though not identical with theirs. There was further discussion of the ways the group had helped them. There was also presentation of things that were not going well, so that ventilation of feelings, problem solving, and review and evaluation were interspersed during this meeting and during the final one. By the end of that session, positive feelings toward the group's ending predominated because the members had seen how they could continue to use what they had learned in facing problems, communicating about their feelings and perceptions of the difficulties, and trying to make decisions that would not create too much conflict.

When group members have had a particularly satisfying experience in working together, they may resist completion of the work if relationships among them have been more satisfying than the achievement of the agreed-upon goals has. Members may delay completing the work in order to prolong the relationships. Some groups desire to continue on a friendship basis after the original purpose has been achieved. Such a decision is often not realistic: it represents a resistance to facing termination and moving out into new experiences in the community. Rather than accede to the members' demands, the need is to face the group with the problem and help them work it through.

A decision to reestablish a group usually means that it has changed its purpose to that of a social, self-help or support group that continues, often without the assistance of a social worker. Greenfield and Rothman refer to a transformation stage beyond termination.[30] Although the members remain together, they still need to face the changes and deal with the separation from the worker and also often from the sponsoring organization. Many self-help and support groups have started with some members who participated in a therapeutic or psychoeducational group and then desired to maintain relationships with people with whom they have shared a particular need. The social worker's role in such groups is to help the members plan for the group and, in some instances, to continue as a consultant or adviser to the group.

In many situations, it is not sufficient that the worker notify and prepare the members of the group for termination and follow-up. In work with children, parents need to participate in the review and evaluation of the child's progress in the group and in the decisions concerning any follow-up services to be provided by the agency or referrals elsewhere. In serving groups within an institutional setting, other staff members who have responsibilities to the members need either to be notified about or to participate in the actual decision to terminate the group service, depending on circumstances. When group work is one part of a constellation of services to a member, the other personnel within the agency or the community need to be involved in the plans for the member after he has left the group. For a group is not an island unto itself: its members are parts of other social systems that may be affected by the discontinuance of the group.

The Ending. The actual termination occurs during the last session of the group. Groups often have a final ritual to symbolize the members' internalization of the experience. In one group of mental patients, there was an exchange of statements of hope that each would be able to get along well and a statement by one member, in behalf of the group, of the meaning the experience had to them and of their appreciation of the help given by the worker. A group of parents brought elaborate refreshments and a thank-you card for the worker to symbolize the ending of that group. In such instances, the worker accepts graciously the members' expressions of appreciation for help given.

The policies of organizations vary concerning follow-up activities. In the actual final disengagement, the social worker makes clear that the door is open if agency policy allows it, that the worker will be available to the members if they feel it necessary to contact him. He assures the members of his continued interest in them, even though they are leaving. The worker's concern for the members does not stop on the last day, and the members need to know this. Hope is held out that the new strengths and outlooks gained through the group experience will provide a base for each member's continued coping in his own way with the problems of daily living.

CONCLUSION

Termination is a dynamic and vital process, not just an end point. If properly understood and managed, it becomes an important force in integrating changes in feeling, thinking, and behaving. In this final stage, knowledge about human behavior and techniques of treatment are used to help the group to terminate in a way that benefits the members. If done successfully, the social worker has prepared the members for other experiences with loss and separation that they will face in the future. When the worker feels that his service has been successful, he will have grown, too. In a sense, he benefits as much from the members as they do from him. They teach him how to be a better social worker. What he learns from serving a particular group should make it possible for him to give better service to the next group. How could it be otherwise? We are all parts of dynamic interacting systems of people who influence and are influenced by each other. We are not islands unto ourselves.

Notes

1. Groups in Social Work Practice

1. William Schwartz, "Group Work and the Social Scene," p. 129.
2. Ashley Montagu, *The Cultured Man*, p. 13.
3. Buddy Silberman, "A New Strain for Social Work," p. 9.
4. Gisela Konopka, "All Lives are Connected to Other Lives: The Meaning of Social Group Work." Paper presented at the Eighth Annual Symposium of Social Work with Groups, Los Angeles, October 24, 1986.
5. For further information, see Wynetta Devore and Elfrieda G. Schlesinger, *Ethnic Sensitive Social Work Practice*, and Barbara Bryant Solomon, *Black Empowerment*.
6. Kenneth L. M. Pray, *Social Work in a Revolutionary Age*, p. 278.
7. National Association of Social Workers. Official Definition prepared for *Congressional Record*. (February 25, 1986), 132(18).
8. Henry S. Maas, *People and Contexts*, p. 3.
9. Robert C. Cook, "Population: Some Pitfalls and Progress," p. 42.
10. Lee P. Dies, *Man's Nature and Nature's Man*, pp. 2–3.
11. Henry and Rebecca Northen, *Ingenious Kingdom*, p. 17.
12. Additional useful references on ecological concepts are as follows: Urie Bronfenbrenner, *Ecology of Human Development;* W. B. Clapham, Jr., *Human Ecosystems;* Donald L. Hardesty, *Ecological Anthropology;* and Andrew P. Vayda, ed. *Environment and Cultural Behavior.* For a recent application to work with groups, see Pallassana R. Balgopal and Thomas V. Vassil. *Groups in Social Work.*
13. Carel B. Germain, ed. *Social Work Practice*, pp. 7–8. See also Germain and Alex Gitterman, *Life Model of Social Work Practice;* Carol H. Meyer, *Social Work Practice;* Meyer, *Clinical Social Work in the Eco-Systems Perspective.*
14. Robert Chin, "Utility of Systems Models," pp. 297–312.
15. For information on these two forms of practice, see: Ronald Toseland, Edmund Sherman, and Stephen Bliven, "The Comparative Effectiveness of Two Group Work Approaches," 137–53.
16. Clara Kaiser, "Characteristics of Social Group Work," p. 157.
17. Mary Louise Somers, "Four Small Group Theories," p. 218.
18. Earle E. Eubank, *The Concepts of Sociology*, p. 163.
19. George Homans, *The Human Group*, p. 3.
20. Mark Davidson, "The Case for Uncommon Sense," *Transcript*, (June, 1983), Los Angeles: University of Southern California, 7–8.
21. William C. Schutz, *Interpersonal Underworld*, p. 1.
22. Raymond J. Corsini and Bina Rosenberg, "Mechanisms of Group Psychotherapy, pp. 406–11.
23. Irvin D. Yalom, *Theory and Practice of Group Psychotherapy*, 1st ed.
24. Irvin D. Yalom, *Inpatient Group Psychotherapy*, p. 45.
25. Irwin D. Yalom, *Theory and Practice of Group Psychotherapy*, 2d. ed.
26. Malcolm Marks, "Group Psychotherapy for Emotionally Disturbed Children," pp. 70–77.

27. National Association of Social Workers (NASW), *Use of Groups in the Psychiatric Setting.*

28. The primary references for this list are as follows: Sidney Bloch, Eric Crouch, and Janet Reibstein, "Therapeutic Factors in Group Psychotherapy," pp. 519–26; Raymond J. Corsini and Bina Rosenberg, "Mechanism of Group Psychotherapy"; Elsbeth Herzstein Couch, *Joint and Family Interviews;* Howard Goldstein, *Social Learning and Change;* William F. Hill, "Further Considerations of Therapeutic Mechanisms," pp. 421–29; NASW, *Use of Groups in the Psychiatric Setting;* Helen Northen, "Selection of Groups"; in Joseph Lassner, Powell, and Finnegan, eds. *Social Group Work,* pp. 19–34; Helen Northen, *Clinical Social Work;* Michael Rohrbaugh and Bryan D. Bartels, "Participants' Perceptions of Curative Factors," pp. 430–56; Saul Scheidlinger, *Focus on Group Psychotherapy;* Lawrence Shulman, *Skills of Helping Individuals and Groups;* Irvin D. Yalom, *Theory and Practice of Group Psychotherapy;* and Yalom, *Inpatient Group Psychotherapy.*

29. Howard Goldstein, *Social Learning and Change.* p. 102.

30. Yalom has summarized the results of research on these forces in *Theory and Practice of Group Psychotherapy,* 3d ed. and in *Inpatient Group Psychotherapy.*

31. Margaret E. Hartford, ed. *Working Papers;* p. 70.

32. Sonia Leib Abels and Paul Abels, "Social Group Work's Contextual Purposes," p. 154.

33. Howard Goldstein, *Social Learning and Change,* p. 185.

34. Frances Caple, "Preventive Social Work Practice."

35. Alex Gitterman and Lawrence Shulman, eds. *Mutual Aid Groups and the Life Cycle.* Margaret E. Hartford, "Group Methods and Generic Practice," pp. 145-74; Naomi Golan, *Passing Through Transitions;* Golan, *The Perilous Bridge;* Sue Henry, *Group Skills in Social Work;* and Helen Northen, *Clinical Social Work.*

36. Elizabeth McBroom, "Socialization through Small Groups," pp. 268–303.

37. Carel B. Germain and Alex Gitterman, *Life Model of Social Work Practice.*

38. Barbara Bryant Solomon, *Black Empowerment,* pp. 322–23.

39. Howard J. Parad, Lola G. Selby, and James Quinlan, "Crisis Intervention with Families and Groups," pp. 304–30.

40. See: Frances Lomas Feldman, *Work and Cancer Health Histories;* Dena Fisher, "The Hospitalized Terminally Ill Patient," pp. 25–45; Harriet C. Johnson and Edmund J. Hart, "Neurological Disorders," pp. 73–118; and Saul Scheidlinger, *Focus On Group Psychotherapy,* pp. 235–38.

2. The Group as a Unit for Social Work Practice

1. Mary Louise Somers, "The Small Group in Learning and Teaching," p. 160.

2. Martin Lakin, ed. "What's Happened to Small Group Research?" pp. 265–429.

3. Charles Cooley, *Social Process;* Earle E. Eubank, *The Concepts of Sociology;* Georg Simmel, *Sociology of Georg Simmel.*

4. A. Paul Hare, *Creativity in Small Groups.*

5. Kurt Lewin, *Field Theory in Social Science,* pp. 239–40.

6. Jacob L. Moreno, *Who Shall Survive?;* Helen Hall Jennings, *Leadership and Isolation.*

7. Robert F. Bales, *Interaction Process Analysis.*

8. George Homans, *The Human Group.*

9. W. R. Bion, *Experiences in Groups;* Helen Durkin, *The Group in Depth;* Sigmund Freud, *An Outline of Psychoanalysis;* Sigmund Freud, *Group Psychology and the Analysis of the Ego;* Fritz Redl and David Wineman, *Controls from Within;* Saul Scheidlinger, *Psychoanalysis and Group Behavior;* Scheidlinger, *Focus on Group Psychotherapy;* S. R. Slavson, *A Textbook in Analytic Group Psychotherapy,* Irvin D. Yalom, *Theory and Practice of Group Psychotherapy.*

10. Lakin, ed. "What's Happened to Small Group Research?"

11. Grace L. Coyle, *Social Process in Organized Groups,* p. 27.

12. Hans Falck, "The Membership Model of Social Work," pp. 155–60; see also Scheidlinger, "Discussion of Individual and Group," pp. 11–15.

13. See, for example: Carel B. Germain, "General Systems Theory and Ego Psychology," pp. 535–50; Carol H. Meyer, *Social Work Practice;* Helen Northen, *Clinical Social Work;* Gerald G. O'Connor, "Small Groups," pp. 145–74.

14. Howard Goldstein, "Cognitive Approaches to Direct Practice," pp. 539–55.

15. Anna Freud, "Emotional and Social Development," pp. 336–52.

16. Harry Grunebaum and Leonard Solomon, "Toward a Peer Theory of Group Psychotherapy," pp. 23–50 and "On the Development and Significance of Peers and Play," pp. 283–308.

17. Erik H. Erikson, *Childhood and Society;* and *Identity, Youth, and Crisis.*

18. Henry S. Maas, *People and Contexts,* p. 4.

19. Tom Douglas, *Group Processes in Social Work.*

20. Marvin E. Shaw, *Group Dynamics,* p. 137.

21. For an excellent presentation of problems in communication, see: Brett A. Seabury, "Communication Problems in Social Work Practice," pp. 40–44. See also Jeannette L. Davis, "Human Communication Concepts and Constructs"; Judith Nelsen, *Communication Theory and Social Work Practice;* Virginia M. Satir, *Conjoint Family Therapy;* Kenneth K. Sereno and C. David Mortensen, *Foundations of Communication Theory.*

22. Pallassana R. Balgopal and Thomas V. Vassil, *Groups in Social Work,* pp. 27–28.

23. For a fuller discussion of purposes and goals, see Margaret E. Hartford, *Groups in Social Work,* pp. 139–58.

24. Shaw, *Group Dynamics,* pp. 293–94.

25. Bernard Berelson and Gary A. Steiner, *Human Behavior,* p. 352; Shaw, *Group Dynamics,* pp. 326–36.

26. For references on affective ties and interpersonal relations, see Grace L. Coyle, *Group Work with American Youth,* pp. 91–132; Durkin, *The Group in Depth;* Hartford, *Groups in Social Work;* Helen Hall Jennings, *Leadership and Isolation;* Scheidlinger, *Psychoanalysis and Group Behavior,* pp. 131–45.

27. Helen U. Phillips, *Essentials of Social Group Work Skill,* p. 93.

28. William C. Schutz, *Interpersonal Underworld.*

29. Urie Bronfenbrenner, *The Ecology of Human Development.*

30. For discussions of transference in groups, see: Durkin, *The Group in Depth,* pp. 139–70 and 183–97; Baruch Levine, *Group Psychotherapy,* pp. 160–64; Scheidlinger, *Psychoanalysis and Group Behavior,* pp. 80–85; Yalom, *Theory and Practice of Group Psychotherapy,* pp. 199–212.

31. Anna Freud, *The Ego and the Mechanisms of Defense,* pp. 117–31.

32. Alice Overton and Katherine Tinker, *Casework Notebook,* p. 162.

33. Major references on status and role are the following: Coyle, *Group Work with American Youth,* pp. 91–132; Neal Gross, Warren S. Mason, and A. W. McEachern, *Explorations in Role Analysis;* Hartford, *Groups in Social Work,* pp. 208–18; Robert K. Merton, *Social Theory and Social Structure,* pp. 281–386; Helen Harris Perlman, *Persona;* Shaw, *Group Dynamics,* pp. 241–47; Herman D. Stein and Richard A. Cloward, eds. *Social Perspectives on Behavior,* pp. 171–262.

34. Bronfenbrenner, *Ecology of Human Development,* p. 85.

35. Stein and Cloward, *Social Perspectives on Behavior,* p. 174.

36. Merton, *Social Theory and Social Structure,* p. 369.

37. Shaw, *Group Dynamics,* pp. 246–47.

38. Norma Radin and Sheila Feld, "Social Psychology for Group Work Practice," pp. 50–69.

39. Hartford, *Groups in Social Work,* p. 218.

40. *Ibid.,* pp. 202–6.

41. For fuller discussion of triads, see Theodore Caplow, *Two Against One.*

42. For an excellent book on the development of norms, see Edgar H. Schein, *Organizational Culture and Leadership.*

43. Muzafer Sherif, "Group Influences Upon the Formation of Norms and Attitudes," pp. 294–362.
44. John W. Thibaut and Harold H. Kelley, *Social Psychology of Groups,* p. 130.
45. Shaw, *Group Dynamics,* pp. 282–85; Serge Moscovisi, *Social Influence and Social Change.*
46. Balgopal and Vassil, *Groups in Social Work,* p. 180.
47. Michael S. Olmsted, *The Small Group,* p. 68.
48. Dorwin Cartwright and Alvin Zander, "Group Dynamics and the Individual," pp. 268–69.
49. Martin L. and Lois Wladis Hoffman, *Review of Child Development Research,* p. 312.
50. Cooley, *Social Process,* p. 39.
51. Walter Buckley, "Society as a Complex Adaptive System," p. 500.
52. For further explanation of constructive conflict, see Saul Bernstein, "Conflict and Group Work," pp. 72–106; Lewis A. Coser, *Functions of Social Conflict;* Morton Deutsch, *Resolution of Conflict;* Evert van de Vliert, "Conflict in Prevention and Escalation," p. 521–51.
53. Nevitt Sanford, *Self and Society,* p. 33.
54. Leslie A. Baxter, "Conflict Management," p. 38.
55. Gertrude Wilson and Gladys Ryland, *Social Group Work Practice,* p. 53.
56. Deutsch, *Resolution of Conflict,* p. 352.
57. James C. Herrick, "Perception of Crisis," pp. 15–30.
58. Mary Parker Follett, *Dynamic Administration,* p. 35.
59. For other definitions of group cohesion, see Cartwright and Zander, eds. *Group Dynamics,* p. 72; Douglas, *Group Processes in Social Work,* p. 58; Hartford, *Groups in Social Work,* pp. 245–60; Sue Henry, *Group Skills in Social Work,* p. 15; Avraham Levy, "Group Cohesion," pp. 28–36; Joseph P. Stokes, "Toward an Understanding of Cohesion in Personal Change Groups,"
60. Charles D. Garvin, William J. Reid, and Laura Epstein, "A Task-Centered Approach," p. 264; Levy, "Group Cohesion," pp. 80–97; Morton A. Lieberman, Irvin D. Yalom, and Matthew B. Miles, *Encounter Groups: First Facts,* pp. 302–13; Shaw, *Group Dynamics,* pp. 200–30; Stokes, "Toward an Understanding of Cohesion in Personal Change Groups"; Yalom, *Theory and Practice of Group Psychotherapy,* 3d ed. pp. 52–56.
61. For a summary of the social work literature citing evidences of group cohesion, see Levy, "Group Cohesion," pp. 37–50.
62. Merton, *Social Theory and Social Structure,* p. 311.
63. Nancy Evans and Paul A. Servis, "Group Cohesion," pp. 359–70; Levy, "Group Cohesion," pp. 98–104.
64. Merton, *Social Theory and Social Structure,* p. 233.
65. Homans, *The Human Group,* p. 453.

3. Social Work Intervention in Groups

1. Group for the Advancement of Psychiatry, *Process of Child Therapy,* pp. 2–3.
2. Mary Louise Somers, "Problem-Solving In Small Groups," pp. 331–68.
3. Helen Harris Perlman, *Social Casework,* p. 91.
4. John Dewey, *How We Think.*
5. Helen Harris Perlman, *Relationship,* p. 23.
6. Helen U. Phillips, *Essentials of Social Group Work Skill,* p. 145.
7. Grace L. Coyle, "Some Basic Assumptions About Social Group Work," p. 100.
8. For discussion of these ingredients in practice, see Pallassana R. Balgopal and Thomas V. Vassil, *Groups in Social Work,* pp. 236–40; Helen Northen, *Clinical Social Work,* pp. 97–102; Perlman, *Relationship,* pp. 155–78; Lawrence Shulman, *The Skills of Helping Individuals and Groups,* pp. 53–57; Ruby B. Pernell, "Identifying and Teaching the Skill Components of Social Group Work," pp. 20–23.
9. Baruch Levine, *Group Psychotherapy,* p. 282.

10. For good discussions of empathy, see Carl R. Rogers, "Empathic," pp. 2–10; Saul Scheidlinger, "Concept of Empathy in Group Psychotherapy," pp. 413–24.

11. Taken from Robert L. Katz, *Empathy, Its Nature and Uses,* p. 1.

12. For descriptions of scales, see Charles B. Truax and Robert R. Carkhuff, *Toward Effective Counseling and Psychotherapy,* pp. 47–56 and pp. 60–67; G. T. Barrett-Lennard, "Dimensions of Therapist Response."

13. For good discussions of the use of transference in groups, see Levine, *Group Psychotherapy,* pp. 260–64; Irvin D. Yalom, *Theory and Practice of Group Psychotherapy,* 3d ed. pp. 201–12.

14. Charlotte Buehler, *Values in Psychotherapy,* p. 1.

15. Gisela Konopka, *Social Group Work,* p. 94.

16. Rogers, "Empathic," pp. 2–10; Richard L. Bednar and G. Frank Lawlis, "Empirical Research in Group Psychotherapy"; Robert R. Carkhuff and Bernard Berenson, *Beyond Counseling and Therapy;* Truax and Carkhuff, *Toward Effective Counseling and Psychotherapy,* pp. 160–61.

17. See Charles B. Truax and Kevin M. Mitchell, "Research on Certain Therapist Interpersonal Skills," pp. 299–344; Morton A. Lieberman, Irvin D. Yalom, and Matthew B. Miles, *Encounter Groups,* pp. 237–64.

18. Paul Pigors, *Leadership or Domination.*

19. Marian F. Fatout, "A Comparative Analysis of Practice Concepts."

20. See Thomas Owen Carlton, *Clinical Social Work in Health Settings;* Urania Glassman and Len Kates, "Techniques of Social Group Work"; pp. 9–38; Florence Hollis and Mary E. Woods, *Casework: A Psychosocial Therapy,* pp. 107–360; Ruth R. Middleman and Gale Goldberg, *Social Service Delivery;* Francis J. Peirce, "A Study of the Methodological Components of Social Work with Groups"; William J. Reid and Laura Epstein, *Task-Centered Casework,* pp. 139–75; Lawrence Shulman, *Skills of Helping Individuals and Groups;* Ronald W. Toseland and Robert F. Rivas, *An Introduction to Group Work Practice,* pp. 77–110.

21. Gideon Horowitz, "Worker Intervention in Response to Deviant Behavior in Groups."

22. See Fritz Schmidl, "A Study of Techniques Used in Supportive Treatment," pp. 413–19; Lola G. Selby, "Supportive Treatment," pp. 400–14; Selby, "Support Revisited," pp. 573–85; Louise A. Frey, "Support and the Group," pp. 35–42.

23. See Ruth R. Middleman, "Relating Group Process to Group Work," pp. 15–26.

24. For further information, see Edward T. Hall, *The Hidden Dimension;* Margaret E. Hartford, *Groups in Social Work,* pp. 173–84; and Brett A. Seabury, "Arrangement of Physical Space in Social Work Settings," pp. 43–49.

25. Yalom, *Theory and Practice of Group Psychotherapy,* 3d ed. pp. 50, 85.

26. This example is taken from Adolph E. Christ and Kalman Flomenhaft, eds., *Psychosocial Family Intervention in Chronic Pediatric Illness.*

27. Barbara Bryant Solomon, *Black Empowerment.*

28. William Schwartz, "The Social Worker in the Group," pp. 146–71.

29. Solomon, *Black Empowerment.*

30. Elizabeth McBroom, "Socialization Through Small Groups," p. 276.

31. Max Siporin, *Introduction to Social Work Practice,* pp. 170–71.

32. Rosalie Kane, "Editorial: Thoughts on Parent Education," p. 2.

33. Reid and Epstein, *Task-Centered Practice,* p. 172.

34. Lieberman, Yalom, and Miles, *Encounter Groups,* pp. 371–73.

35. Eric Sainsbury, *Social Work with Families.*

36. Inger P. Davis, "Advice-Giving in Parent Counseling," pp. 343–47.

37. Alice Overton and Katherine Tinker, *Casework Notebook,* p. 68.

38. David Hallowitz et al., "Assertive Counseling Component of Therapy," p. 546.

39. Robert M. Nadel, "Interviewing Style and Foster Parents' Verbal Accessibility," p. 211.

40. Yalom, *Theory and Practice of Group Psychotherapy,* 2d. ed., pp. 19–44.

41. Nicholas Hobbs, "Sources of Gain in Psychotherapy," pp. 741-47.

42. R. W. Heine, "A Comparison of Patients' Reports."

43. Lieberman, Yalom, and Miles, *Encounter Groups.*

44. Warren G. Bennis, "Personal Change Through Interpersonal Relations," pp. 357–94.

45. Arthur Blum, "The 'Aha' Response as a Therapeutic Goal," pp. 47–56.

46. Robert A. Brown, "The Technique of Ascription," p. 73. For an article based on the dissertation, see Robert A. Brown, "Feedback in Family Interviewing," pp. 52–59.

47. Joan M. Hutten, "Short-Term Contracts," p. 617.

48. *Ibid.*

49. Lieberman, Yalom, and Miles, *Encounter Groups.*

4. Use of Activity-Oriented Experiences

1. For references on the benefits of activities, see: Pallassana R. Balgopal and Thomas V. Vassil, *Groups in Social Work,* pp. 143–48; Ken Heap, *Process and Action in Work with Groups;* Sue Henry, *Group Skills in Social Work;* Ruth R. Middleman, *The Nonverbal Method;* James K. Whittaker, "Program Activities," pp. 217–50; Gertrude Wilson and Gladys Ryland, *Social Group Work Practice,* Part II.

2. Sallie R. Churchill, "Social Group Work," pp. 581–88; Fritz Redl, "Diagnostic Group Work," pp. 53–67; Martin Sundel, Norma Radin, and Sallie R. Churchill, "Diagnosis in Group Work," pp. 117–39.

3. Henry W. Maier, "Play Is More than a Four Letter Word."

4. For references on role playing, see Roger Etcheverry, Max Siporin, and Ronald W. Toseland, "Uses and Abuses of Role Playing"; Alan F. Klein, *Role Playing in Leadership Training;* Middleman, *The Nonverbal Method,* p. 102; Lawrence Shulman, *Skills of Helping Individuals and Groups,* pp. 168–69.

5. For examples, see Mary E. Sheridan, "Talk Time for Hospitalized Children," pp. 40–45.

6. Jane A. Waldron, Ronaele R. Whittington, and Steve Jensen, "Children's Single Session Briefings," pp. 101–9.

7. Kathleen Decker, "Puppets Help Children."

8. Nicholas Mazza and Barbara D. Price, "When Time Counts," pp. 53–66.

9. This example is adapted from Marian F. Fatout, "Group Work with Severely Abused and Neglected Latency Age Children: Special Needs and Problems." Unpublished paper, November 1986.

10. Roger Lauer and Michael Goldfield, "Creative Writing in Group Therapy," pp. 248–51.

11. Heap, *Process and Action in Work with Groups,* p. 75.

12. Quentin A. Rae-Grant, Thomas Gladwin, and Eli M. Bower, "Mental Health, Social Competence, and the War on Poverty."

13. Heap, *Process and Action in Work with Groups,* p. 93.

14. Henry W. Maier, ed., *Group Work as Part of Residential Treatment,* p. 28.

15. Howard Goldstein, *Social Work Practice,* p. 101.

16. Julianne L. Wayne and Barbara B. Feinstein, "Group Work Outreach to Parents," pp. 345–51.

17. Audrey Oppenheimer, "Triumph over Trauma," p. 356.

18. James K. Whittaker, "Developmental-Educational Approach to Child Treatment," p. 180.

19. Elaine Pinderhughes, "Empowerment for Our Clients," pp. 331–38; Barbara Bryant Solomon, *Black Empowerment.*

20. Derryl Lubell, "Living with a Lifeline," pp. 283–96.

21. Toby Berman-Rossi, "The Fight Against Homelessness," pp. 323–58.

22. Harold Lipton and Sidney Malter, "The Social Worker as Mediator on a Hospital Ward."

23. Judith A. B. Lee. "No Place to Go," pp. 245–62.

24. Carel B. Germain and Alex Gitterman, *Life Model of Social Work Practice*, p. 316.
25. Charles Garvin, *Contemporary Group Work*, pp. 176–87.
26. Ibid.
27. Ruby B. Pernell, "Empowerment in Social Group Work," pp. 107–18; Solomon, *Black Empowerment*.
28. Ruth Bittner, "Therapeutic Mother-Child Groups," pp. 154–61.
29. Melvin Delgado, "Activites and Hispanic Groups," pp. 85–96.
30. E. Daniel Edwards, Margie E. Edwards, Gari M. Davies, and Francine Eddy, "Enhancing Self-Concept and Identification with Indianness of American Indian Girls," pp. 309–18.
31. For discussion of activities in varied stages of group development, Henry, *Group Skills in Social Work;* Middleman, *The Nonverbal Method*, pp. 113–29; Andrew L. Ross and Norman D. Bernstein, "A Framework for the Therapeutic Use of Group Activities," pp. 627–40.
32. See, for example: Andrew Fluegelman, ed., *The New Games Book;* Fluegelman, ed., *More New Games;* Middleman, *The Nonverbal Method;* Terry Orlick, *The Second Cooperative Sports and Games Book;* Gerrold Lee Shapiro *Methods in Group Psychotherapy and Encounter;* Wilson and Ryland, *Social Group Work Practice*, pp. 197–346.

5. Planning: Purposes of Groups in Social Context

1. Max Siporin, *Introduction to Social Work Practice*, p. 39.
2. Carol H. Meyer, *Social Work Practice*, p. 167.
3. Roselle Kurland, "Planning: the Neglected Component," p. 173.
4. Marjorie White Main, "Selected Aspects of the Beginning Phase," p. 114.
5. Roselle Kurland, "A Model of Planning."
6. Irvin D. Yalom, *Inpatient Group Psychotherapy*, p. x.
7. For a good article on the subject, see Irving Miller and Renee Solomon, "The Development of Group Services for the Elderly," pp. 74–106.
8. For further information, see Elaine Cooper Lonergan, *Group Intervention;* Robert H. Klein, "Some Problems of Patient Referral," pp. 229–39.
9. See Carel B. Germain, "Social Context of Clinical Social Work," pp. 54–65.
10. Grace L. Coyle, *Group Experience and Democratic Values*, p. 47.
11. Harold M. Proshansky, William H. Ittelson, and Leanne G. Rivlin, eds., *Environmental Psychology*, p. 28.
12. For further information, see Alex Gitterman, "Delivering a New Group Service," pp. 53–74. See also Carel B. Germain and Alex Gitterman, *Life Model of Social Work Practice*, pp. 297–342; George Brager and Stephen Holloway, *Changing Human Service Organizations*.
13. Michael Katch, "Commentary," pp. 121–24.
14. See, for example, June H. Brown et al., *Child/Family/Neighborhood;* Child Welfare League of America, *Group Methods and Services in Child Welfare;* Elsbeth Herzstein Couch, *Joint and Family Interviews;* Family Service Association of America, *Use of Group Techniques;* Gisela Konopka, *Social Group Work*, pp. 191–97.
15. Grant Loavenbruch and Paul Keys, "Settlements and Neighborhood Centers," NASW, pp. 556–61.
16. Wendy Glasgow Winters and Freda Easton, *Practice of Social Work in Schools*.
17. National Association of Social Workers, *Use of Groups in the Psychiatric Setting:* Harleigh B. Trecker, ed., *Group Work in the Psychiatric Setting;* Konopka, *Social Group Work*, pp. 200–9.
18. Yalom, *Inpatient Group Psychotherapy*, p. 33.
19. Bernard Rosen et al., "Clinical Effectiveness in 'Short' versus 'Long' Psychiatric Hospitalization," pp. 1316–22.
20. Yalom, *Inpatient Group Psychotherapy*.

21. Raymond C. Lerner, "The Therapeutic Social Club," p. 6.
22. Louise A. Frey, ed., *Use of Groups in the Health Field;* Abraham Lurie, Gary Rosenberg, and Sidney Pinsky. *Social Work with Groups in Health Settings.* Helen Northen, "Social Work with Groups in Health Settings," pp. 107–21, and Commentaries by Michael Katch and Phyllis Mervis, pp. 123–28.
23. Hans Falck, "Social Work in Health Settings," p. 401.
24. Konopka, *Social Group Work,* pp. 209–12; Elliot Studt, "Correctional Services," pp. 219–25.
25. Saul Bernstein, *Youth in the Streets;* Irving Spergel, *Street Gang Work.*
26. See Diane Meadow, "The Use of Groups"; David Siegel, "Social Work with Groups"; and Joel Walker and Paul Keys, "Industrial and Organizational Group Work."
27. This material is adapted from Northen, *Clinical Social Work,* pp. 67–74.
28. Carel B. Germain and Alex Gitterman, *The Life Model of Social Work Practice,* pp. 77–136; Naomi Golan, *Passing Through Transitions;* Golan, *The Perilous Bridge.*
29. Howard J. Parad, Lola G. Selby, and James Quinlan, "Crisis Intervention," pp. 304–30.
30. For good discussions, see Jack Rothman, "Analyzing Issues in Race," pp. 24–37; Barbara Bryant Solomon, *Black Empowerment.* Kenneth L. Chau, "A Model of Practice with Special Reference to Ethnic Minority Populations," paper presented at the Symposium on Social Work with Groups, October 1986.
31. Valerian J. Derlega, *Communication, Intimacy, and Close Relationships.*
32. American Psychiatric Association, *Diagnostic and Statistical Manual III-R.*
33. James K. Whittaker, "Causes of Childhood Disorders," pp. 91–96.
34. Ben A. Orcutt, "Family Treatment of Poverty Level Families," p. 92.
35. For elaboration of these ideas, see Pallassana R. Balgopal and Thomas V. Vassil, *Groups in Social Work,* pp. 130–35; Margaret E. Hartford, *Groups in Social Work,* pp. 139–58; Louis Lowy, "Goal Formulation in Social Work Groups," pp. 116–44; Janice H. Schopler, Maeda J. Galinsky, and Mark D. Alicke, "Goals in Social Work Practice," pp. 140–58; and Rosamond P. Tompkins and Frank T. Gallo, "Social Group Work," pp. 307–17.
36. Max Siporin, *Introduction to Social Work Practice,* p. 258.
37. Julianna Schmidt, "The Use of Purpose,"pp. 36, 77–84.
38. Gerald Raschella, "Evaluation of the Effect of Goal Congruence."
39. Charles D. Garvin, "Complementarity of Role Expectations in Groups," pp. 127–45.
40. Rosalie Kane, "Editorial Thoughts on Parent Education," pp. 2–4.
41. Ronald W. Toseland and Robert F. Rivas. *An Introduction to Group Work Practice.*

6. Planning: Composition, Structure, Content

1. Fritz Redl, "The Art of Group Composition," pp. 76–96.
2. *Ibid.*
3. Baruch Levine, *Group Psychotherapy,* p. 13.
4. Levine, "Factors Related to Interpersonal Balance."
5. Charles D. Garvin and Beth Glover Reed, "Gender Issues in Social Work," pp. 3–19.
6. Barbara Sabin Daley and Geraldine Suzanne Koppenaal, "The Treatment of Women," pp. 343–57.
7. Barbara Bryant Solomon, *Black Empowerment.*
8. Ralph Kolodny, *Peer-Oriented Group Work.*
9. Ronald A. Feldman et al., "Treating Delinquents in Traditional Agencies," pp. 71–78.
10. Edward N. Peters, Muriel W. Pumphrey, and Norman Flax, "Comparison of Retarded and Nonretarded Children," pp. 87–89; David Preininger, "Reactions of Normal Children to Retardates," pp. 75–78.
11. Irvin D. Yalom, *Theory and Practice of Group Psychotherapy,* 3d ed., p. 237.

12. Alfred Kadushin, *The Social Work Interview,* pp. 254–60.
13. Solomon, *Black Empowerment,* pp. 299–313.
14. Annette K. Boer and James E. Lantz, "Adolescent Group Therapy Membership Selection," pp. 172–81.
15. Levine, *Fundamentals of Group Treatment,* pp. 14–15.
16. Margaret E. Hartford, *Groups in Social Work,* p. 162. For other research on size of groups, see A. Paul Hare et al., eds., *Small Groups,* pp. 495–510; Edwin Thomas and Clinton Fink, "Effects of Group Size," in *ibid,* pp. 525–35; Bernard Berelson and Gary A. Steiner, *Human Behavior,* pp. 358–59.
17. Yalom, *Theory and Practice of Group Psychotherapy,* 3d ed., p. 283.
18. Robert F. Bales et al., "Structure and Dynamics of Small Groups," p. 394.
19. One entire issue of a journal deals with the issue of co-leadership, *Social Work with Groups* (Winter 1980), vol. 3, no. 4. Each author presents many references on the subject. For an excellent analysis of the positive and negataive aspects of co-leadership, see Maeda J. Galinsky and Janice H. Schopler, "Structuring Co-leadership," pp. 51–63.
20. See Ruth R. Middleman, "Co-leadership and Solo Leadership," *ibid,* pp. 39–50.
21. Beth Glover Reed, "Women Leaders in Small Groups," in *ibid,* p. 41.
22. Kolodny, "The Dilemma of Co-leadership," in *ibid,* pp. 31–34.
23. Dane Archer, "Ethical Problems in Small Group Observation," pp. 222–43.
24. This is reported in Ellen Waldman, "Co-Leadership as a Method of Training: A Student's Point of View," pp. 51–58.
25. *Ibid,* p. 52.
26. Beryce W. MacLennan, "Co-therapy," pp. 154–66.
27. David G. Rice, William F. Fey, and Joseph Kepecs, "Therapist Experience and Style," pp. 1–12.
28. Beulah Rothman, "Study of Patterns of Leadership," pp. 11–17.
29. Group for the Advancement of Psychiatry, *The Field of Family Therapy.*
30. Alan S. Gurman, "Effects and Effectiveness of Marital Therapy," pp. 145–70.
31. Robert R. Dies, "Clinical Implications of Research on Leadership," p. 59.
32. Barry Friedman, "Cotherapy: A Behavioral and Attitudinal Survey," pp. 228–34.
33. Alex Gitterman, "Delivering a New Group Service: Strategies and Skills," p. 68.
34. For further views on the values of co-therapy, see Elsa Leichter and Gerda Schulman, "The Family Interview as an Integrative Device," pp. 335–45; Levine, *Group Psychotherapy,* pp. 296–302.
35. Eldon Marshall, "Use of Aides in Activity Group Treatment," pp. 333–44.
36. See Robert Ziller, "Toward a Theory of Open and Closed Groups," pp. 164–82; Hartford, *Groups in Social Work,* pp. 135–36.
37. Sue Henry, *Group Skills in Social Work,* p. 303.
38. Janice H. Schopler and Maeda J. Galinsky, "Meeting Practice Needs," pp. 3–22; and Schopler and Galinsky, "The Open-Ended Group," pp. 87–100.
39. William F. Hill and L. A. Gruner, "Study of Development in Open and Closed Groups," pp. 355–81.
40. For a report of research on open-ended groups, see Maeda J. Galinsky and Janice H. Schopler, "Practitioners' Views of Assets and Liabilities of Open-Ended Groups," In Joseph Lassner, Kathleen Powell, and Elaine Finnegan, eds. *Social Group Work,* pp. 83–98.
41. Hartford, *Groups in Social Work,* pp. 181–90.
42. See Anne E. Fortune, *Task-Centered Practice;* Charles D. Garvin, William J. Reid, and Laura Epstein, "A Task-Centered Approach," pp. 238–67.
43. See, for example, Naomi D. Bloom and Joseph G. Lynch, "Group Work in a Hospital Waiting Room," pp. 48–63; Lisa Rae Block, "On the Potentiality and Limits of Time," pp. 81–100; Jane A. Waldron, Ronaele R. Whittington, and Steve Jensen, "Children's Single Session Briefings," pp. 101–9; Alma R. Weisberg, "Single Session

Group Practice in a Hospital," pp. 99–112. Yalom, *Inpatient Group Psychotherapy;* Tryne Retholz, "The Single Session Group," pp. 143–46.

44. Norman Epstein, "Brief Group Therapy," pp. 33–48.

45. Wynetta Devore and Elfrieda G. Schlesinger, *Ethnic-Sensitive Social Work Practice.*

46. See, for example Dorthea Lane, "Psychiatric Patients Learn a New Way of Life," pp. 114–23; Edith Tufts, *Group Work with Young School Girls.*

47. See Hartford, *Groups in Social Work,* pp. 184–85; Josephine Klein, *The Study of Groups,* pp. 90–94.

48. Yalom, *Inpatient Group Psychotherapy,* pp. 74–82.

49. For references on the importance of space, see Hartford, *Groups in Social Work,* pp. 167–81; Brett A. Seabury, "Arrangement of Physical Space," pp. 43–49; Max Siporin, *Introduction to Social Work Practice,* pp. 177–78.

50. Henry, *Group Skills in Social Work,* p. 45.

7. Selection and Preparation of Members

1. Richard A. Cloward, "Agency Structure as a Variable," pp. 30–44.

2. Alvin W. Gouldner, "Red Tape as a Social Problem," pp. 410–18.

3. Ronald W. Toseland, "Increasing Access," pp. 227–34, 227.

4. Linda H. Kilburn, "An Educational/Supportive Group Model," pp. 53–63.

5. For fuller information on assessment, see Helen Northen, "Assessment in Direct Practice," pp. 171–83.

6. Max Siporin, *Introduction to Social Work Practice,* p. 224.

7. Mary Richmond, "Some Next Steps in Social Treatment," in Mary Richmond, *The Long View,* p. 487.

8. California Chapter, National Association of Social Workers, "Social Work Intervention Guide."

9. Allen Frances, John F. Clarkin, and Samuel Perry, *Differential Therapeutics in Psychiatry.*

10. For excellent material on how this concept applies to residential settings, see Henry W. Maier, "Social Group Work Method," pp. 26–44.

11. Gerald Caplan, *Support Systems and Community Mental Health,* pp. 216–17.

12. Henry Grunebaum and Leonard Solomon, "Toward a Peer Theory," p. 40.

13. Shirley Jenkins, *The Ethnic Dilemma in Social Services.*

14. Doman Lum, *Social Work Practice and People of Color,* pp. 3–37.

15. Elaine J. Cooper and Margarita Hernandez Cento, "Groups and the Hispanic Prenatal Patient," pp. 689–700.

16. Beulah Roberts Compton and Burt Galaway, eds. *Social Work Processes;* Howard Goldstein, *Social Work Practice;* Allen Pincus and Anne Minahan, *Social Work Practice;* Max Siporin, *Introduction to Social Work Practice;* Ronald W. Toseland and Robert F. Rivas, *Introduction to Group Work Practice.*

17. Toseland and Rivas, ibid.; Gertrude Wilson and Gladys Ryland, *Social Group Work Practice.*

18. Siporin, *Introduction to Social Work Practice;* Toseland and Rivas, *Introduction to Group Work Practice.*

19. Walter Hudson, *The Clinical Measurerment Package;* John L. Leavitt and William J. Reid, "Rapid Assessment Instruments," pp. 13–20; Toseland and Rivas, *Introduction to Group Work Practice,* pp. 306–23.

20. Helen Harris Perlman, "The Problem-Solving Model in Social Casework," in Robert W. Roberts and Robert H. Nee, eds. *Theories of Social Casework,* pp. 129–180; Mary Louise Somers, "Problem-Solving in Small Groups," pp. 331–67.

21. Harold Lewis, *Intellectual Base of Social Work Practice.*

22. Cervando Martinez, "Community Mental Health," pp. 595–601.

23. Barbara Bryant Solomon, *Black Empowerment,* p. 306.

24. Lewis, *Intellectual Base of Social Work Practice.*

25. Siporin, *Introduction to Social Work Practice,* pp. 239–41.

26. Baruch Levine, *Group Psychotherapy*, pp. 45–48.
27. Frances Louise Boatman, "Caseworkers' Judgments of Clients' Hope,"; David Fanshel, "a Study of Caseworkers' Perceptions," pp. 543–51; Lilian Ripple, "Factors Associated with Continuance," pp. 87–94; Irvin D. Yalom, *Theory and Practice of Group Psychotherapy*, 2d ed. pp. 6–7; Serapio R. Zalba, "Discontinuance during Social Service Intake."
28. Diane Ammund Meadow, "Effects of Client-Focused Pregroup Preparation Interview," pp. 52–134.
29. Yalom, *Theory and Practice of Group Psychotherapy*, 3d ed, pp. 295–96.
30. William Schwartz, "The Social Worker in the Group," pp. 146–71.
31. John Dewey, *Democracy and Education*, p. 104.
32. Lynette Beall, "The Corrupt Contract," pp. 77–81.
33. Donald E. Wallens, "Congruence," pp. 207–16.
34. Robert H. Klein, "Therapy Group for Adult Inpatients," pp. 291–319.

8. Group Development

1. Bruce W. Tuckman, "Developmental Sequence," pp. 384–99.
2. Robert F. Bales, *Interaction Process Analysis*.
3. Tuckman and M. A. C. Jensen, "Stages of Group Development Revisited," pp. 419–27.
4. Roy B. Lacoursiere, *Life Cycle of Groups*.
5. James K. Whittaker, "Models of Group Development," pp. 308–22.
6. *Ibid.*, p. 308.
7. James A. Garland, Hubert E. Jones and Ralph L. Kolodny, "Model for Stages of Development," pp. 17–71.
8. Garland and Louise A. Frey, "Application of Stages of Group Development," pp. 1–33.
9. Garland, Jones, and Kolodny, "Model for Stages of Development," p. 29.
10. Helen Northen, *Social Work with Groups*.
11. Margaret E. Hartford, *Groups in Social Work*.
12. Rosemary Sarri and Maeda Galinsky, "Conceptual Framework," pp. 71–88.
13. Pallassana R. Balgopal and Thomas V. Vassil, *Groups in Social Work;* Charles D. Garvin, *Contemporary Group Work;* William Schwartz "Between Client and System," pp. 171–97; Robert W. Toseland and Robert F. Rivas, *Introduction to Group Work Practice;* Emanuel Tropp, "A Developmental Theory," pp. 198–237; O'Connor also has a three-stage model that differs from the others in that he does not include an ending or termination stage. Gerald G. O'Connor, "Small Groups: A General System Model," pp. 145–74.
14. Arthur M. Cohen and R. Douglas Smith, *The Critical Incident in Growth Groups*, pp. 209–10.
15. Joseph D. Anderson, *Counseling Through Group Process;* Garland, Jones, and Kolodny, "Model for Stages of Development"; Hartford, *Groups in Social Work;* Sue Henry, *Group Skills in Social Work;* Alan F. Klein, *Effective Group Work;* Baruch Levine, *Group Psychotherapy;* Northen, *Social Work with Groups;* O'Connor, "Small Groups: A General System Model."
16. Garland, Jones, and Kolodny, ibid.; Klein, ibid.; Anderson, ibid.
17. Henry, *Group Skills in Social Work*.
18. Harleigh B. Trecker, *Social Group Work*.
19. Sarri and Galinsky, "A Conceptual Framework."
20. Lacoursiere, *Life Cycle of Groups*.
21. Balgopal and Vassil, *Groups in Social Work*, p. 195.
22. Hartford, *Groups in Social Work*, pp. 87–93.
23. Levine, *Group Psychotherapy*, pp. 65–69.
24. *Ibid.*, p. 68.
25. Urania Glassman and Len Kates, "Authority Themes and Worker-Group Transactions;" pp. 33–52.

26. Warren G. Bennis and Herbert A. Shepard, "A Theory of Group Development," pp. 127–53.
27. William C. Schutz, *Interpersonal Underworld.*
28. O'Connor, "Small Groups: A General System Model."

9. Stage I: Orientation-Inclusion

1. Grace Coyle, *Group Work With American Youth,* p. 45.
2. Erving Goffman, *Behavior in Public Places,* p. 16.
3. Dorothy Stock Whitaker, *Using Groups To Help People,* pp. 37–40.
4. William Schwartz, "Between Client and System," pp. 186–88.
5. Meyer Williams, "Limitations, Phantasies, and Security Operations," pp. 15–62.
6. Erik H. Erikson, *Childhood and Society,* pp. 219–34.
7. Irving Spergel, *Street Gang Work,* p. 73.
8. Jerome Frank, *Persuasion and Healing,* p. 132.
9. Barbara Bryant Solomon, *Black Empowerment,* p. 308.
10. Shirley A. Cooper, "A Look at the Effect of Racism," p. 76; For other important references, see Larry E. Davis, "Group Work Practice with Ethnic Minorities," pp. 324–45; Melvin and Denise Humm-Delgado, "Hispanics and Group Work;" pp. 85–96; Man Keung Ho, "Social Group Work with Asian Pacific Americans," pp. 49–61; Doman Lum, *Social Work Practice and People of Color.*
11. Joan Velasquez et al., "Framework for Establishing Social Work Relationships," pp. 197–203.
12. Ignacio Aguilar, "Initial Contacts with Mexican-American Families," pp. 66–77.
13. D. Corydon Hammond, "Cross-cultural Rehabilitation," pp. 34–36.
14. George Nakama, "Japanese-Americans' Expectations of Counseling."
15. Alfred Kadushin, "Racial Factor in the Interview," pp. 88–98.
16. Solomon, *Black Empowerment,* pp. 324–25.
17. Henry S. Maas, "Group Influences on Client-Worker Interaction," pp. 70–79; H. Aronson and B. Overall, "Treatment Expectations of Patients," pp. 35–41.
18. Morris B. Parloff, Irene E. Waskow, and Barry E. Wolfe, "Research on Therapist Variables," p. 262.
19. Ibid., p. 273.
20. Hazel Osborn, "Some Factors of Resistance," pp. 1–14.
21. Ronald C. Bounous, "Study of Client and Worker Perceptions," pp. 94–95; Max Siporin, *Introduction to Social Work Practice,* p. 208.
22. Margaret E. Hartford, "The Social Group Worker and Group Formation."
23. Helen M. Levinson, "Use and Misuse of Groups," pp. 66–73.
24. Judith A. B. Lee, "No Place To Go," pp. 245–62.
25. Irvin D. Yalom, *Theory and Practice of Group Psychotherapy,* pp. 115–34.
26. Leonard N. Brown, "Social Workers' Verbal Acts."
27. Charles D. Garvin, "Complementarity of Role Expectations in Groups," pp. 127–45.
28. Scott Briar, "Family Services," pp. 14–15 and 21–27.
29. Edgar H. Schein, *Organizational Culture and Leadership,* pp. 224–26.
30. See Judith A. B. Lee and Danielle N. Park, "Group Approach to Depressed Adolescent Girl," pp. 516–27.
31. Aaron Rosen and Dina Lieberman, "Experimental Evaluation of Interview Performance," pp. 395–412.
32. Martha Gentry, "Initial Group Meetings."
33. Ann W. Shyne, "What Research Tells Us," pp. 223–31; Frances B. Stark, "Barriers to Client-Worker Communication," pp. 177–83.
34. Norman A. Polansky and Jacob Kounin, "Clients' Reactions to Initial Interviews," pp. 237–64.
35. Marsha Worby, "Adolescent's Expectations," pp. 19–59.

36. John E. Mayer and Aaron Rosenblatt, "The Client's Social Context," pp. 511–18.
37. Anthony N. Maluccio and Wilma D. Marlow, "Case for the Contract," pp. 28–36.

10. Stage II: Dissatisfaction and Power Conflict

1. James A. Garland, Hubert E. Jones, and Ralph Kolodny, "Model for Stages of Development," pp. 43–45.
2. Barbara Bryant Solomon, *Black Empowerment,* pp. 28–29. See also Gisela Konopka, "Formation of Values," pp. 86–96.
3. Wilfred R. Bion, *Experiences in Groups.*
4. Sheila Thompson and J. H. Kahn, *The Group Process,* p. 63.
5. Baruch Levine, *Group Psychotherapy,* p. 75.
6. The examples are from Judith A. B. Lee and Danielle N. Park, "Group Approach to the Depressed Adolescent Girl," pp. 516–27; for another reference to work with depressed clients, see Baruch Levine and Judith Schild, "Group Treatment of Depression," pp. 49–52.
7. Helen Northen, "Social Group Work," pp. 60–69.
8. For biopsychosocial knowledge about mental disorders, see Francis J. Turner, ed., *Adult Psychopathology.*
9. Florence Clemenger, "Congruence Between Members and Workers."
10. Marjorie White Main, "Selected Aspects of the Beginning Phase."
11. Julianna Schmidt, "The Use of Purpose," pp. 77–84.
12. Robert Paradise, "The Factor of Timing," pp. 524–30.
13. This is an example from Tonia Tash Lasater and Frank F. Montalvo, "Understanding Mexican-American Culture," pp. 23–25.
14. See Margaret E. Hartford, "The Social Group Worker"; George H. Wolkon and Henry Tanaka, "Outcome of a Social Rehabilitation Service," pp. 55–61; Irvin D. Yalom, "Study of Group Therapy Drop-Outs," pp. 393–414.
15. Elaine Cooper Lonergan, *Group Intervention,* p. 7.
16. Norman A. Polansky, Ronald Lippitt, and Fritz Redl, "Investigation of Behavioral Contagion," pp. 319–48.
17. Robert F. Bales and Philip E. Slater, "Functional Roles of Group Members," in Talcott Parsons and Bales, eds., *Family: Socialization and Interaction Process,* pp. 259–306; Kenneth D. Benne and Paul Sheats, "Functional Roles of Group Members," pp. 41–49; Grace L. Coyle, *Group Work with American Youth,* pp. 91–132.
18. Gisela Konopka, *Social Group Work,* pp. 490–51.
19. Mark Anstey, "Scapegoating in Groups," pp. 51–63; Florence B. Powdermaker and Jerome D. Frank, *Group Psychotherapy,* p. 137; 162–63; Saul Scheidlinger, "On Scapegoating," pp. 131–43; Lawrence Shulman, "Scapecoats, Group Workers," pp. 37–43; Eugene Toker, "The Scapegoat as an Essential Group Phenomenon," pp. 320–32.
20. This incident is taken from Grace Ganter, "The Group Worker in the Child Guidance Center," pp. 33–34.
21. Shulman, *The Skills of Helping Individuals and Groups,* 2d ed., pp. 268–69.
22. Hartford, *Groups in Social Work,* p. 218.
23. Hartford, "The Social Group Worker."
24. Taken from Elaine Cooper Lonergan and Gaetana M. Manuele, "A Group for Relatives and Friends of Patients," pp. 357–79.
25. Henry W. Maier, "Play Is More than a Four-Letter Word," pp. 65–74.
26. Fritz Redl, "Strategy and Technique of the Life Space Interview," pp. 1–18.
27. For a model of such an approach, see June H. Brown et al., *Child/Family/Neighborhood.*
28. Sue Henry, *Group Skills in Social Work,* pp. 194–95.
29. Charles D. Garvin, "Complementarity of Role Expectations in Groups," p. 145.
30. Leonard N. Brown, "Social Workers' Verbal Acts."

31. Irvin D. Yalom et al., "Preparation of Patients," p. 426.
32. Dorwin Cartwright and Alvin Zander, eds., *Group Dynamics,* 3d ed., p. 72.

11. Stage III: Mutuality and Work

1. Valerian J. Derlega, "Self-Disclosure in Intimate Relationships," pp. 1–9.
2. L. M. Horowitz, "Cognitive Structure of Interpersonal Problems," pp. 5–15.
3. Edgar H. Schein in *Organizational Culture and Leadership* explains how this happens.
4. Florence B. Powdermaker and Jerome D. Frank, *Group Psychotherapy,* p. 433.
5. For further information, see Janice Perley, Carolyn Winget, and Carlos Placci, "Hope and Discomfort as Factors," pp. 557–63.
6. Nathan Ackerman, *Treating the Troubled Family,* p. 88.
7. Pallassana R. Balgopal and R. F. Hull, "Keeping Secrets," pp. 334–36.
8. Pallassana R. Balgopal and Thomas V. Vassil, *Groups in Social Work,* p. 129.
9. Schein, *Organizational Culture and Leadership,* p. 206.
10. Georg Simmel, *Conflict,* p. 46.
11. Irvin D. Yalom, *Theory and Practice of Group Psychotherapy,* 3d ed., pp. 52–55.
12. *Ibid.,* p. 67.
13. *Ibid.,* pp. 361–62.
14. Erik H. Erikson, "Identity and the Life Cycle," pp. 18–164.
15. Judith A. B. Lee and Danielle N. Park, "A Group Approach to the Depressed Adolescent Girl," p. 523.
16. William Schwartz, "The Social Worker in the Group," p. 148.
17. David Hallowitz et al., Assertive Counseling Component," p. 546.
18. Barbara Bryant Solomon, *Black Empowerment,* pp. 311–13.
19. Arthur Blum, "The A-ha Response as a Therapeutic Goal," pp. 47–56.
20. Yalom, *Theory and Practice of Group Psychotherapy,* 3d ed., pp. 143–80.
21. Gisela Konopka, "The Significance of Social Group Work," p. 128.
22. Grace L. Coyle, "Social Group Work," p. 29.
23. William J. Reid, "Client and Practitioner Variables," pp. 586–92.
24. Lee and Park, "A Group Approach to the Depressed Adolescent Girl," p. 522.
25. Konopka, *Social Group Work,* p. 104.
26. For references on crisis intervention in groups, see Jean M. Allgeyer, "Resolving Individual Crises," pp. 159–67; Jean M. Allgeyer, "The Crisis Group," pp. 235–46. Howard J. Parad, Lola G. Selby, and James Quinlan, "Crisis Intervention," p. 305.
27. Joyce E. Williams and Karen A. Holmes, *The Second Assault,* pp. 87–89.
28. Erik H. Erikson, *Childhood and Society;* Henry S. Maas, *People and Contexts.*
29. Alline Del Valle and Felton Alexander, Project Enable," pp. 633–38.

12. Stage IV: Separation, Termination, Transition

1. Gordon Hamilton, *Theory and Practice of Social Case Work,* p. 236.
2. Irvin D. Yalom, *Theory and Practice of Group Psychotherapy,* 3d ed., p. 373.
3. Erik H. Erikson, *Identity, Youth, and Crisis,* pp. 99–141; Constance Hoenk Shapiro, "Termination," pp. 13–19; Henry S. Maas, *People and Contexts.*
4. Pallassana R. Balgopal and Thomas V. Vassil, *Groups in Social Work,* p. 212.
5. See Yalom, *Theory and Practice of Group Psychotherapy,* 3d ed. for a fuller discussion of dropouts, pp. 230–44; Roselle Kurland, "Planning: The Neglected Component," pp. 173–78.
6. Dorothy Fahs Beck and Mary Ann Jones, *Progress in Family Problems;* Elizabeth Kerns, "Planned Short-term Treatment," *Social Casework* (June 1970), 51(6):340–46; Norman Epstein, "Brief Group Therapy," pp. 33–48; William J. Reid and Ann W. Shyne, *Brief and Extended Casework.*
7. Nazneen Mayadas and Paul Glasser, "Termination," p. 253.
8. See Evelyn Fox, Marion Nelson, and William Bolman, "The Termination Process," pp. 53–63; James A. Garland, Hubert E. Jones, and Ralph L. Kolodny, "A Model

for Stages of Development," pp. 17–71; Carel B. Germain and Alex Gitterman, *Life Model of Social Work Practice,* pp. 258–78; Margaret E. Hartford, *Groups in Social Work,* pp. 87–93; Shirley C. Hellenbrand, "Termination in Direct Practice," pp. 765–69; Sue Henry, *Group Skills in Social Work,* pp. 243–87; Mary Beit-Hallahmi Lackey, "Termination"; Helen Northen, *Clinical Social Work,* pp. 274–83; Lawrence Shulman, *Skills of Helping* pp. 278–91.

9. Garland, Jones, and Kolodny, "Model for Stages of Development," pp. 57–58; Northen, *Clinical Social Work,* p. 282.

10. Paul Bywaters, "Ending Casework Relationships (2)," p. 337.

11. John Bowlby, "Separation Anxiety," p. 102.

12. For a more thorough discussion of separation crises, see Baruch Levine, *Group Psychotherapy,* pp. 224–40.

13. Garland, Jones, and Kolodny, "Model for Stages of Development," pp. 57–58.

14. Saul Scheidlinger and Marjorie A. Holden, "Group Therapy of Women," pp. 174–89.

15. Sheldon K. Schiff, "Termination of Therapy," p. 80.

16. *Ibid.*

17. William Schwartz, "Between Client and System," p. 192.

18. In a content analysis of four adult groups, Lackey found many expressions of positive feelings about termination. See Lackey, "Termination."

19. Germain and Gitterman, *Life Model of Social Work Practice,* p. 258.

20. Jane K. Bolen, "Easing the Pain of Termination," pp. 519–27; Richard D. Casey and Leon Cantor, "Group Work with Hard-to-Reach Adolescents," pp. 9–22; Mona Eklof, "The Termination Phase," pp. 565–71.

21. For a task-centered approach to work with groups, see Charles D. Garvin, William J. Reid, and Laura Epstein, "A Task-Centered Approach," pp. 238–67.

22. Mayadas and Glasser, "Termination," p. 252.

23. Benjamin F. Lewis, "Examination of the Final Phase," pp. 507–14.

24. Lackey, "Termination."

25. Lydia Rapoport, "Crisis Intervention," p. 236.

26. For similar formulations of tasks, see Charles D. Garvin, *Contemporary Group Work,* pp. 208–9; Ronald W. Toseland and Robert F. Rivas, *Introduction to Group Work Practice,* pp. 333–41.

27. Robert Chin, "Evaluating Group Movement," p. 42.

28. Gordon Hearn, *Theory Building in Social Work,* p. 28.

29. Hamilton, *Theory and Practice of Social Case Work,* p. 81.

30. Wilma L. Greenfield and Beula Rottman, "Termination or Transformation," pp. 51–66.

Bibliography

Abels, Sonia Leib and Paul Abels. "Social Group Work's Contextual Purpose." In Sonia Leib Abels and Paul Abels, eds. *Proceedings, 1979 Symposium on Social Work with Groups,* pp. 146–60. Louisville, Ky.: Committee for the Advancement of Social Work with Groups, 1979.

Ackerman, Nathan. *Treating the Troubled Family.* New York: Basic Books, 1966.

Aguilar, Ignacio. "Initial Contacts with Mexican-American Families." *Social Work* (May 1972), 17(3):66–70.

Albee, George W. and Justin M. Jaffee, eds. *Primary Prevention of Psychopathology,* vol. 1. Hanover, N.H.: University Press of New England, 1977.

Akabas, Sheila H. and Paul A. Kurzman, eds. *Work, Workers, and Work Organizations.* Englewood Cliffs, N.J.: Prentice-Hall, 1982.

Alissi, Albert S., ed. *Perspectives on Social Group Work Practice.* New York: Free Press, 1980.

Allgeyer, Jean M. "Resolving Individual Crises Through Group Methods." In Howard J. Parad, H. L. P. Resnik, and Libbie G. Parad, eds. *Emergency and Disaster Management,* pp. 159–67. Bowie, Md.: Charles Press, 1976.

Allgeyer, Jean M. "The Crisis Group: Its Unique Usefulness to the Disadvantaged." *International Journal of Group Psychotherapy* (April 1970), 20(2):235–40.

Allport, Gordon. *The Nature of Prejudice.* Garden City, N.J.: Doubleday Anchor, 1985.

Anstey, Mark. "Scapegoating in Groups: Some Theoretical Perspectives and a Case Record of Intervention." *Social Work with Groups* (Fall 1982), 5(3):51–63.

American Psychiatric Association. *Diagnostic and Statistical Manual of Mental Disorders, III-R.* Washington, D.C.: American Psychiatric Association, 1987.

Anderson, Joseph D. *Counseling Through Group Process.* New York: Springer, 1984.

Archer, Dane. "Ethical Problems in Small Group Observation." *Small Group Behavior* (May 1974), 5(2):224–43.

Aronson, H. and B. Overall. "Treatment Expectations of Patients in Two Social Classes." *Social Work* (January 1966), 11(1):35–41.

Baker, Ron. "The Multirole Practitioner in the Generic Orientation to Social Work Practice." *British Journal of Social Work* (Autumn 1976), 6(3):327–52.

Baker, Ron. "Toward Generic Social Work Practice: A Review and Some Innovations." British Journal of Social Work (Summer 1975), 5(2):193–215.

Bales, Robert F. *Interaction Process Analysis: A Method for the Study of Small Groups.* Cambridge, Mass.: Addison Wesley, 1950.

Bales, Robert F. et al. "Structure and Dynamics of Small Groups: A Review of Four Variables." In Joseph Gittler, ed., *Review of Sociology: Analysis of a Decade.* New York: Wiley, 1957.

Balgopal, Pallassana R. and R. F. Hull. "Keeping Secrets: Group Resistance for Patients and Therapists." *Psychotherapy: Theory, Research, and Practice* (Winter 1973), 10(4):334–36.

Balgopal, Pallassana R. and Thomas V. Vassil. *Groups in Social Work: An Ecological Perspective.* New York: Macmillan, 1983.

Barker, Roger. *Ecological Psychology.* Palo Alto; Stanford University Press, 1968.

Barrett-Leonard, G. T. "Dimensions of Therapist Response as Causal Factors in Therapeutic Change." *Psychological Monographs* (1962), 73(3):entire issue.
Baxter, Leslie A. "Conflict Management: An Episodic Approach." *Small Group Behavior* (February 1982), 13(1):23–42.
Beall, Lynette. "The Corrupt Contract: Problems in Conjoint Therapy with Parents and Children." *American Journal of Orthopsychiatry* (January 1972), 42(1):77–81.
Beck, Ariadne P. "A Study of Group Phase Development and Emergent Leadership." *Group* (Winter 1981), 5(4):48–54.
Beck, Dorothy Fahs and Mary Ann Jones. *Progress in Family Problems.* New York: Family Service Association of America, 1973.
Bednar, Richard L. and G. Frank Lawlis. "Empirical Research in Group Psychotherapy." In Allen E. Bergin and Sol L. Garfield, eds., *Handbook of Psychotherapy and Behavior Change,* pp. 812–38. New York: Wiley, 1971.
Benne, Kenneth D. and Paul Sheats. "Functional Roles of Group Members." *Journal of Social Issues* (Spring 1948), 4(2):41–49.
Bennis, Warren G. "Personal Change Through Interpersonal Relations." In Bennis et al., eds. *Interpersonal Dynamics,* pp. 357–94.
Bennis, Warren G. and Herbert A. Shepard. "A Theory of Group Development." In Graham S. Gibbard, John H. Hartman, and Richard Mann, eds., *Analysis of Groups. Contributions to Theory, Research, and Practice,* pp. 127–53. San Francisco: Jossey-Bass, 1974.
Bennis, Warren G. et al., eds. *Interpersonal Dynamics: Essays and Readings on Human Interaction.* Homewood, Ill.: Dorsey Press, 1968.
Bennis, Warren G., Kenneth D. Benne, and Robert Chin. *The Planning of Change.* New York: Holt, Rinehart and Winston, 1962.
Berelson, Bernard and Gary A. Steiner. *Human Behavior: An Inventory of Scientific Findings.* New York: Harcourt, Brace and World, 1964.
Berkovitz, Irving, ed. *Adolescents Grow in Groups: Clinical Experiences in Adolescent Group Psychotherapy.* New York: Brunner/Mazel, 1972.
Berman-Rossi, Toby. "The Fight Against Homelessness and Despair." In Alex Gitterman and Lawrence Shulman, eds., *Mutual Aid Groups and the Life Cycle,* pp. 323–58. Itasca, Ill.: Peacock, 1986.
Bernstein, Saul. "Conflict and Group Work." In Saul Bernstein, ed., *Explorations in Group Work,* pp. 72–106.
Bernstein, Saul. *Youth in the Streets: Work with Alienated Groups.* New York: Association Press, 1954.
Bernstein, Saul, ed. *Explorations in Group Work.* Boston: Boston University School of Social Work, 1965, Milford House, 1973.
Bernstein, Saul, ed. *Further Explorations in Group Work.* Boston: Milford House, 1973.
Bertcher, Harvey J. *Group Participation: Techniques for Leaders and Members.* Beverly Hills: Sage, 1979.
Bertcher, Harvey J. "Guidelines for the Group Worker's Use of Modeling." *Social Work with Groups* (Fall 1978), 1(3):235–46.
Bertcher, Harvey J. and Frank Maple. *Creating Groups.* Beverly Hills: Sage, 1978.
Biddle, Bruce and Edwin J. Thomas, eds. *Role Theory: Concepts and Research.* New York: Wiley, 1966.
Bion, Wilfred R. *Experiences in Groups and Other Papers.* London: Tavistock, 1961.
Bittner, Ruth. "Therapeutic Mother-Child Groups: A Developmental Approach." *Social Casework* (March 1984), 65(3):154–61.
Blanck, Gertrude and Rubin Blanck. *Ego Psychology: Theory and Practice.* New York: Columbia University Press, 1974.
Bloch, Sidney, Erik Crouch, and Janet Reibstein. "Therapeutic Factors in Group Psychotherapy." *Archives of General Psychiatry* (May 1981), 38(5):516–26.
Block, Lisa Rae. "On the Potentiality and Limits of Time: The Single Session Group and the Cancer Patient." *Social Work with Groups* (Summer 1985), 8(2):81–100.
Bloom, Naomi D. and Joseph G. Lynch. "Group Work in a Hospital Waiting Room." *Health and Social Work* (August 1979), 4(3):48–63.

Blum, Arthur. "The 'Aha' Response as a Therapeutic Goal." In Henry W. Maier, ed. *Group Work as Part of Residential Treatment*, pp. 47–56. New York: National Association of Social Workers, 1965.

Boatman, Frances Louise. "Caseworkers' Judgments of Clients' Hope: Some Correlates Among Client-Situation Characteristics and Among Workers' Communication Patterns." D.S.W. dissertation, Columbia University, 1975.

Boehm, Werner W. "The Nature of Social Work." *Social Work* (April 1958), 3(2): 10–18.

Boer, Annette K. and James E. Lantz. "Adolescent Group Therapy Membership Selection." *Clinical Social Work Journal* (Fall 1974), 2(3):172–81.

Bolen, Jane K. "Easing the Pain of Termination for Adolescents." *Social Casework* (November 1972), 53(9):519–27.

Boulding, Kenneth. *Ecodynamics: A New Theory of Societal Evolution*. Beverly Hills: Sage, 1978.

Bounous, Ronald C. "A Study of Client and Worker Perceptions in the Initial Phase of Casework Marital Counseling." Ph.D. dissertation, University of Minnesota, 1965.

Bowlby, John. "Separation Anxiety." *International Journal of Psychoanalysis* (March–June 1960), 41(2):89–113.

Bradford, Leland, ed. *Group Development*. Washington, D.C.: National Training Laboratory, National Education Association, 1961.

Bradford, Leland, Dorothy Stock, and Murray Horowitz. "How To Diagnose Group Problems." In Bradford, ed., *Group Development*, pp. 37–50.

Brager, George and Stephen Holloway. *Changing Human Service Organizations*. New York: Free Press, 1978.

Brenner, Charles. *An Elementary Textbook of Psychoanalysis*. Rev. ed. Garden City, N.Y.: International Universities Press, 1973.

Briar, Scott. "Family Services." In Henry S. Maas, ed. *Five Fields of Social Service: Reviews of Research*, pp. 9–50. New York: National Association of Social Workers, 1966.

Bronfenbrenner, Urie. *The Ecology of Human Development: Experiments by Nature and Design*. Cambridge, Mass: Harvard University Press, 1979.

Brown, John A. "Clinical Social Work with Chicanos: Some Unwarranted Assumptions." *Clinical Social Work Journal* (October 1979), 7(4):256–66.

Brown, John A. "Group Work with Low-Income Black Youths." *Social Work with Groups* (Fall 1984), 7(3):111–24.

Brown, June H. et al. *Child/Family/Neighborhood: A Master Plan for Social Service Delivery*. New York: Child Welfare League of America, 1982.

Brown, Leonard N. "Social Workers' Verbal Acts and the Development of Mutual Expectations with Beginning Client Groups." D.S.W. dissertation, Columbia University, 1971.

Brown, Robert A. "Feedback in Family Interviewing." *Social Work* (September, 1973), 18(5):52–59.

Brown, Robert A. "The Technique of Ascription." D.S.W. dissertation, University of Southern California, 1971.

Buckley, Lola Elizabeth. "The Use of the Small Group at a Time of Crisis: Transition of Girls from Elementary to Junior High School." D.S.W. dissertation, University of Southern California, 1970.

Buckley, Walter. *Sociology and Modern Systems Theory*. Englewood Cliffs, N.J.: Prentice-Hall, 1967.

Buckley, Walter. "Society as a Complex Adaptive System." In Buckley, ed. *Modern Systems Research*, pp. 490–513.

Buckley, Walter, ed. *Modern Systems Research for the Behavioral Scientist*. Chicago: Aldine, 1968.

Budman, Simon H., ed. *Forms of Brief Therapy*. New York: Guilford Press, 1981.

Buehler, Charlotte. *Values in Psychotherapy*. New York: Free Press, 1962.

Burnside, Irene Mortenson. *Working with the Elderly: Group Process and Techniques*. 2d ed. Monterey, Calif.: Wadsworth Press, 1984.

Butler, Timothy and Addie Fuhriman. "Curative Factors in Group Therapy: A Review of Recent Literature." *Small Group Behavior* (May 1983), 14(2):131–42.
Bywaters, Paul. "Ending Casework Relationships (1)." *Social Work Today* (August 1975), 6(10)301–4.
Bywaters, Paul. "Ending Casework Relationships (2)." *Social Work Today* (September 1975), 6(11):336–38.
California Chapter, National Association of Social Workers. "Social Work Intervention Guide: Descriptions and Codes for Problems of Social Functioning." Sacramento: NASW, March 1984.
Caplan, Gerald. *Principles of Preventive Psychiatry.* New York: Basic Books, 1964.
Caplan, Gerald. *Support Systems and Community Mental Health.* New York: Behavioral Publications, 1974.
Caple, Frances. "Preventive Social Work Practice: A Generic Model for Direct Service on Behalf of Children." Ph.D. dissertation, University of Southern California, 1982.
Caplow, Theodore. *Two Against One: Coalitions in Triads.* Englewood Cliffs, N.J.: Prentice-Hall, 1968.
Carkhuff, Robert R. and Bernard Berenson. *Beyond Counseling and Therapy.* New York: Holt, Rinehart, and Winston, 1967.
Carlton, Thomas Owen. *Clinical Social Work in Health Settings. A Guide to Professional Practice with Exemplars.* New York: Springer, 1984.
Cartwright, Dorwin and Alvin Zander. "Group Dynamics and the Individual." In Warren Bennis et al., eds. *The Planning of Change.* New York: Holt, Rinehart, and Winston, 1962.
Cartwright, Dorwin and Alvin Zander, eds. *Group Dynamics: Research and Theory.* 2d ed. Evanston, Ill.: Row Peterson, 1960.
Casey, Richard D. and Leon Cantor. "Group Work with Hard-to-Reach Adolescents: The Use of Member-Initiated Program Selection." *Social Work with Groups* (Winter 1983), 6(1):9–22.
Chau, Kenneth. "A Model of Practice with Special Reference to Ethnic Minority Populations." Paper presented at the Symposium on Social Work with Groups, October 1986.
Chestang, Leon W. "The Issue of Race in Casework Practice." In *Social Work Practice, 1972,* pp. 114–26. New York: Columbia University Press, 1972.
Child Welfare League of America. *Group Methods and Services in Child Welfare.* New York: Child Welfare League of America, 1963.
Chin, Robert. "Evaluating Group Movement and Individual Change." In National Association of Social Workers, *Use of Groups in the Psychiatric Setting,* pp. 34–45. New York: NASW, 1960.
Chin, Robert. "The Utility of Systems Models and Developmental Models for Practitioners." In Warren G. Bennis et al., *The Planning of Change,* pp. 201–14. New York: Holt Rinehart and Winston, 1962.
Christ, Adolph E. and Kalman Flomenhaft, eds. *Psychosocial Family Interventions in Chronic Pediatric Illness.* New York: Plenum Press, 1982.
Churchill, Sallie R. "Social Group Work: A Diagnostic Tool in Child Guidance." *American Journal of Orthopsychiatry* (April 1965), 35(3):581–88.
Clapham, W. B., Jr. *Human Ecosystems.* New York: Macmillan, 1981.
Clemenger, Florence. "Congruence Between Members and Workers on Selected Behaviors of the Role of the Social Group Worker." D.S.W. dissertation, University of Southern California, 1965.
Clement, Robert G. "Factors Associated with Continuance and Discontinuance in Cases Involving Problems in Parent-Child Relationships." Ph.D. dissertation, University of Chicago, 1964.
Cloward, Richard A. "Agency Structure as a Variable in Service to Groups." In *Group Work and Community Organization, 1956.* Selected Papers, 83rd Annual Forum, National Conference on Social Welfare. *New York: Columbia University Press, 1956.*
Coelho, George et al., eds. *Coping and Adaptation.* New York: Basic Books, 1974.

Cohen, Arthur M. and R. Douglas Smith. *The Critical Incident in Growth Groups: A Manual for Group Workers.* La Jolla, Calif.: University Associates, 1976.

Collins, Alice H. and Diane L. Pancoast. *Natural Helping Networks: A Strategy for Prevention.* Washington, D.C.: National Association of Social Workers, 1976.

Compton, Beulah Roberts and Burt Galaway, eds. *Social Work Processes.* 2d ed. Homewood, Ill.: Dorsey Press, 1979.

Cook, Robert C. "Population: Some Pitfalls of Progress." In Sylvan Kaplan and Everlyn Kivy-Rosenberg, eds., *Ecology and the Quality of Life.* Springfield, Ill.: Charles C. Thomas, 1973.

Cooley, Charles. *Social Process.* New York: Scribner's 1918.

Cooper, Elaine J. and Margarita Hernandez Cento. "Groups and the Hispanic Prenatal Patient." *American Journal of Orthopsychiatry* (October 1977), 47(4):689–700.

Cooper, Shirley A. "A Look at the Effect of Racism on Clinical Work." *Social Casework* (February 1973), 54(2):76–84.

Cooper, Shirley A. and Leon Wasserman. *Children in Treatment.* New York: Brunner/Mazel, 1977.

Corsini, Raymond J. and Bina Rosenberg. "Mechanisms of Group Psychotherapy: Process and Dynamics." *Journal of Abnormal and Social Psychology* (1955), 51(4): 406–11.

Coser, Lewis A. *The Functions of Social Conflict.* Glencoe, Ill.: Free Press, 1956.

Cotter, Hinsberg J. "Termination of Residential Treatment of Children." *Child Welfare* (October 1970), 49(8):443–47.

Couch, Elsbeth Herzstein. *Joint and Family Interviews in the Treatment of Marital Problems.* New York: Family Service Association of America, 1969.

Coyle, Grace L. *Group Experience and Democratic Values.* New York: Woman's Press, 1947.

Coyle, Grace L. *Group Work with American Youth.* New York: Harper, 1948.

Coyle, Grace L. "Social Group Work: An Aspect of Social Work Practice." *Journal of Social Issues* (1952), 8(1):21–35.

Coyle, Grace L. *Social Process in Organized Groups.* New York: Smith, 1930.

Coyle, Grace L. "Some Basic Assumptions About Social Group Work." In Marjorie Murphy, ed., *The Social Group Work Method in Social Work Education,* pp. 88–105. New York: Council on Social Work Education, 1959.

Cumming, John and Elaine. *Ego and Milieu: Theory and Practice of Environmental Therapy.* New York: Atherton Press, 1962.

Daley, Barbara Sabin and Geraldine Suzanne Koppenaal. "The Treatment of Women in Short-Term Women's Groups." In Simon H. Budman, ed. *Forms of Brief Therapy,* pp. 343–57. New York: Guilford Press, 1981.

Davidson, Mark. "The Case for Uncommon Sense." *Transcript* (June 1983), pp. 7–8. Los Angeles: University of Southern California.

Davies, Bernard. *The Use of Groups in Social Work Practice.* London: Routledge and Kegan Paul, 1975.

Davies, Martin. "The Assessment of Environment in Social Work Research." *Social Casework* (January 1974), 55(1):3–12.

Davis, Inger P. "Advice-Giving in Parent Counseling." *Social Casework* (June 1975), 56(6):343–47.

Davis, L. Jeannette. "Human Communication Concepts and Constructs: Tools for Change as Applied to Social Work Practice Theory." D.S.W. dissertation, University of Southern California, 1976.

Davis, Larry E. "Group Work Practice with Ethnic Minorities of Color." In Martin Sundel et al., eds. *Individual Change Through Small Groups,* pp. 324–44. New York: Free Press, 1986.

Decker, Kathleen. "Puppets Help Children Shed Horrors of Abuse." Los Angeles *Times,* April 1985.

Delgado, Melvin. "Activities and Hispanic Groups: Issues and Suggestions." *Social Work with Groups* (Spring 1983), 6(1):85–96.

Delgado, Melvin. "Hispanic Cultural Values: Implications for Groups." *Small Group Behavior* (February 1981), 2(1):69–80.

Delgado, Melvin. "Hispanics and Psychotherapeutic Groups." *International Journal of Group Psychotherapy* (October 1983), 33(4):507–20.

Delgado, Melvin and Denise Humm-Delgado. "Hispanics and Group Work: A Review of the Literature." *Social Work with Groups* (Fall 1984), 7(3):85–96.

Del Valle, Alline and Felton Alexander. "Project Enable: Effects of the Project on Family Service Agencies and Urban Leagues." *Social Casework* (December 1967), 48(1):633–38.

Derlega, Valerian J., ed. *Communication, Intimacy, and Close Relationships*. Orlando, Fla.: Academic Press, 1984.

Derlega, Valerian J. "Self-Disclosure in Intimate Relationships." In *ibid.*, pp. 1–9.

Deutsch, Morton. *The Resolution of Conflict*. New Haven, Conn.: Yale University Press, 1973.

Devore, Wynetta and Elfrieda G. Schlesinger. *Ethnic-Sensitive Social Work Practice*. St. Louis: C. V. Mosby, 1981.

Dewey, John. *Democracy and Education*. New York: Free Press (paperback ed.), 1966.

Dewey, John. *How We Think*. Boston: Heath, 1910.

Dies, Lee P. *Man's Nature and Nature's Man: The Ecology of Human Communication*. Ann Arbor: University of Michigan Press, 1955.

Dies, Robert R. "Clinical Implications of Research on Leadership in Short-Term Group Psychotherapy." In Robert F. Dies and K. Roy MacKenzie, eds. *Advances in Group Psychotherapy*, pp. 27–78. New York: International Universities Press, 1983.

Dillon, Carolyn L. "A Study of Goal Formulation and Implementation." *Smith College Studies in Social Work* (June 1968), 38(3):169–84.

Donovan, James M., Michael J. Bennett, and Christine M. McElroy. "The Crisis Group: Its Rationale, Format, and Outcome." In Simon H. Budman, ed. *Forms of Brief Therapy*. New York: Guilford Press, 1981.

Douglas, Tom. *Group Processes in Social Work: A Theoretical Synthesis*. New York: Wiley, 1979.

Douglas, Tom. *Groupwork Practice*. New York: International Universities Press, 1976.

Drenth, Pieter J. D., ed. *Handbook of Work and Organizational Psychology*. New York: Wiley, 1984.

Durkin, Helen. "Change in Group Psychotherapy and Practice: A Systems Perspective." *International Journal of Group Psychotherapy* (October 1982), 32(4):431–39.

Durkin, Helen. *The Group in Depth*. New York: International Universities Press, 1964.

Durkin, James E. *Living Groups: Group Psychotherapy and General Systems Theory*. New York: Brunner/Mazel, 1981.

Edwards, E. Daniel, Margie E. Edwards, Geri M. Davies, and Francine Eddy. "Enhancing Self-Concept and Identification with 'Indianness' of American Indian Girls." *Social Work with Groups* (Fall 1978), 1(3):309–18.

Eklof, Mona. "The Termination Phase in Group Therapy: Implications for Geriatric Groups." *Small Group Behavior* (November 1984), 15(4):565–71.

Epstein, Norman. "Brief Group Therapy in a Child Guidance Clinic." *Social Work* (July 1970), 15(3):33–48.

Erikson, Erik H. *Childhood and Society*. 2d ed. New York: Norton, 1963.

Erikson, Erik H. "Identity and the Life Cycle." In *Psychological Issues*, pp. 18–164. New York: International Universities Press, 1959.

Erikson, Erik H. *Identity, Youth, and Crisis*. New York: Norton, 1968.

Etcheverry, Roger, Max Siporin, and Ronald W. Toseland. "The Uses and Abuses of Role Playing." In Paul H. Glasser and Nazneen S. Mayadas, eds., *Group Workers at Work: Theory and Practice in the 80s*. Totowa, N.J.: Rowman and Littlefield, 1986.

Eubank, Earle E. *The Concepts of Sociology*. Boston: D. C. Heath, 1932.

Evans, Nancy and Paul A. Servis. "Group Cohesion: A Review and Revaluation." *Small Group Behavior* (November 1980), 11(4):359–70.

Ewalt, Patricia L., ed. *Toward a Definition of Clinical Social Work: Conference Proceedings*. Washington, D.C.: National Association of Social Workers, 1980.

Ewalt, Patricia L. and Janice Kutz."An Examination of Advice-Giving as a Therapeutic Intervention." *Smith College Studies in Social Work* (November 1976), 47(1): 3–9.

Falck, Hans. "Social Work in Health Settings." *Social Work in Health Care* (Summer 1978), 3(4):395–403.

Falck, Hans. "The Membership Model of Social Work." *Social Work* (March 1984), 29(2):155–60.

Family Service Association of America. *Use of Group Techniques in the Family Service Agency.* New York: Family Service Association of America, 1959.

Fanshel, David. "A Study of Caseworkers' Perceptions of Their Clients." *Social Casework* (December 1958), 39(10):543–51.

Farber, Deborah Ann. "A Study of Clients' Reactions to Initial Contacts with a Community Mental Health Center: Another Look." *Smith College Studies in Social Work* (November 1975), 46(1):44–45.

Fatout, Marian F. "A Comparative Analysis of Practice Concepts Described in Selected Social Work Literature." D.S.W. dissertation, University of Southern California, 1975.

Feinberg, Norma. "A Study of Group Stages in A Self-Help Setting." *Social Work with Groups* (Winter 1983), 3(1):41–49.

Feldman, Frances Lomas. *Work and Cancer Health Histories.* Oakland, Calif.: California Division, American Cancer Society, 1980.

Feldman, Ronald A. and John S. Wodarski. *Contemporary Approaches to Group Treatment.* San Francisco: Jossey-Bass, 1975.

Feldman, Ronald A. et al. "Treating Delinquents in Traditional Agencies." *Social Work* (September 1972), 17(5):71–78.

Fisher, Dena. "The Hospitalized Terminally Ill Patient: An Ecological Perspective." In Carel B. Germain, ed. *Social Work Practice: People and Environments.* New York: Columbia University Press, 1979.

Flanzer, Jerry. "Conintegration: The Concurrent Integration of Treatment Modalities in Social Work Practice." D.S.W. dissertation, University of Southern California, 1973.

Fluegelman, Andrews, ed. *The New Games Book.* New York: Doubleday-Dolphin, 1976.

Fluegelman, Andrew, ed. *More New Games.* New York: Doubleday-Dolphin, 1981.

Fogelman, Eva and Bella Savran. "Therapeutic Groups for Children of Holocaust Survivors. *International Journal of Group Psychotherapy* (April 1979), 29(2):211–36.

Follett, Mary Parker. *Dynamic Administration.* New York: Harper, 1942.

Fong, Stanley L. M. "Assimilation and Changing Social Roles of Chinese Americans." *Journal of Social Issues* (1973), 29(2):115–27.

Forgays, Donald D., ed. *Primary Prevention of Psychopathology,* vol. 2: *Environmental Influences.* Hanover, N.H.: University Press of New England, 1978.

Fortune, Anne E. *Task-Centered Practice with Families and Groups.* New York: Springer, 1984.

Fox, Evelyn, Marion Nelson, and William Bolman. "The Termination Process: A Neglected Dimension in Social Work." *Social Work* (October 1969), 14(4):53–63.

Frances, Allen, John F. Clarkin, and Jean Paul Marachi. "Selection Criteria for Outpatient Group Psychotherapy." *Hospital and Community Psychiatry* (April 1980), 31(4):245–50.

Frances, Allen, John F. Clarkin, and Samuel Perry. *Differential Therapeutics in Psychiatry: The Art and Science of Treatment Selection.* New York: Brunner/Mazel, 1984.

Frank, Jerome. *Persuasion and Healing: A Comparative Study of Psychotherapy.* Baltimore: The John Hopkins Press, 1961.

Freud, Anna. *The Ego and the Mechanisms of Defense.* New York: International Universities Press, 1946.

Freud, Anna. "Emotional and Social Development." In *The Writings of Anna Frued,* 1967, pp. 336–52.

Freud, Sigmund. *An Outline of Psychoanalysis.* Rev. ed. New York: Norton, 1949.

Freud, Sigmund. *Group Psychology and the Analysis of the Ego.* London: International Psychoanalytical Press, 1922.

Frey, Louise A. "Support and the Group: Generic Treatment Form." *Social Work* (October 1962), 7(3):35–42.

Frey, Louise A., ed. *Use of Groups in the Health Field.* New York: National Association of Social Workers, 1966.

Friedman, Barry. "Cotherapy: A Behavioral and Attitudinal Survey of Third Year Psychiatric Residents." *International Journal of Group Psychotherapy* (April 1973), 23(2):228–34.

Furness, Anne-Marie. "Some Facets of Similarity and Difference Between the Social Work Methods of Casework and Group Work." D.S.W. dissertation, University of Southern California, 1971.

Galinsky, Maeda J. and Janice H. Schopler. "Patterns of Entry and Exit in Open-ended Groups." *Social Work with Groups* (Summer 1985), 8(2):67–80.

Galinsky, Maeda J. and Janice H. Schopler. "Practitioners' Views of Assets and Liabilities of Open-Ended Groups." In Joseph Lassner, Kathleen Powell, and Elaine Finnegan, eds., *Social Group Work: Competence and Values in Practice.* New York: Haworth Press, 1987.

Galinsky, Maeda J. and Janice H. Schopler, "Structuring Co-leadership in Social Work Training." *Social Work with Groups* (Winter 1980), 3(4):51–63.

Galinsky, Maeda J. and Janice H. Schopler. "Warning: Groups May Be Dangerous." *Social Work* (March 1977), 22(2):89–94.

Ganter, Grace. "The Group Worker in the Child Guidance Center." In Harleigh B. Trecker, ed. *Gorup Work in the Psychiatric Setting,* pp. 33–36. New York: Whiteside and William Morrow, 1956.

Ganter, Grace, Margaret Yeakel, and Norman A. Polanksy. *Retrieval from Limbo: The Intermediary Group Treatment of Inaccessible Children.* New York: Child Welfare League of America, 1967.

Garfield, Sol and Allen E. Bergin, eds. *Handbook of Psychotherapy and Behavior Change.* New York: Wiley, 1978.

Garland, James A. and Louise A. Frey. "Application of Stages of Group Development to Groups in Psychiatric Settings." In Saul Bernstein, ed. *Further Explorations in Group Work,* pp. 1–33. Boston: Milford House, 1973.

Garland, James A., Hubert E. Jones, and Ralph L. Kolodny. "A Model for Stages of Development in Social Work Groups." In Saul Bernstein, ed., *Explorations in Group Work,* pp. 17–71. Boston: Boston University School of Social Work, 1965; Milford House, 1973.

Garland, James A. and Ralph Kolodny. "Characteristics and Resolution of Scapegoating." In Saul Bernstein, ed., *Further Explorations in Group Work,* pp. 55–74. Boston: Milford House, 1973.

Gartner, Alan S. and Frank Riessman. *Self-Help in the Human Services.* San Francisco: Jossey-Bass, 1977.

Garvin, Charles D. "Complementarity of Role Expectations in Groups: The Member-Worker Contract." In *Social Work Practice, 1969,* pp. 127–45. New York: Columbia University Press, 1969.

Garvin, Charles D. *Contemporary Group Work.* 2d ed. Englewood Cliffs, N.J.: Prentice-Hall, 1987.

Garvin, Charles D. and Beth Glover Reed. "Gender Issues in Social Work: An Overview." *Social Work with Groups* (Fall/Winter 1983), 6(3/4):3–19.

Garvin, Charles D., William J. Reid, and Laura Epstein. "A Task-Centered Approach." In Robert W. Roberts and Helen Northen, eds. *Theories of Social Work with Groups.* New York: Columbia University Press, 1976.

Gentry, Martha. "Initial Group Meetings: Member Expectations and Information Distribution Process." Ph.D. dissertation, Washington University, 1974.

Germain, Carel B., ed. *Advances in Clinical Social Work Practice.* Silver Spring, Md.: National Association of Social Workers, 1985.

Germain, Carel B. "General Systems Theory and Ego Psychology: An Ecological Perspective." *Social Service Review* (December 1978), 52(4):535–50.

Germain, Carel B. "Social Context of Clinical Social Work." In Patricia L. Ewalt, ed. *Toward a Definition of Clinical Social Work,* pp. 54–65. Washington, D.C.: American Association of Social Workers, 1980.

Germain, Carel B., ed. *Social Work Practice: People and Environments: An Ecological Perspective.* New York: Columbia University Press, 1979.

Germain, Carel B. and Alex Gitterman. *The Life Model of Social Work Practice.* New York: Columbia University Press, 1980.

Getzel, George. "Group Work with Kin and Friends Caring for the Elderly." *Social Work with Groups* (Summer 1982), 5(2):91–102.

Getzel, George. "Poetry Writing Groups for the Elderly: A Reconsideration of Art and Social Group Work." *Social Work with Groups* (Spring 1983), 6(1):65–76.

Gibbard, Graham S., John Hartman, and Richard D. Mann, eds. *Analysis of Groups: Contributions to Theory, Research, and Practice.* San Francisco: Jossey-Bass, 1974.

Gitterman, Alex. "Delivering a New Group Service: Strategies and Skills." In Alex Gitterman and Lawrence Shulman, eds. *Mutual Aid Groups and the Life Cycle,* pp. 53–74. New York: Free Press, 1986.

Gitterman, Alex. "Group Work in the Public Schools." In William Schwartz and Serapio R. Zalba, eds. *The Practice of Group Work,* pp. 45–72. New York: Columbia University Press, 1971.

Gitterman, Alex. "The Use of Groups in Health Settings." In Abraham Lurie, Gary Rosenberg, and Sidney Pinsky, *Social Work with Groups in Health Settings,* pp. 6–24. New York: Prodist, 1982.

Gitterman, Alex and Lawrence Shulman, eds. *Mutual Aid Groups and the Life Cycle.* Itasca, Ill.: Peacock, 1986.

Gittler, Joseph, ed. *Review of Sociology: Analysis of a Decade.* New York: Wiley, 1957.

Glasser, Paul H. and Nazneen S. Mayadas, eds. *Group Workers at Work: Theory and Practice in the 80s.* Totowa, N.J.: Rowman and Littlefields, 1986.

Glassman, Urania and Len Kates. "Authority Themes and Worker-Group Transactions: Additional Dimensions to the Stages of Group Development." *Social Work with Groups* (Summer 1983), 6(2):33–52.

Glassman, Urania and Len Kates. "Techniques of Social Group Work: A Framework for Practice." *Social Work with Groups* (Spring 1986), 9(1):9–38.

Goffman, Erving. *Behavior in Public Places.* New York: Free Press, 1963.

Golan, Naomi. *Passing Through Transitions.* New York: Free Press, 1981.

Golan, Naomi. *The Perilous Bridge: Helping Clients Through Mid-Life Transitions.* New York: Free Press, 1986.

Golan, Naomi. *Treatment in Crisis Situations.* New York: Free Press, 1978.

Goldstein, Eda G. *Ego Psychology and Social Work Practice.* New York: Free Press, 1984.

Goldstein, Howard. "Cognitive Approaches to Direct Practice." *Social Service Review.* (December 1982), 56(4):539–55.

Goldstein, Howard. *Social Learning and Change.* Columbia, S.C.: University of South Carolina Press, 1981.

Goldstein, Howard. *Social Work Practice: A Unitary Approach.* Columbia, S.C.: University of South Carolina Press, 1973.

Goroff, Norman, ed., *Reaping from the Field: From Practice to Principle.* Proceedings of the Third Annual Symposium for the Advancement of Social Work with Groups. Hartford, Conn.: Committee for the Advancement of Social Work with Groups, 1982.

Gouldner, Alvin W. "Red Tape as a Social Problem." In Robert Merton, et al., eds. *Reader in Bureaucracy,* pp. 410–18. Glencoe, Ill.: Free Press, 1952.

Greenfield, Wilma L. and Beulah Rothman. "Termination or Transformation? Evolving Beyond Termination in Groups," In Joseph Lassner, Kathleen Powell, and Elaine Finnegan, eds. *Social Group Work: Competence and Values in Practice.* New York: Haworth Press, 1987.

Greer, Colin, ed. *Divided Society: The Ethnic Experience in America.* New York: Basic Books, 1974.
Gross, Neal, Warren S. Mason, A. W. McEachern. *Explorations in Role Analysis: Studies of the School Superintendency Role.* New York: Wiley, 1958.
Group for the Advancement of Psychiatry. Report No. 78. *The Field of Family Therapy* (March 1970), 7:531–644.
Group for the Advancement of Psychiatry. *The Process of Child Therapy.* New York: Brunner/Mazel, 1982.
Grunebaum, Henry and Leonard Solomon. "Toward a Peer Group Theory of Group Psychotherapy, I." *International Journal of Group Psychotherapy* (January 1980), 30(1):23–50.
Grunebaum, Henry and Leonard Solomon. "On the Development and Significance of Peers and Play." *International Journal of Group Psychotherapy* (July 1982), 32(3): 283–308.
Gurman, Alan S. "The Effects and Effectiveness of Marital Therapy: A Review of Outcome Research." *Family Process* (June 1973), 12(2):145–70.
Hall, Edward T. *The Hidden Dimension.* Garden City, N.Y.: Doubleday, 1966.
Hallowitz, David. "Advocacy in the Context of Treatment." *Social Casework* (July 1974), 55(7):416–20.
Hamilton, Gordon. *Theory and Practice of Social Case Work.* 2d ed. New York: Columbia University Press, 1951.
Hamilton, Gordon. *Theory and Practice of Social Case Work.* 2d ed. New York: Columbia University Prerss, 1951.
Hammond, D. Corydon. "Cross-cultural Rehabilitation." *Journal of Rehabilitation* (September-October 1971), 37(5):34–36.
Hardesty, Donald L. *Ecological Anthropology.* New York: Wiley, 1977.
Hare, A. Paul. *Creativity in Small Groups.* Beverly Hills: Sage, 1982.
Hare, A. Paul. *Handbook of Small Group Research.* 2d ed. New York: Free Press, 1976.
Hare, A. Paul, Edgard F. Borgatta, and Robert F. Bales, eds. *Small Groups: Studies in Social Interaction.* New York: Knopf, 1955.
Hartford, Margaret E. "Group Methods and Generic Practice." In Robert W. Roberts and Helen Northen, eds. *Theories of Social Work with Groups.* pp. 45–74. New York: Columbia University Press, 1976.
Hartford, Margaret E. *Groups in Social Work.* New York: Columbia University Press, 1971.
Hartford, Margaret E. "The Social Group Worker and Group Formation." Ph.D. dissertation, University of Chicago, 1962.
Hartford, Margaret E., ed. *Working Papers: Toward a Frame of Reference for Social Group Work.* New York: National Association of Social Workers, 1964.
Hartmann, Heinz. *Ego Psychology and the Problem of Adaptation.* New York: International Universities Press, 1958.
Heap, Ken. *Process and Action in Work with Groups. The Preconditions for Treatment and Growth.* New York: Pergamon Press, 1979.
Heap, Ken. "Purposes in Social Work with Groups—Their Interrelatedness with Values and Methods: A Historical and Prospective View." *Social Work with Groups* (Spring 1984), 7(1):21–34.
Heap, Ken. *The Practice of Social Work with Groups: A Systematic Approach.* London: George Allen and Unwin, 1985.
Hearn, Gordon. *Theory Building in Social Work.* Toronto: University of Toronto Press, 1958.
Hearn, Gordon, ed. *The General Systems Approach: Contributions Toward a Holistic Conception of Social Work.* New York: Council on Social Work Education, 1968.
Heine, R. W. "A Comparison of Patients' Reports on Psychotherapeutic Experience with Psychoanalytic, Nondirective, and Adlerian Therapists." Ph.D. dissertation, University of Chicago, 1950.
Hellenbrand, Shirley C. "Termination in Direct Practice." In National Association of

Social Workers. *Encyclopedia of Social Work,* pp. 765–69. 18th ed. Silver Spring, Md.: NASW, 1987.

Henry, Sue. *Group Skills in Social Work: A Four-Dimensional Approach.* Itasca, Ill.: Peacock, 1981.

Herrick, James C. "The Perception of Crisis in a Modified Therapeutic Community." D.S.W. dissertation, University of Southern California, 1966.

Hill, William F. "Further Considerations of Therapeutic Mechanisms in Group Therapy." *Small Group Behavior* (November 1975), 6(4):421–29.

Hill, William F. and L. A. Gruner. "A Study of Development in Open and Closed Groups." *Small Group Behavior* (August 1973), 4(3):355–81.

Hinchman, Madison. "Social Work Practice with Children and Youth: A Content Analysis of Social Work Practice Literature, 1947–1973." DSW dissertation, University of Southern California, 1977.

Hirayama, Hisashi and Kasumi Hirayama. "Empowerment Through Group Participation: Process and Goals." In Marvin Parnes, ed. *Innovations in Social Group Work: Feedback from Practice to Theory.* New York: Haworth Press, 1986.

Ho, Man Keung and Eunice McDowell. "The Black Worker–White Client Relationship." *Clinical Social Work Journal* (Fall 1973), 1(3):161–67.

Hobbs, Nicholas. *The Futures of Children: Categories, Labels, and Their Consequences.* San Francisco: Jossey-Bass, 1975.

Hobbs, Nicholas. "Sources of Gain in Psychotherapy." *American Psychologist* (October 1962), 17(1):741–47.

Hoffman, Martin L. and Lois Wladis Hoffman. *Review of Child Development Research.* New York: Russell Sage Foundation, 1964.

Hollis, Florence and Mary E. Woods. *Casework: A Psychosocial Therapy.* 3d ed. New York: Random House, 1981.

Homans, George. *The Human Group.* New York: Harcourt-Brace, 1950.

Horowitz, Gideon. "Worker Interventions in Response to Deviant Behavior in Groups." Ph.D. dissertation, University of Chicago, 1968.

Horowitz, L. M. "Cognitive Structure of Interpersonal Problems Treated in Psychotherapy." *Journal of Consulting and Clinical Psychology* (1979), 47:5–15.

Hudson, Walter. *The Clinical Measurement Package.* Homewood, Ill.: Dorsey Press, 1982.

Hutten, Joan M. "Short-Term Contracts IV. Techniques: How and Why To Use Them." *Social Work Today* (August 1976), 6(20):614–18.

Hutten, Joan M. *Short-Term Contracts in Social Work.* London: Routledge and Kegan Paul, 1977.

Ishikawa, Wesley. "Verbals Acts of the Social Worker and Their Variations Through Time in Release Planning Discussion Group Meetings." D.S.W. dissertations, University of Southern California, 1968.

Jacobs, Alfred and W. W. Spradlin, eds. *The Group as Agent of Change.* New York: Behavioral Publications, 1974.

Jenkins, Shirley. *The Ethnic Dilemma in Social Services.* New York: Free Press, 1981.

Jennings, Helen Hall. *Leadership and Isolation: A Study of Personality in Interpersonal Relations.* New York: Longmans Green, 1950.

Johnson, Harriet C. and Edmund J. Hart. "Neurological Disorders." In Francis J. Turner, ed. *Adult Psychopathology. A Social Work Perspective,* pp. 73–118. New York: Free Press: 1984.

Jolesch, Miriam. "Strengthening Intake Practice Through Group Discussion." *Social Casework* (November 1959), 40(9):504–10.

Kadushin, Alfred. "The Racial Factor in the Interview." *Social Work* (May 1972), 17(3):88–98.

Kadushin, Alfred. *The Social Work Interview.* New York: Columbia University Press, 1972.

Kahn, Alfred J. "Therapy, Prevention and Developmental Provision: A Social Work Strategy." In Council on Social Work Education. *Public Health Concepts in Social Work Education,* pp. 132–48. New York: CSWE, 1962.

Kahn, Alfred J., ed. *Issues in American Social Work.* New York: Columbia University Press, 1959.

Kahn, Alfred J., ed. *Shaping the New Social Work.* New York: Columbia University Press, 1973.

Kaiser, Clara. "Characteristics of Social Group Work." In National Conference of Social Work. *The Social Welfare Forum.* New York: Columbia University Press, 1957.

Kane, Rosalie. "Editorial: Thoughts on Parent Education." *Health and Social Work* (February 1981), 6(1):1–4.

Kaplan, Sylvan J. and Everlyn Kivy-Rosenberg, eds. *Ecology and the Quality of Life.* Springfield, Ill.: Charles C. Thomas, 1973.

Katch, Michael. "Commentary." In Gary Rosenberg and Helen Rehr, eds. *Advancing Social Work Practice in the Health Care Field,* pp. 121–24. New York: Haworth Press, 1983.

Kauff, Priscilla A. "The Termination Process: Its Relationship to the Separation-Individuation Phase of Development." *International Journal of Croup Psychotherapy* (January 1977), 27(1):3–18.

Katz, Robert L. *Empathy, Its Nature and Uses.* New York: Free Press, 1963.

Katz, Alfred H. and Eugene Bender. *The Strength in Us: Self-Help Groups in the Modern World.* New York: New Viewpoints, 1976.

Keefe, Thomas. "Empathy: The Critical Skill." *Social Work* (January 1976), 21(1): 10–15.

Kerson, Toba Schwaber. *Social Work in Health Settings: Practice in Context.* New York: Longmans, 1982.

Kilburn, Linda H. "An Educational/Supportive Group Model for Intervention with School-Age Parents and Their Children." *Social Work with Groups* (Spring 1983), 6(1):53–63.

Klein, Alan F. *Effective Group Work: An Introduction to Principle and Method.* New York: Association Press, 1972.

Klein, Alan F. *Role Playing in Leadership Training and Group Problem Solving.* New York: Association Press, 1956.

Klein, Alan F. *Society, Democracy, and the Group.* New York: Women's Press and William Morrow, 1953.

Klein, Josephine. *The Study of Groups.* London: Routledge and Kegan Paul, 1967.

Klein, Robert H. "A Therapy Group for Adult Inpatients in a Psychiatric Ward." In Max Rosenbaum, ed. *Handbook of Short-Term Therapy Groups,* pp. 291–319. New York: McGraw-Hill, 1983.

Klein, Robert H. "Some Problems of Patient Referral for Outpatient Group Psychotherapy." *American Journal of Group Psychotherapy* (April 1983), 33(2):29–39.

Kluckhohn, Florence. "Family Diagnosis: Variations in the Basic Values of Family Systems." *Social Casework* (February 1958), 39(2):66–69.

Kolodny, Ralph L. *Peer-Oriented Group Work for the Physically Handicapped Child.* Boston: Charles Rivers Books, 1976.

Kolodny, Ralph L. "The Dilemma of Co-leadership." *Social Work with Groups* (Winter 1980), 3(4):31–34.

Konopka, Gisela. "Formation of Values in the Developing Person." *American Journal of Orthopsychiatry.* (January 1973), 43(1):86–96.

Konopka, Gisela. *Group Work in the Institution: A Modern Challenge.* New York: Whiteside, Morrow, 1954.

Konopka, Gisela. *Social Group Work: A Helping Process.* 3d ed. Englewood Cliffs, N.J.: Prentice-Hall, 1983.

Konopka, Gisela. "The Significance of Social Work Based on Ethical Values." *Social Work with Groups* (Summer 1978), 1(2):123–31.

Konopka, Gisela. *Young Girls.* Minneapolis: University of Minnesota Press, 1976.

Kurland, Roselle. "A Model of Planning for Social Work with Groups." Ph.D. dissertation, University of Southern California, 1980.

Kurland, Roselle. *Group Formation: A Guide to the Development of Successful Groups.*

Albany, N.Y.: Continuing Education Program, School of Social Welfare, State University of New York at Albany and United Neighborhood Centers of America, 1982.

Kurland, Roselle. "Planning: The Neglected Component of Group Development." *Social Work with Groups* (Summer 1978), 1(2):173–78.

Kurland, Roselle, George Getzel, and Robert Salmon. "Sowing Groups in Infertile Fields." In Marvin Parnes, ed. *Innovations in Social Group Work: Feedback from Practices to Theory.* New York: Haworth Press, 1986.

Lackey, Mary Beit-Hallahmi. "Termination: The Crucial Stage of Social Work." D.S.W. dissertation, University of Southern California, 1981.

Lacoursiere, Roy B. *The Life Cycle of Groups: Group Development Stage Theory.* New York: Human Sciences Press, 1980.

Lakin, Martin, ed. "What's Happened to Small Group Research?" *Journal of Applied Behavioral Science* (July-August-September 1979), 15(3):265–429.

Lane, Dorthea. "Psychiatric Patients Learn a New Way of Life." In National Association of Social Workers. *New Perspectives on Services to Groups,* pp. 114–23. New York: NASW, 1961.

Lang, Norma. "A Broad-Range Model of Practice in the Social Work Group." *Social Service Review* (January 1972), 46(1):76–89.

Lang, Norma. "A Comparative Examination of Therapeutic Uses of Groups in Social Work and in Adjacent Human Service Professions." Part I. *Social Work with Groups* (Summer 1979), 2(2):101–115; Part II. (Fall 1979), 2(3):197–221.

Lasater, Tonia Tash and Frank F. Montalvo. "Understanding Mexican-American Culture: A Training Program." *Children Today* (May-June 1982), 11(3):23–25.

Lasky, Robert G. and Arthur E. Dell Orto. *Group Counseling and Physical Disability.* Belmont, Calif.: Wadsworth, 1979.

Lassner, Joseph, Kathleen Powell, and Elaine Finnegan, eds. *Social Group Work: Competence and Values in Practice.* New York: Haworth Press, 1987.

Lauer, Roger and Michael Goldfield. "Creative Writing in Group Therapy." *Psychotherapy: Theory, Research and Practice* (Winter 1970), 7(4):248–51.

Leavitt, John L. and William J. Reid. "Rapid Assessment Instruments in Social Work Practice." *Social Work Research and Abstracts* (Spring 1981), 17(1):13–20.

Lee, Judith A. B. "No Place To Go: Homeless Women." In Alex Gitterman and Lawrence Shulman, eds. *Mutual Aid Groups and The Life Cycle,* pp. 245–62. Itasca, Ill.: Peacock, 1986.

Lee, Judith A. B. and Danielle N. Park. "A Group Approach to the Depressed Adolescent Girl in Foster Care." *American Journal of Orthopsychiatry* (July 1978), 48(3): 516–27.

Lee, Judith A. B. and Carol R. Swanson. "The Concept of Mutual Aid." In Gitterman and Shulman, eds. *Mutual Aid Groups,* pp. 361–80.

Leichter, Elsa and Gerda Schulman. "The Family Interview as an Integrative Device in Group Therapy with Families." *International Journal of Group Psychotherapy* (July 1963), 13(3):335–45.

Lerner, Raymond C. "The Therapeutic Social Club: Social Rehabilitation for Mental Patients." *International Journal of Social Psychiatry* (1960), p. 6.

Levine, Baruch. "Factors Related to Interpersonal Balance in Social Work Treatment Groups." Ph.D. dissertation, University of Chicago, 1968.

Levine, Baruch. *Fundamentals of Group Treatment.* Chicago: Whitehall, 1967.

Levine, Baruch. *Group Psychotherapy. Practice and Development.* Englewood Cliffs, N.J.: Prentice-Hall, 1979.

Levine, Baruch and Judith Schild. "Group Treatment of Depression." *Social Work* (October 1969), 14(4):46–52.

Levinson, Helen M. "Use and Misuse of Groups." *Social Work* (January 1973), 18(1):66–73.

Levinson, Hilliard L. "Termination of Psychotherapy: Some Salient Issues." *Social Casework* (October 1977), 48(8):480–89.

Levy, Avraham. "Group Cohesion." Ph.D., dissertation, University of Southern California, 1984.

Levy, Charles S. *Social Work Ethics.* New York: Human Sciences Press, 1976.

Lewin, Kurt. *Field Theory in Social Science, Selected Theoretical Papers.* Dorwin Cartwright, ed. New York: Harper, 1951.

Lewis, Benjamin F. "An Examination of the Final Phase of a Group Development Theory." *Small Group Behavior* (December 1978), 9(4):507–17.

Lewis, Harold. *The Intellectual Base of Social Work Practice: Tools for Thought in a Helping Profession.* New York: Haworth Press, 1982.

Lieberman, Florence. "Clients' Expectations, Preferences and Experiences of Initial Interviews in Voluntary Social Agencies." D.S.W. dissertation, Columbia University, 1968.

Lieberman, Florence. *Social Work with Children.* New York: Human Sciences Press, 1979.

Lieberman, Morton A. "The Implications of Total Group Phenomena Analysis for Patients and Therapists." *International Journal of Group Psychotherapy* (January 1967), 17(1):71–81.

Lieberman, Morton A., Irvin D. Yalom, and Matthew B. Miles. *Encounter Groups: First Facts.* New York: Basic Books, 1973.

Lindzey, Gardner and Elliott Aronson, eds. *Handbook of Social Psychology.* Reading, Mass.: Addison-Wesley, 1968.

Lippitt, Ronald, Jeanne Watson, and Bruce Westley. *The Dynamics of Planned Change.* New York: Harcourt Brace, 1958.

Lipton, Harold and Sidney Malter. "The Social Worker as Mediator on a Hospital Ward." In William Schwartz and Serapio R. Zalba, eds. *The Practice of Group Work,* pp. 97–121. New York: Columbia University Press, 1971.

Loavenbruch, Grant and Paul Keys, "Settlements and Neighborhood Centers." In *Encyclopedia of Social Work,* pp. 556–61, 18th ed. Silver Spring, Md.: National Association of Social Workers, 1987.

Loevinger, Jane. *Ego Development.* San Francisco: Jossey-Bass, 1976.

Lonergan, Elaine Cooper. *Group Intervention. How To Begin and Maintain Groups in Medical and Psychiatric Settings.* New York: Jason Aronson, 1982.

Lonergan, Elaine Cooper and Gaetana M. Manuele. "A Group for Relatives and Friends of Patients Hospitalized in an Acute Care Service." In Max Rosenbaum, ed. *Handbook of Short-Term Therapy Groups,* pp. 357–79. New York: McGraw-Hill, 1983.

Lowy, Louis. "Goal Formulation in Social Work Groups." In Saul Bernstein, ed., *Further Explorations in Group Work,* pp. 116–44. Boston: Milford House, 1973.

Lubell, Derryl. "Living with a Lifeline: Peritoneal Dialysis Patients," In Carel B. Germain, ed. *Social Work Practice: People and Environments.* New York: Columbia University Press, 1979.

Luft, Joseph. *Group Processes: An Introduction to Group Dynamics.* Palo Alto: Mayfield, 1970.

Lum, Doman. *Social Work Practice and People of Color: A Process-Stage Approach.* Monterey, Calif.: Brooks/Cole, 1986.

Lurie, Abraham, Gary Rosenberg, and Sidney Pinsky, eds. *Social Work with Groups in Health Settings.* New York: Prodist, 1982.

Maas, Henry S., ed. *Five Fields of Social Service; Reviews of Research.* New York: National Association of Social Workers, 1966.

Maas, Henry S. "Group Influences on Client-Worker Interaction," *Social Work* (April 1964), 9(2):70–79.

Maas, Henry S. *People and Contexts. Social Development from Birth to Old Age.* Englewood Cliffs, N.J.: Prentice-Hall, 1984.

Mackey, Richard A. "Developmental Processes in Growth-Oriented Groups." *Social Work* (January 1980), 25(1):26–31.

McBroom, Elizabeth. "Socialization Through Small Groups." In Robert W. Roberts and Helen Northen, eds., *Theories of Social Work with Groups,* pp. 268–303. New York: Columbia University Press, 1976.

McCaughan, Nano, ed. *Group Work: Learning and Practice.* London: Allen and Unwin, 1978.

MacLennan, Beryce W. "Co-therapy." *International Journal of Group Psychotherapy* (April 1965), 13(2):154–66.

MacLennan, Beryce W. and Naomi Felsenfeld. *Group Counseling and Psychotherapy with Adolescents.* New York: Columbia University Press, 1968.

Macon, Lilian. "A Comparative Study of Two Approaches to the Treatment of Marital Dysfunction." D.S.W. dissertation, University of Southern California, 1975.

Maier, Henry W., ed. *Group Work as Part of Residential Treatment.* New York: National Association of Social Workers, 1965.

Maier, Henry W. "The Social Group Work Method and Residential Treatment." In Maier, ed. *Group Work as Part of Residential Treatment,* pp. 26–44.

Maier, Henry W. "Play Is More than a Four Letter Word: Play and Playfulness in the Interaction of People." In Paul Glasser and Nazneen Mayadas, eds. *Group Workers at Work: Theory and Practice in the 80s,* pp. 65–74. Totowa, N.J.: Rowman and Littlefield, 1986.

Main, Marjorie White. "Selected Aspects of the Beginning Phase of Social Group Work." Ph.D. dissertation, University of Chicago, 1964.

Maluccio, Anthony N. "Planned Use of Life Experiences." In Aaron Rosenblatt and Diane Waldfogel, eds. *Handbook of Clinical Social Work,* pp. 134–53. San Francisco: Jossey-Bass, 1983.

Maluccio, Anthony N. and Wilma D. Marlow. "The Case for the Contract." *Social Work* (January 1974), 19(1):28–36.

Maluccio, Anthony N., ed. *Promoting Competence in Clients.* New York: Free Press, 1981.

Marks, Malcolm. "Group Psychotherapy for Emotionally Disturbed Children." In National Conference of Social Work. *Group Work and Community Organization,* pp. 70–77. New York: Columbia University Press, 1956.

Marshall, Eldon. "Use of Aides in Activity Group Treatment." *Social Work with Groups* (Winter 1978), 1(4):333–44.

Martinez, Cervando. "Community Mental Health and the Chicano Movement." *American Journal of Orthopsychiatry* (July 1973), 43(4):595–610.

Mayadas, Nazneen and Paul Glasser. "Termination: A Neglected Aspect of Social Group Work." *Social Work with Groups* (Spring/Summer 1981), 4(1/2):193–204.

Mayer, John E. and Aaron Rosenblatt. "The Client's Social Context: Its Effect on Continuance in Treatment." *Social Casework* (November 1964), 45(9):511–18.

Mazza, Nicholas and Barbara D. Price. "When Time Counts: Poetry and Music in Short-Term Group Treatment." *Social Work with Groups* (Summer 1985), 8(2):53–66.

Meadow, Diane A. "The Preparatory Interview: A Client-Focused Approach with Children of Holocaust Survivors." *Social Work with Groups* (Fall/Winter 1981), 4(3/4):135–45.

Meadow, Diane A. "The Effects of a Client-Focused Pregroup Preparation Interview on the Formation of Group Cohesion and Members' Interactional Behavior." Ph.D. dissertation, University of Southern California, 1982.

Meadow, Diane A. "The Use of Groups To Facilitate Coping with Life in a Shift Work Family." Paper presented at the Eighth Annual Symposium on Social Work with Groups. Los Angeles, 1986.

Merton, Robert K. *Social Theory and Social Structure.* Glencoe, Ill.: Free Press, 1949.

Mervis, Phyllis. "Commentary." In Gary Rosenberg and Helen Rehr, eds., *Advancing Social Work Practice in the Health Care Field,* pp. 125–28. New York: Haworth Press, 1983.

Meyer, Carol H., ed. *Clinical Social Work in the Eco-Systems Perspective.* New York: Columbia University Press, 1983.

Meyer, Carol H. *Social Work Practice: The Changing Landscape.* New York: Free Press, 1976.
Middleman, Ruth R. "Co-leadership and Solo Leadership in Education for Social Work with Groups." *Social Work with Groups* (Winter 1980), 3(4):39–50.
Middleman, Ruth R. *The Nonverbal Method in Working with Groups.* New York: Association Press, 1968.
Middleman, Ruth R. "Relating Group Process to Group Work." *Social Work with Groups* (Winter 1978), 1(1):15–26.
Middleman, Ruth R. and Gale Goldberg. *Social Service Delivery: A Structural Approach to Social Work Practice.* New York: Columbia University Press, 1974.
Middleman, Ruth R. and Gale Goldberg. "Social Work Practice with Groups." In National Association of Social Workers. *Encyclopedia of Social Work,* pp. 714–29, 18th ed. Silver Spring, Md.: NASW, 1987.
Miller, Irving and Renee Solomon. "The Development of Group Services for the Elderly." *Journal of Gerontological Social Work* (Spring 1980), 2(3):241–58.
Miller, James Grier. *Living Systems.* New York: McGraw-Hill, 1978.
Mills, Theodore M. and Stan Rosenberg, eds. *Readings in the Sociology of Small Groups.* Englewood Cliffs, N.J.: Prentice-Hall, 1970.
Montagu, Ashley. *The Cultured Man.* Cleveland: World, 1958.
Moore, Edith E. "The Group-in-Situation as the Unit of Attention in Social Work with Groups." *Social Work with Groups* (Summer 1983), 6(2):19–32.
Moos, Rudolph. *Evaluating Treatment Environments: A Social Ecological Approach.* New York: Wiley, 1974.
Moos, Rudolph. *Human Adaptation.* London: Heath, 1976.
Moos, Rudolph. *The Human Context: Environmental Determinants of Behavior.* New York: Wiley, 1976.
Moreno, Jacob L. *Who Shall Survive? A New Approach to the Problem of Human Interaction.* Washington, D.C.: Nervous and Mental Disease Publishing Co., 1934.
Moscovisi, Serge. *Social Influence and Social Change.* London, New York: Academic Press, 1976.
Moss, Sidney Z. and Miriam S. "When a Caseworker Leaves an Agency: The Impact on Worker and Client." *Social Casework* (July 1967), 48(7):433–37.
Murphy, Marjorie, ed. *The Social Group Work Method in Social Work Education: A Project Report of the Curriculum Study,* vol. 11. New York: Council on Social Work Education, 1959.
Nadel, Robert M. "Interviewing Style and Foster Parents' Verbal Accessibility." *Child Welfare.* (April 1967), 46(4):207–13.
Nakama, George. "Japanese-Americans' Expectations of Counseling: An Exploratory Survey." D.S.W. dissertation, University of Southern California, 1980.
National Association of Social Workers (NASW). *Building Social Work Knowledge.* New York: NASW, 1964.
National Association of Social Workers. *Code of Ethics.* 1980.
National Association of Social Workers. *New Perspectives on Services to Groups.* New York: NASW, 1961.
National Association of Social Workers. *Social Work with Groups, 1959.* New York: NASW, 1959.
National Association of Social Workers. *The Family Is the Patient: The Group Approach to the Treatment of Family Health Problems.* Monograph VII. New York: NASW, 1965.
National Association of Social Workers. *The Psychiatric Social Worker as Leader of a Group.* New York: NASW, 1959.
National Association of Social Workers. *Use of Groups in the Psychiatric Setting.* New York: NASW, 1960.
Nelsen, Judith. *Communication Theory and Social Work Practice.* Chicago: University of Chicago Press, 1980.
Nicholas, Mary W. *Change in the Context of Group Therapy.* New York: Brunner/Mazel, 1984.
Nixon, Howard L. *The Small Group.* Englewood Cliffs, N.J.: Prentice-Hall, 1979.

Northen, Helen. "Assessment in Direct Practice." National Association of Social Workers, *Encyclopedia of Social Work,* pp. 171–83. 18th ed. Silver Spring, Md.: NASW, 1987.
Northen, Helen. *Clinical Social Work.* New York: Columbia University Press, 1982.
Northen, Helen. "Psychosocial Practice in Small Groups." In Robert W. Roberts and Helen Northen, eds. *Theories of Social Work with Groups,* pp. 116–52. New York: Columbia University Press, 1976.
Northen, Helen. "Selection of Groups as the Preferred Modality of Practice." In Joseph Lassner, Kathleen Powell, and Elaine Finnegan. *Social Group Work: Competence and Values in Practice,* pp. 19–34. New York: Haworth Press, 1987.
Northen, Helen. "Social Group Work: A Tool for Changing the Behavior of Disturbed Acting-out Adolescents." In National Association of Social Workers. *Social Work with Groups, 1958,* pp. 61–74. New York: NASW, 1958.
Northen, Helen. "Social Work with Groups in Health Settings: Promises and Problems." In Gary Rosenberg and Helen Rehr, eds. *Advancing Social Work Practice in the Health Care Field,* pp. 107–21. New York: Haworth Press, 1983.
Northen, Helen. *Social Work with Groups.* New York: Columbia University Press, 1969.
Northen, Henry and Rebecca. *Ingenious Kingdom. The Remarkable World of Plants.* Englewood Cliffs, N.J.: Prentice-Hall, 1970.
O'Connor, Gerald G. "Small Groups: A General System Model." *Small Group Behavior* (May 1980), 11(2):145–74.
Olmsted, Michael S. *The Small Group.* New York: Random House, 1959.
Olson, David H., ed. *Treating Relationships.* Lake Mills, Iowa: Graphic, 1976.
Oppenheimer, Audrey. "Triumph over Trauma in the Treatment of Child Abuse." *Social Casework* (June 1978), 59(6):352–58.
Orcutt, Ben A. "Family Treatment of Poverty Level Families." *Social Casework* (February 1976), 58(2):92–100.
Orlick, Terry. *The Second Cooperative Sports and Games Book.* New York: Random House, 1982.
Osborn, Hazel. "Some Factors of Resistance Which Affect Group Participation." In Dorothea Sullivan, ed. *Readings in Group Work.* New York: Association Press, 1952.
Overton, Alice and Katherine Tinker. *Casework Notebook.* St. Paul, Minn.: Greater St. Paul Community Chests and Councils, 1957.
Papell, Catherine P. "Group Work in the Profession of Social Work: Identity in Context." In Norma Lang and C. Marshall, eds. *Patterns in the Mosaic.* Proceedings of the 4th Annual Symposium for the Advancement of Social Work with Groups, pp. 1193–1209. Toronto, Canada: Committee for the Advancement of Social Work with Groups, 1983.
Papell, Catherine P. and Beulah Rothman. "Relating the Mainstream Model of Social Work with Groups to Group Psychotherapy and the Structured Group Approach." *Social Work with Groups* (Summer 1980), 3(2):5–23.
Papell, Catherine P. and Beulah Rothman. "Social Group Work Models: Possession and Heritage." *Journal of Education for Social Work* (Fall 1966), 2(2):66–77.
Parad, Howard J., H. L. P. Resnik, and Libbie G. Parad. *Emergency and Disaster Management.* Bowie, Md.: Charles Press, 1976.
Parad, Howard J., Lola G. Selby, and James Quinlan. "Crisis Intervention with Families and Groups." In Robert W. Roberts and Helen Northen, eds., *Theories of Social Work with Groups,* pp. 304–30. New York: Columbia University Press, 1976.
Paradise, Robert. "The Factor of Timing in the Addition of New Members to Established Groups." *Child Welfare* (November 1968), 47(9):524–30.
Parloff, Morris B., Irene E. Waskow, and Barry E. Wolfe. "Research on Therapist Variables in Relation to Process and Outcome." In Sol Garfield and Allen Bergin, eds., *Handbook of Psychotherapy and Behavior Change,* pp. 233–82. New York: Wiley, 1978.
Parnes, Marvin, ed. *Innovations in Social Group Work: Feedback from Practice to Theory.* New York: Haworth Press, 1986.
Parsloe, Phyllida. "What Social Workers Say in Groups of Clients." *British Journal of Social Work* (1971), 1(1):39–62.

Parsons, Talcott and R. F. Bales. *Family: Socialization, and Interaction Process.* Glencoe, Ill.: Free Press, 1955.

Peirce, Francis J. "A Study of the Methodological Components of Social Work with Groups." D.S.W. dissertation, University of Southern California, 1966.

Perley, Janice, Carolyn Winget, and Carlos Placci. "Hope and Discomfort as Factors Influencing Treatment Continuance." *Comprehensive Psychiatry* (November 1971), 12(6):557–63.

Perlman, Helen Harris. *Persona. Social Role and Personality.* Chicago: University of Chicago Press, 1968.

Perlman, Helen Harris. *Relationship, the Heart of Helping People.* Chicago: University of Chicago Press, 1979.

Perlman, Helen Harris. *Social Casework: A Problem-Solving Process.* Chicago: University of Chicago Press, 1957.

Pernell, Ruby B. "Identifying and Teaching the Skill Components of Social Group Work." In Council on Social Work Education, *Educational Developments in Social Group Work,* pp. 18–36. New York: CSWE, 1962.

Pernell, Ruby B. "Empowerment in Social Group Work." In Marvin Parnes, ed. *Innovations in Social Group Work: Feedback from Practice To Theory.* New York: Haworth Press, 1986.

Peters, Edward N., Muriel W. Pumphrey, and Norman Flax. "Comparison of Retarded and Nonretarded Children on the Dimensions of Behavior in Recreation Groups." *American Journal of Mental Deficiency* (July 1974), 79(1):87–89.

Phillips, Helen U. *Essentials of Social Group Work Skill.* New York: Association Press, 1957.

Pigors, Paul. *Leadership or Domination.* Boston and New York: Houghton-Mifflin, 1935.

Pincus, Allen and Anne Minahan. *Social Work Practice: Model and Method.* Itasca, Ill.: Peacock, 1973.

Pinderhughes, Elaine. "Empowerment for Our Clients and for Ourselves" *Social Casework* (June 1983) 64(6):331–38.

Pines, Malcolm and Lisa Rafaelsen, eds. *The Individual and the Group: Boundaries and Interrelations.* New York: Plenum Press, 1982.

Polansky, Norman A. *Integrated Ego Psychology.* Chicago: Aldine, 1982.

Polansky, Norman A., Ronald Lippitt, and Fritz Redl. "An Investigation of Behavioral Contagion in Groups." *Human Relations* (1950), 3:319–48.

Polansky, Norman A. and Jacob Kounin. "Clients' Reactions to Initial Interviews: A Field Study." *Human Relations* (1956), 9:237–64.

Polansky, Norman A., Ronald Lippitt, and Philip E. Slater. "Functional Roles of Group Members." In Talcott Parsons and Robert F. Bales, eds. *Family, Socialization and Interaction Process,* pp. 259–306. Glencoe, Ill.: Free Press, 1955.

Powdermaker, Florence B. and Jerome D. Frank. *Group Psychotherapy, Studies in Methodology of Research and Therapy.* Cambridge, Mass.: Harvard University Press, 1953.

Pray, Kenneth L. M. *Social Work in a Revolutionary Age.* Philadelphia: University of Pennsylvania Press, 1949.

Preininger, David. "Reactions of Normal Children to Retardates in Integrated Groups." *Social Work* (April 1968), 13(2):75–78.

Proshansky, Harold M., William H. Ittelson, and Leanne G. Rivlin, eds. *Environmental Psychology: Man and His Physical Setting.* New York: Holt, Rinehart, and Winston, 1970.

Rabin, Herbert M. "Preparing Patients for Group Psychotherapy." *International Journal of Group Psychotherapy* (April 1970), 20(2):135–45.

Radin, Norma and Sheila Feld. "Social Psychology for Group Work Practice." In Martin Sundel et al., eds. *Individual Change Through Small Groups,* pp. 50–69. 2d ed. New York: Free Press, 1985.

Rae-Grant, Quentin A. F., Thomas Gladwin, and Eli M. Bower. "Mental Health, Social Competence, and the War on Poverty." *American Journal of Orthopsychiatry* (July 1966), 36(4):652–64.

Rapoport, Lydia. "Crisis Intervention as a Mode of Brief Treatment." In Robert W. Roberts and Robert H. Nee, eds. *Theories of Social Casework*, pp. 267–311. Chicago: University of Chicago Press, 1970.

Raschella, Gerald. "An Evaluation of the Effect of Goal Congruence Between Client and Therapist on Premature Client Dropout from Therapy." Ph.D. dissertation, University of Pittsburgh, 1975.

Redl, Fritz. "Diagnostic Group Work." *American Journal of Orthopsychiatry* (January 1944), 14(1):53.

Redl, Fritz. "Strategy and Technique of the Life Space Interview. *American Journal of Orthopsychiatry* (January 1959), 29(1):1–18.

Redl, Fritz. "The Art of Group Composition." In Suzanne Schulze, ed., *Creative Group Living in a Children's Institution*, pp. 76–96. New York: Association Press, 1953.

Redl, Fritz and David Wineman. *Controls from Within: Techniques for the Treatment of the Aggressive Child.* Glencoe, Ill.: Free Press, 1952.

Reed, Beth Glover. "Women Leaders in Small Groups: Social-Psychological, Psychodynamic, and Interactional Perspectives." *Social Work with Groups* (Fall/Winter 1983), 6(3/4):35–42.

Reid, Kenneth E. *From Character Building to Social Treatment: The History of the Use of Groups in Social Work.* Westport, Conn.: Greenwood Press, 1981.

Reid, William J. "Client and Practitioner Variables Affecting Treatment," *Social Casework* (December 1964), 53(10):586–92.

Reid, William J. "Process and Outcome in Treatment of Family Problems." In William J. Reid and Laura Epstein, eds., *Task-Centered Practice*, pp. 58–77. New York: Columbia University Press, 1977.

Reid, William J. and Laura Epstein. *Task-Centered Casework.* New York: Columbia University Press, 1972.

Reid, William J. and Laura Epstein, eds. *Task-Centered Practice.* New York: Columbia University Press, 1977.

Reid, William J. and Barbara L. Shapiro. "Client Reactions to Advice." *Social Service Review* (June 1969), 43(2):165–73.

Reid, William J. and Ann W. Shyne. *Brief and Extended Casework.* New York: Columbia University Press, 1969.

Resnick, Herman and Benson Jaffee. "The Physical Environment and Social Welfare." *Social Casework* (June 1982), 63(6):354–62.

Retholz, Tryne. "The Single Session Group: An Innovative Approach to the Waiting Room." *Social Work with Groups* (Summer 1985), 8(2):143–46.

Reynolds, Bertha C. *Social Work and Social Living.* New York: Citadel Press, 1951.

Reynolds, Mildred M. "Threats to Confidentiality." *Social Work* (April 1976), 21(2):108–13.

Rice, David G., William F. Fey, and Joseph G. Kepecs. "Therapist Experience and Style as Factors in Co-therapy." *Family Process* (March 1971), 11(1):1–12.

Richmond, Mary. "Some Next Steps in Social Treatment." *The Long View.* New York: Russell Sage Foundation, 1930.

Ripple, Lilian. "Factors Associated with Continuance in Casework Service." *Social Work* (January 1957), 2(1):87–94.

Ripple, Lilian, Ernestina Alexander, and Bernice W. Polemis. *Motivation, Capacity, and Opportunity: Studies in Casework Theory and Practice.* Chicago: School of Social Service Administration, University of Chicago, 1964.

Roberts, Robert W. and Robert H. Nee, eds. *Theories of Social Casework.* Chicago: University of Chicago Press, 1970.

Roberts, Robert W. and Helen Northen, eds. *Theories of Social Work with Groups.* New York: Columbia University Press, 1976.

Rogers, Carl R. "Empathic: An Unappreciated Way of Being." *Counseling Psychologist* (April 1976), 5(2):2–10.

Rohrbaugh, Michael and Bryan D. Bartels. "Participants' Perceptions of Curative Factors in Therapy and Growth Groups." *Small Group Behavior* (November 1975), 6(4):430–56.

Rokeach, Milton. *The Nature of Human Values.* New York: Free Press, 1973.
Rose, Sheldon D. *Group Therapy: A Behavioral Approach.* Englewood Cliffs, N.J.: Prentice-Hall, 1977.
Rosen, Aaron and Dina Lieberman. "The Experimental Evaluation of Interview Performance of Social Workers." *Social Service Review* (September 1972), 46(3):395–412.
Rosen, Bernard, Arnold Katzoff, Charles Corrillo, and Donald F. Klein. "Clinical Effectiveness in "Short" vs. "Long" Psychiatric Hospitalization." *Archives of General Psychiatry* (November 1976), 33(11):1316–1322.
Rosenbaum, Max. *Handbook of Short-Term Therapy Groups.* New York: McGraw-Hill, 1983.
Rosenberg, Gary and Helen Rehr, eds. *Advancing Social Work Practice in the Health Care Field.* New York: Haworth Press, 1983.
Rosenblatt, Aaron and Diane Waldfogel, eds. *Handbook of Clinical Social Work.* San Francisco: Jossey-Bass, 1983.
Ross, Andrew L. and Norman D. Bernstein. "A Framework for the Therapeutic Use of Group Activities." *Child Welfare* (November 1976), 55(9):627–40.
Rothman, Beulah. "Study of Patterns of Leadership in Group Work Field Instruction." *Social Work with Groups* (Winter 1980), 3(4):11–17.
Rothman, Jack. "Analyzing Issues in Race and Ethnic Relations." In Rothman, ed. *Issues in Race and Ethnic Relations,* pp. 24–37.
Rothman, Jack, ed. *Issues in Race and Ethnic Relations.* Itasca, Ill.: Peacock, 1977.
Rubenstein, Hiasura and Mary Henry Bloch. *Things That Matter: Influences on Helping Relationships.* New York: Macmillan, 1982.
Rubin, Gerald K. "General Systems Theory: An Organismic Conception for Teaching Modalities of Social Work Intervention." *Smith College Studies in Social Work* (June 1973), 43(3):206–19.
Rutter, Michael. *Helping Troubled Children.* New York: Plenum Press, 1975.
Sager, Clifford and Helen Kaplan, eds. *Progress in Group and Family Therapy.* New York: Brunner/Mazel, 1972.
Sainsbury, Eric. *Social Work with Families.* London: Routledge and Kegan Paul, 1975.
Sanford, Nevitt. *Self and Society: Social Change and Individual Development.* New York: Atherton Press, 1966.
Sarri, Rosemary and Maeda Galinsky. "A Conceptual Framework for Group Development." In Paul Glasser, Rosemary Sarri, and Robert Vinter, eds. *Individual Change Through Small Groups,* pp. 71–88. New York: Free Press, 1974.
Satir, Virginia M. *Conjoint Family Therapy: A Guide to Theory and Technique.* Palo Alto: Science and Behavior Books, 1964.
Scheidlinger, Saul. "Discussion of Individual and Group." In Malcolm Pines and Lisa Rafaelsen, eds. *The Individual and the Group: Boundaries and Interrelations,* pp. 11–15. New York: Plenum Press, 1982.
Scheidlinger, Saul. *Focus on Group Psychotherapy: Clinical Essays.* New York: International Universities Press, 1982.
Scheidlinger, Saul. "Identification, the Sense of Belonging and of Identity in Small Groups." *International Journal of Group Psychotherapy* (July 1964), 14(3):291–306.
Scheidlinger, Saul. "On Scapegoating in Group Psychotherapy." *International Journal of Group Psychotherapy* (April 1982), 32(2):131–44.
Scheidlinger, Saul. *Psychoanalysis and Group Behavior.* New York: Norton, 1952.
Scheidlinger, Saul, ed. *Psychoanalytic Group Dynamics: Basic Readings.* New York: International Universities Press, 1980.
Scheidlinger, Saul. "The Concept of Empathy in Group Psychotherapy." *International Journal of Group Psychotherapy* (October 1966), 16(4):413–24.
Scheidlinger, Saul and Marjorie A. Holden. "Group Therapy of Women with Severe Character Disorders: The Middle and Final Phases." *International Journal of Group Psychotherapy* (April 1966), 16(2):174–89.
Schein, Edgar H. *Organizational Culture and Leadership.* San Francisco: Jossey-Bass, 1985.

Schiff, Sheldon K. "Termination of Therapy: Problems in a Community Psychiatric Outpatient Clinic." *Archives of General Psychiatry* (January 1962), 6(1):77–82.

Schmidl, Fritz. "A Study of Techniques Used in Supportive Treatment." *Social Casework* (December 1950), 32(8):413–19.

Schmidt, Julianna. "The Use of Purpose in Casework Practice." *Social Work* (January 1969), 4(1):77–84.

Schopler, Janice H. and Maeda J. Galinsky. "Meeting Practice Needs: Conceptualizing the Open-Ended Group, *Social Work with Groups* (Summer 1984), 7(2):3–22.

Schopler, Janice H. and Maeda J. Galinsky. "The Open-Ended Group." In Martin Sundel et al., eds. *Individual Change Through Small Groups,* pp. 87–100. 2d ed. New York: Free Press, 1986.

Schopler, Janice H., Maeda J. Galinsky, and Mark D. Alicke. "Goals in Social Group Work Practice: Formulation, Implementation, and Evaluation." In Martin Sundel et al., eds. *Individual Change Through Small Groups,* pp. 140–58.

Schulze, Suzanne, ed. *Creative Group Living in a Children's Institution.* New York: Association Press, 1951.

Schutz, William C. *Interpersonal Underworld.* Palo Alto: Science and Behavior Books, 1966.

Schwartz, Marc. "Situation/Transition Group: A Conceptualization and Review." *American Journal of Orthopsychiatry* (October 1975), 45(5):744–55.

Schwartz, William. "Between Client and System: The Mediating Function." In Robert W. Roberts and Helen Northen, eds. *Theories of Social Work with Groups,* pp. 171–97. New York: Columbia University Press, 1976.

Schwartz, William. "Group Work and the Social Scene." In Alfred J. Kahn, ed. *Issues in American Social Work,* pp. 110–37. New York: Columbia University Press, 1959.

Schwartz, William. "The Social Worker in the Group." In *The Social Welfare Forum, 1961,* pp. 146–71. New York: Columbia University Press, 1961.

Schwartz, William and Serapio R. Zalba, eds. *The Practice of Group Work.* New York: Columbia University Press, 1971.

Seabury, Brett A. "Arrangement of Physical Space in Social Work Settings." *Social Work* (October 1971), 16(4):43–49.

Seabury, Brett A. "Communication Problems in Social Work Practice." *Social Work* (January 1980), 25(1):40–44.

Selby, Lola G. "Supportive Treatment: The Development of a Concept and A Helping Method." *Social Service Review* (December 1956), 30(4):400–414.

Selby, Lola G. "Support Revisited." *Social Service Review* (December 1979), 53(4):573–85.

Sereno, Kenneth K. and C. David Mortensen. *Foundations of Communication Theory.* New York: Harper and Row, 1970.

Shapiro, Constance Hoenk. "Termination: A Neglected Concept in the Social Work Curriculum." *Journal of Education for Social Work* (Summer 1980), 16(2):13–19.

Shapiro, Jerrold Lee. *Methods of Group Psychotherapy and Encounter.* Itasca, Ill.: Peacock, 1978.

Shaw, Marvin E. *Group Dynamics: The Psychology of Small Group Behavior.* 3d ed. New York: McGraw-Hill, 1981.

Sheridan, Mary E. "Talk Time for Hospitalized Children." *Social Work* (January 1975), 20(1):40–45.

Sherif, Muzafer. "Group Influences Upon the Formation of Norms and Attitudes." In Guy E. Swanson, ed. *Readings in Social Psychology.* Rev. ed. New York: Holt, 1952.

Sherman, Sanford N. "The Choice of Group Therapy for Casework Clients." In *Social Work Practice, 1962,* pp. 174–86. New York: Columbia University Press, 1962.

Shulman, Lawrence. "Scapegoats, Group Workers, and Pre-emptive Intervention." *Social Work* (April 1967), 12(2):37–43.

Shulman, Lawrence. *The Skills of Helping Individuals and Groups.* Itasca, Ill.: Peacock, 1979.

Shyne, Ann W. "What Research Tells Us About Short-Term Cases in Family Agencies." *Social Casework* (May 1957), 38(5):223–31.

Siegel, David. "Social Work with Groups in an Industrial Setting." Paper presented at the Eighth Annual Symposium for the Advancement of Social Work with Groups, Los Angeles, October 1986.

Silberman, Buddy. "A New Strain for Social Work." Paper presented at the Annual Meeting of the Group for the Advancement of Doctoral Education, October 1982.

Silverman, Phyllis. *Mutual Help Groups: Organization and Development.* Beverly Hills: Sage, 1980.

Silverman, Phyllis. "The Client Who Drops Out: A Study of Spoiled Helping Relationships." Ph.D. dissertation, Brandeis University, 1969.

Simmel, Georg. *Conflict.* Translated by Kurt H. Wolff. Glencoe, Ill.: Free Press, 1955.

Simmel, Georg. *The Sociology of Georg Simmel.* Edited and translated by Kurt H. Wolff. Glencoe, Ill.: Free Press, 1950.

Siporin, Max. *Introduction to Social Work Practice.* New York: Macmillan, 1975.

Slavson, S. R. *A Textbook in Analytic Group Psychotherapy.* New York: International Universities Press, 1964.

Smith, Peter B., ed. *Small Groups and Personal Change.* London: Methuen, 1980.

Smith, Larry. *Crisis Intervention: Theory and Practice.* Washington, D.C.: University Press of America, 1976.

Sobey, Francine, ed. *Changing Roles in Social Work Practice.* Philadelphia: Temple University Press, 1977.

Solomon, Barbara Bryant. *Black Empowerment: Social Work in Oppressed Communities.* New York: Columbia University Press, 1976.

Somers, Mary Louise. "Four Small Group Theories: An Analysis and Frame of Reference for Use in Social Group Work." D.S.W. dissertation, Western Reserve University, 1957.

Somers, Mary Louise. "Group Process Within the Family Unit." In National Association of Social Workers, *The Family Is the Patient: The Group Approach to the Treatment of Family Health Problems,* pp. 22–39. Monograph VII. New York: NASW, 1965.

Somers, Mary Louise. "Problem-Solving in Small Groups." In Robert W. Roberts and Helen Northen, eds. *Theories of Social Work with Groups,* pp. 331–67. New York: Columbia University Press, 1976.

Somers, Mary Louise. "The Small Group in Learning and Teaching." In *Learning and Teaching in Public Welfare.* Report of the Cooperative Project on Public Welfare Staff Training, I. Washington, D.C.: Bureau of Family Services, Welfare Administration, U.S. Department of Health, Education, and Welfare, 1963.

Soo, Edward S. "Premature Termination in Activity Group Therapy." *International Journal of Group Psychotherapy* (January 1979), 29(1):115–18.

Spergel, Irving. *Street Gang Work, Theory and Practice.* Reading, Mass.: Addison-Wesley, 1966.

Stamm, Isabel L. "Ego Psychology in the Emerging Theoretical Base of Casework." In Alfred J. Kahn, ed. *Issues in American Social Work.* New York: Columbia University Press, 1959.

Stark, Frances B. "Barriers to Client-Worker Communication at Intake." *Social Casework* (April 1959), 40(4):177–83.

Stein, Aaron. "Group and Individual Boundaries in Group Psychotherapy: Theoretical and Technical Considerations." In Malcolm Pines and Lisa Rafaelsen, eds. *The Individual and the Group: Boundaries and Interrelations,* pp. 209–23. New York: Plenum Press, 1982.

Stein, Herman D. and Richard A. Cloward, eds. *Social Perspectives on Behavior: A Reader in Social Science for Social Work and Related Professions.* Glencoe, Ill.: Free Press, 1958.

Stein, Irma L. *Systems Theory, Science, and Social Work.* Metuchen, N.J.: Scarecrow Press, 1974.

Stein, Irma L. "The Systems Model and Social Systems Theory." In Herbert S. Strean, ed. *Social Casework: Theories in Action,* pp. 123–95. Metuchen, N.J.: Scarecrow Press, 1971.

Stempler, Benjamin. "A Group Work Approach to Family Group Treatment." *Social Casework* (March 1977), 58(3):143–52.

Stokes, Joseph Powell. "Components of Group Cohesion: Intermember Attraction, Instrumental Value, and Risk Taking." *Small Group Behavior* (May 1983), 14(2):163–73.

Stokes, Joseph Powell. "Toward an Understanding of Cohesion in Personal Change Groups." *International Journal of Group Psychotherapy* (October 1983), 33(4):449–67.

Studt, Elliot. "Correctional Services." In Harry L. Lurie, ed. *Encyclopedia of Social Work,* pp. 219–25. New York: National Association of Social Workers, 1965.

Sugar, Max, ed., *The Adolescent in Group and Family Therapy.* New York: Brunner/Mazel, 1975.

Sundel, Martin, Paul Glasser, Rosemary Sarri, and Robert Vinter, eds. *Individual Change Through Small Groups.* 2d ed. New York: Free Press, 1986.

Sundel, Martin, Norma Radin, and Sallie R. Churchill. "Diagnosis in Group Work." In Paul Glasser, Rosemary Sarri, and Robert Vinter, eds. *Individual Change Through Small Groups,* pp. 105–25. New York: Free Press, 1974.

Sullivan, Dorothea, ed. *Readings in Group Work.* New York: Association Press, 1952.

Swanson, Guy E., ed. *Readings in Social Psychology.* Rev. ed. New York: Holt, 1952.

Taber, Richard H. "A Systems Approach to the Delivery of Mental Health Services in Black Ghettos." *American Journal of Orthopsychiatry* (July 1970), 40(3):702–9.

Tennant, Violet. "The Caseworker's Experience in Working with Groups." D.S.W. dissertation, University of Pennsylvania, 1968.

Thibaut, John W. and Harold H. Kelley. *The Social Psychology of Groups.* New York: Wiley, 1959.

Thomas, Edwin and Clinton Fink. "Effects of Group Size." In A. Paul Hare et al., eds. *Small Groups; Studies in Social Interaction.* New York: Knopf, 1955.

Thompson, Sheila and J. H. Kahn. *The Group Process as a Helping Technique.* Oxford, England: Pergamon Press, 1970.

Tiktin, Emily A. and Catherine Cobb. "Treating Post-Divorce Adjustment in Latency Age Children: A Focused Group Paradigm." *Social Work with Groups* (Summer 1983), 6(2):53–66.

Toker, Eugene. "The Scapegoat as an Essential Group Phenomenon." *International Journal of Group Psychotherapy* (July 1972), 22(3):320–32.

Tompkins, Rosamond P. and Frank T. Gallo. "Social Group Work: A Model for Goal Formulation." *Small Group Behavior* (August 1978), 9(3):307–17.

Toseland, Ronald W. "Increasing Access: Outreach Methods in Social Work Practice." *Social Casework* (April 1981), 62(4):227–34.

Toseland, Ronald W. and Robert F. Rivas. *An Introduction to Group Work Practice.* New York: Macmillan, 1984.

Toseland, Ronald, Edmund Sherman, and Stephen Bliven. "The Comparative Effectiveness of Two Group Work Approaches to the Development of Mutual Support Groups Among the Elderly." *Social Work with Groups* (Spring/Summer 1981), 4(1/2):137–53.

Trecker, Harleigh B. *Social Group Work—Principles and Practices.* Rev. ed. New York: Whiteside, 1973.

Trecker, Harleigh B., ed. *Group Work in the Psychiatric Setting.* New York: Whiteside and Morrow, 1956.

Tropp, Emanuel. "A Developmental Theory." In Robert W. Roberts and Helen Northen, eds. *Theories of Social Work with Groups,* pp. 198–237. New York: Columbia University Press, 1976.

Truax, Charles B. and Robert R. Carkhuff. *Toward Effective Counseling and Psychotherapy: Training and Practice.* Chicago: Aldine, 1967.

Truax, Charles B. and Kevin H. Mitchell. "Research on Certain Therapist Interpersonal Skills in Relation to Process and Outcome." In Allen E. Bergin and Sol L. Garfield, eds. *Handbook of Psychotherapy and Behavior Change: An Empirical Analysis,* pp. 299–344. New York: Wiley, 1971.

Tuckman, Bruce W. "Developmental Sequence in Small Groups." *Psychological Bulletin* (June 1965), 63(6):384–99.

Tuckman, Bruce W. and M. A. C. Jensen. "Stages of Small Group Development Revisited." *Group and Organizational Studies* (January 1977), 2(1):419–27.

Tufts, Edith. *Group Work with Young School Girls.* Los Angeles: Los Angeles Area Council, Camp Fire Girls, 1968.

Turner, Francis J., ed. *Adult Psychopathology. A Social Work Perspective.* New York: Free Press, 1984.

Turner, Francis J. "Psychosocial Approach." In National Association of Social Workers. *Encyclopedia of Social Work,* pp. 397–405. 18th ed. Silver Spring, Md.: NASW, 1987.

Turner, Francis J. *Psychosocial Therapy: A Social Work Perspective.* New York: Free Press, 1978.

Turner, Francis J., ed. *Social Work Treatment: Interlocking Theoretical Approaches.* New York: Free Press, 1974.

van de Vliert, Evert. "Conflict in Prevention and Escalation." In Pieter J. D. Drenth, ed. *Handbook of Work and Organizational Psychology,* pp. 521–55. New York: Wiley, 1984.

Vayda, Andrew P., ed. *Environmental and Cultural Behavior: Ecological Studies in Cultural Anthropology.* Garden City, N.Y.: Doubleday, 1969.

Velasquez, Joan et al. "A Framework for Establishing Social Work Relationships Across Racial Ethnic Lines." In Beulah Roberts Compton and Burt Galaway, eds. *Social Work Processes,* pp. 197–203. Homewood, Ill.: Dorsey Press, 1979.

von Bertalanffy, Ludwig. *A General Systems Theory.* New York: Braziller, 1968.

von Bertalanffy, Ludwig. "General Systems Theory and Psychiatry." In Silvano Arieti, ed., *American Handbook of Psychiatry.* pp. 1095–1117. New York: Basic Books, 1976.

Waldman, Ellen. "Co-Leadership as a Method of Training: A Student's Point of View." *Social Work with Groups* (Spring 1980), 3(1):51–58.

Waldron, Jane A., Ronaele R. Whittington, and Steve Jensen. "Children's Single Session Briefings: Group Work with Military Families Experiencing Parents' Deployment." *Social Work with Groups* (Summer 1985), 9(2):101–9.

Walker, Joel and Paul Keys. "Industrial and Organizational Group Work." Paper presented at the Eighth Annual Symposium for the Advancement of Social Work with Groups, Los Angeles, October 1986.

Wallens, Donald E. "Congruence." *American Journal of Psychotherapy* (January 1969), 23(1):207–16.

Wayne, Julianne L. and Nancy Avery. "Activities as a Tool for Group Termination." *Social Work* (January 1979), 24(1):58–62.

Wayne, Julianne L. and Barbara B. Feinstein. "Group Work Outreach to Parents by School Social Workers." *Social Casework* (June 1978), 59(6):345–51.

Weiss, Robert. *Loneliness: The Experience of Emotional and Social Isolation.* Cambridge, Mass.: MIT Press, 1973.

Wexler, Joan and Thomas Steele. "Termination of One Therapist in Co-led Group Psychotherapy." *Clinical Social Work Journal* (September 1978), 6(3):211–20.

Whitaker, Dorothy Stock. *Using Groups To Help People.* London: Routledge and Kegan Paul, 1985.

Whitaker, Dorothy Stock and Morton A. Lieberman. *Psychotherapy Through the Group Process.* New York: Atherton Press, 1964.

Whittaker, James K. "A Developmental-Educational Approach to Child Treatment." In Francine Sobey, ed., *Changing Roles in Social Work Practice,* pp. 176–96. Philadelphia: Temple University Press, 1977.

Whittaker, James K. "Causes of Childhood Disorders: New Findings." *Social Work* (March 1976), 21(2):91–96.

Whittaker, James K. "Differential Use of Program Activities in Child Treatment Groups." *Child Welfare* (August 1976), 55(7):459–67.

Whittaker, James K. "Models of Group Development: Implications for Social Group Work Practice." *Social Service Review* (September 1970), 44(3):308–22.

Whittaker, James K. "Program Activities: Their Selection and Use in a Therapeutic Milieu." In Martin Sundel et al., eds. *Individual Change Through Small Groups*, pp. 217–50. 2d ed. New York: Free Press, 1986.

Whittaker, James K. *Social Treatment: An Approach to Interpersonal Helping*. Chicago: Aldine, 1974.

Whittington, Ronaele. "Group Process in Social Work Treatment." D.S.W. dissertation, University of Southern California, 1976.

Williams, Joyce E. and Karen A. Holmes. *The Second Assault: Rape and Public Attitudes*. Westport, Conn.: Greenwood Press, 1981.

Williams, Meyer. "Limitations, Phantasies, and Security Operations of Beginning Group Therapists." *International Journal of Group Psychotherapy* (April 1966), 16(2):15–62.

Wilson, Gertrude. "From Practice to Theory: A Personalized History." In Robert W. Roberts and Helen Northen, eds., *Theories of Social Work with Groups*, pp. 1–44. New York: Columbia University Press, 1976.

Wilson, Gertrude. *Group Work and Case Work: Their Relationship and Practice*. New York: Family Welfare Association of America, 1941.

Wilson, Gertrude and Gladys Ryland. *Social Group Work Practice*. Boston: Houghton-Mifflin, 1949.

Wilson, Gertrude. "The Social Worker's Role in Group Situations." In Marjorie Murphy, ed. *The Social Group Work Method in Social Work Education*, pp. 129–68. New York: Council on Social Work Education, 1959.

Winters, Wendy Glasgow and Freda Easton. *The Practice of Social Work in Schools*. New York: Free Press, 1983.

Wolkon, George H. and Henry Tanaka. "Outcome of a Social Rehabilitation Service for Released Psychiatric Patients: A Descriptive Study," *Social Work* (1966), 11(2):53–61.

Worby, Marsha. "The Adolescents' Expectations of How a Potentially Helpful Person Will Act." *Smith College Studies in Social Work* (1955), 26:29–59.

Yalom, Irvin D. "A Study of Group Therapy Drop-outs." *Archives of General Psychiatry* (1966), 14:393–414.

Yalom, Irvin D. *Inpatient Group Psychotherapy*. New York: Basic Books, 1983.

Yalom, Irvin D. *The Theory and Practice of Group Psychotherapy*. New York: Basic Books, 1970; 2d ed. 1975; 3d ed. 1985.

Yalom, Irvin D. et al. "Preparation of Patients for Group Therapy." *Archives of General Psychiatry* (1967), 17(4):416–27.

Zalba, Serapio R. "Discontinuance During Social Service Intake." Ph.D. dissertation, Western Reserve University, 1971.

Ziller, Robert. "Toward A Theory of Open and Closed Groups." *Psychological Bulletin* (1965), 43:164–82.

Index